TOUGH PLANTS
for
TOUGH PLACES

TOUGH PLANTS
for
TOUGH PLACES

GARY VERGINE &
MICHAEL JEFFERSON-BROWN

CB
CONTEMPORARY BOOKS

Cataloging-in-Publication Data

is available from the United States Library of Congress

First published in the United Kingdom by David & Charles
Brunel House, Newton Abbot, Devon

This edition published 1998 by Contemporary Books
An imprint of NTC/Contemporary Publishing Company
4255 West Touhy Avenue, Lincolnwood (Chicago), Illinois 60464-1975 U.S.A

Printed in Italy.

CONTENTS

INTRODUCTION

Not quite Eden

No garden has perfect conditions, and often if they are right for one plant they are tricky for another. In some gardens the conditions are more extreme, which can lead to difficulties in getting plants established and growing. By matching plants to conditions and using sensible cultivation techniques it is possible to overcome most problems. This book identifies key problem areas and suggests solutions. There are no hard and fast rules, each problem must be looked at individually: just as no single elixir will cure all medical disorders, so each horticultural trouble has its own range of remedies.

Difficulties! What difficulties?

Difficulties may be caused by climatic factors, by soils, by surrounding buildings or maybe just the competition of other plants. Usually it is a combination of factors that renders one garden site difficult and another relatively easy. Often what might appear to be problems are merely opportunities waiting to be exploited. Soggy wet areas give a chance to grow a series of fascinating and dramatic plants that gardeners with drier terrain can only wonder at. Of course, it is always the way that the gardener with limy soil yearns to grow lime-hating plants such as rhododendrons, and where these grow like weeds, the gardener wants to specialize in growing lime-loving alpines and other calcifrages. Sometimes you have to live with what you have got.

Although 'horses for courses' is an apt slogan for the philosophy of this book, which aims to match plants to conditions rather than conditions to plants, there will always be some tinkering and work to be done to make conditions the best possible for the plants. After all this is what gardening is about. Most gardens will be improved by the addition of mulches, composts and other nutritious plant foods, which is simple enough for the gardener to fix, but some conditions are not easy to alter. Any rushed attempt to change the acidity or alkalinity of your soil, for example, will not meet with much success. The pH scale runs from 0 to 14 with 7.0 being neutral and 0 being extreme acid. To change the value of your garden soil 1 point either way will take a huge amount of effort and may just not be worth while. It is best to work with what you have got and choose plants that suit. In any case, readings above 8.5 or below 4.5 are rare and most plants will happily grow in a pH between 6.0 and 7.0.

TOUGH PLACES?

The naïve might suppose that gardening, away from flower shows of course, is a relatively uncompetitive undertaking. It may be so but gardeners are humans and most of us have some of the competitive spirit. This may be exemplified by the way in which two gardeners will vie in the description of their weed problems, each declaring their weeds the worst. Similarly their clay will be the heavier, the ground the most ill-drained and their garden the more windswept. It seems to give each comfort to know that they are dealing with the worse problem.

The tough places dealt with in this book range from the dry to the wet, the sunny to the shady. We cover clay both under normal conditions and where it never, or rarely, dries out. Clay is the most frequently quoted garden problem soil and supposedly one that is difficult to overcome, even though almost all 'clay' soils have some sand or humus in them and increasing the amount of these will often soften their character. Sand, which has its own set of special needs, is also considered.

TOUGH PLANTS?

Most gardeners know that it is possible to kill most plants. It is just that some plants can be killed more easily than others and that some gardeners are more adept at finding the methods. Just what is meant by

A Mediterranean garden combining palm trees with tough plants such as eschscholzia, alyssum and clarkia

'tough'? Tough, in the way it is used here, is a plant that once placed in the right environment can be expected to flourish with the minimum of cosseting and trouble. As the dictionary suggests, our 'tough' means 'flexible, tenacious and able to endure hardship'. Some plants are of their nature hardier souls, so the secondary definition can also be considered; our tough might be a 'street ruffian', able and willing to fight back.

Our planet is inhabited by those plants that have adapted to and survived in the particular environmental niches in which they are found or for which they have been bred. By considering the mini-environment of our garden and choosing plants that are adapted to it because their homeland offers the same conditions, we can expect the plants to be happy. A great part of this book concentrates on matching plants to environments as this is the surest way to success. In some cases it is easy to pair plant and place, in others, it may need a little more ingenuity and a little adjustment. However, the overriding rule we have adopted is that the plant should be able to fend for itself once set in an appropriate place.

The choice of plants

The choice of plants is wide and varied. Nothing is ruled out as unfashionable or too idiosyncratic. Old favourites appear cheek-by-jowl with novelties and 'stars'. The many garden-worthy plants found in every garden centre are not forgotten, but we also take a look at our humble native plants. Annuals and biennials that are rarely praised in horticultural circles, but may be the answer to certain difficult corners, are all considered on their merit. Ground cover plants have been much lauded as labour saving in past decades, the best are excellent, some that have been suggested are really little more than normal border plants. The better ones are considered here, as are those plants such as ferns and grasses that can be planted singly or in sweeps and create newly fashionable ensembles. Hardworking plants that naturalize by seed or other means are given a welcome, and the whole is balanced to encourage wildlife, especially birds, moths, butterflies and useful animals such as toads and frogs.

It is important that groups of plants can survive happily together, but also vital for gardens is that, in doing so, they present an interesting and beautiful picture so that all the year, or as much of it as possible, will find each part of the garden filled with interest. Everyone has their own ideas on this, but it is usually the case that neighbouring plants should be picked to make a show of each other. Juxtaposition is the code word. Leaf shape, colour, size, texture and individual habits can be highlighted by contrasting neighbours. Flower colours are important and are given due consideration, but the long-term appearance of the plants, their leaves and form, are perhaps even more important: the party should run a twelve-month!

PLANT COMMUNITIES

One of the sub-plots of this book is the plant community. Nature's success depends on plant associations and communities to build up and function together, and these can help to suggest a plan to follow in the garden, either using the same species or, more likely, selected cultivars. Present and past gardening practice are both considered to see what has proved successful. Very popular ideas are not ignored just because they are commonplace, their widespread use is likely to be because they work and look good. Suggestions are made of groupings of plants that will grow together well even if they have arrived in our gardens from the four corners of the world or from the plots of plant breeders.

WILDLIFE

An ideal garden environment is a balance of plant and animal life. Although rabbits and moles are not often invited in, birds are welcome. Some, such as bullfinches, may take a toll with fruit buds but this is a small price to pay for the presence of such attractive birds. Birds may be actively encouraged into the garden by providing bushes and plants that give succour with seeds and other fruits. And various feeding stations can be positioned around the garden. Many birds work for us in culling pests such as aphids, slugs and snails. Birdsong in the garden gives it an extra lively dimension.

Bees, moths and butterflies can also be actively encouraged. Keeping hive bees may be an option. They are certainly fascinating creatures and will be busy pollinating plants in the vegetable and pleasure garden. Lists of plants that attract different flying insects and other visitors are given in margin notes.

ENVIRONMENTAL CONCERNS

The dedicated gardener looks also to the earth and thinks of it as a living thing, a vast complicated eco-mass that is crammed with tiny forms of life many microscopically small and ranging up to the familiar range of earthworms (although there is the occasional pest, currently the much despised flatworms from New Zealand which live off wholly beneficial worms). It is perhaps a good idea to think of gardening as a tending of the soil rather than the plants, encouraging the formation of a soil structure that is healthy and teeming with life, which will then pass its health on to our precious specimens.

The book

The book is divided into five main sections:

Section 1 Too Dry
Section 2 Too Wet
Section 3 Other Difficult Conditions
Section 4 Solving Everyday Problems
Section 5 More Tough Plants

Sections 1 to 3 deal with problem conditions that you might face, either as a general rule throughout your whole garden or in isolated areas within your garden. Consideration is given to extremes such as wet and shady or dry and sunny where particular care is required to get plants to succeed. Section 4 looks at more specific areas of gardens and at types of gardens. Here you will find ideas for small gardens or large ones, and solutions for planting particular areas such as banks or beside paths. There are details of how to reduce the amount of work in a garden, and how to create something from nothing. There are also chapters dealing with choosing plants for conservatories or hanging baskets. Section 5 features some good all-rounders from the wide selection available.

All sections are introduced with a discussion of the particular problems faced. Some consideration is given to the forms and functions of specific plants that help to explain how they cope with the conditions: what makes one plant revel in hot sun whereas another collapses almost instantly. We also take a look at the type of plant communities that cope with, or even enjoy, the natural environment dominated by these main factors.

Within sections 1–4, each chapter includes a detailed study of the type of site, the causes of the problems, the variations that may occur and the range of methods available to maximize the growing opportunities. Each site variation is accompanied by suggestions of plants that will survive the conditions, and ideas are given for successful groupings and associations.

Throughout the book, a number of plants are recommended through plant profiles. These have been selected as suitable for the conditions and are the 'Tough Plants' of the title. However, as space allows only a comparative few to be featured in such a way, there are supplementary lists of the many others that may also be used in the conditions described. And, yet more plants are described in the body of the book itself.

HARDINESS

In this book fully hardy means the plant will survive temperatures down to -15°C (5°F), frost hardy plants can survive to -5°C (23°F) and half hardy ones to 0°C (32°F). More tender plants, or ones that do not fit these labels, are given a minimum temperature, below which they cannot survive or will not thrive.

SEASONS

Just as conditions vary in every garden so do the seasons. It is rarely possible to say with certainty 'this flowers in May', one can be sure that a gardener in a mild area will have it in bloom in April. Therefore, assuming that gardeners know the relative climate of their own gardens, the seasons are given instead. These roughly correspond to the months as follows:

Early winter: December
Midwinter: January
Late winter: February
Early spring: March
Mid-spring: April
Late spring: May
Early summer: June
Midsummer: July
Late summer: August
Early autumn: September
Mid-autumn: October
Late autumn: November

TOO DRY

AVAILABILITY OF WATER – too little, too much, or just enough – is the most important influence on plants. Miserable soil, direct exposure to sun or wind, deep shade or excessive competition are just as hard on plants as drought, and, particularly in the case of poor soil, these factors can often be more difficult to identify. When combined with dryness, therefore, they need some care to overcome. There are two basic approaches to lessening the impact of too little water: use simple techniques to alleviate the effects of dryness; and choose plants that are adapted to a dry environment. Identifying a drought problem is the first step towards dealing with it. This section highlights key dry spots in the garden and suggests ways to deal with them. To find out whether you are likely to have a drought problem read on.

Is your garden too dry?

WEATHER

Your plant choices should take local climate into account. Weather is governed mainly by the prevailing wind and the amount of cloud and rain. Where prevailing winds blow off the sea, cloud will be common and rainfall high. As the air travels across the countryside dropping rain as it goes, it becomes less moisture-laden, so the last land it crosses receives the least rain. Mountains and hills produce a similar effect to land by the sea. The slopes that face the prevailing wind have a higher rainfall than those over the other side. Wet or dry weather can also be very local. On the side of the country away from the prevailing wind or on high ground that is sheltered from it, there is relatively low rainfall.

Wind will help dry a site, so windswept sites can be short of water. Wind dries exposed wet but also leaches water from the leaves of the vegetation. Wind brings other problems which are considered on pages 108-117.

Gardens badly subject to frosts will feel the effects throughout the year. The last spring frost and the first serious autumn one controls the timing of everything you and your plants can do: they truncate the growing season. On the positive side a dry

If you have low rainfall or other drought-related conditions, it pays to choose plants that relish the environment. In this paved garden, lavender, thyme, *Verbascum thapsus*, fennel and *Alchemilla mollis* are in their element naturalizing in any available crack or crevice

site may be less vulnerable to frost damage; the plants themselves contain less water so their tissue is more frost-damage-resistant.

SLOPES

The shape of the surrounding land helps to mould the garden environment. Plants on slopes facing the sun will feel its full strength. In these conditions you can create a garden for the sun-lovers from the Mediterranean, the southern states of America, the Australasian subtropics and southern Africa (see margin lists). Despite the dry conditions that these countries experience, not everything is like a cactus. In the autumn, *Nerine bowdenii* opens flowers that are sparkling and crisp. *Amaryllis bella-donna* is even more dramatic and dew-drop fresh. The fleshy, low leaves of mesembryanthemums are succulent beneath their scintillating many-coloured carpets of flowers.

Ground sloping away from the sun will be a lot less hot and dry in summer. It will also be very slow

GENISTA AETNENSIS
Mount Etna broom

G. lydia

Description: A very hardy shrub from Sicily with aspirations to grow rapidly into a tree; a rounded one with lots of thin green arching branches almost without leaves – the branches aid photosynthesis – so the effect is of an evergreen. In midsummer its typical pea-like flowers transform it into a cloud of yellow.

Uses: A quick-growing focal point in a sunny spot in front of dark evergreen trees or walls. Behind other shrubs it will grow up and create a colourful picture.

Colour: Bright golden-yellow.

Size: 8m (25ft) high, spread 9m (28ft).

Flowering time: Through summer.

Relatives: Most genistas are only a fraction of this giant size. Do not overlook the value of *G. hispanica*, the Spanish gorse, a shrub that forms hedgehog-spiny cushions of green, 45-75cm (18-30in) high. Late spring and early summer low golden blossom smothers these rounded mounds. *G. lydia* (pictured) makes a mound about 45cm (18in) high but wider and covers itself with masses of smallish golden flowers. Dramatic in a large rock garden or tumbling over a wall.

Cultivation: Best in sun and well-drained soil.

Propagation: Seed or layering.

to warm up after the winter and will receive scant benefit from the winter sun which, if it reaches it at all, will do so at a very low angle. Here, with less contrast between the seasons and less stressful heat on the plants, flowering periods can be prolonged and of a subtler beauty.

Geranium pratense (meadow cranesbill), will flourish in such a site, relishing any sunshine and coping

SUN-LOVING PLANTS
Perennials
Anthemis punctata

Anthyllis montana

Echinops spp.

Eryngium spp.

Euphorbia spp.

Geranium endressii

G. sanguineum var. *striatum*

Linum spp.

Oenothera spp.

Persicaria affinis

Saponaria ocymoides

Sedum forms

Shrubs
Carpenteria californica

Caryopteris forms

Cistus spp.

Erythrina crista-galli

Euphorbia characias subsp.
  wulfenii

Fremontodendron 'California
  Glory'

Grevillea forms

Hibiscus forms

Olearia forms

Phlomis spp.

Sophora davidii

Trees
Arbutus spp.

Celtis australis

Cladrastis lutea

Eucalyptus spp.

Fraxinus spp.

Genista aetnensis

Gleditsia spp.

Quercus spp.

Sophora japonica

Umbellularia californica

BASIC RAINFALL PATTERN

Clouds formed over the sea drop rain as they travel across land. Slopes facing the prevailing wind tend to get most rainfall.

ARMERIA MARITIMA
Thrift

Description: A hardy evergreen perennial found wild on cliff tops. It forms a tight mound of grass-like deep green leaves which, in late spring, sprouts wiry stems with perky pompom heads made of clusters of tiny flowers.

Uses: Its sculptural shape gives definition to path edges and adds some solidarity to a bed of rockery plants. Grows contentedly between paving.

Wildlife: Attracts bees and other insects.

Colour: The usual pinks are augmented by whites and reds.

Size: 15cm (6in) high, spread 30cm (12in).

Flowering time: Late spring into early summer.

Relatives: 'Alba' white, 'Dusseldorf Pride' crimson, 'Glory of Holland', with large pink flowers, is half as big again as the type, 'Splendens' is carmine and 'Vindictive' is rich rose-pink.

A. juniperifolia (syn. *A. caespitosa*) makes neat cushions of leaves and produces umbels of bright pink flowers resting on the foliage. It is excellent in rock garden crevices or in trough gardens.

Cultivation: Deep roots dislike disturbance.

Propagation: By seed or cuttings in summer.

with much dryness, whereas they would flag under an unmitigated baking. The pure blue species is extremely garden-worthy and there are some wonderful forms: *G. pratense* 'Mrs Kendall Clark' has large saucer-shaped silvery blue blooms; *G. pratense* 'Plenum Caeruleum' has double flowers like miniature blue peonies; *G. pratense* 'Plenum Violaceum' is another double but this time in violet-maroon. In fact the geranium genus is full of plants that are easy to grow, persistent, attractive in foliage, generous of bloom and very well able to look after themselves (see margin list page 13).

Cold air flows downward, just like water, to collect in pockets and pools below. Where barriers impede air flow, frost pockets may form on slopes – your fabulous yew hedge is better with a gap for 'frost drainage'. Frost pockets restrict the choice of plants; the earliest flowers, particularly, should be bone-hardy ones such as snowdrops and winter aconites.

ALTITUDE

Does your garden stand high or low? Height gives a shorter season: knock 1°C off your mean temperature for every rise of 600m above sea level (2°F for every 2,000ft). Drying winds are more likely on higher ground. Alpine plants cope by keeping close to the soil. Ground-hugging *Dryas octopetala* (mountain avens), mound-forming *Armeria* (thrift) species and miniature rosettes of saxifrages demonstrate distinct adaptation for high mountains. Luckily, most mountain-top plants are also happy in low altitude gardens.

SOIL TYPES

Shallow soil over poor subsoil or underlying rock will afford little water storage. The soil will be less 'alive'. There are wide-spreading shallow-rooters and deep-delving tap-rooted alpines, which drill their way through difficult layers into the debris below, and these may cope. Deep soil will nurture almost every plant, although smaller ones could be overwhelmed by more rumbustious neighbours.

Heavy clay cracks as it dries, exposing delicate roots and allowing the air to suck up the last traces of water. However, when properly managed, clay is a 'fat' soil in which a good range of plants can grow strongly. Many of the more suitable plants are large and dramatic versions of familiar favourites, like *Inula magnifica* with huge rich orangey-yellow daisy flowers (see margin list).

Sandy soil usually drains very rapidly and has no long-term water reserves. With little organic matter of its own, it has an unlimited appetite for added compost and manure. There are plants that enjoy such sites: *Limonium vulgare* (sea lavender) and related species, together with *Eryngium maritimum* (sea holly) flourish in sand (see margin list).

Soft dark loam is for the fortunate few and must be treated with reverence. If it is shallow, add to it whatever and whenever you can. It will repay your offerings with healthy plants. Some specials that ought to be considered are listed in the margin.

DROUGHT SPOTS

Some gardeners produce or inherit man-made dry areas. Walls and hedges in particular are likely places for over-dry soil.

Walls often shelter the ground immediately around them from rain; soil at their feet can be very dry indeed. Some walls are made of materials that can suck up soil water and then allow it to evaporate. Walls also reflect the sun's heat and cause even more dryness. However, slightly tender climbers, such as carpenterias will survive more happily against a sun-facing wall than elsewhere and *Geranium* 'Kashmir White' and *G.* 'Kashmir Purple' bask at ground level.

Hedges and trees have root systems that thirst for water and, spreading out from their base, they can dry a considerable area. Privet hedges produce an extraordinary mass of greedy roots, leyland hedges are almost as bad.

SEDUM SPECTABILE
Ice Plant

S. spectabile 'Autumn Joy'

Description: Flowering for many weeks right at the end of the growing season, this hardy plant is a must for most gardens. New spring foliage unfolds silver-grey and bedewed. Summer is all plump opulent succulence. Wide shallow domes of autumn blossom are almost top-heavy and composed of crowded tiny flowers.

Uses: Any well-drained site with plenty of sun. Ideal for an autumn border.

Wildlife: One of the most popular of butterfly plants; also crowded with bees and other insects.

Colour: White, pink, cerise, carmine, magenta.

Size: 60cm (2ft) high and across.

Flowering time: Late summer, through autumn.

Relatives: 'Autumn Joy' (pictured) is a rich pink that darkens to coppery bronze. 'Brilliant' is bright pink, 'Iceberg' is the best white. *S. acre*, the common stonecrop, is a scrambling, low-growing plant that will colonize a stone wall with its small swollen leaves and bright golden starry flowers. A single leaf falling on the ground can soon develop into a new plant. On walls it is useful, though in the rock garden or other more classy spots it can be a persistent nuisance.

Cultivation: Placed in well-drained soil in a sunny spot, it is virtually maintenance-free.

Propagation: Plants can be split in early spring, stems will root and leaves removed from the stem will also root and form new plants.

DROUGHT-RESISTANT GERANIUMS

G. cinereum

G. dalmaticum

G. incanum

G. macrorrhizum

G. maculatum

G. pratense

G. sanguineum

G. thunbergii

PLANTS FOR SANDY SOILS

Bulbs

Fritillaria spp.

Iris bulbous

Tulipa forms

Shrubs

Ballota spp.

Brachyglottis spp.

Callistemon spp.

Cistus spp.

Cytisus forms

Genista spp.

Grevillea forms

Halimodendrum spp.

Hibiscus forms

Indigofera ambylantha

Lavatera forms

Lespedeza thunbergii

Potentilla fructicosa

Robinia spp.

Romneya coulteri

Santolina chamaecyparissus

PLANTS FOR GOOD LOAM

Most herbaceous plants

Most bulbs

Most shrubs

How plants cope with dryness

Every variation in plant structure, form and colour has evolved for a reason. The shape of the whole plant, the shape of parts such as leaves, the make-up and surfaces of the parts, the type of root system, and the periods during which the plant grows all influence performance.

In dry places plants have to maximize water use, minimize water wastage and find other ways to survive droughts. They have to deal with a lack of water to the roots a well as with dry air around stems, leaves and flowers. The greater the air movement, the greater the water loss.

PLANT SHAPES

Low-growing plants crouch out of the wind. Mound-formers such as *Armeria maritima* (thrift) establish a solid hummock which spreads outwards projecting only a streamlined bump to any wind.

Mat- or cushion-makers are plastered against the soil. Creeping thymes are typical mat-formers and grow along hugging the ground. They rely on there being no competition from other plants which might smother them. Where stronger plants may overwhelm low-creepers, some have evolved a variation – the trailing habit. Trailers are permanently low-growing and *Convolvulus sabatius* is a typical example. If its territory is threatened by other plants, its trailing stems reach out to light perhaps by scrambling up its competitors, using them to find its place in the sun.

Other plants use other means for overcoming taller surrounding growth. Rosette-formers stay low with their close-knit clump of leaves but then come right out and hit a high note when flowering and seeding. They hoist flowers up to attract pollinators and their elevation helps seed dispersal. Many rosetted plants are biennials such as *Verbascum thapsus* (mullein), germinating one year and concentrating on making leaves and roots to build up their strength. All the reserves in leaves and strong roots are spent the following year in growing the tall flowering stems and to distribute huge numbers of seeds. This technique enables an early claim to a patch of

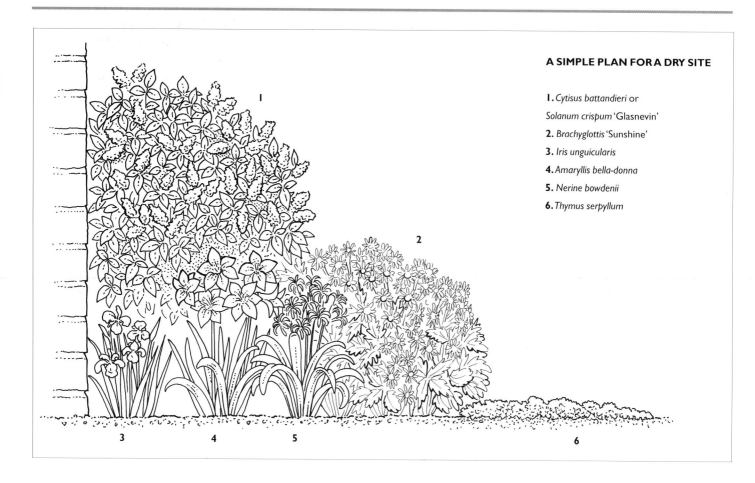

A SIMPLE PLAN FOR A DRY SITE

1. *Cytisus battandieri* or *Solanum crispum* 'Glasnevin'

2. *Brachyglottis* 'Sunshine'

3. *Iris unguicularis*

4. *Amaryllis bella-donna*

5. *Nerine bowdenii*

6. *Thymus serpyllum*

ground before the rush of other seeding plants at the end of each growing season.

Some perennials make use of similar tactics; all mulleins are rosetted but some are perennial and, although discarding their flowered rosettes after the working season, will keep producing a succession of rosettes from the permanent rootstock.

LEAF CHARACTERISTICS

Leaves have many uses, but the main fundamental one is to utilize the sun's energy. Water evaporation from their surfaces aids photosynthesis, moderates the plant's temperature and helps pump the sap around it.

For the gardener foliage is vital. It allows us to experiment with size, shape, form, colour, texture, scent, transparency, reflectivity and wind-stirred movement. Leaves are evergreen or deciduous and may have dramatic seasonal colour changes. They may give shade and shelter, help smother weeds and, when fallen, may be gathered up to convert into precious leaf mould.

In plants that have to adapt to dry areas, the leaves are an important factor in their survival. One form that drought-resistant leaves take is to be thick and fleshy to allow increased water storage; a good

ERIGERON KARVINSKIANUS (SYN. *E. MUCRONATUS*)
Mexican daisy

Description: A low-profile high-performance plant from Mexico but hardy in most places through Europe. It spreads across the ground with scrambling low stems and soon starts seeding itself into walls and all sorts of odd spots. It has a crowd of daisy flowers in a very long succession and intricate light green foliage.

Uses: All open spots, on walls, in paving, in containers and hanging baskets.

Colour: Opening white, the flowers become pink and turn reddish before dying.

Size: Only 10-15cm (4-6in) high, but spread is without measure.

Flowering time: Throughout summer well into autumn and not adverse to winking open a few flowers in winter and spring.

Relatives: All popular relatives are much larger border plants.

Cultivation: Once planted it will take care of itself. Any exposed plants that are killed by excessively bad weather are soon replaced by seedlings.

Propagation: Easy by seed. Self sown seedlings can be moved when young, thereafter the deep main root prevents this. Late spring cuttings root quickly.

HELICHRYSUM BRACTEATUM
Everlasting flower, Immortelle

Description: This well-known plant is the annual that produces upright branching growth with pointed rather crisp-looking leaves and then for many weeks a series of daisy flowers with shiny papery petals. An Australian plant, it is grown as a half hardy annual though, rarely, it will last longer.

Uses: It will grow in poor soil and can make a useful filler in such sites. The flowers can be cut for use as indoor decoration. Pick them fresh before the flowers have been opened enough to display their centres. You will get the biggest harvest by removing individual heads to dry and mount on florist's wires. Decapitation encourages further flowering.

Colour: Occurs in any number of shades and colour combinations involving creams, yellows, pinks, oranges and reds.

Size: Dependent on soil and site, up to a height and spread of over 1m (3ft) but the strains usually sold are likely to be only half this.

Flowering time: Summer into autumn.

Relatives: Each seedhouse seems to have their own strains, some quite dwarf. The genus is a varied one with plenty of perennials and subshrubs and some fully fledged shrubs.

Propagation: Sow seed in spring in sunny well-drained soil. The plants will grow rapidly, doing best if thinned out to allow each plenty of elbow room. If you are anxious to get a quick start, seedlings can be raised in individual pots and planted out in mid-spring.

Verbascum thapsus are so hairy they are almost woolly. In other plants, it is essential oils and other chemicals in leaves that are the defence against water loss. The aromatic leaves of thymes, rosemary and lavender saturate the air around the plant and inhibit transpiration.

Inefficient energy collection by restricting the supply of sunlight to the leaves is a rather extreme adaptation, but, in areas with strong sunshine, leaves can afford to cut back on the supply. This they do with small leaves, light-resistant hairy coverings and tough opaque filtering layers. Shiny leathery leaves reflect surplus light and heat. Blue leaves, such as those on *Melianthus major*, one of the most attractive of all foliage plants, reject the most energetic wavelengths of sunlight.

example of this is *Sedum spectabile* (see page 13), which has succulent grey-green leaves.

Small leaves are common in dry areas; the thin, needle-like leaves of heather, lavender, rosemary and brooms have less surface area from which water can evaporate, thus reducing water loss.

Leaf surfaces may be adapted to prevent moisture loss. Fine hairs create a thin blanket of still air next to the working surface and this helps to minimize water loss. These leaves often appear silvered from the reflection of light by the many tiny hairs. *Brachyglottis* 'Sunshine' has white-silver leaves that gradually become dark green on top; those of

Nestling below a South African mountain, this garden shows just how lush a dry, sunny site can look. However, water is unlikely to be in short supply here

BELOW THE GROUND

Deep roots are a response to dry conditions, delving down towards distant reserves. Root stores of water, such as carrots and potatoes, are common, tucking away spare supplies for use when needed.

Bulbs, corms and tubers are all energy stores. In hard times, the soil is a safe retreat from the difficulties above. Life below can exist without the 'running expenses' of the open air and such plants simply await the arrival of reasonable growing conditions. Nerine and amaryllis retreat from baking drought, lilies hide from cold, and woodland species retire before the canopy of leaves above makes life too difficult. Some clever plants, such as colchicums, flower in autumn then duck the bad weather before producing leaves in spring.

Seed is the last resort. The plant abandons the battle to maintain its complete structure and invests its energy in producing seed that will ensure its genes survive for a further generation. Some seed can remain viable in the soil for many years: poppy seed survives for over eighty years. Annuals are permanently committed to this life plan and one particularly successful practitioner is *Eschscholzia* (Californian poppy).

VERBASCUM THAPSUS
Great mullein

V. 'Artic Summer'

Description: Strong growing biennial that is native to all countries of northern Europe, including Britain. In the first year it produces a large rosette of broadly spear-shaped leaves apparently made out of a thick white felt, which also clothes the stems and flower buds. In the second year, a tall stout stem appears with many closely clasped, flat, five-petalled flowers opening in succession up the long spike.

Uses: Impressive in a wild garden.

Colour: White downy leaves; mid-yellow flowers.

Size: 2m (6ft) high, spread 45cm (18in).

Flowering time: Through summer.

Relatives: *V.* 'Arctic Summer' (pictured) has white flowers. *V. chaixii* is a perennial species with nettle-shaped leaves much silvered with hairs and slender spikes of yellow flowers; height 1m (3ft).

Cultivation: Introduce by seed. The first year rosettes are handsome and it could be grown for these alone. If the flowers are allowed to seed, a stem can produce enough to cover a county.

Propagation: By seed.

COLOUR CLUE

Many plants adapted to heat and strong sunlight have a blue tinge. Eucalypts are an example. Sometimes the blue is masked by stronger tints or coverings: grey-leaved artemisias are blue beneath their silvery hairs.

DRY AND SUNNY

ORIGANUM VULGARE
Wild marjoram

O. vulgare 'Aureum'

Description: Marjorams are very useful plants, not the kind to make headlines, but quietly to gain affection through their quiet charms. They are neat in growth and easy to grow, having pleasingly scented leaves and long seasons of modest flowers. Fully hardy.

Uses: For pots or in beds near the house where its fragrant leaves can be appreciated.
Wildlife: Attracts flying insects such as butterflies.
Colour: Mauve.
Scent: Aromatic leaves.
Size: Height and spread 45cm (18in).
Flowering time: Summer.
Relatives: The species is usually represented in the garden in the golden-leaved form, *O.v.* 'Aureum' (pictured), an excellent foliage plant in glowing primrose-gold, perhaps best with a little shade so that the leaves do not get too burnt. *O. laevigatum* is a spreading sub-shrub with small leaves and lots of small cone-shaped flowers in cherry-pink.
Cultivation: Easy in well-drained, sunny soil, preferably slightly alkaline.
Propagation: Division in spring.

DRY, SUNNY sites with the almost mythical free-draining, moisture-retentive soil, give ideal growing conditions. Under these circumstances the plants enjoy enough light, water, air and food; they can manage through lean seasons with stockpiled food and accumulated strength. Real life, however, can be more brutal. In years of little rain and water shortages, everyone has problems, but if drought is a recurrent theme – you live in a dry area or the weather has been on the dry side for a few years – and you feel obliged to be constantly watering, you can and should look for ways of lessening the hardship. One simple, sensible and straightforward method is to adapt your planting schemes to the conditions in your garden. By growing plants from any of the three groups detailed on page 21, you will be choosing those that enjoy the difficult aspects of these conditions and, as a result you will have a good-looking garden that is a good deal easier to look after.

Do you have a dry sunny site?

This is likely to be obvious. Its open aspect to sun will be clear; if it also slopes towards the sun, the soil will get that much warmer and drier. While it can be dry on the surface, some sites may be relatively wet underneath. Digging at different times will soon reveal the truth. If plant growth is slow or stunted you can assume dry conditions below. Areas below sunny walls or at the fringe of trees or hedges can be desperately dry, but sometimes walls can shed a lot of rainfall onto the ground and in high rainfall districts these sites may well be wet.

Coping with a dry sunny site

A benefit of dry sunny spots is that the relative dryness and warmth can stretch the growing seasons; with shelter and protection from excessive damp, frost and cold, many plants will bloom earlier, late performers will carry on even later and other plants may donate out-of-season bonuses.

If your dry sunny site is limited to an area that is close to the house, in a pleasant spot, do not give it all to plants, save a place for yourself. Lay paving, brick paviors or any other hard surface underfoot. Ensure that all paving is securely laid on fast-draining hardcore and that any slope is away from the house so that surface water is taken away. Low retaining walls will provide good plant sites and will tend to increase the sense of an outdoor room and of seclusion. A partial screen of trellis will further this sense of privacy and shelter, and provides an opportunity to grow climbing plants such as honeysuckles, jasmines, clematis species and hybrids, and the less aggressively armed roses. The trellis may provide some shade, certainly a pergola will, especially if draped with strong climbers such as vines.

Use hard landscaping to make a micro-climate for yourself and your plants. It can produce a warmer, less humid, quicker drying, less frost-prone, ice-free, more human-friendly area. In such

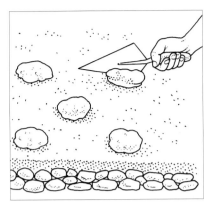

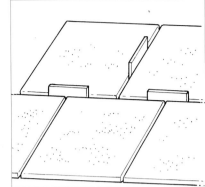

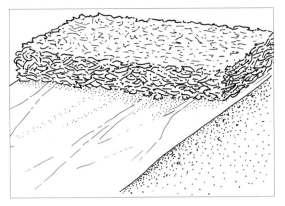

PRACTICAL TIP

• Choose paving that dries quickly so that you do not get wet feet after rain showers.

• Lay paving on blobs of mortar above a granite

waste layer, but allow cracks wide enough for a weeding knife and for inserting thymes and other scented creepers in a gritty mix.

MULCHING

• Lay a porous membrane over well prepared soil then cover this with the mulch material.

protected sites tender plants can bloom unseasonably and insects can enjoy the warmth that gives them energy. Around the perimeters of patios, walls and paths, the ground is softer during cold spells, with frosts kept at bay by the stored heat of gravel, brick and paving stones. Birds of the thrush family search for worms and other juicy items; other birds follow. In warmer weather lizards may bask in the sun. You may create thermal air currents for larger birds. In the evening, swallows and martins may stay longer over these sites, swooping after flies; then with dusk come the hawking bats.

IMPROVING CONDITIONS WITH GRAVEL, MULCHES AND MEMBRANES

Soil is best protected from the elements, so where flower beds are too dry mulch them. A dry top layer of soil is less biologically active than that below; by spreading a shallow skin over this layer you can reactivate it. In dry weather, mulches let rain penetrate to the soil but prevent sun and air drying it. Soil organisms prosper in the protected humidity and they are able to continually refresh the soil. During less dry weather, exposed wet soil creates a humid layer above it as moisture evaporates. When very cold, this humid air may damage the tissue of more tender plants. Gravel mulches separate the damp soil from the air. In times of frost, the mulches mitigate the effects of the expansion of soil in damaging roots.

The most effective form of mulching is two-fold. First, lay a membrane of a sheet material that is

GAZANIA

G. 'Blackberry Ripple'

Description: A South African genus of a couple of dozen perennial species, but usually represented in gardens by hybrids

often grown as annuals. Half hardy.

Uses: Excellent in warm, well-drained spots in borders, in containers or in walls.

Colours: White, yellows, oranges and purples usually with dark marks.

Size: Height and spread 30cm (12in).

Flowering time: Summer.

Varieties: Sold as mixed seedlings or named cultivars such as 'Blackberry Ripple' (pictured) and 'Daybreak', which has daisy flowers of orange, gold, rose pink, bronze and white. While many will close in dull weather and later in the day, 'Daybreak' remains open.

Cultivation: Plant out after frosts in a sandy, sunny spot.

Propagation: By cuttings in spring and summer. Keep young plants under glass out of frost over winter.

pervious to moisture and air but impervious to root growth; this vastly improves the weed suppressing efficacy of mulches. Next, spread over the layer of mulch material. There are many mulches to choose from including shredded bark and leaf mould, which can provide food for the soil and the plants; there are also mulches of grit, gravel or crushed stone. It is important to match mulches to conditions. In hot, dry spots use hard materials: gravel or crushed stone. The soil below the membrane will be left to its own

ERYSIMUM 'BOWLES' MAUVE'
(SYN. *CHEIRANTHUS*
'BOWLES' MAUVE')
Perennial wallflower

Description: A bushy perennial but not long lived. Typical narrow pointed cheiranthus leaves in a dark shade and lots of rounded posies of open, four-petalled flowers. It is on the borderline of hardiness with hard-grown plants of dryish spots standing a better chance of coming through bad weather unscathed.

Uses: Larger rock gardens. Below sunny walls.

Colour: Rich purple-mauve flowers from buds that can be buff.

Scent: Some scent.

Size: 45-75cm (18-30in) high, spread to 45cm (18in).

Flowering time: Mid-spring into summer.

Relatives: *E.* 'Bredon' bright rich yellow, *E. cherii* 'Harpur Crewe' double rich golden and well scented.

Cultivation: Grow in the open in good soil that is well-drained and do not over-stimulate with nitrogenous fertilizer.

Propagation: Seed sown in spring will give variable offspring; increase named clones by greenwood cuttings in summer.

PLANT POINTER
Grow cistuses in positions where you can see them from the sunward side. This is where all their flowering is concentrated and the direction in which all the flowers face. (Other flowers also tend to face the sun.)

devices so it is sensible to do whatever you can to improve it before all is covered over. You will not be digging here for the foreseeable future so try to get as much air into the soil as possible now. If it is very compacted, break it up. Whatever the soil conditions, extra humus will improve it, opening up heavy soils, bulking up light ones and improving water retention, especially in fast-draining sands. Humus is the basis of all living soils.

Material is needed that is likely to add air to the soil structure, particularly important on poorly-drained clay, which may be improved by adding very coarse grit; sand and rounded pea gravel are of very little use. Don't worry about digging very deep, you can turn grit and humus into just the top layers of soil – a lot of organic material far underground is of limited use. Even just leaving grit and humus spread evenly on the soil surface can be highly beneficial: rain and worms will soon incorporate it in the vital top layer.

A fairly satisfactory temporary mulch can be formed with a layer of grit 5cm (2in) deep. This will work well for a period but will become incorpo-rated into the top soil over twelve months. Allow this to happen and then spread your membrane sheet and cover with a coarser stone or bark mulch.

Making the most of it

There are various types of dry, sunny spots. Each can be approached in a slightly different way. One that is in a prominent location, perhaps near the house or patio, will need to be tackled so that it looks reasonable at all times, but more out of the way spots are suitable for a collection of cornfield and allied plants that look their best through the summer months and manage on soils that are not all that well endowed with nutrients and good structure. More prominent spots will need shrubs and plants to furnish the area permanently. *Cistus lauri-folius*, standing up to 2m (6ft) high and wide and with dark green aromatic evergreen leaves, looks good with or without its large golden-centred white flowers. *Brachyglottis* 'Sunshine' would make a good contrasting shrub; bright, light, silver-grey against the dark mass of the cistus. The plants listed in the margins on the following pages are divided by cultural needs into three groups. There is plenty of choice and by choosing from just one of these groups you are more likely to create a natural

environment that will look good and in which the plants will thrive.

Group 1 (margin) is garden-worthy plants that naturally grow in extreme conditions in otherwise moderate climates: their performance can be more spectacular than that of 'ordinary' plants. From this group you can choose cliff- or mountain-dwellers to jostle with 'tough' plants from hay- and cornfields.

Group 2, page 23, includes aromatic herbs from the scrubby Mediterranean Maquis and Californian grasslands. These plants are used to summer droughts and are able to grow and bloom well despite a lack of water. In fact, without a summer baking, they could not survive: your 'problem area' really suits them.

Group 3 plants, page 25, find dry sunny sites a haven from fatal winter wet. Species often assumed to be frost tender can survive freezing cold conditions so long as they have dry feet. In this group are the bulbs from Africa and the plants from the high mountains. Among these are those plants that produce large exciting flowers which look exotic among smaller blooms of hardier species.

BROOMS AND GORSES

Plants from the genera *Cytisus*, *Genista*, *Spartium* and *Ulex* – the brooms and the gorses – are wonderful for dry, sunny spots. They grow rapidly and bloom copiously from their earliest years. They are undemanding and tough and always look green and fresh although it is the stems rather than the small branch-clasping leaves that give the colour.

Genista aetnensis (Mount Etna broom, see profile page 11) grows to a young tree and adds height to a planting, without casting much shade. *Spartium junceum* (Spanish broom) is considered weedy by some gardeners but it is very quick and easy from seed and will help fill gaps while slower, more prestigious shrubs are getting established. It has green stems and bright golden flowers.

Some of the smaller species are choicer. *Genista lydia*, syn. *G. spathulata* (Bulgarian broom), is a real star whose wide, low-mounded form is lost under a

HALIMIUM OCYMOIDES

Description: Evergreen shrub belonging to a genus closely related to *Cistus* (rock rose). It has slender oval, grey leaves on wiry stems that reach upwards from a spreading shub and carry a succession of wide saucer-shaped flowers for weeks in summer.
Uses: A good shrubs for a hot spot with less than abundant supplies of water.
Colour: Very bright yellow with a dramatic, dark mahogany or purple-red blotch at the base of each petal and a central boss of golden stamens.
Size: 30-45cm (12-18in) high, to 75cm (30in) across.
Flowering time: Early to midsummer.
Relatives: x *H. ocymoides* 'Susan' has wide-petalled, yellow flowers with rich blotching. Intergeneric hybrids with *Cistus* are listed as x *Halimiocistus*. x *H. wintonensis* has white flowers with a dark red-ringed, gold centre. It grows to 60cm (2ft) high.
Cultivation: Easy in sun with good drainage.
Propagation: Semi-ripe cuttings in summer.

PLANTS FOR DRY SUNNY SITES

Amaryllis bella-donna
Chaenomeles forms
Gladiolus nanus forms
Gladiolus spp.
Hyacinthus orientalis
Iris unguicularis
Narcissus tazetta forms
Nerine bowdenii
Watsonia spp.

GROUP I PLANTS FROM EXTREME LOCAL CONDITIONS

Armeria maritima
Dryas octopetala
Genista pilosa
Geranium sanguineum var. *striatum*
Hippophaë rhamnoides
Pulsatilla vulgaris
Salix reticulata
Saxifraga oppositifolia
Scilla autumnalis
S. verna
Silene maritima
Tamarix spp.

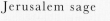

PHLOMIS FRUTICOSA
Jerusalem sage

P. italica

Description: A spreading evergreen shrub which can be dramatic with strongly sculptured, coarse and hairy grey-green leaves, above which are borne whorls of hooded flowers for several weeks. It needs space to make its effect; a tough looking character that it is a mistake to try to restrain severely. Borderline hardy.
Uses: It makes a bold focal point and is especially good for dry spots.
Colour: Golden flowers, grey-green leaves.
Size: 1.4m (4½ft) high, spread fractionally less.
Flowering time: Early and midsummer.
Relatives: *P. russeliana* is an evergreen perennial with strongly textured heart-shaped leaves and whorls of mid-yellow flowers on strong erect stems. Good ground cover. *P.* 'Edward Bowles' is a robust hybrid subshrub with paler yellow flowers than *P. fruticosa*. *P. italica* (pictured) is an evergreen shrub with pink blossom: a good colour contrast with the grey foliage.
Cultivation: Easy in well-drained soil in sunshine.
Propagation: By seed sown in autumn, by softwood cuttings in summer. *P. russeliana* can be divided in early spring.

plethora of bright yellow blossom. *Cytisus × kewensis* splays itself low over the ground, across rocks or down banks with a frothing mass of creamy blossom. *Genista hispanica* (Spanish gorse) makes a very spiny hedgehog bush of green, almost lost beneath a mass of rich golden flowerheads. Tiny in comparison is *G. pilosa* (hairy greenwood) which may only make 15cm (6in). *G. sagittalis* (winged broom) is only a little larger, with procumbent winged stems that turn their ends up to offer clusters of yellow pea-flowers.

All these brooms and gorses grow quickly from seed and can be very useful for awkward sunny spots in need of a quick fix. Tree lupins are similarly rapid and could be grown alongside.

Blue and mauve go well with broom and gorse colours, producing a regal effect with the gold and a more subtle harmony with the cream. *Erysimum* 'Bowles' Mauve' (page 20) is a distinguished perennial wallflower with the most beautiful lavender-blue flowers over a firm mound of linear glaucous leaves. Very quick to make a reasonable size, perhaps up to 60cm (2ft) in a year, its size and habit are not dissimilar to that of the smaller brooms. A sterile hybrid, it will stay almost permanently in flower as it strives unsuccessfully to produce seed. Even a normal year will find it blooming for six to eight months, and in a balmy one it can carry right through one flowering season into the next! Little wonder it is short-lived, it flowers itself to death. A bad winter may kill it off, however, a succession of cuttings will ensure replacements.

There are other less well-known plants of which good use can be made. Do not ignore the annuals (see also below, page 26). Although it may seem a chore to have to sow seed of these each year, they will often do the job for you, self sowing happily after once being introduced.

Hibiscus trionum is a delectable annual that is found growing in some of the tough wild spots of New Zealand. The cream flowers have deep plum-purple centres, making them real eye-catchers, and they go well with the wallflower and the brooms. It is a mistake to use it sparsely; splash out and plant it in bold drifts to arrest you and any visitors walking the garden.

A very good plant to associate with brooms, growing under and around them, is catnip (*Nepeta racemosa*, syn *N. mussinii*). The floppy habit seems in keeping with a casual approach to life but its blue-grey foliage works well with yellows. Where you have the room for rather bolder effects try the larger *N.* 'Six Hills Giant', height 60cm (2ft). *N. × faassenii*, the familiar catmint, is useful and can make dense masses of foliage as well as providing long-lasting crops of lavender-coloured blossom. Catnip is less thick-growing, so other plants should be planted with it to help in the weed-suppressing role. To keep work to a minimum, all gaps in the flower beds should be filled before nature does its own filling with a range of weeds; we can choose our own weeds. Some of these can be very effective. *Hieracium aurantiacum* (fox-and-cubs or orange hawkweed) is a European grassland flower with runners and flat rosettes of hairy leaves. It will be happy to occupy niches between catnip. It blooms over a long summer period with stiff stems rising from each rosette to 15-20cm (6-8in) high to open a bunch of flat vividly orange-gold flowers, brighter and smaller than dandelions: and not so invasive from seed.

SHRUBBY HERBS

Herbs of the more shrubby variety are very heat-resistant and can be used to form a solid understorey. Lavender is always desirable, its evergreen-silvery-blue clump and spiky flower stems giving texture and shape as well as colour through the year. Scent from its foliage and the hazy-blue flowers, which encourage the flutter and buzz of busy wings in summer, all earn it a place in the garden, whether as a clipped hedge, steered towards formality, or as ageing, rugged individual specimens. *Convolvulus sabatius* echoes all its colours while contrasting in its growth pattern. Planted at the base of lavender, it will scramble around and into the lower foliage where it spreads its wide funnel-discs of flowers. The touch of winter protection given by the lavender will do no harm to the convolvulus in colder areas.

Rosemary (*Rosmarinus officinalis*) is another familiar shrubby plant often mentally linked with lavenders. While foliage and flower form vary relatively little among the different cultivars, the plant itself can be fairly severely upright, as in the aptly named 'Miss Jessopp's Upright', or low growing as in the Prostratus Group, which includes 'Jackman's Prostrate'. 'Benenden Blue' is a popular worthwhile clone. The grey-green leaves of all rosemaries are effectively highlighted by the vivid cool silvery blue foliage of rue (*Ruta graveolens*, see plant profile page 26). And shrubby hyssop could be brought into a herb mix, together with some of the taller thymes.

The marjorams and oreganos are splendid plants, if at first glance rather ordinary looking. The common majoram (*Origanum vulgare*) acts as a magnet for butterflies such as the small copper. The golden-leaved version, *O.v.* 'Aureum', is a real winner. Like the rest, it likes a place in the light, but will be best with a touch of protection from the fiercest sun to stop its leaves getting scorched brown.

GROUP 2 MEDITERRANEAN AND CALIFORNIAN GRASSLAND TYPE PLANTS

Agave americana

Allium spp.

Artemisia spp.

Carpenteria californica

Cistus spp.

Colchicum spp.

Crocus spp.

Cytisus battandieri

Epilobium latifolium

Eschscholzia californica

Fritillaria spp.

Gaillardia spp.

Genista aetnensis

Halimium spp.

Iris bulbous forms

Lavandula dentata

L. trimestris

Rosmarinus spp.

Sternbergia spp.

Thymus spp.

Tulipa spp.

Yucca spp.

This Mediterranean-style courtyard in England shows how effective a few carefully chosen plants and hard materials are in recreating the atmosphere of gardens of another climate

SMALL EVERGREEN SHRUBS

Small evergreen shrubs fill the same garden role as our culinary and medicinal herbs. They provide stronger bones for the overall design and widen the choice of colours and forms as well as increasing the range of flowering times.

Winter-flowering heathers are very welcome throughout the year because by planting a selection of cultivars you can have flower colour from mid- or late autumn until mid-spring. Heathers always look tidy and can manage through periods of drought without looking peaky. Their growth is so dense that very few weeds are likely to challenge their territorial hold. Conifers, such as the prostrate junipers, also play a role, there is no questioning their weed-suppressing abilities. Hebes are evergreen. The hardiest will survive any weather, the taller hybrids with beautiful purple, blue and white flowers may be a touch more tender but are not normally badly mauled by the winter and if they get killed one winter in ten or twenty they are soon replaced, cuttings grow quickly into substantial rounded bushes.

HYSSOPUS OFFICINALIS
Hyssop

H. officinalis subsp. *aristatus*

Description: One of the group of classic small shrubby herbs which includes rosemary, lavender and thyme. This is less often grown, probably because its uses are more medicinal than culinary. A pleasing hardy plant with narrow oval dark aromatic leaves and long spires of small crowded twin-lipped flowers for many weeks.

Uses: Decorative from the second half of summer into autumn and can make a low hedge. Adds unusual tang to soups or salads and leaves can be added to cooked fruits. Infusions of the leaves used to relieve coughs and catarrh..

Wildlife: Flowers attract bees and other flying insects.

Colour: Usually bright blue, also rich pinks, purples and white.

Scent: Flower perfume attracts bees, leaves sharply aromatic.

Size: To 60cm (2ft) high, spread slightly more.

Flowering time: Midsummer well into autumn.

Relatives: *H. officinalis* f. *albus* is white, *H.officinalis.* f. *roseus* is pink. Subsp. *aristatus* (pictured) is a much more narrowly upright shrub with bright green leaves.

Cultivation: Needs full sun and best in good, fertile, well-drained soils.

Propagation: Softwood cuttings in summer or seed sown in autumn.

POTENTILLAS

The potentilla genus is a diverse one, but it is basically of two halves: the shrubby and the herbaceous. The shrubs are an easy lot managing well enough on poor rations, surviving in poorish soils that are not all that deep, and despite difficult conditions they are able to husband their resources, take all the sun that comes, and last out almost all droughts. *Potentilla fruticosa* is native to all countries of northern Europe, including Britain where it is a rather rare plant. It makes a spreading very twiggy bush up to 1m (3ft) tall and at least twice as wide, the whole having a somewhat downy appearance due to the hairy narrow leaflets that make up the pinnate leaves. It can be found wild in a variety of habitats, often wet ones in wild hollows by river sides but also in hilly terrain in rocky spots. The usual flower colour is a bright gold, but nowadays, thanks to the huge number of cultivars, the palette is expanded, ranging from white through lots of pale primrose shades to deep gold into oranges and near reds; pinks are also available. As there are over a hundred cultivars to choose from it might be best to visit a comprehensive collection to see them in flower (in Britain the National Collection is at Webbs Garden Centre, near Bromsgrove) before making your choice.

HERBACEOUS PERENNIALS

No matter what conditions are in your garden, there is always something to be found among the herbaceous perennials to add floral relish to the year-round display. In dry areas, the choice includes some of the herbaceous potentillas, such as the rock cinquefoil (*Potentilla rupestris*) a white-faced angel looking to heaven. Some forms have larger flowers than others which, truthfully, are rather mean for the garden. The foliage is a light green, perhaps even yellowish, which is fine so long as you are expecting it and do not start worrying about jaundice. Familiar faces like those of the ox-eye daisy (*Leucanthemum vulgare*) can be great: remember just how strong a colonizer it can be. The harebell (*Campanula rotundifolia*) is such a lightweight plant with thin leaves and thread-like stems that it will always be welcome and never become a pest. *Campanula portenschlagiana* (syn. *C. muralis*) is another matter. It might be a wonder scrambling over a wall but given a centimetre it would like a kilometre. Campanulas do tend to sort themselves out into the three categories of plants: the pernicious, the perennial and the pernickety, so be careful with your choice!

Other plants from the wild, such as musk mallow (*Malva moschata*) and its white form, are good garden plants with pleasing foliage and much more refined flowers – pale rose pink and icy white – than the more familiar roadside *M. sylvestris*, admirable in its wild place but too rampant for any but the largest parkland garden.

In a dry spot it is certainly worth importing sun-loving irises, of which there are no end, from among the bulbous and rhizomatous kinds. *I. pallida* is a pleasing mid-blue bearded iris; its variegated forms, *I. p.* 'Argentea Variegata' and *I. p.* 'Variegata', have strikingly white-striped foliage. It is also an excellent idea to dip into the flora of South Africa to find a wealth of sun-worshippers that will do well if given excellent drainage. The vivid daisies of gazanias add a really exotic touch; osteospermums may look a little more cool and refined but don't let them fool you, they hail from the same country and like to open their daisy faces to the sun.

Silver grey sea hollies (*Eryngium* species and forms) evolved in sand dunes, hence 'sea'. Their prickly leaves account for 'holly', but, of course, they are herbaceous perennials not shrubs, and prefer to be below ground when winter seas storms are raging. There are many scintillating characters among the sea hollies and these are worth placing carefully. In silver and steel shades, they look almost metallic, though in some the blue of the flowers can tend to run down the stems.

The qualities of the hardy geraniums must be constantly lauded: *G. riversleaianum* 'Mavis Simpson' for its wide circle of soft grey foliage and the quantities of pink flowers it displays against this backcloth all through the summer until autumn or winter. The flowers are worth a second glance to appreciate the delicate veining in darker shades. Pink and grey make a good colour pairing, and, as 'Mavis Simpson' will spread from an overwintered crown to a circular mat 1m (3ft) across, she is a splendid item.

From some of the higher, tougher mountainsides of New Zealand, *Hebe pinguifolia* 'Pagei', which is strictly speaking a prostrate shrub, extends the grey idea with tough, neatly-packed, oval leaves of steely-grey highlighted, rather than dissipated, by its many heads of small white flowers poked just above the foliage mass. It associates well with the geranium,

CISTUS × PURPUREUS
Sun rose

C. creticus

Description: One of the best of a genus of fast-growing evergreen Mediterranean shrubs. Strong with narrowish grey-green rough-textured leaves and wide saucer-blooms for many weeks. Frost hardy.

Uses: Grows easily in poorer well-drained soils and can withstand lots of wind. A useful seaside shrub.

Colour: Rich purplish pink flowers each centred by a showy dark crimson blotch.

Size: Height and spread 1m (3ft).

Flowering time: Summer.

Relatives: *C. x purpureus* 'Alan Fradd' and 'Betty Taudevin' are two selected clones with particularly good-sized and showy flowers. *C. creticus* (pictured) has plain purplish pink flowers. *C. laurifolius* can make a formidable bush 2m (6ft) high and wide and has showy white flowers centred with gold.

Cultivation: Plant out then leave undisturbed. Cut away dead wood but avoid hard pruning.

Propagation: Hybrids by softwood cuttings in summer. Species by seed.

the texture of the foliage is a complete contrast – hard against soft. This is a plant that is worth grouping: three specimens will more than treble the effect. Its formal appearance can be exploited by border edges, or patio beds.

As in all areas of life, there are the yeomen plants, never hitting the headlines but doing a good job nevertheless; the calamints are among these. The large *Calamintha grandiflora*, stays low to the ground with greyish leaves up to 7cm (3in) long and producing thyme-like purplish flowers in loose racemes in summer. It is an introvert, sedate, bushy plant rather

Sand and coastal plants, such as thrift, have been cleverly used to create this seaside garden

similar to its relative hyssop but with more rounded, blue, aromatic, crinkled leaves. A cloud of bees descends on the flowers when they open in late summer, transforming them to buzzing spikes of pale blue. This type of plant makes a good companion for some of the allium species, including the smaller crimson-pink *A. oreophilum* (syn. *A. ostrowskianum*) at 15cm (6in), the taller *A. sphaerocephalon* with hard oval heads of purple-red at 60cm (2ft) and major players such as *A. aflatunense* with purplish rose round drumstick heads standing up to 1m (3ft) high.

ANNUALS

Annuals give easy extra colour, an instant morale boost for the garden. Hardy ones are the easiest, growing quickly, even in poor soils, and thereafter self sowing. Meadow foam (*Limnanthes douglasii*) is a Californian grassland plant (see plant profile page 233). Sown on the top of a slope, it may well try colonizing, and self sown plants will bloom earlier than those from your sowing. The yellow with some white looks good with blue-flowered plants.

Cornfield weeds were once a source of much joy to walkers, if not to farmers. Selective sprays have wiped out most, but they can be reintroduced into the garden scene. Creating a cornfield patch is not

difficult where there is open worked soil in a sunny spot with good drainage. As long as you prevent stronger plants colonizing and keep at least a proportion of the soil open and stirred around, you can expect to get generation after generation of seedlings. Choose cornflower (*Centaurea cyanus*), which is pure blue in the type but also available in white, pink and redder shades in cultivated strains. The common field poppy (*Papaver rhoeas*) is probably the best known of cornfield flowers and is sometimes still seen in wide stretches. Now there are pleasing pastel shades available as Shirley poppies. *P. commutatum* is orange-red with a conspicuous black centre; it is sometimes erroneously marketed under the name 'Ladybird'.

Corncockle (*Agrostemma githago*) is well worth growing. Allowed to scramble upwards through other plants, its slender stems present their really silky purple-pink flowers for admiration. They are delicate with a certain refinement: dotted lines mark veins and point to the darker centre of each rounded bloom cradled in long green needle-shaped sepals. A collection of these cornfield species should include *Viola tricolor*, the wild pansy or heartsease, a small-flowered merry imp with lots of faces gazing upwards in sunny colour schemes of yellows and mauves. A particularly desirable variant is *V.* 'E. A. Bowles' (syn. *V.* 'Bowles' Black') in deepest velvety violet-black with a small golden eye. Corn marigold (*Chrysanthemum segetum*) is an 8cm (3in) golden disc with a big soft heart. It is one of the plants often found in mixed packets of annuals for children, but

---

RUTA GRAVEOLENS
Rue, Herb of grace

Description: An upright or leaning sub-shrub, this herb has pungent leaves which are sometimes used medicinally; be careful of handling foliage as some people experience allergic reactions and the white sap can cause skin problems particularly in sunlight. The silver blue-grey much-divided foliage is its main claim to fame. Flowers are poor little yellowish buttony bits.

Uses: Foliage plant.

Colour: Grey-green or silver-blue foliage, yellowish flowers.

Scent: Leaves pungent.

Size: 60cm (2ft) high and across.

Flowering time: Summer.

Relatives: *R. graveolens* 'Jackman's Blue' is the usual garden plant, and is very glaucous with nearly white foliage. 'Variegata' is variable with leaves splashed with differing amounts of cream.

Cultivation: Wants sun and good well-drained soil. Cut back in early spring to keep tidy.

Propagation: By seed or midsummer softwood cuttings.

older gardeners can join in the fun too.

Ornamental grasses mix well with all these annuals. It is best to mark where you sow them otherwise they may be weeded out. Anyone who has introduced love-in-the-mist (*Nigella damascena*) into their garden knows how cheekily it seeds itself around, but no matter, its light green filigree foliage is as pleasing as the blue flowers and inflated seedheads. *Lavatera trimestris*, an annual mallow, has sizeable trumpets through the summer and autumn, a contrast in size to some of the smaller-flowered cornfield species. *L. t.* 'Loveliness' can reach 1.2m (4ft) and is striking in deep rose, at the other end of the scale is *L. t.* 'Silver Cup', only some 12cm (5in) high bearing abundant pale pink flowers with deeper coloured veins radiating from the dark centres.

Natural communities

Dry habitats make up a large part of the world, but some are rich in plant life. Even desert areas given a fall of rain will come quickly to life with plants that get through their growing cycle in treble-quick time to leave behind a crop of seed before normal waterless conditions are resumed. Although desert plants are unlikely to be suitable there are plants such as the *Delosperma (Mesembryanthemum)* forms from South Africa that are brilliant in bright sunny hot spots in the garden. Other South Africans such as gladioli, *Watsonia* spp., *Gazania* forms, osteospermums and pelargoniums may or may not be completely hardy in climates cooler than their homeland, but they are

certainly doing better with the warmer, dryer summers of recent years.

Other groups of plants may be found in temperate parts of the world but in areas that are environmentally very challenging. Cliff-hangers, mountain-top dwellers and some hayfield plants are in this category.

CLIFFS AND MOUNTAINS

Plants that cling to the apparently inhospitable refuges of cliff and mountainside have evolved their own methods of coping. Where land joins sea, all the

PEROVSKIA ATRIPLICIFOLIA
Russian sage

Description: Somewhat like rosemary or lavender. A hardy upward-striving subshrub with slender narrow silvery stems and narrow serrated, silvery-white foliage. Long, narrow spikes of twin-lipped flowers for many weeks.

Uses: Light colouring and airy effect in border or shrubbery.

Colour: Lavender-blue flowers, silvery plant.

Scent: Leaves aromatic if crushed.

Size: Dependent on management, with time can be up to 1.2m (4ft) high and 1m (3ft) across.

Flowering time: From late summer through autumn.

Relatives: *P.* 'Blue Spire' bears prolific much-branched spikes of violet-blue.

Cultivation: Needs sun and perfectly drained soil. Cut top growth back by two thirds at end of winter to stimulate fresh growth.

Propagation: Take cuttings of soft wood in late spring.

SOME SEEDS NEEDING STRATIFICATION

Acer (some)

Amelanchier

Betula

Carya

Cotoneaster

Euonymus

Fagus

Hippophaë

Ilex

Rosa

Sorbus

Viburnum (some)

SEA HOLLIES AND RELATIVES

Eryngium alpinum 75-90cm (30-36in) high

E. bourgatii 45cm (18in) high

E. giganteum, biennial, 1-1.2m (3-4ft) high

E. x *oliverianum* 60-90cm (24-36in) high

E. maritimum, true sea holly, 30-60cm (12-24in) high

E. x *tripartitum* 1-1.2m (3-4ft) high

E. variifolium 45cm (18in) high

HELIANTHEMUM 'WISLEY PRIMROSE'
Rock rose

Description: In appearance like the low growing smaller cistuses but these procumbent much-branched shrubby plants are hardier. Species grow throughout Europe, including Britain, often on poor moorland or thin pasture as well as on cliffs. In gardens the selected hybrid forms are grown. Buds burst to display crumpled silks in various colours, but quickly these iron out to open saucers looking very bright and covering the plants.

Uses: Rock garden plants but especially useful for trailing down a retaining wall.

Colour: Primrose-yellow flowers, grey-green leaves.

Size: 20-30cm (8-12in) high, 30-45cm (12-18in) wide or more.

Flowering time: Summer.

Relatives: 'Ben More' orange-red, 'Fire Dragon' scarlet, 'Raspberry Ripple' white with irregular crimson centres, 'Wisley Pink', 'Wisley White'.

Cultivation: Not too rich soil in full sun. After flowering clip back to keep neat and encourage fresh growth.

Propagation: Seed gives differing results. Cuttings are reliable, take semi-ripe wood in summer.

erosive forces of nature combine. Wind sweeps off the sea, laden with salt and buffeting the plants. This stress limits their size. Sun shines strongly with its effects intensified by reflected heat and glare from the water's surface. There are no trees for shelter. At night, heat radiation is severe. Temperatures fluctuate wildly. Soil is likely to be poor and shallow. There may be only the thinnest skin of recently deposited litter with no chance of building a proper soil layer. Wind and rain bear away any beginnings. But here

sea campion (*Silene maritima*) and thrift (*Armeria maritima*) flourish and make a familiar pattern of white and pink in spots where nothing can grow.

Alpines live in a harsh world. Icy-cold water from the snow melt is followed by little except morning mists. They have to resort to drilling deep into the rock with penetrating roots to find the moisture they need. As cold is the normal form, they must bloom and seed quickly during the brief warm days. To attract the vital pollinating insects, they are brilliant in flower; tiny leaves of saxifrages and phloxes can be lost under a blanket of bloom.

HAYFIELDS
Hayfields are often grazed well into the winter, losing fertility all the while. When new growth is at its most nutritious it is cut and carted away. Little is left to be recycled and build up the topsoil fertility. However, the mowing does keep in check the stronger plants, the shrubs and the trees that would otherwise invade. The natural path of succession of plant life is frozen. However, in this hard environment there are low-growing plants that manage to make a living. The creeping bugle, *Ajuga reptans*, is an example. It manages to crouch low and only pokes its flowers upwards; it is safe in hayfields or grazed meadows. The harebell, *Campanula rotundifolia*, is another such plant. The ox-eye daisy, *Leucanthemum vulgare*, comes into bloom early and may shed some seed before the hayfield is cut; it is likely to produce some later bloom which will double its chances of distributing fresh seed around.

Creating shade

Shade is often a blessing although it can be a problem in some situations (see pages 32-43). Many of our most attractive garden plants originate in mixed habitats in the wild where they will certainly have enjoyed at least partial shade. Where gardens are open and bare the creation of shade becomes an urgent necessity, or rather, it is shade, along with some shelter, that is needed. A third desirable feature of shade, or shade-producing plants, may well be screening – not everything that is visible from the homestead may please the eye.

Trees and shrubs are usually the most satisfying answers to these three desiderata. They screen the distant prospect of the gasworks, they break some of

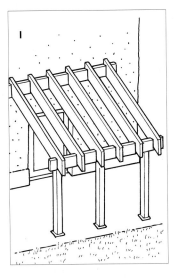

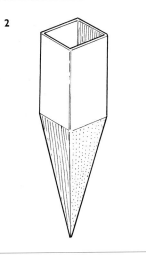

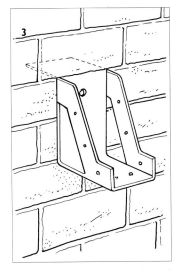

MAKING A PERGOLA

You may be especially thankful for a pergola in dry, sunny gardens to provide shade as well as give opportunities for growing a range of climbing plants. In a small or medium-sized garden you may not need to build brick columns; wooden posts will be quite adequate.

1 For uprights use 10 x 10cm (4 x 4in) posts. Assuming a modest pergola width

of about 1m (3ft), use cross-beams of 1.3m length and 20 x 7.5cm cross-section (50 x 8 x 3in). For the runners going the length of the pergola use wood approximately 1.5-2m (5-6ft) long and not less than 15 x 7.5cm (6 x 3in) cross-section.

2 Secure uprights in metal housings that have been accurately driven or buried into the ground so that when the posts are entered they are upright and all reach the same height. Alternatively,

the posts can be secured with a concrete base that is at least 60cm (24in) deep and 45cm (18in) wide. Remember that these uprights are going to hold up the superstructure and will also have to cope with the stresses of winds and gales that will be pulling at it and all the wind-catching climbers on it.

3 Galvanized joist hangers are useful for securing the cross-beams to the house wall. Alternatively a wall plate can be used.

4 Runners and cross-beams can be interlocked by cutting slots in both members so that the completed joint is flush. Alternatively, the slots may be a little less than half the depths so that the runners ride across the top some few centimetres proud.

5 Use timber that has been treated with preservative, or treat it yourself. Use strong nails or screws – brass screws do not rust.

---

the force of the prevailing south west winds, they help provide the microclimates for some smaller garden treasures, and they do all this while giving generously of their own beauty, producing more leaves for the compost heap or for mulching and growing root systems that delve deep to exploit latent sources of food and on the way improving the natural structure of the soil.

Light shade is most suitable for supporting other plant life; thicker more dense growth is best restricted to the outer perimeters of the garden, where screening, more than anything else, is the aim. Depending on your needs, choose from thin-crowned deciduous trees and shrubs, to allow light through to the ground below, which will allow you to grow smaller plants in their shade, to the heaviest of conifers, which may create desert dryness beneath but come into their own in the winter months when the deciduous trees are mere silhouettes. There is a place for all.

There is no reason to pick huge trees that belong in the forest. There is a wide variety of deciduous trees suitable for the garden. Among the lightest are the rowan-type *Sorbus* species and hybrids, The white-beam *Sorbus* types are somewhat heavier but can make impressive focal points. Choose the birches to ensure that your shade will also allow plenty of light through. They have attractive foliage, bark and form. The weeping kinds, such as the familiar silver birch (*Betula pendula*), have varying shapes but the bark of all takes on a silvery papered look in a few seasons; as they age the lower part of the trunk can become increasing dark and black. *B. utilis* has bark in shades of buff-cream and pink as well as the predominant silver-white. It is an open upright tree with little or none of the weeping form of the silver birches. *B. utilis* var. *jacquemontii* is the form most often planted. It is outstanding for its trunks and branches that look as if someone has just walked away after painting a luminous brilliant white all over.

PLANT NAMES

The name Bowles recurs throughout this book. Mr Bowles was a dedicated gardener and plantsman who grew, collected, wrote about and bred plants in his garden near London until the 1950s. He had a good eye for plants and grew many interesting curiosities, and he was thoughtful and kind, giving encouragement to many, including myself as a young man.

FLOWERING TREES FOR LIGHT SHADE

Amelanchier lamarckii

Betula spp.

Crataegus spp. (thorns)

Malus spp. (apples)

Prunus spp. (cherries)

Robinia pseudoacacia 'Frisia'

Sorbus spp. (rowans)

Flowering trees that cast light shade include ornamental cherries (*Prunus*) and apples (*Malus*) as well as lesser known genera (see margin list).

TOUGH TREES FOR TOUGH PLACES

Transplanted trees, either bare-rooted or pot-grown ones, do not establish so well as trees grown in situ by seed. The restricted, possibly spiralling roots of the potted specimen will take some time to get unravelled and to settle into their new surroundings. If the all-important tap roots are damaged, they are unlikely to recover fully, and in some species will be permanently crippled, meaning that the tree will never get as deep an anchoring system as it would naturally. Consequently, as it grows taller it is more threatened by high winds, which may even blow it over to reveal the catastrophic lack of a sound, deep root system, just at a time when it should be approaching its most treasured mature beauty.

Consider sowing seeds in tough places; probably the best time to sow is the autumn. Be sensible and work out the mature size of the trees and choose some likely positions for sowing. Then give the seeds a good start by cultivating the chosen spots, removing a few handfuls of soil and replacing this with sterilized seed compost. After sowing, surround the area with a plastic weed mat. As the seeds germinate, thin to the best one early on. Control weed growth from the time of sowing through the first few formative years.

Scarification or stratification helps to break the dormancy of some tree seeds. The seed packet or a good manual should give details for the species.

Some fresh seed will grow immediately because the chemical inhibitors that are designed to delay germination are only formed as the seed dries. So collecting fresh seed and sowing early can pay dividends. Other seed, particularly small or fragile

DOROTHEANTHUS SPECIES AND VARIETIES

Mesembryanthemum, Ice plant, Livingstone daisy

Description: Grown as half hardy annuals these succulent-leaved low-carpeting plants from South Africa have daisy flowers in colours that will dazzle the sun itself.

Uses: Unbeatable for very dry sunny spots.

Colours: White, white tipped yellow, cream, yellows, pink tipped, fully pink, purples, magentas and reds.

Size: 7-10cm (3-4in) high, spread 30cm (12in).

Flowering time: Flowers open in summer sunshine, close in poor weather.

Varieties: Choose from a selection of various seed strains.

Cultivation: Best on poor soil which further encourages an already extraordinary generosity of bloom.

Propagation: Sow under glass in early spring, prick out and then plant out in mid-spring. Can also be raised by seed in situ if sown mid-spring. Prolong flowering by dead-heading.

kinds, such as the flaky seed of birches, are certainly best sown immediately and only very lightly covered. If collecting seed outside your domain, obtain permission from the owner; you will not need much. Remember that seed is not necessarily free for the taking, some cannot be legally harvested, even with permission.

Pre-germination of seed is another option. Such seed is available commercially or you can do it yourself under controlled conditions in a greenhouse or coldframe, or even in your home. Here, you can keep an eye on the seed and it is easier to keep the

PRACTICAL TIP

Keep your eyes open for nurseries and institutions like horticultural training colleges that have sales of bare-rooted trees in the autumn or early winter. Bare-rooted trees can often get away quicker and make better specimens in garden conditions than similarly sized container-grown ones. And they are a lot cheaper. I have planted many birches, *Sorbus*, ornamental apples (*Malus*) and ornamental cherries (*Prunus*) very successfully as bare-rooted plants. It is not so long ago that this was the standard practice. Container-grown stock only took over the main role some three or so decades ago.

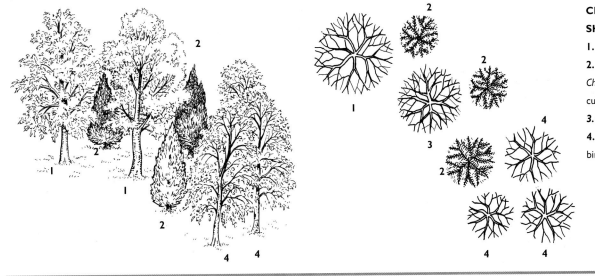

CREATING LIGHT SHADE

1. *Sorbus aria* (Whitebeam)

2. Evergreens such as *Chamaecyparis lawsoniana* cultivars

3. *Betula utilis jacquemontii*

4. *Betula pendula* (Silver birch)

seedling clear of any competition from foreign species. By potting on the young seedlings and growing them yourself you avoid any danger of the roots getting pot-bound. When nicely growing, the sapling can be placed in its permanent quarters. The benefit of this is that you will have a marked plant to guard, which may be easier than keeping weed-free a seed-sown station.

When seedlings have appeared and been thinned to one per station or once you have planted out your pot-reared sapling, think of protecting the youngster from any dangers in the environment – weed encroachment, gnawing rabbits, squirrels, deer and the unhelpful attentions of dogs. A cut-down plastic tree protection tube will not only manage this but will help the plant with moisture accrual and save it from too much drying and damage from wind, as well as encouraging it to grow up straight.

Weed mats to control weed growth around young trees is almost essential. The growth above ground can be bad enough, but below ground the competition is fierce and it is this that may hold back a young tree. A weed mat, stretching at least 1m (3ft) around the plant, will help create a neutral buffer zone where the privileged youngster can make its own way and establish a healthy root system.

It is of course possible to manage perfectly well with transplanted specimens, if for any reason sowing in situ is impossible. Choose young established plants; under no circumstances should you buy anything with roots going round and round the inside of the pot. Such specimens either never make good plants or take a long while to overcome this initial handicap. Neither should you buy specimens that have been cut back strongly once or twice to make them look within the bounds of their container. Whatever the 'special' price, these are not bargains.

OSTEOSPERMUM

Description: A hybrid from the genus of South African daisy-flowered woody perennials. In milder winters it will survive outside. It usually scrambles and has narrowly oval leaves and a long succession of bright, large, daisy flowers. 'Buttermilk' is rather more upright than most cultivars.

Uses: Splendid in containers, in larger hanging baskets, in raised beds or grown in warm spots in borders/beds.

Colours: Grey-green leaves and pale yellow flowers deeper at the petal tips than the bases where they are nearly white to contrast with the dark brown central discs.

Size: 60cm (2ft) high, spread 30cm (12in).

Flowering time: Midsummer until frosts.

Varieties: Breeding these is a real growth industry. There are whites, blues, purples, magentas and pinks all with contrasting dark centres. 'Whirligig' is a striking bluish white with each petal starting wide at the flower centre then being restricted to a narrow quill which opens to a spoon-shaped end.

Cultivation: Choose a sunny spot with warm well-drained soil and plant out in mid-spring when bad frosts should be in the past. Tidy in early spring but see Propagation.

Propagation: By cuttings of unflowered stems in midsummer. Keep a few under glass over winter in case of calamitous frosts.

DRY AND SHADY

AUCUBA JAPONICA
'VARIEGATA'
Spotted laurel

Description: Strong evergreen weather-resistant hardy shrub with handsome but tough polished foliage – oval and pointed leaves 15-20cm (6-8in) long and up to 7-8cm (3in) wide. Flowers are inconspicuous but berries are bright (see below).

Uses: Probably the most valuable of evergreen shrubs for difficult dry shady places. Looking healthy in the most unpropitious spots.

Wildlife: Affords shelter for birds and other animal life.

Colour: Foliage polished bright green and gold, tiny purple flowers and later some red fruits like oval cherries.

Size: 2.7m (9ft) high, spread a little more.

Flowering time: Mid-spring, inconspicuous.

Relatives: *A. japonica* 'Gold Dust' a female form with glossy leaves dusted generously with golden spots. 'Crotonifolia', a female with bright red berries, is very popular for its large leaves on which the dark green is outmanoeuvred by golden mottling.

Cultivation: Grows in any site from full sun to deep shade. If planted from a pot ensure that the receiving hole is well dug over and thoroughly wet to give the plant a start. Little care is necessary except where it has overgrown an allotted space. Takes kindly to being cut back – evenly if severely.

Propagation: Easiest from semi-ripe cuttings in summer, but even winter cuttings can be successful.

DRY SHADE is quite possibly the worst disaster area in the garden. With too little water and low light levels, the essentials for plant life are in very short supply. To a small degree, however, the benefit of shelter tempers the austere nature of the environment. Any plants that manage here are likely to have a slow rate of metabolism, coping with a limited input of life-giving energy from the sun and the poorest of water resources to enable the chemistry of plant activity; growth is tamped down to one of the lowest rates at which plant life can be sustained.

There are some benefits in dry shade. With little water there is unlikely to be many active rampant weeds. Gluttons will not be rushing for places here.

Those that can manage may have a less stressful, less competitive life than elsewhere. If sunshine is in abundant supply, it demands that the other essential resources of water, air and food are also readily available so that life can proceed comfortably. A shortage of any one ingredient makes a sunny place a tough place. In sites with low light levels the urgency is less. Although the requirements are still there and must be met, everything is slower and there is more time for the plants to find what they need.

Sheltered areas that are free of frost allow a wider range of plants to be grown. A certain amount of dryness can be a help to some marginally hardy plants. Because water is rationed to the plant tissue, much of this tissue will actually be short of water so in times of frost will be less liable to freezing and thus to damaged cells. Shade under thin-crowned trees, such as birch or rowan, can be used to foster less hardy treasures like more delicate understorey rhododendrons. Low on the ground, collections of cyclamen welcome tree roots sucking up excess water which could threaten their shallow corms.

Do you have a dry shady site?

Begin by assessing the extent of the dry shade problem, then tackle it in our two standard ways: ameliorate the conditions and build up a community of plants that thrive in these conditions.

Look carefully at larger trees and shrubs and see whether the shade they cast is too dense for life below. Check the soil beneath them, it may be damp on the surface but bone dry just below. In an area of shade caused by trees and shrubs, the root systems of such inhabitants will mean that much, if not all, of the soil's food resources are earmarked. Little is left for others, although the late winter and spring rains may mobilize a momentary surplus that can be used by small bulbs and other plants below.

It will normally be fairly obvious where the dry, shady sites are, but you may need to explore the soil around to decide just how far the factors causing the dryness and shade are exerting their influence; this may be some way beyond what you initially imagine. Woodland areas can be both dry and shady. The tree cover prevents much rain penetrating the soil below, and the trees will also be taking vast quantities of moisture from the soil themselves. Artificial structures such as houses, fences and walls will cast shade but will often also shed much falling rain to the windward side. A shady wall can deprive the area beneath it of much sunlight and the same area will not receive any falls of rain borne by winds coming from the sunny side.

Coping with a dry shady site

CLEARING OVER-GROWTH

If you conclude that you do have a shade and dry soil problem, consider whether it is possible to thin growth to allow more light and moisture to the ground. The specimen trees of the garden with branches down to soil level look wonderful but in reality they are unnaturally perfect. In the wild, they would normally be competing with neighbours, with the result that the liveliest branches would be

Early flowering bulbs and plants like forget-me-nots do well under deciduous trees

This rock garden has enough sun during the day to allow for a colourful display of flowers

those reaching for the light above; the lower ones would die away. In parkland, the very lowest branches are kept cropped by stock. It is possible to take a saw and achieve a similar arrangement by cutting away lower branches to give a length of clean trunk – something many gardeners would think entirely right and aesthetically proper, doing no harm to the majestic effect of the tree and doing a good deal to allow light, air and maybe some more moisture on to the soil below. Rain can sweep in under the branches and light can filter through much more easily. The higher the shade canopy, the easier life will be at ground level, all other factors

being equal. Even the tree will benefit from a little space at its feet. Remember to ensure that your trimming will not sabotage wind shelter, and take care not to spoil appearances by indiscriminate or over-enthusiastic lopping.

PROVIDING WATER

Water is essential for all the organic life of the soil as well as being a vehicle to pass soluble food to the plants. An apparently lifeless soil quickly turns lively when water is added: after rain, desert areas go into a quick cycle of growth making the most of the temporary water supply. In temperate climates

ANEMONE NEMOROSA
Windflower, Wood anemone

A. sylvestris

Description: A dainty and discrete herbaceous perennial with thin spreading slender rhizomes. Attractive, divided, roughly triangular leaves are held on slender stems and die back a few weeks after blooming. Very hardy native of all countries of northern Europe including Britain.

Uses: Naturalizes in woodland or semi-woodland conditions and carpets between shrubs. Its shortish upper cycle of growth is finished before the dense canopy of large plants and trees obscures light and lessens water supply.

Colour: Usually white flowers, pink in bud; also pink and blue forms.

Scent: Faint.

Size: 15cm (6in) high, spread soon to 30cm (12in) but will colonize given encouragement.

Flowering time: Early to mid-spring, sometimes later.

Relatives: A. nemorosa 'Allenii' and 'Robinsoniana' are soft lavender-blue forms. 'Wilks' Giant' is a large single white. 'Vestal' is a splendid neat double white. Anemone sylvestris (pictured) is a rarer species which is very similar but taller and tolerates sun.

Cultivation: Best installed from pot-grown plants: dried rhizomes that are offered maybe too dried. Keep moist until established.

Propagation: Lift and divide the spreading rhizomes just as foliage is turning yellow in late spring or early summer.

there are also plenty of organisms that can go into a state of rest only to burst into life when better conditions – and this usually means water – return. These organisms can be both beneficial and malign: some nematodes that can be disastrous to bulbous plants can hibernate in an inactive cyst-like mode in times of want.

So in shady, dry areas it is vital to ensure that water can reach the plants. Clearing away surplus branches will help but it may be that an artificial source needs to be arranged as a top up measure, perhaps a pipeline through which water can be flushed at intervals.

COTONEASTER 'CORNUBIA'

C. dammeri

Description: This is a hybrid of *C. frigidus* and is a hardy, large and strong, spreading shrub that can grow into small trees with time. It has pointed oval evergreen or semi-evergreen leaves and after blooming prolifically in the spring bears spectacular crops of bunched berries that last for months, sometimes until it is ready to bloom again.

Uses: Good in mixed shrub plantings for its colour year round; a good member of a group of screening or shelter shrubs. Copes well in dry spots.

Wildlife: Berry-eating birds do not appear to relish the fruit, or only begin to take it when there is little else.

Colours: Rich evergreen foliage, wide clusters of creamy blossom followed by large bunches of bright red berries.

Size: 6m (20ft) high and across.

Flowering/ fruiting time: Flowers early summer, fruit autumn through till spring.

Relatives: *C. x watereri* hybrid series bred between *C. frigidus* and *C. henryanus* are all evergreens of spreading vigorous habit, 6m (20ft) high and wider. With similar leaves and appearance, the fruits of some can be fractionally larger than that of 'Cornubia'. *C. dammeri* (pictured) is at the opposite end of the scale size-wise. It is a prostrate shrub, moulding itself over the ground, over rocks or low walls, to create a tight mass of branches and neat rounded dark leaves. Its tightly clasped flowers in white and pink are followed by round red fruits. 'Skogholm' is a hybrid which may reach 45-60cm (18-24in) high but in doing this will spread some 3m (10ft). It is evergreen, has white flowers, and a scatter of bright red fruits.

Cultivation: Plant out potted specimens early spring or early autumn and water in thoroughly. Thereafter it will probably manage without further attention. It grows strongly in all soil except permanently sodden ones.

Propagation: By semi-ripe cuttings early summer or by ground or air-layering.

Supplying our gardens with water is going to be more and more of a problem as overall demands for water escalate year by year. It makes good common, as well as ecological, sense to provide ourselves with a personal supply of water from the rain that falls. Land can be landscaped to incorporate one or more ponds. Drainage pipes can be laid towards such ponds. Waterbutts can be stationed by the house, by the garage, by the greenhouse and by any other area that sheds rainfall which can be directed by guttering. These 'reservoirs' can be used periodically to replenish some of the moisture lost or needed in particularly dry areas. Even without butts it is possible to lead water down fall pipes into pipes

VERY DEEP SHADE

To make up for a lack of plant growth consider enlivening these dark corners with pieces of sculpture, painted fences and gates, and trellis supports for climbers such as the honeysuckles that may manage to produce growth and some flower in conditions not so far removed from natural woodland sites.

below ground to areas subject to drought conditions, and thereby water plants that would otherwise perish.

MULCHING

Organic mulches are likely to be the best bet in the work to improve conditions at soil level. Their bulky mass will eventually rot down due to the action of micro-organisms. Building up this mulched organic layer will help retain what moisture there is and will make the ingress of moisture easier. It will also act as insulation, keeping the temperatures below it as

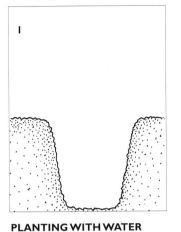

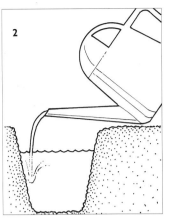

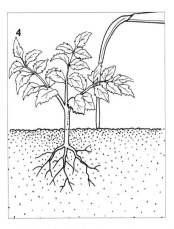

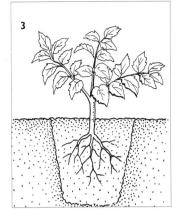

PLANTING WITH WATER

Most likely the biggest problem when planting up a shaded dry spot is the provision of enough water to the roots while the plant is getting its toes into its new home and establishing a root system extensive enough for it to be able to gather such moisture as it needs.

Give plants the best chance you can by planting at a suitable time: late autumn or early winter, seasons that are the most likely to produce a surplus of water.

1 Dig out the planting hole a few days before you plan to plant.
2 Fill the hole up a number of times with water. This ensures that water reaches the surrounding soil, ready for the new plant to it take up. If you wait till after planting, it is unlikely that you are doing much more than moistening a thin top layer of soil, which may encourage roots to turn towards the surface and means you will need to carry on watering for much longer to be successful.

3 Having planted, it makes good sense with most specimens to trim off some top growth, thus allowing the roots to get going without being over-burdened by an over-opulent superstructure.
4 Finally, give another thorough watering and very importantly, mulch heavily around the plant for a wide area and place weed-resistant matting.

Ivies and lamiums (dead nettles) mangaging well in a dry spot

CYCLAMEN COUM

Description: Very hardy tuberous perennial with delicate looking, rounded flowers robust enough to stand the worst of the weather along with and after the snowdrops. Leaves appear before flowers and are more or less round or heart-shaped, a dark matt green. Rooting is from the underside of the flattened corm.

Uses: Naturalize where winter and early spring colour will be appreciated and where the original and seedling corms can be left undisturbed, in beds or borders, by the base of trees or between shrubs. They will grow in dry awkward spots.

Wildlife: Field and other mice enjoy collecting the seedpods and burying them. Ants will also collect the sticky seeds.

Colour: Rich carmine-pink with a much darker stain at the puckered mouth.

Scent: Sweet.

Size: 10cm (4in) high, spread 7-10cm (3-4in).

Flowering time: Midwinter to spring.

Relatives: *C. coum album* is particularly effective with snow-white flowers, each petal marked with a crimson-maroon spot at the tiny mouth.

Cultivation: Easy in all except very wet soil. Leave tubers undisturbed. Keep free of dominant weeds. Will grow well in light grass.

Propagation: By seed that is allowed to drop on the soil or gathered and sown in summer as soon as ripe.

equable as possible. Every scrap that is added goes towards making the situation that little bit better (see also pages 19-20).

Making the most of it

In inherited dry shade you may, initially, be faced with some dusty rather boring stalwarts, perhaps ordinary ivy and the fleshy-leaved creeping perennial *Pachysandra terminalis* with stems only 10cm (4in) high but providing dense ground cover and seemingly able to exist in most dark dry places once established. They need not be ignored and we should be thankful for their determined stand in adversity, but it is probably a good idea to add a lighter touch, maybe not all gay abandon but at least some interest. Even the trusty *Pachysandra terminalis* can be somewhat more festive as there is a form 'Variegata' with cream variegated leaves at the stem ends. In the driest spots these slow growers can be covered with dust and look rather weary and pedestrian.

Although it is not possible to create the vivid herbaceous border colours in deep, dry shade, by

PRACTICAL TIP

The adult ivy was a favourite shrub of Victorian times and is certainly worth considering for any dark, dry place. A notable one is *Hedera helix* ssp. *poetarum* (syn. *H. helix* 'Poetica Arborea') with a rounded shrubby form and beautiful glossy and veined foliage, but the real prize is the orange berries rather than the usual black, making it an interesting and somewhat less sombre shrub. A few specialist nurseries offer shrub ivies or you can take cuttings from the adult wood and rear your own.

Even in their juvenile form, ivies certainly do not need to look dull, there are hundreds of different variegated forms available. An excellent kind is *H. helix* 'Buttercup' with completely yellow leaves. Perhaps they are not the golden-yellow of wild buttercups but they are no less pleasing, nevertheless, in soft but bright shades. Although the brightest colour is on the new leaves, and these are produced more freely on well-watered specimens it is still worth trying the cultivar in difficult spots. It will clothe trunks, cover low or high walls and can even be trained up wire supports to make topiary specimens in fanciful shapes.

TREES OVERGROWN WITH IVY

I like ivy and am not one of those who rush to remove all scraps of it from walls or trees. It can beautify a not-too-pretty wall and certainly make it warmer as well as provide new nesting sites for birds. It will not destroy mortar and does keep wall and mortar drier and safer than if left unclad. Growing up

trees, it can lend mass and colour to the winter silhouette of deciduous trees. However, old trees that are losing some of their zest for life may be overendowed with ivy. Its weight can help to make them less stable, especially when the ivy has produced a mass of adult, non-clinging growth high up. Prevention is better than cure. Branches can be severed low to

the ground. You can cut through as few or as many as you wish. If this is done before matters have become threatening it will be a very simple matter indeed. The severed branches will be left with brown, dead foliage for a while. Later they can be pulled away. Alternatively, some of the heavy masses of adult growth can be pruned away to lighten the load.

using well variegated foliage and some of the paler coloured flowers a lot can be done to achieve an interesting atmosphere. Variegated plants come in all types; the best are often those with strong variegation, such as well-marked margins or centres, that emphasize the form of the leaves. Avoid plants in which the variegation makes them look sickly; they will never look better. A few of the ferns that can stand drier conditions may help. Good choices include *Dryopteris felix-mas* in all its forms and the common polypody (*Polypodium vulgare*) and its cultivars.

Then there are the ivies.

IVY

Ivy's very commonness blinds us to its extraordinary qualities, its powers of endurance and its doggedness. Seedlings germinate and, in the most forbidding of terrains in deepest shade and on tinder-dry soil, they manage to exploit the minutest of resources. Waiting for better days, the rooted shoots slowly, centimetre by centimetre, make their progress. Once ivy finds support, it seems to discover new strength and starts on its way upwards, often scaling the very plant that has been keeping it in subjugation. Then, as it attains the heights where it lays claim to a fair share of light and moisture, it

DAPHNE MEZEREUM
Mezereon

D. mezereum f. *alba*

Description: A deciduous, rather upright small shrub of light woodland. Pale fawn or grey wood, long oval leaves of matt grey-green. Four-pointed star blooms enwreath the leafless twigs in midwinter. It is noted for its scent. Not necessarily long-lived but produces an abundance of round fleshy fruits which can provide plenty of offspring. A hardy native of Europe to Turkey and Siberia.
Uses: Good winter colour in shaded

and dry spots where and when there is not a long queue of showy plants waiting to take up residence.
Wildlife: Birds may take fruits.
Colour: Rich mauvey-pink flowers. Glossy scarlet fruit.
Scent: Exceptionally powerful and sweet perfume so position it where you will get the benefit.
Size: 60-90cm (2-3ft) high, spread less but can be made more if growing points of young seedlings are nipped out to force more 'lateral thinking'.
Flowering time: Mid- and late winter.
Relatives: *D. mezereum* f. *alba* (pictured) is white-flowered but the size and clarity of the flower colour varies; golden fruits.
Cultivation: Plant only young potted specimens. Shrubs very much resent root disturbance. The rather gaunt upright stance can be mitigated by grouping perhaps three plants near each other or by careful finger pruning of top shoots of very young plants.
Propagation: By seed, sown when ripe.

EUPHORBIA AMYGDALOIDES VAR. ROBBIAE
Mrs Robb's spurge

Description: An indestructibly hardy evergreen herbaceous plant with vigorous rhizomatous rootstock and many upright stems with dark green leaves outward pointing and sitting atop of the stems like rosettes. For weeks and months rounded airy heads of flowers lighten the whole.

Uses: One of the few plants that can be unreservedly recommended for dark dry places. It can manage under yew and holly!

Wildlife: Shelter for ground-foraging birds.

Colour: Very dark green leaves, bracts surrounding the tiny flowers are lime-yellow.

Scent: Slight musky scent.

Size: 35-60cm (14-24in) high, spreads quickly to 60cm (2ft) and then beyond.

Flowering time: Prolonged, end of winter through spring.

Relatives: E. amygdaloides is the wood spurge native to much of northern Europe, including Britain, and is a little lighter in weight. 'Purpurea' has attractive foliage much suffused with purplish red, a good colour combination with the lime flowers. Rather prone to mildew.

Cultivation: var. robbiae can be almost too easy to grow; wonderful for dark dry spots. If it is allowed into posher places it can run riot.

Propagation: By division of roots, but will also self seed freely given an undisturbed soil.

reaches adulthood and its demeanour changes; gone is the fighting crawling clinging mode, a new dress is donned, the leaves change shape, and the stems produce no adventitious roots; now it becomes a respectable shrub with shining leaves and a much branched form. To crown its success, it bears rounded heads of creamy flowers and dark blue-black berries.

If shade is heavy and unremitting and the site is dry you do have a problem but even so there are solutions. An appearance of healthy colour can be given by planting the very amenable *Aucuba japonica* in one of its brightest golden-spotted modes. Often called the spotted laurel, it may be looked down upon by those who search for the rare and exotic. Don't let snobbery prevail: this bush is a proper treasure. It clothes itself with shining healthy leaves making a rounded mound from ground level up. It really does look very good in a dark site and can be pruned as you wish.

Where the sun is very hot, such as in this Mediterranean garden, even sun-lovers appreciate some shade during the day

Stonecrop or wallpepper
(*Sedum acre*) tolerates some
shade and will grow where
water is hardly ever seen

If all else fails in deep shade, the soil surface can be covered with creeping plants such as periwinkle (*Vinca minor* and *V. major*) perhaps in their variegated forms, and by the brightest ivies you can find. These variegated plants may not be as bright in heavy shade as they would be in the sun but nor will they be as dark as the ordinary ivy. Other trailing plants such as the silver-leaved forms of dead nettle (*Lamium*) will manage with little light, provided they have some moisture.

Early colour can usually be achieved by planting some of the hardiest of bulbs, predominantly snowdrops and winter aconites. Later in the year, it may be possible to get a group of *Lilium martagon* or *L. hansonii* to come into bloom; we have managed these is some really quite dark areas and, provided they get wet at the beginning of their growing season, it is surprising how much drought they can manage.

GERANIUM ROBERTIANUM
Herb Robert

Description: One of the prettiest of annual or biennial weeds with much divided fern-like colourful leaves and a light airy branching habit. Stems and flower buds are hairy. Many five-petalled, smallish flowers are bright and perky. Fully hardy.
Uses: For naturalizing in dry awkward spots. Can make a good living off a broken wall or a discarded pile of bricks or rubble.

Colours: Foliage, stems and flower buds are green much flushed with red and sometimes completely glowing orange red. Flowers are pink with white stripes.
Size: 15-22cm (6-9in) high, 22-30cm (9-12in) across.
Flowering time: Early summer well into mid-autumn.
Relatives: *G. robertianum* 'Celtic White' has fresh green leaves and white flowers. 'Album' has white flowers usually with green stems and leaves though some have red stems and flushed foliage. *G. pylzowianum* is a slender-stemmed plant growing to about 30cm (12in) high, 5cm (2in) wide, with dark, divided leaves and purplish pink flowers. Its rootstocks are running underground rhizomes with rounded tubers. *G. sanguineum* var. *striatum* is a favourite tidy form of the bloody cranesbill that forms a mound of leaves divided into many narrow, long lobes; through these are displayed in a continuing summer succession the rounded, rose-pink flowers. Height to 15cm (6in) and spread about double.
Cultivation: No further care needed.
Propagation: Seeds itself.

Natural communities

As in all conditions and positions the success is more likely if the plants grown are adapted to their surroundings and grow in harmony with each other. If you get the balance right, the plants you choose will eventually create their own environment, one in which they can thrive.

Below trees, shrubs such as *Aucuba japonica* and the Portuguese laurel (*Prunus lusitanica*) together with *Mahonia aquifolium*, are good subjects for difficult

LAMIUM MACULATUM 'BEACON SILVER'
Variegated deadnettle

Description: Scrambling evergreen perennial that roots as it spreads and makes carpets of foliage that look well through the year. Leaves are typical nettle shape, tough in texture and prettily coloured. Bunches of hooded flowers are produced in short-stemmed whorls. It is reliably hardy provided it does not get completely dried out in summer or swamped with stagnant water in winter.

Uses: Makes an attractive ground cover in woodland areas or shady places.

Colour: Foliage is green, suffused mauve and with much of the surface overpainted silver. Margins may be green. Flowers are pale mauve-pink.

Size: To 20cm (8in) high, over 1m (3ft) across.

Flowering time: Summer.

Varieties: *L. maculatum* 'Album' has green leaves with silvered centres and pure white flowers, 'White Nancy' has white blossom and leaves of mid-green more evenly overall painted white.

Cultivation: Easy; does not require rich soil.

Propagation: By taking rooted divisions in early spring or early autumn.

sites. Butcher's broom (*Ruscus aculeatus*), with its bright red winter berries, the common box (*Buxus sempervirens*), together with its relatives from the *Sarcococca* genus, which have white flowers and blue-black berries, are useful evergreens that can be called into play.

In some of the worst of spots, *Euphorbia amygdaloides* var. *robbiae* can form drifts of evergreen dark foliage topped with limy flowers for long periods in the spring. It has almost the effect of a low shrub but spreads by its energetic rhizomatous roots just below the soil surface. Other herbaceous plants that can be added to the community are the strong comfrey, *Symphytum ibericum* (syn. *S. grandiflorum*) with strong low rough leaves and creamy flowers. In a particularly dry sheltered spot, we have managed to get a drift of self-perpetuating honesty (*Lunaria annua*) to take over. It makes a brilliant annual flower display of lovely purple-mauves and white. Early in the year some of the strong bulbs cope well enough. Try snowdrops, bluebells, winter aconites and wood anemones in some of the less dark spots.

SANDY SOIL

This display garden, created for the Chelsea Flower Show, provides plenty of inspiration for coping with a sandy site

SANDY SOIL is light, normally very free draining and with poor nutrient resources. It will respond quickly to seasonal changes, warming up rapidly in spring and cooling quickly with winter. It may be an easier soil for tender plants to survive in, being likely to keep them that bit drier and so less prone to frost damage as water freezes in cold weather, but this is no absolute rule as frost pockets can occur as easily on sand as on other soils.

Air in soil is important for the health of roots, but without humus to hold moisture there may only be short periods when there is water readily available to the plants, after a rain shower or thorough watering. The need for humus in the soil is paramount; it is needed for water retention and for food. It will also help to stabilize temperatures.

ROBINIA HISPIDA
Rose acacia

Description: Deciduous hardy shrub of lax arching habit. The stems are brittle and armed with fierce bristles, and the dark green pinnate leaves can have up to thirteen leaflets. It produces hanging wide bunches of pea flowers.

Uses: Grows easily in open sites in sandy, often poor, soil.

Colour: Dark foliage and glowing rich pink flowers with just a hint of lilac.

Size: 2.7m (9ft) high, spread 2.5m (8ft).

Flowering time: Late spring into early summer.

Relatives: *R. pseudoacacia* is the fast-growing false acacia tree whose most popular garden manifestation is the yellow-leaved 'Frisia'.

Cultivation: Easy in most soils that are not sodden. Cut away broken twigs and branches.

Propagate: By seed, from suckers or from winter root cuttings.

Do you have sandy soil?

It is normally fairly obvious if you have sandy soil. It dries quickly and is easily dug. In contrast to clay soils, you are able to move out on to it soon after rain and start work without any excuses. If you take a sample of clay soil and shake it up with water in a test tube or even a narrow glass jar you will find that the small clay particles float in the water a long time but eventually settle as the top layer. Sand falls quickly to the bottom. A clay soil is likely to have a narrow band of sand at the bottom of the settled test tube contents. A similar sample of sandy soil will reveal a band of 50% or more of sand with only a narrow band of clay. An extremely sandy soil will benefit from the addition of clay as many nutrients

in the soil tend to join with clay particles rather than get washed clean away, one of the reasons that sand is such a hungry medium.

Coping with sandy soil

The benefits of sandy soil include the possiblity of being able to grow a wider range of slightly tender plants which might be much more difficult to succeed with on heavier soils. The soil is fast to dry out after rain and warm up after winter, so that you are able to get out and work on it more quickly and sooner. It will also be fairly easy to dig. It is normally possible to plant out a little earlier into sandy soils, especially when the aspect is sunny and gets the benefits of warm sunshine. In extremely sandy soils shrubs, trees and larger plants may well be better planted in late autumn and allowed to get their roots established before the winter. In spring the possibility of summer drought is too threatening.

Be wary of trying to grow plants that need ample water, unless you can easily supply this, otherwise you will become a watering slave or, in times of

AMARYLLIS BELLA-DONNA

A. bella-donna 'Johannesburg'

Description: Large bulb that produces, while leafless, large trumpet flowers on red-purple stems in autumn. A well-established group in a warm spot can be spectacular in bloom. Leaves appear after flowering perhaps in late winter or early spring and are typical of this family: strap-like and more or less erect. A South African plant, it is only frost hardy and needs shelter and warmth.

Uses: For sudden showy colour in the

autumn this is really worthwhile. Grow near a wall or in sheltered warm areas.

Colour: Shocking pink.

Size: 50-75cm (20-30in) high, spread 30-45cm (12-18in).

Flowering time: Autumn.

Relatives: *A. bella-donna* 'Hathor' has flowers of shining white with golden throats and maybe a whispered blush of pink on the outside. 'Johannesburg' (pictured) has paler pink flowers.

Cultivation: Plant bulbs in a well-drained sunny spot with 8cm (3in) of soil over their tops: usually done in the late summer. They may take a season to settle down and flourishing groups are best left alone until hopelessly over-crowded or when a new settlement is planned.

Propagation: By division of the bulbs in late spring/early summer after leaves have faded, or in late summer before the flowering shoots appear.

TREES AND SHRUBS FOR SANDY SOILS

Atraphaxis frutescens
Ballota acetabulosa
Betula spp.
Brachyglottis forms
Callistemon citrinus
Cistus spp.
Cytisus forms
Genista spp.
Grevillea forms
Hibiscus forms
Indigofera amblyantha
Juniperus spp.
Lavatera forms
Lespedeza thunbergii
Potentilla fruticosa
Robinia spp.
Romneya coulteri
Santolina chamaecyparissus

water restriction, subject to real frustration. Choose instead from among the dry- and sun-loving plants: Mediterranean, Australian and South African plants that can help to make the garden undemanding and exotic.

IMPROVING CONDITIONS

Almost the whole focus of attempts to improve sandy soil is going to be on the addition of humus. All types of humus will help; use as much bulky organic matter as possible: traditional farmyard manure, compost, leaf and bracken litter, peat, coir, spent hops, shredded garden rubbish and mulches such as shredded bark. Plastic mats over the soil surface together with mulches further the efforts in water conservation.

It is virtually impossible to add too much humus. The micro-organisms in the soil are ready to pounce on any new source of it and will rapidly incorporate it into the soil structure where it will then get used up in supporting plant growth. There is a constant need to replenish it by adding more. It can be worked into the top few centimetres/inches and added as a mulch to try to improve water retention and produce more stable temperature levels. A regular compost-making routine may well be the most crucial, life-giving heart of all your gardening operations. Use all the material the garden and house can provide, and also look to the windfalls of autumn – gather fallen leaves (sometimes those swept up in public places are available). Obtain bales of straw and use this to bulk up the material. In rural areas you may also be able to get permission to harvest the young unfurling fronds of bracken, which can be added to the mix. They are particularly rich in potash.

PLANTING SHELTER BELTS

The choice of trees and shrubs for shelter belts will depend on the prevailing conditions. Choose the hardiest of kinds and plant them at half the normal recommended distance apart. Make three lines of trees or shrubs only separated by perhaps a couple of metres; their close proximity will help them to protect each other as they gain size. It is cheaper to start with 'whips', young single-stemmed specimens, and plant these with plastic anti-rabbit collars. If you want to get ahead a little bit more quickly, you can plant rather larger specimens but avoid trying to get very big specimens. These not only make the job expensive but smaller specimens soon catch up with the larger ones and could even overtake them. A temporary fence built to give some shelter to the young plants can help establish shelter more easily.

CRINUM × POWELLII

Description: A hugely tough hybrid of the South African species *C. bulbispermum* and *C. moorei*, members of the same family as *Amaryllis bella-donna* (see page 45) but much larger and having luxurious foliage at flowering time. Bulbs are at rest through the winter and then make strong growth through summer, peaking with an exuberant flowering display at the end of the summer or in early autumn – often over a dozen large trumpet-shaped flowers to a 60cm (2ft) stem. Spreading strap-like leaves, up to 10cm (4in) wide at their bases and possibly over 1m (3ft) long, form an arching mass of greenery. Frost hardy.

Uses: A bold focal point end of summer/early autumn in a warm sunny position.

Colour: Rich shade of rosy pink.

Scent: Good warm scent.

Size: 1m (3ft) high, spread 75cm (30in).

Flowering time: End of summer into autumn.

Relatives: *C. x. powellii* 'Album' is a very impressive large plant with six-pointed trumpet flowers of pure white.

Cultivation: Plant the huge bulbs with their necks just level with the soil surface as soon as available in early spring in a well-worked rich deep soil that is well-drained and in a sunny sheltered site. Arrange for a plentiful supply of humus deep down. Make sure the supply is good for a number of years: the longer they can be left undisturbed the better they bloom.

Propagation: By detaching offsets from the main clump at the winter's end and replanting. If a clump has become overcrowded or has to be moved, the opportunity can be taken to split the bulbs up.

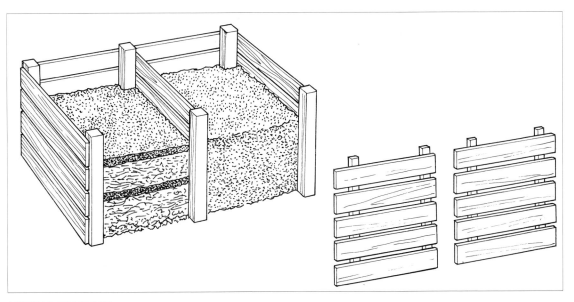

MAKING COMPOST

Compost making is not difficult. It is a lot easier with a variety of different materials to mix together. A heap of undiluted grass cuttings is not ideal: they need mixing with coarser weeds, leaves, straw and kitchen waste. If you have to manage mainly with the lawn cuttings, lay out about a 7-10cm (3-4in) layer of grass cuttings/mixed waste, then scatter a thin layer of soil over to introduce soil bacteria, and add further layers of grass/waste. If the waste is very dry give it a dousing of water before adding the next layer. The rotting process may be accelerated by the addition of a thin scatter of sulphate of ammonia or one of the commercial preparations. In the warmer months the rotting takes place much more quickly. If the weather is very dry the heap may be helped by a top layer of old carpet, sacking or even polythene to keep the whole warm and moist. When the rotting process has obviously proceeded well, the heap can be turned upside down with outer parts thrown in the centre and all given a thorough mixing. After a relatively short time you will be left with a dark crumbly medium that will be caviare to your plants.

SHELTER BELTS

Winds whistling over the garden increase the amount of moisture drawn from light soil and cause more dryness. Shelter belts and a good balance of shrubs inside the garden will help to stop the immediate drying of the surface by wind as well as somewhat reducing the transpiration rates of the plants, so they will use up less water. Trees and shrubs that are likely to manage well in sandy soils are listed in the margin.

Trees for screening could include *Acer platanoides* (Norway maple), *A. pseudoplatanus* (sycamore), *Alnus cordata* (Italian alder), *Fagus sylvatica* (beech), *Fraxinus excelsior* 'Westhof's Glorie' (ash), *Populus nigra* 'Italica' (poplar), *Prunus serotina* (rum cherry), *Quercus robur* (oak), *Tilia cordata* (lime).

Shrubs for screening could include *Berberis* × *stenophylla*, *Buxus sempervivens* forms (box), *Cotoneaster* species such as *C. lacteus*, *Elaeagnus* forms, *Escallonia* forms, *Euonymus* forms, *Ilex* (holly), *Olearia* species, *Viburnum tinus*.

Eucalyptus normally grow easily in sandy soils. Being evergreen they are serviceable all round the year as shelter-belt trees, and they will help with screening and shelter without being too heavy. They are mostly attractive trees with leaves of silver, white or steely-grey and many have decorative bark. *E. pauciflora* subsp. *niphophila* (syn. *E. niphophila*) is white-barked when young but the older parts become patterned with jigsaw shapes of olive, buff, brown and lots of other shades. In others the bark peels. Crushed leaves of most eucalyptus have the typical eucalyptus scent. Flowers of the hardy kinds are likely to be creamy powder-puffs and are followed by hard nutty seedpods. *E. gunnii* tends to grow tall quickly and will make a more interesting shape if cut back close to the ground as a young specimen perhaps in its second year. *E. pauciflora* subsp. *niphophila* can make a large tree but does not bolt skywards to the same degree. It is probably the hardiest of all the eucalyptus and very tough. *E. dalrympleana* is another useful species and this, again, may be made into a more interesting tree by being cut back after two or three seasons to encourage it to produce several trunks.

Celtis australis, the nettle tree, is a deciduous spreading tree with oval, sharply pointed, dark leaves, a contrast to the silvery grey of the eucalyptus. While not commonly seen, it is an easy tree even on very dry sunny sites. It is deciduous, and in winter the smooth pale grey trunks and branches look very ornamental; through the growing months there is a dense mass of pointed oval leaves to provide formidable wind shelter. *Quercus canariensis*, Mirbeck's oak, is not wholly deciduous or evergreen; it makes a narrow tree that will broaden with age. Most of its large rich green leaves turn yellow with autumn but are often held through the winter, aiding the shelter potential. This, too, is a tree that will thrive in dry, sunny spots.

Natural communities

A look at natural plant communities in your local area will nearly always come up with some sugges-

tions for your garden. Plants that thrive naturally may have relations that will be ideal for using, or they may be perfect themselves.

DUNE AND SEASIDE PLANTS

Although it is only a very few gardeners who will be having to cope on dunes, there are some lessons to be learned even here. The silvery grey marram grass, *Ammophila arenaria* (syn. *A. arundinacea*), is used for stabilizing dunes; its tough spreading rhizomes and strong foliage will grow in difficult sandy garden soils, and it will at least provide good weed-proof silvery cover in areas where its strong growth can be accommodated or kept in check. The vast majority of the plants of these areas will grow equally well on soils with a bias towards acid or alkaline and they are able to cope with more salt in the soil than most. One effect of their uptake of common salt is that their rate of water transpiration is reduced.

Coastal plants that are hardy natives of many countries of Europe including Britain, such as sea holly (*Eryngium maritimum*), sea lavender (*Limonium vulgare*) and the horned poppy (*Glaucium flavum*), are

The impoverished soil created by years of hay harvesting provides the ideal enviroment for plants like poppies

excellent garden plants in their own right. A very effective seaside atmosphere can be created by using a selection of these plants, especially with a clump of marram grass as a complementary planting, and perhaps adding some smooth boulders, like the sea-rounded ones you might find by the shore, to complete the design. And there are plenty of other plants that are equally as good for fostering the illusion, including thrift (*Armeria maritima*, see page 12) and sea campion (*Silene maritima*).

There are other native and more tropical species that flourish in seaside gardens and which can be pressed into service in sandy gardens. The brightly coloured *Erythrina crista-galli* (cock's spur or coral tree), with its vivid crimson spikes of pea-flowers, is from Brazil and almost hardy although it looks so exotic. The *Brachyglottis* from New Zealand are not quite so flamboyant, but there is something slightly alien about the grey-silver-leaved familiar shrub, *B.* 'Sunshine' with its oval leaves and summer bunches of yellow daisies. Also useful is *B. monroi*, again with yellow daisies but an altogether tighter, more compact shrub, making an evergreen mound of dark

CARYOPTERIS × *CLANDONENSIS*

Description: A hybrid series of deciduous subshrubs bred from *C. mastacanthus* and *C. mongholica* and usually outstripping their parents in performance and hardiness. Pointed oval leaves are lightly serrated and furnish upward-reaching stems in pairs. Towards the end of the growing months a generous display of bloom features rounded clusters of small flowers as terminal cymes but much reinforced by others from the leaf axils of the upper parts of each stem. The plants are tidy in form with pleasing foliage and splendid blossom. Frost hardy.

Uses: Mixed border or in a collection of shrubs; also a possibility for a raised or terrace bed. Could be grown near the house where its habit can be admired.

Colour: Violet shaded blue flowers, grey-green leaves.

Size: 75cm (30in) high and across.

Flowering time: Late summer well into autumn.

Relatives: *C.* x *clandonensis* 'Arthur Simmonds' is a leafy bushy plant with rather narrow leaves and rich blue flowers. 'Heavenly Blue' is free growing with a mass of blossom; an established favourite. 'Pershore Seedling' is newer. It is a compact plant which covers itself with a generous cloak of rich blue blossom with a lavender tint.

Cultivation: Best in a light soil in a open sunny spot. Cut back hard at the end of the winter. It will grow strongly and blooms on current growth.

Propagation: By cuttings in summer.

SHRUBS FOR SANDY SOIL

Atriplex halimus (tree purslane)

Ballota acetabulosa

Brachyglottis monroi

B. repanda

B. 'Sunshine'

Bupleurum fruticosum

Callistemon

Cistus

Colutea arborescens (bladder senna)

Grevillea

Hebe

Hibiscus

Lespedeza thunbergii

Lupinus arboreus (tree lupin)

Olearia x *haastii* (daisy bush)

O. nummulariifolia

O. stellulata

Phlomis fruticosa

P. italica

Potentilla fruticosa

Romneya coulteri

Sophora davidii

Spartium junceum

GLAUCIUM FLAVUM
Horned poppy

Description: A very hardy native of most countries of northern Europe including Britain. Often seen wild as a seaside plant. An impressive biennial that slowly builds up an erect stance with longish leaves tending to clasp the stem, each leaf a sculptured shape with rounded lobes. Typical poppy flowers followed by extraordinary curved seed-pods up to 30cm (12in) long.

Uses: Grown for the distinctive silvery foliage and bright poppy flowers over a long period. In the wild it will thrive in waste areas and places where soil has been moved and laid bare. In the garden it can colonize open areas of soil.

Colour: Usually rich deep gold but the shade is variable: orange or red is possible, leaves are a silvery grey-green.

Size: 30-60cm (12-24in) high, spread 45cm (18in).

Flowering time: Usually for some weeks through end of summer into autumn.

Relatives: *G. corniculatum* has red or orange flowers. *G. grandiflorum* has bigger flowers of dark orange to crimson with dark-spotted bases.

Cultivation and propagation: Like all poppies these short-lived plants have thick roots that should not be disturbed. Probably best grown in situ and seedlings thinned out or, alternatively, sown under glass in pots or large modules and resulting seedlings thinned to one. Place in permanent quarters before the main root escapes from drainage hole.

green leaves with waved edges and white undersurfaces. *B. repanda* is totally distinct and is capable of making a large shrub or small tree up to 6m (20ft). Although they have white undersurfaces, its leaves are much larger, 10-30cm (4-12in) long, and they are attractively lobed and a shining rich green perhaps touched with purple. Ivory or greenish white, sweet-scented flowers are packed into intricately branched panicles, 30cm (12in) long and rather wider. There is a purple-leaved form. In the wild these are plants found in coastal communities growing on sandy or poor soils.

Among shrubs that are hardy in sandy soils are the *Tamarix* species. *T. ramosissima* has pinky red crowded small flowers in long spikes from late summer well into autumn – a typical tamarisk but more so! It has the characteristic feathery green foliage of all tamarisks and a wide branched robust habit with long-reaching stems. *T. anglica* is the English tamarisk; *T. gallica* is similar and wild in France. See margin for other shrubs for sandy conditions.

HEATHLAND

Heathlands are usually characterized by poor sandy acid soils. Often heathland sites have a restricted natural community with relatively few plants dominating all. Silver birch (*Betula pendula*) is common, there may also be pines and junipers. At ground level there will be acres of ling, or heather, *Calluna vulgaris* along with plenty of gorse (*Ulex europaeus*) and broom (*Cytisus scoparius*). In wetter spots there are rushes and smaller plants such as harebell (*Campanula rotundifolia*), petty whin (*Genista anglica*), and the occasional exciting little orchid.

Taking a lead from these wild communities, it is simple to create a glorified and more varied picture by calling upon some of the more showy relatives of these species and gathering them into bolder plantings. There are the brooms: *Cytisus* × *kewensis*, *C.* × *praecox* 'Allgold', *Genista hispanica*, the very procumbent *G. pilosa* 'Vancouver Gold', *G. tinctoria* 'Flore Pleno'; and there is double gorse (*Ulex europaeus* 'Flore Pleno'). Combine these with the best cultivars of the heather *Calluna vulgaris* such as the pink-flowered 'Annemarie' or the mauve 'Blazeaway' whose foliage changes from green to orange and red through the winter. If you have the space add the more stagey birch *Betula utilis* var. *jacquemontii*, eventually quite a substantial tree but taking its time to get very large and always looking in the spotlight with shining white trunk and branches. Some of the small lily species and hybrids, including the tall American *L. pardalinum*, with its dark-spotted, dark red flowers, and the Pixie Series, which comes in a range of colours, can help to complete this gentrification of the heathland.

GRASSLANDS

Grasslands in temperate countries are the meadows and pastures which by artificial means consist predominantly of grasses and other small plants, such as small primroses, gentians, campanulas and vetches. The soils are of various types, with chalks and sands being somewhat more natural than loams and clays which are more likely to have been exploited in arable farming. In a sandy garden, it is possible to try to recreate an ideal grassland mix of plants, or

Heathers can make a real splash of colour when there is little else about. Here, *Erica* x *darleyensis* 'Margaret Porter' is flowering happily despite frost

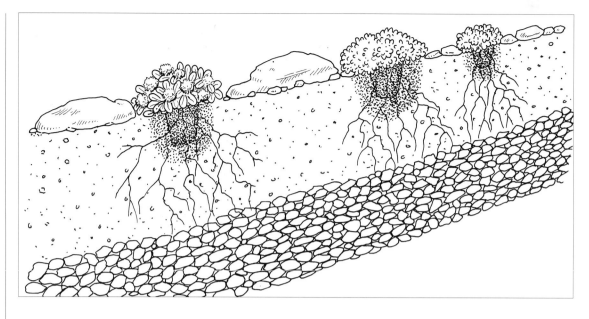

PLANTING TIP

The poor soil conditions in screes make things very difficult for plants that have been used to the easy life in pots and containers. Try to allow a little more soil around the lower roots, but more importantly keep the area well watered until the plants have got their roots running into the scree mix. Scree dwellers are famous for their fantastically long root runs, and once established they should be able to cope with most problems.

even develop the idea further and aim at an alpine meadow, although the latter is dependent for its success on a somewhat greater supply of water than is perhaps available to us, but we could manage this by using the more spartan species such as *Armeria caespitosa*, the sedums, sempervivums and pea family dwarfs such as the rest harrows, *Ononis* species.

Assuming the aim is for a wild grassland effect, the first thing to realise is that the richest soil in the garden is not needed: the designated area can be stripped of its top few centimetres/inches of soil, possibly by cutting away the turf. Removing the top soil achieves several things: it reduces fertility, to discourage strong growth and more rapacious plants; it also removes grass and assorted growing weeds; and it takes away a high proportion of banked weed seeds. The exposed soil can then be worked lightly and the grassland species introduced by seed or as established plants. If you wish to have a background of grass, sow the finest seed mix and reduce the rate of sowing it to a fifth or even a tenth of what is recommended for a creating lawn.

Grasslands in the garden do not need to be restricted to the obvious grassland plants. It is in order to have cowslips and primroses to help the

early spring display. You can introduce such leguminous favourites as bird's foot trefoil (*Lotus corniculatus*) and its relative bird's foot, *Ornithopus perpusillus*, together with its orange counterpart, *O. pinnatus*. The slightly more shrubby rest harrow (*Ononis repens*), with its very attractive pea-flowers in pink, is a very pleasing midsummer to autumn flower that will fit well in the scheme.

Other wild grassland plants you ought to consider introducing are field scabious (*Knautia arvensis*), the very pretty centaury (*Centaurium erythraea*), with its pure rose-pink flowers, and the knapweeds, *Centaurea nigra* and *C. scabiosa*. Lady's bedstraw (*Galium verum*) with masses of tiny mustard flowers above ferny fresh green filigree foliage is another possibility as is dyer's greenwood (*Genista tinctoria*), which is a mass of golden blossom often continuing into late summer and autumn and is low-growing, not an upright shrub like most of its relatives. The strong blue of viper's bugloss (*Echium vulgare*), which is pink in bud, is an excellent choice for encouraging insect activity. Decide just how much of your garden you want to turn over to a wild grassland effect. Mark the margins by a stone path, a mowed edge or by shrubs. The grassland area itself should not be fertilized and

GLEDITSIA TRIACANTHOS
Honey locust

Description: Deciduous shrubs eventually growing into substantial trees and prized for their attractive foliage. The flowers are insignificant but are sometimes followed by large pea pods. The dark green foliage is much divided and ferny. Trunk and stems are formidably armed with thorns. Young specimens may be better for some frost protection, thereafter they should cope well enough.

Uses: Fine specimen bushes or trees.

Colour: Type has dark green foliage which turns to yellow before leaf fall.

Size: Eventually to 10m (35ft) high, spread 6m (20ft).

Flowering time: Early summer.

Relatives: *G. triacanthos* f. *inermis* is thornless as is 'Skyline' with particularly good rich gold autumn colour. 'Sunburst' is the most popular clone with young foliage a rich yellow for many weeks, greening for summer and again turning yellow before dropping leaves.

Cultivation: Best in warm spots and likes sandy drained soils.

Propagation: Grows quite quickly from seed. Named forms are usually increased by budding on to stock of the type.

should be mown in late autumn once or twice to remove most of the top growth but perhaps leaving one or two clumps of grasses or other plants that still look attractive in their dead plumage. The area can be mown lightly again in early spring to start the season tidily. For the rest of the time let nature rule.

LIGHT WOODLAND
Most sandy soils are fairly amenable for the quick creation of a bit of light woodland. Do this by planting groups of silver birch (*Betula pendula*) perhaps with some eucalyptus for evergreen effect. Do not overdo the eucalyptus; they seem to inhibit the growth of plants below.

In more open areas you can deploy shrubby plants such as the quick growing *Buddleja globosa*, with its fragrant round clusters of yellow flowers, or some of the *B. davidii* hybrids, together with lots of the taller brooms rapidly raised from seed or young pot-grown specimens. In a woodland patch you can introduce bulbs such as bluebells, scillas, ornithogalums, small daffodils and even some tulip species at the sunnier edges.

SCREES
A well-drained sandy soil provides the chance of creating a scree garden; most of the hard work has been done for you: you have the required drainage. Choose a site in an open unshaded spot. Excavate and replace soil with a mix of 60% grit, crushed rock or gravel chippings – either as one or as mixed ingredients – 20% good loam and 20% leaf mould or well rotted compost. To have the finished scree level with the surrounding areas, an excavation 20-30cm (8-12in) will suffice. If the scree is being made in heavier soil, the depth would have to be greater for more effective drainage.

The scree might be an adjunct to a rock garden and could have its surface level somewhat higher than the surrounding level ground.

The plants of a scree are rather like icebergs but more so! There is a lot more of them below ground than above. Roots travel for huge distances and so can withstand periods of drought better than surface rooters. Above ground the foliage is often closely clamped together in cushions or tight mounds to offer as little resistance to wind and weather as possible. They all expect to have instant drainage from around their necks.

SCREE PLANTS
Anacyclus pyrethrum var. *depressus*
Anchusa caespitosa
Androsace, various
Aquilegia bertolonii
A. flabellata var. *nana*
A. scopulorum
Asperula suberosa
Callianthemum kernerianus
C. rutifolium
Convolvulus sabatius
Daphne blagayana
Edraianthus, various
Erinus alpinus
Erodium, various
Frankenia laevis
F. thymifolia
Globularia, various
Haplopappus brandegeei
Helichrysum bellidioides
H. coralloides
H. milfordiae
Myosotis rupicola
Ononis fruticosa
O. natrix
O. rotundifolia
Origanum amanum
O. laevigatum
Raoulia, various
Sedum, various
Sempervivum, various
Silene acaulis
S. elisabethae
S. schafta

CLAY SOIL

TREAT A CLAY soil well and it will reward you; abuse it and it will become impossibly intransigent. It is like a mule with its own agenda: ignore this fact and you will find yourself punished. Allow it to get too wet and it is almost impossible to get on it to do anything. Allow it to dry out in a drought and it can bake dry, as hard as bricks.

Clay soils are stuffed full of nutrients. Clay is made up of very tiny particles; it is the finest ground of all the mineral materials we meet in the garden. Finely ground means it is easily broken down and ready to donate its food store to plants for transformation into burgeoning growth. It is fast food, but unless it is attended to sympathetically it can deteriorate into indigestible mush.

Do you have clay soil?

Many gardeners grumble about their garden soil being 'stiff clay' when in fact it is merely somewhat on the heavy side and there is a good proportion of clay. Such soils are usually highly productive. A very clay soil will be one which has 25% of clay particles. Those with 10% only of clay will be silty or sandy ones. Clay particles are very small, 0.002mm ($\frac{1}{16,000}$in), which compares with sand particles one thousand times larger, 2mm ($\frac{1}{16}$in) in diameter. The small clay particles bind together easily and form a poorly drained soil that becomes sticky when wet. If you take a handful of normal soil and try to compress it, the resulting lump will fall apart easily; a clay soil will take on the imprint of your hand and remains as a lump. It can be rolled into balls.

Coping with clay

The most important thing in managing clay is to avoid compacting it. Walking on it in wet weather is disastrous. With all its particles being the same almost microscopic size, it can pack tight – very tight. Once this happens there is no room between the particles for air, water or roots. Water cannot drain away into compacted soil, and if the soil is very dry it runs off the top, collecting in all the wrong places and not reaching plant roots.

In the garden all the effort with clay is directed towards improving its unrelenting structure to make it into a more open healthy soil. It is clay that requires winter digging, leaving the lumpy bare soil for the frost to break up. Clay is the only soil that seems to really benefit from this routine, and there are doubts as to whether it really is that useful by itself. Frost action tries to get clay particles to join into groups: to flocculate. But this happy state can only be maintained if extra work is done by adding grit and humus, and perhaps using lime, which also makes clay particles group themselves into large units. Any resulting improvement needs to be safely guarded with a constant regime that will avoid any backsliding of the soil towards it former impacted and glutinous state. The best regime to follow is one

AJUGA REPTANS
Bugle

Description: Bugle is an indomitable perennial which forms ground-hugging rosettes of semi-evergreen leaves with a long season of sturdy flowering spikes. New plants are usually quick to spread by runners. A native plant and a frequent weed in the lawn, it is completely hardy. In ornamental beds and borders it is best to use cultivars selected for the particularly rich purple shining leaves.
Uses: A reliable small non-threatening but energetic ground cover. Front of borders, wild garden, bolder rock gardens.
Colour: Bright blue flower spikes, choice of leaf colours and variegations.
Size: 10cm (4in) high, spread to 45cm (18in).
Flowering time: Mid-spring flush with intermittent spikes through until late autumn.
Relatives: *A. reptans* 'Catlin's Giant', taller than average and richly coloured. 'Jungle Beauty' up to 38cm (15in) high, spread 60cm (24in), bold foliage suffused purple. 'Multicolor' ('Rainbow', 'Tricolor') with variegated foliage of purple, pink and cream splashes. *A. pyramidalis* is a similar species with spoon-shaped leaves, height to 15cm (6in) and spread 45cm (18in).
Cultivation: Good humoured, tolerant plant; it is best in moist soils and can cope with boggy sites. Grows well in sun, semi- or full shade.
Propagation: Detach rooted runners and replant where needed.

of continual top-dressing with humus-rich material. This will certainly help to improve the vital topsoil as it is worked on by bacteria and is physically integrated into the soil by worms and other animals.

DRAINAGE

Soil structure needs to be improved. Look first to the drainage; even the driest gardens get some rainfall, and to be fully exploited clay soils need to have their drainage looked at and this means looking to the soil itself. We may have to lay field drain pipes down to a lower area, to a large soak away or to a major drain. A drop of one in fifty is plenty, but ensure that pipes do not get quickly clogged up by clay getting through the joins. Lay pipes on and surround them by a generous layer of rough gravel or crushed rock covered with a layer of plastic mesh to prevent all getting rapidly silted up. If the lengths are considerable and the cost of pipes too much, then make cleanly dug out channels with a steady gentle fall and fill these channels with a generous depth of hardcore, eg crushed rock, covered with plastic mesh. The main trench can be fed by a series of shorter echelon trenches falling at the same rate and pointing towards the lower area.

TOP-DRESSING

The worst of clays are the blue marls, alkaline clays of infractible plasticity. Gardeners with this problem may decide to tackle the situation by top-dressing in a very liberal manner, using every possible combination of humus together with some grit and laying this on the top of the clay without working the clay below. You hope for some integration by the encouragement of worms and other organisms. Plants are installed in the built-up soil. To cover the whole garden with sufficient depth of top dressing is not something that is likely to be contemplated except as

Flowering currants such as *Ribes sanguineum* 'Brocklebankii' are among the many shrubs that cope and flourish on clay soil

ASTER AMELLUS
Michaelmas daisy

A. x *frikartii* 'Mönch' and rudbeckia

Description: These are dwarfer than the big Michaelmas daisies (A. *novi-belgii*) but they have the inestimable advantage of being mildew-resistant, and are fully hardy. Neat foliage and growth close to the ground and lots of upright stems carrying loads of blossom.

Uses: Excellent autumn colour for borders and can be left in place for a few seasons without any worry.

Wildlife: Seed-eating birds will sometimes peck at the ripe seedheads; butterflies, bees and other insects visit flowers to search for pollen and nectar.

Colour: Limited but attractive range: purples and violets shading to mauves and some close to blue, some approach pink.

Size: 40-60cm (16-24in) high, spread 60cm (24in).

Flowering time: Late summer till almost the end of autumn.

Relatives: A. *amellus* 'Brilliant' has bright pink flowerheads, 'King George' has rich violet petals with smallish yellow centres. A. x *frikartii* 'Mönch' (pictured) is one of the outstanding plants of late summer and autumn. It is taller than the amellus types and has branching stems bearing a widespread galaxy of mauve-blue flowers with yellow centres. A. *novae-angliae* 'Alma Potschke' has poker-stiff stems 60cm (24in) or more high with clusters of rich pink daisies.

Cultivation: Best in sun or partial shade in good drained soil which does not dry out. Can be left undisturbed for several seasons before being lifted and good divisions planted in fresh or renewed soil.

Propagation: By division of clumps or by cuttings in early spring. Do not attempt this in the autumn, you may find the roots rot and you lose your plants.

CHAENOMELES SPECIOSA
Cydonia, Japonica

Description: Tough winter- and spring-flowering deciduous shrub. Fully hardy. Bowl-shaped flowers often begin to open early winter and can continue until the spring comes so that the last flush will be accompanied by the freshly unfurled leaves.

Uses: Most commonly trained against a wall where the support helps it to make stronger upward growth and helps ripen the wood to produce copious flower buds. Can also be grown in open or among other shrubs.

Colour: Reds, oranges, pinks and white.

Wildlife: Birds may choose to nest in its intricate branching.

Size: To 2.5m (8ft) high, spread 4-5m (12-15ft)
Flowering time: Early winter–spring

Relatives: C. speciosa 'Apple Blossom' is pink and white, 'Moerloosei' is pink and white with arching stems, 'Nivalis' is tall and brilliantly white, 'Simonii' deepest scarlet-red flowers often with extra petals and making a rather lower bush of interlocking branches. Consider also the nearly related C. x superba hybrids such as 'Crimson and Gold' and 'Knap Hill Scarlet'.

Cultivation: In warm, well-drained soils these shrubs grow well. The most taxing job will be to prune them back to prevent them swamping other plants and encouraging wood to be close to the ripening effect of warm walls and so to stimulate the production of flower buds.

Propagation: By layers, air layers, or by softwood cuttings in summer.

a lifetime's ideal. The humus rich top-dressing is confined to the areas you wish to plant and the added height protected from dispersion by walls or brick, stone, railway sleepers, logs or peat blocks.

One of the most pleasing gardens I knew as a child was built on the site that had been used to extract clay for brick making. The soil was a thick orange clay with little humus in it. The owner started to improve matters by arranging a series of bonfires encased with clay. By the time that one of these fires had burnt itself out – a matter of days rather than hours – the clay that had been built up over the fire was thoroughly burnt and broke up into a crumbly mass that might have been the result of the hammering of earthenware pots. This material when incorporated into the soil with the addition of humus built up a well drained highly nutritious topsoil in which a amazing collection of rare and wonderful plants flourished.

Whilst many may complain loudly of their heavy clay soil, most complaints are exaggerated. These soils are packed with nutrients and need only careful tending by eliminating very badly drained spots and improving the soil structure by continual incorporation of humus and possibly grit into the top few centimetres/inches or by a continuous programme of mulching with humus which the soil organisms will work on and incorporate into the soil below.

Making the most of it

Working with nature, which is what this book advocates, it makes sense to avoid the more intensive forms of gardening when dealing with heavy clay. For instance, it is not very sensible to opt for annual bedding plants. These require a lot of work to get going properly and to maintain by deadheading. They are unlikely to be able to be planted up as early in clay soils as in better drained ones and will probably take longer to get going. Such plants are better enjoyed in containers where the soil and other conditions are more under control (see pages 196–219). A very much more practical plan on clay soil is to rely heavily on shrubs with some trees, and to underplant with bulbs and a few really heavy-weight perennials.

SHRUBS

Summertime blossom from brooms, evergreen *Osmanthus* species and hybrids, lilacs and a host of other shrubs, can prove the point that there are many shrubs which can usually cope well with clay if given a little help to start with and then given a regular allocation of top-dressing, with various mulches, to improve the topsoil, guard against soil-cracking in the heat of summer and prevent weed growth. Even winter stars such as the witch hazels (*Hamamelis*) can cope with heavy soil within a fair range of pH levels if given the reasonable start they deserve. This means preparing a generous hole and using humus-rich compost to fill it. Although there are over sixty named cultivars and species now available, *Hamamelis mollis* and the Wisley-raised cultivar 'Pallida' are still two of the most excellent choice shrubs, producing very generous amounts of yellow blossom in the depths of winter – all happily frost-proof and long lasting. The species has petals of golden mini-ribbons, those of 'Pallida' are lemony. There are a lot of orange- and red-flowered cultivars, some very attractive ones, but these should be planted where you will see them close by,

pH levels

pH is a measure of the acidity or alkalinity of the soil. The scale is from 1 to 14, 7 being neutral, above 7 alkaline, below 7 aciditic. Most garden soils are within one or two full units of neutral. The easiest way of measuring the pH of your soil is to make a sensible sample to test (take a spadeful, mix it thoroughly and then use a portion of this). Follow the directions on a soil sampling kit. You may have to repeat the process for different parts of the garden to make sure that you have a full correct picture.

Acidity can be lessened by applying calcium in the form of lime. Severe alkalinity can be modified by the application of repeated dosages of humus material.

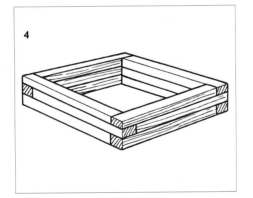

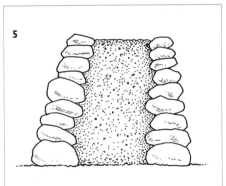

RAISED BEDS

The problem of difficult soils may be partially solved by using raised beds. In dry gardens on clay soils this will mean building up a relatively modest height above the heavy soil, perhaps the equivalent of three courses of bricks, somewhere in the 20-30cm (8-12in) range. The soil mix used within the raised bed should be heavily biased in favour of humus material – 50% or more would not be too much.

It will be sensible to contain the raised bed safely by bricks, rocks, railway sleepers, other timber or tree branches (silver birch can be useful and pleasing). This helps to contain moisture.

1 Mark out bed area.
2 Remove pernicious weed.
3 Lightly dig over the surface and leave it rough.
4 Position the 'walls'. Stone walls should slope inwards

for stability. Railway sleepers can be arranged with vertical sides.
5 Fill the raised bed with a mix that is approximately 50% humus material, 30% healthy garden soil, 20% grit. (It is acceptable to take the healthy garden soil from the garden with its high clay content.)
6 Introduce the plants and then topdress with humus as compost, leaf mould or, most likely, shredded bark.

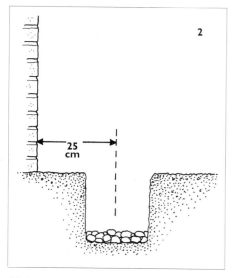

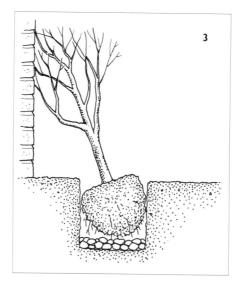

GROWING PEACHES

Peaches are one of the most rewarding of wall fruits. You just cannot compare a freshly picked ripe peach from your own garden with those that masquerade as peaches in the supermarkets. They are an easy fruit to grow if you take note of one or two of the following points.

*There is a selection of cultivars. I reckon 'Peregrine' to be still the most wonderful. Saliva glands start working at the thought.

1 They enjoy a sunny wall.

2 They grow well on clay into which has been incorporated a generous amount of rubble or hardcore. Soil may be slightly acid, neutral or just a little alkaline. Dig a hole about 25cm (10in) from the wall.

3 The tree should be planted with its trunk at soil level leading to the with roots pointing away.

4 Pin back and prune branches so that they can be fanned across the wall and attached to supports in the form of tensed wires or trellis.

5 Fix a batten of wood to the wall across the top of the whole spread of the tree. To this, from leaf-fall until early spring, should be fixed a polythene curtain. This will prevent the ingress or germination of the spores of the leaf-curl disease which is the bane of peaches and the only real reason for them not being more widely grown. Remove the curtain as growth starts in spring.

Peonies and forget-me-nots enjoyed the shelter of *Viburnum davidii* in this spring border

as the colour does not shine out in the distance as the yellows do. 'Diane' has excellent dark mahogany-red flowers and, like most of its relatives, it has a second season of glory with the autumn colours its leaves turn before they drop. *H. mollis* foliage turns gold but that of 'Diane' becomes various shades of deep red and crimson.

Roses are traditionally thought of as lovers of heavy clay soils. This penchant has been rather overstated in the past, but there is no doubt that they can flourish for many years in heavier soils. Beds devoted entirely to roses are somewhat of a rarity in smaller private gardens. This is partly because the months when they consist only of bare twigs put them at a real disadvantage in places where everything has to earn its keep, and although they can be underplanted with spring bulbs and other useful auxiliaries, the effect never seems entirely satisfactory. However, it is worth considering bush roses as 'normal' shrubs and planting them in herbaceous and mixed borders as individual specimens in groups of three. The English roses bred by David Austin, with their old-fashioned looks but modern robustness and free flowering habit are ideal.

Another genus well worth considering is *Viburnum*. It is full of good trustworthy shrubs. The Victorian's favourite, *V. tinus*, is a real workhorse, giving really windproof dark evergreen shelter and making a magnificent hedging plant, in bloom from autumn through till spring. The deciduous *V. × bodnantense* series are invaluable for their winter blossom, which opens from the autumn and

MAKING USE OF WALLS AND FENCES

Walls or strong fences can be enlivened by some of the many firethorns (*Pyracantha* cultivars). These spreading, spiny shrubs or woody climbers are evergreen and look decorative for much of the year, with quantities of wide creamy panicles of bloom in spring and fantastic loads of autumn berries – in shades of gold, orange or red – which many will be displaying fully by the end of the summer and will retain until early spring. Next door to these a bush of the dark evergreen *Garrya elliptica* would look effective, with its autumn and winter catkins in silvers, greys and greens; some catkins can be 20cm (8in) to over 30cm (12in) long.

INULA HELENIUM
Elecampane

Description: Strong herbaceous perennial widespread through Europe in wet sites, found in Britain but maybe an introduced plant. Tall, hardy and bold, it has large rough serrated basal leaves to 40cm (16in) long, elliptical or somewhat heart shaped and closely clasped up the tall flower stems. Large daisy flowers have wide central discs and rather narrow strips for outer disc petals.

Uses: One or a group in a wet place will be very bold and lend a sense of scale.

Colour: Golden.

Size: 1-1.2m (3-4ft) high, 75cm (30in) across.

Flowering time: Mid- to late summer.

Relatives: *I. ensifolia* is much smaller with spear-shaped leaves and many golden daisies in late summer. *I. hookeri*, another hairy plant with golden flowers, is distinguished by the greater number of long narrow petals radiating from the darker central disc. *I. magnifica* is a giant with huge leaves and stems towering to 1.8m (6ft) and perhaps needing support. It has very narrow petalled golden daisies.

Cultivation: Once planted it may be safely left to do its heavyweight thing.

Propagation: By seed or division in early spring.

remains around for months. 'Dawn' is the most widely available and with lots of pink and white scented posies generously covering the framework of the shrub, its popularity is well earned. 'Charles Lamont' and 'Deben' are siblings, the latter rather whiter in blossom and a somewhat more spare upright shrub. All three have deservedly been honoured with the Royal Horticultural Society's Award of Garden Merit: AGM is something to look out for in catalogues, as the award is not lightly bestowed.

Some of the berberis flourish on clay, certainly the excellent evergreens, *B. darwinii* and the hybrid series *B. × stenophylla* are top favourites. Other evergreens include the escallonia hybrids such as 'Apple Blossom' and richer pink 'Langleyensis'. The spotted laurel, *Aucuba japonica*, is again in the list of shrubs happy in a difficult spot. If the soil is not alkaline you can introduce rhododendrons; they are shallow rooted so will need the help of humus-rich mulches. Most brooms will manage happily.

Deciduous shrubs include the many sweet-scented philadelphus species and hybrids, the deutzias,

SHRUBS FOR CLAY SOIL

Aucuba japonica cultivars
Berberis, various
Choisya ternata, and others
Colutea × media cultivars
Cotinus coggygria cultivars
Cytisus cultivars
Deutzia, various
Escallonia cultivars
Magnolia, various including
    M. stellata forms
Osmanthus cultivars
Prunus glandulosa 'Alba Plena'
Rhododendron, various
Ribes sanguineum cultivars
Sambucus nigra, coloured-
    leaved forms
Spiraea cultivars
Syringa cultivars
Viburnum davidii, and others
Weigela cultivars

Berberis are content on many soil types. Here, *B. thunbergii* 'Dart's Red Lady' is shown in full autumn glory

SAMBUCUS RACEMOSA
Red-berried elder

S. racemosa Aurea 'Plumosa'

Description: Easy hardy deciduous shrub, its typical elder pinnate leaves having five oval leaflets. Small flowers in thick terminal clusters. Round red fruits in summer and autumn.

Uses: Grows well in moist soils in full sun or light shade. Will quickly make a mature bush.

Colour: Creamy flowers, red fruits.

Size: Height and spread 3m (10ft).

Flowering time: Mid-spring.

Relatives: *S. racemosa* 'Plumosa' has deeply cut leaves, which are almost fern-like as are those of 'Plumosa Aurea' (pictured) but this has bronzed young foliage maturing to gold.

Cultivation: Plant in a moist spot. Can be cut back severely every other winter to give fresh stems with bright foliage and plenty of bloom.

Propagation: Cuttings taken in autumn, some 30-45cm (12-18in) long, and pushed two-thirds down into the ground, preferably in gritty soil. Either in a nursery section or where the mature plant is wanted.

ribes, lilacs, and spiraeas such as the robust *S. × vanhouttei*. (See margin list page 59.)

WALLS AND FENCES

A lot of shrubs can be encouraged to grow up walls in clay soils. Recommendations about the ones to try and how to do this are to be found in the chapters on fences and walls (see pages 170 and 176). However, here is an idea.

PERENNIALS

Herbaceous perennials that flourish on clay include asters of the Michaelmas daisy clan, the solidago hybrids, better known as golden rod, and the daisies such as rudbeckia, helenium and heliopsis. The monardas, astilbes and astrantias also cope well, together with the rather more unusual *Cimicifuga simplex* with its tall, narrow white spikes held well above attractive divided fern-like foliage.

TREES

Many fine trees revel in clay so long as it is not

Natural communities

Trees found naturally growing on clay soils include horse chestnuts, English oaks, beeches, poplars and limes. With them are the smaller and more shrubby hawthorns, elders and viburnums with possibly brooms and gorse.

Perennial plants found in such conditions are wide ranging but are likely to be some of the polygonums, nettles, poppies, fumitories and knapweeds along with ox-eye daisies, valerian and yarrows.

Where ground has been left untended, brambles and wild roses begin to colonize and take over stretches perhaps vying with rosebay willowherb for dominance. They do not sound like plants for the gardener but the communities give clues to what to plant; there are plenty of attractive relatives of brambles and roses as well as polygonums, daisies, poppies and even nettles.

permanently waterlogged. Familiar ones include the horse chestnut, *Aesculus hippocastanum*, the grey alder, *Alnus incana*, the English oak, *Quercus robur*, and the hornbeam, *Carpinus betulus*, of which 'Fastigiata' is a splendid upright form. There are also plenty of good conifers that welcome a clay such as *Abies koreana*, 10m (30ft), *Chamaecyparis lawsoniana* forms, 15m (50ft), *Pinus aristata*, 8m (25ft), *Pinus peuce*, 18m (60ft), *Pinus thunbergii*, 12m (40ft), *Taxodium distichum*, 20m (70ft), *Taxus baccata*, 12m (40ft), or for smaller kinds *Pinus mugo* forms or *Thuya occidentalis* forms.

The Indian bean tree, *Catalpa bignonioides*, is impressive as a small specimen and gets more impressive as it grows, up to some 12m (40ft) in time. The golden-leaved *C. b.* 'Aurea' is a lovely tree flamboyant in colour and bold in leaf, even when a young specimen; it can be pruned back to keep it within reasonable bounds.

Other ornamentals that will be quite happy in clay include decorative apples such as *Malus hupehensis* or the hybrid series of magnolias gathered under the name *Magnolia* × *soulangeana*.

PHILADELPHUS 'BELLE ETOILE'
Mock orange

P. 'Virginal'

Description: Easy, hardy, deciduous shrub of arching demeanour and very free flowering with open, four-petalled, scented blooms. Bright green pointed oval leaves.

Uses: Reliable for borders in sun or light shade.

Colour: Snow-white with a maroon spot at the base of each petal and a boss of golden stamens.

Scent: Typically generously perfumed mock-orange.

Size: Height and spread to 2m (6ft) but can be pruned to less.

Flowering time: Late spring–early summer.

Relatives: There are any number of relatives, both species and hybrids, most with white flowers and the exotic perfume. *P.* 'Beauclerk' has large flowers with each white petal having a tiny purple basal spot. *P.* 'Virginal' (pictured) is a very robust upright shrub to 3m (10ft) high, much-scented, rounded, double or semi-double white blossom, *P. coronarius* 'Aureus' is less free with modest clusters of smallish flowers but with very pleasing yellow spring foliage, still yellowish in summer 1.2m (4ft) x 90cm (3ft). *P. microphyllus* is very floriferous, with very perfumed, smallish, white single flowers. It grows 1.2m (4ft) high and across. 'Avalanche' and 'Manteau d'Hermine' are also recommended.

Cultivation: Easy in well drained fertile soils. For best results cut back flowering twigs and branches after blooming.

Propagation: Hardwood winter cuttings.

SECTION TWO
TOO WET

Too much water can be just as much a problem for most plants as too little. It makes things less pleasant for humans as well: dank mists, soaking rainfall, mud underfoot, midges. On the other hand, a plentiful supply of water gives the chance of creativity that is impossible in drier conditions. Water means life; plenty of water can mean an abundance of life.

Handled with sympathy and imagination, a water-saturated site can be a place of magic all the year round. There is endless activity and fascination above and below the water. In summer, visitors find a green burgeoning haven in the dry landscape; luxuriant vegetation is reflected in the calm mirror surface of a pool, dragonflies fly low over the water, swallows skim the surface to sip in full flight, plants fulfill their potential unstressed. Shapes move below the water surface, and at dusk the leaping arcs of golden orfe bear witness to their fly-catching successes. In spring there is the croaking of courting frogs. In the presence of pools, waterfalls or streams, human senses come alive: vision is saturated with colour, nostrils are filled with perfumes and ears relax to the murmur of moving water.

Is your garden too wet?

Usually it is easy to recognise a garden that has problems with too much water. It may be less easy to find the reason for the surplus. It may be that the excess is a seasonal occurrence, perhaps becoming apparent after times of particularly heavy or persistent rainfall. A permanent high water table may affect a number of sites, others may be fed by a spring or springs. Some soils are heavy and 'claggy' meaning that any water they receive stays put and does not drain away.

PREVAILING WEATHER
Different areas, and locales within those areas, all have their own climates (New Zealand has 17 distinct climate types). In islands countries like Britain, gardeners moving from the west coast to the east quickly learn that there is a very considerable difference in climatic conditions; in Britain the west is well-known for its high rainfall whereas the east is very much drier. Greater rainfall is often combined with heavy cloud cover, providing conditions that

With a little imagination and effort a wet site can be transformed into a lush paradise

favour the retention of water. Wetter areas encourage the growth of a wide range of plants; only a relatively small proportion of plants are in danger of rotting or being disfigured by wet-induced diseases. The real sun-loving plants from low rainfall areas are, however, unlikely to do really well: those blue- or grey-leaved beauties with hairy leaf surfaces that are too often sodden with wet will not live long. Instead it is necessary to look to the moisture lovers that will flourish in full tumescent magnificence.

Rain-carrying clouds arriving with the winds will begin to shed their rain as they move over the land, and especially where they encounter hill ranges that force the air movement upwards, which stimulates the formation of the heavy droplets that lead to precipitation. Where soils are retentive of water the ground can soon become waterlogged. Low-lying ground is obviously vulnerable, with surplus water moving from high to low areas. Springs can appear in the areas below slopes. Streams and rivers at valley bases or on flat land can overflow and create marshland or at the very least conditions similar to the water meadows that are expected to flood at least once a year.

MYOSOTIS SCORPIOIDES
Water forget-me-not

Description: A hardy perennial that dies back each autumn. It quickly forms spreading mounds of slender leaves and tops these with a continuous supply of small forget-me-not flower sprays through the summer.
Uses: Shallow water or marginal plant for pond or stream.
Colour: Blue.
Size: To about 20cm (8in) high, spread 45cm (18in) or more.
Flower time: Through summer.
Relatives: *M. scorpioides* 'Mermaid' is perhaps a little more compact than most, a good free-flowering form.
Cultivation: No problems.
Propagation: Will self seed.

SLOPING SITES

Slopes can have surprisingly wet soils. Spring lines form around slopes at points where the underlying rock formations act as funnels, directing ground water to the surface. Quite steep slopes can be almost covered by a sheet of slow seeping water, either on the surface or just below. For example, melting snow-water can slide under the thin topsoil of a mountain slope creating startling boggy conditions where good drainage might reasonably be expected. In the garden a little work can channel this type of widely dispersed water into a faster running stream that will be an attractive feature, and will enable all sorts of plants to be grown around it.

Naturally wet slopes often have boggy bases, where the water has gathered at the lowest point. Such a site can be cleared to form a pond that will be replenished by nature. The soil around ponds like this is likely to be permanently sodden and poorly aerated. Many plants will not appreciate such conditions, however, there are those that are adapted to wet areas, and these can be used to great effect.

PLANTS FOR
WATERLOGGED CLAY

Caltha palustris, king cup, marsh marigold
Cornus alba 'Elegantissima', variegated dogwood
Dipsacus fullonum, teasel
Fritillaria meleagris, snake's head fritillary
Lysichiton americanus, yellow skunk cabbage
Lysimachia nummularia, creeping Jenny
Monarda, bergamot
Myosotis scorpioides, water forget-me-not
Rodgersia, various
Scrophularia auriculata 'Variegata', variegated figwort
Viburnum opulus, guelder rose

PARNASSIA PALUSTRIS
Grass of Parnassus

Description: A classy member of the saxifrage family, a native of Northern Europe. It forms a neat basal arrangement of heart-shaped somewhat succulent leaves in matt mid-green. On slender wiry stems, way above the foliage, the plant unfurls open five-petalled stars.
Uses: For moist spots in rock garden, stream- or pondside.
Colour: Petals pure white but with delicate veining in dark green or light purple.
Size: Flowers reach 20cm (8in) high, but leaves are a third of this, spread 6-8cm (2-3in).
Flowering time: Late spring and early summer, but odd flowers can appear later.
Cultivation: Needs sunshine and moisture.
Propagate: By fresh seed sown in autumn.

ALTITUDE

Low lying areas are the obvious places for wet land: valley bottoms particularly, collect water. However, sodden conditions here are normally offset by the increased depth of soil which the levelling teamwork of erosion and gravity have, over time, brought down from higher ground. The soil surface in some valleys has been overlaid by a layer of peaty materials from many centuries of boggy growth. With the artificial lowering of the water table by ditches and drainage, this ground can be exploited as a wonderful growing medium.

SOIL TYPES

Clay is the classic wet soil. Wet weather waterlogs clay making it a solid, structureless, airless pudding which suffocates roots and crowns.

Peaty soils are created by wet conditions in which there has been vegetation. Peat has long been renowned as a soil improver, but that is to improve soils that basically consist of other materials. These benefit from all forms of rotted vegetable matter which is what forms humus. A solely peaty soil is another matter. Heavy drainage could dry it out too much and result in it being blown away. Those who live on or near peat fens are familiar with the dark clouds of peat that can be spread for miles in windy conditions. Nature would normally have all such soils covered with a layer of vegetation.

Peat is not necessarily loaded with nutriment; it more often acts like a sponge, holding huge quantities of acid water which may or may not have a balanced supply of nutrients. It can be as hungry a soil as a sandy one. The actual level of a peaty soil will fall year by year if it is cropped without returning the equivalent humus. And peaty soil is incurably acid. It is pointless trying to grow lime-loving plants on it. On the other hand, almost every wet-loving plant likes acid conditions.

Other indicators of waterlogging

A soil may be waterlogged below while the surface seems free of surplus water. This can be perplexing because many plants will only signal that their roots are drowning by dropping leaves. The most obvious example of this is overwatered pot plants. Often the dropping of leaves is taken as a sign that the plant is short of water and so the watering can is used, only to make bad matters worse. So starts a vicious spiral that can lead to the death of the plant.

In your garden, if leaf dropping happens only occasionally, there can be a number of causes. However, if it happens regularly and especially on a particular stretch of ground, then suspect waterlogging. Dig an exploratory hole. Try to get at least 60cm (2ft) deep and then leave the hole open. Inspect it regularly. A high water table results in the hole being full or partially full for prolonged periods. If in digging you come across a particularly hard layer of soil, an almost impermeable pan, this could be making it difficult for water to drain away. Or you may find that the ground has an unsuspected high water table, meaning that rising water covers and drowns questing roots or stops them penetrating soil below a certain modest depth.

A high water level like this may not be a permanent feature, it could be something that happens in the winter when you are less likely to notice the phenomena as the deciduous plants are without the leaves that would signal distress in the summer. The drowning of roots during this period may well be enough to cause mysterious deaths later. Plants that have been deprived of any deep roots are going to be dependent on shallow roots which will be all the more vulnerable to drought conditions.

Plant form and Function – how plants cope

THE SHAPES OF PLANTS

Many wetlands have an abundance of all the things that a plant needs – sunlight, water and food. So growth should not be restricted by lack of resources and should be vigorous. The main problem will be the struggle to reach the light first and shade out the competition. Thus many wetland plants grow very large.

OSMUNDA REGALIS
Royal fern

Description: The largest fern in Britain with fronds from 60cm to 1.8m (2-6ft) long and, in wet sites, when established, capable of impressive size, with each frond up to 1m (3ft) wide. Deciduous, its dead winter fronds are warm buff shades; the delightful new crosiers held upright and then uncurling.
Uses: Waterside or wetland.
Wildlife: Shelter for ducks and other aquatic life.
Colour: From pale green unfurling crosiers, with orange scales, to fresh green mature fronds. Fertile fronds are rusty, drying and dead fronds buff-brown.
Size: To 2m (6ft) high, spread 2-3m (6-10ft).
Flowering time: No real flowers.
Cultivation: Once planted in a permanently wet place, needs little further care. You may wish to clear away old dead fronds at the winter's end to leave new growth better viewed.
Propagation: Try dividing a clump at the end of the year. Alternatively, fresh spores can be sown as soon as ripe (see page 89).

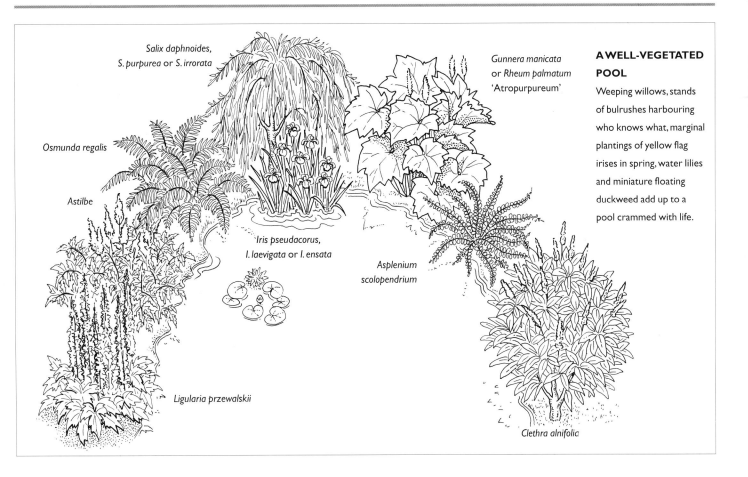

A WELL-VEGETATED POOL
Weeping willows, stands of bulrushes harbouring who knows what, marginal plantings of yellow flag irises in spring, water lilies and miniature floating duckweed add up to a pool crammed with life.

Lady's smock (*Cardamine pratensis*) brightens up this wooded pool

FILIPENDULA ULMARIA 'AUREA'
Meadowsweet

F. rubra

Description: This is the yellow-leaved form of the common meadowsweet that is a familiar sight in ditches and ill-drained pastures. A native of Britain and northern Europe. Its divided almost ferny foliage is particularly bright in spring but is still attractive in flowering midsummer. Clusters or plumes of flowers.

Uses: At home in any wet spot. A useful foliage plant.

Colour: Foliage primrose-yellow in spring then limy in summer; flowers creamy white.

Scent: Rather musky perfume.

Size: 30-40cm (12-16in) high and across.

Flowering time: Midsummer.

Relatives: The species has dark green, divided, creased foliage and is a strong plant. *F. rubra* (pictured) is huge, to 2.5m (6ft), with fragrant deep pink flowers.

Cultivation: Easy in moist soils.

Propagation: Division in early spring.

LEAF CHARACTERISTICS

With such an ample water supply, the plants can expand freely and support a lot of leaf surface, it is not a problem to replace large amounts of water lost through these larger areas of transpiration. Gunneras and rheums are two large-leaved plants that love the wet.

Rheum (rhubarb) is a typical lush wetland plant. When winter arrives it retreats to crowns, its food reserves safely tucked into the soil during the cold weather and its massive underground roots holding ample resources ready to be utilized when it leaps into action with spring. Then it surges forth with thick stems water-bloated and carrying huge

umbrella leaves to outshade its neighbours. The gunnera is even larger and more dominant in its own territory.

Even those plants that are somewhat more restrained have plenty of foliage; *Iris pseudacorus* (page 76) is energetic with many sword leaves catching

the light as they thrust upwards. Lower down by the stream or poolside, the marsh marigold replaces its first tentative tiny leaves with a succession of larger round ones, glistening with health. The broad buckler fern, *Dryopteris dilatata*, sends out pristine fronds to look intricate, sparkling, beautiful and still.

DIPSACUS FULLONUM
Teasel

Description: A tall strong biennial or perennial. Stems and most parts prickly, especially the seedheads that were used in 'teasing' fabrics. Light green leaves are long, serrated and pointed; the basal ones are much broader than the smaller ones up the stems. Their surfaces are covered with white pimples. Rosettes of leaves are established before blooming and wither before flowers open. The tight teasel flowerheads are showy in blossom and persist through the winter as seedheads held by the skeleton stems. Native to Germany, France and Britain.

Uses: Makes a stately impressive stand as a group on poor soils or other bare places, especially from midsummer when its starts blooming and through the winter till spring. Excellent in wild garden among grasses, with shrubs and at rear of larger borders.

Colour: Leaves and stems silvery green, flowers pale violet.

Size: 2m (6ft) high, spread 45cm (18in) across.

Flowering time: Midsummer onwards.

Cultivation: Grows in most soils including wet or dryish ones. In the wild favours moist spots. Seedlings planted out should be given at least 45cm (18in) spacing and can then be left alone.

Propagation: Saved seed germinates easily in open or in pots. Seedlings in pots need to be pricked out when small and the potted ones planted out as soon as they have got established.

PLANTS FOR RICH WATERLOGGED SITES, MARSH AND PONDSIDE

Achillea ptarmica, sneeze wort, of which 'The Pearl' is quite outstanding

Caltha palustris, Marsh marigold

C. palustris 'Flore Pleno', fine double form

Cardamine pratensis, cuckoo flower, lady's smock

Filipendula ulmaria, meadowsweet

Lychnis flos-cuculi, ragged robin

Lythrum salicaria, purple loosestrife

Myosotis scorpioides, water forget-me-not

Parnassia palustris, grass of Parnassus

Petasites fragrans, winter heliotrope

P. hybridus, butter-burr

PLANT POINTER

Lythrum salicaria, **purple loosestrife, has special cells like white spongy swellings within its stems and its roots to enable it to breathe in waterlogged soils. Like many plants that revel in wet places, it can be surprisingly adaptable. I have grown this pleasing plant successfully in a dry garden in shallow soil over rock, not the first place one would choose for it. Of course, it was not as tall as it would have been in wet soils.**

LYCHNIS FLOS-CUCULI
Ragged robin

L. chalcedonica

Description: A branched, leaning and upward-stretching perennial, growing wild in all countries of northern Europe including Britain, with hairy stems and foliage. The leaves are narrow and mid-green; the flowers have five petals each divided into four pointed lobes.

Uses: Great in the wild garden, by hedgerows, in damp and even marshy spots as well as in mixed borders.

Colours: Vivid pink flowers.

Size: Dependent on site but around 60cm (2ft) high and across.

Flowering time: Can start in late spring and still be producing blossom at the end of the summer.

Relatives: *L. flos-cuculi albiflora* is a white-flowered form. *Lychnis chalcedonica* (pictured) is often called the Jerusalem or Maltese cross. It makes a neat, erect plant up to 1m (3ft) or more and half as much across. Bright green foliage is topped by broad, tight, flat heads of scarlet flowers in early summer.

Cultivation: Sow seed or plant out specimens in moist soils in light conditions and allow to naturalize.

Propagation: Easy from fresh seed.

ROOTS AND CROWNS

The overwintering mound of the royal fern, *Osmunda regalis*, keeps this shallow-rooting plant above the main soil and water levels so that it has air around its breathing roots. In spring it bestirs itself and from this crouching rootstock sends out crosiers like up-ended yo-yos, their ends unfurling magically.

The swamp cypress, *Taxodium distichum*, is an expert in dealing with the most waterlogged of conditions; it can cope even with oxygen-starved water. This trick it manages by growing extensions up from its roots, pushing up into the air. These 'knees' function as air-breathing snorkels for the roots in the stagnant water below.

Plant communities from wet habitats

There are three major wetland habitats: marshland, water meadows, and bogs. Each has somewhat different conditions and in any particular site one can merge into another so that there is a lack of very clear-cut rules when you are in the field. It is much tidier in this book!

MARSHLAND

Marsh occurs on waterlogged ground where the water is rich in dissolved chemicals. Plant growth is vigorous and in the wild there are many plants that have become familiar friends in the garden. *Myosotis scorpioides*, the water forget-me-not, is the largest flowered of its kind but we like it by a pool or in its shallows, taking advantage of its marsh-loving habit. The marsh marigold, *Caltha palustris*, is also a marsh-land dweller that has come into the garden; so are many others. See margin list page 67.

Poolside The side of a pond or lake may provide a strip of ground with conditions similar to marsh-land, unless particular conditions make it closer to a fen or bog (see below).

WATER AND FLOOD MEADOWS

These are drier than marshes and have less of the waterside reeds and rushes. Although it is usual to differentiate between water meadows and flood meadows, they differ only in that in one the flooding is a natural phenomenon and in the other, it is artificially engineered. Here, the ground is likely to be rich, even very rich, as the flood water brings with it successive fresh supplies of nutrient-laden silt. Often these meadows are flooded in winter months and return to normality with the late spring, and by the summer they could even by quite dry. The cutting of the herbage for hay will maintain the plant population that has become established. In Britain, one or two of these meadows are a springtime magnet for

VIBURNUM OPULUS
Guelder rose

V. opulus 'Roseum'

Description: A hardy deciduous upright and spreading shrub that can aspire to small tree status, with wide, lobed leaves. Flowers are in wide, almost flat, umbel-like clusters, the outer ones being conspicuous and large while the inner ones are small and fertile. The display is followed in the autumn by spectacular crops of large bunches of juicy berries.

Uses: Wet soils but also normal ones. Good in mixed plantings of shrubs, in shelter belts or screens.

Colours: Flowers white, berries shiny scarlet. Leaves orange and red in autumn.

Size: To 4m (12ft) high and wide.

Flowering time: Late spring and early summer.

Relatives: V. opulus 'Compactum' is half the size. 'Notcutt's Variety' is particularly free of flower and fruit. 'Xanthocarpum' loads itself with innumerable bunches of golden berries bordering pale orange. 'Roseum' (pictured) is a form with all sterile flowers – the heads are rounded snowballs that tend to turn pink with age.

Cultivation: Easy in normal or damp soils. Will not object to being cut back strongly if necessary.

Propagation: Species can be grown from seed; forms from cuttings in summer or by layers.

plant lovers. In Gloucestershire, near the village of Cricklade, is one that is famous for its population of wild fritillaries (*Fritillaria meleagris*), a heart-warming sight when their mauves, purples and whites are mixed with the golden blossom of less rare dandelions. Other plants that flourish in wet meadows include the delicate lady's smock (*Cardamine pratensis*) and the more hefty dyer's greenweed (*Genista tinctoria*). See also margin list, right.

Streamside Streamside species have to manage with moving water and periodic dunking under strong flood waters. Some compensation will be that the water is well oxygenated, the temperature fairly constant and nutrients are not in short supply.

You might expect to find the same species here as listed for wet meadows and waterlogged conditions. *Trollius europaeus*, the globe flower, could be added.

BOG

Now we move to rather different conditions. Where before the plants were buoyed up by plentiful supplies of food, here the soil water is normally acid and holds much less plant nutrients. Dead plant material has been submerged below water where the acid conditions have prevented a complete rotting process. This material might be described as 'preserved', like pickle. As the material builds up, the dark fibrous peaty material, spongy with moisture, forms the bog.

Even here conditions are not absolutely even, there could be some spots of slightly higher ground which are a little better served and where ericaceous shrubs may take hold. *Erica tetralix*, the cross-leaved heath, for example, and *Calluna vulgaris*, the widespread heather or ling. The royal fern, *Osmunda regalis* (page 65), may cope well enough with wet acid conditions.

Fenland This is similar to bog: it has the same peaty layers of only partially rotted plant remains, but much of the water comes from underlying rocks of limestone or chalk so there is an important alkaline input. The pH of the two environments is dramatically different, something that is reflected in the differing plant communities. The plants of fenland are a different set from the bog plants, although there are familiar friends from marshland conditions.

PLANTS OF WET MEADOWS

Achillea ptarmica, sneezewort

Ajuga reptans, bugle

Caltha palustris, marsh marigold

Cardamine pratensis, cuckoo flower, lady's smock

Fritillaria meleagris, snake's head fritillary

Genista tinctoria, dyer's greenweed

Lychnis flos-cuculi, ragged robin

Lythrum salicaria, purple loosestrife

Myosotis scorpioides, water forget-me-not

PLANTS OF FEN CONDITIONS – PEATY SOIL BUT ALKALINE WATER

Alnus glutinosa, alder

Angelica sylvestris, angelica

Betula pubescens, downy birch

Eupatorium cannabinum, hemp agrimony

Fraxinus excelsior, ash

Geum rivale, water avens

Lysimachia nummularia, creeping Jenny

Menyanthes trifoliata, bog bean, buckbean

Sparganium, bur reeds

Typha latifolia

T. minima

Viburnum opulus, guelder rose

WET AND SUNNY

PLENTY OF MOISTURE, plenty of light; so why is it a tough place? As with all the garden situations dealt with in this book, for the plants that have adapted themselves to the particular conditions, this is not a difficult situation at all. However, if you try to grow plants here which are not suited to the conditions, they will rapidly die. Think how unlikely you would be to grow most alpines or rockery plants in a place where they would have permanent wet feet. Most gardeners can see the limitations of a wet site, but it also has as many opportunities. The moisture-rich garden is one that may be thought of as doubly endowed. Apart from the splendid plant life that it will support, all manner of birds and animal life will come to enjoy the water and the abundant life that it brings. From the annual excitement of tadpoles and frogs, to birds of all kinds, and with some stretches of clear water there may even be visiting ducks.

The problem with a wet sunny site arises because the ample and permanent water squeezes out another essential element – air. Lack of air is not usually a difficulty in most other conditions. Plants need air around their leaves to breathe and carry on the food producing processes of photosynthesis. But roots, too, need air: without enough air they drown, much as animal life would.

Seasonal drought is another problem that affects some wet sites. It is a case of feast or famine; excessive wet can be replaced by really thirsty times. And such a problem can be difficult to cope with. Usually there is plenty of water when the plants need it least – in the cool of winter and periods of abundant rain. Then the weather warms up and the

An open sunny spot is ideal for a wildlife pond, the dense surrounding growth providing plenty of cover for mammals and birds

sun and wind start curtailing the water supply just as the plants begin to grow more busily and transpire large quantities into the air.

Seasonal drought can be overcome by using plants that plunge their roots deeply to make use of deep water resources. Choosing plants that have their main period of activity and display early in the year before the threat of drought shrivelling leaves or wilting flowers also avoids problems.

Do you have a wet and sunny site?

Try digging – your sunny site may be dry on the surface but wet below. Abundant moisture below may be suspected if the growth of plants and weeds is on the generous side of respectable. Pulling up the weeds will declare the soil to be wet. You could verify your suspicions by digging a hole and seeing whether it remains moist below (see page 64).

Coping with wet and sunny sites

If you are surrounded with very wet ground and feel that each time you venture outside you are in danger of being lost forever in a quagmire, some work needs to be done to change the environment. However, do not be in too big a hurry to have all the apparently excess moisture drained completely away. You have a site that many other gardeners will covet. Some of the most magnificent of plants are thirsty moisture lovers; huge *Gunnera manicata*, the royal fern, *Osmunda regalis*, the ligularias and many other striking foliage plants, such as the rodgersias, will flourish here and produce a lush wonderful atmosphere.

POOLS AND PONDS

There is the opportunity to produce waterscapes without the extra bother and constant maintenance that those with more arid ground will have to face.

A healthy pond, both in terms of animal and plant life, is very much easier to maintain if it is not too small. A small and shallow pool can fluctuate violently and rapidly in temperature and oxygen content, vastly more so than larger bodies of water. The larger pond more quickly reaches a level of natural organic equilibrium than a small one. If

ANEMONE HUPEHENSIS

Description: Tough, perennial herbaceous species, one of the main parents of the important hybrids formerly known as *A. japonica* and now gathered under the collective title *A.* x *hybrida*. Plants form steadily enlarging crowns from which dark green, deeply divided leaves with well serrated leaflets are produced. The erect stems divide and produce a wealth of upward-facing, rounded, anemone flowers over a long period. It is a long-lived plant that is best given a generous patch to make its own.

Uses: Permanent planting, especially in moist soil; able to cope with heavy soils. Could be incorporated in semi-wild situations, in sun or semi-shade, not deep shade.

Colour: Rich pink, softened by the somewhat velvety texture. Central ring of golden anthers.

Size: 60-75cm (24-30in) high, spread 45-60cm (18-24in).

Flowering time: From late summer well into autumn.

Relatives: There are many good cultivars of which the following are excellent: 'Bowles' Pink', a well formed old favourite; 'Hadspen Abundance'; 'Prinz Heinrich'; 'September Charm'. The *A.* x *hybrida* series includes the well known 'Honorine Jobert', an outstanding snow-white.

Cultivation: Plant from pot into permanent site.

Propagation: Careful division in early spring.

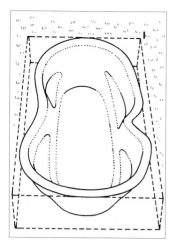
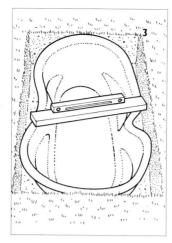

SITING A PREFORMED POND

Preformed ponds are widely available in a range of sizes and shapes; there is something to suit every pocket, and to fit any garden.

1 Mark out the area that the preform will need.
2 Dig the soil to the correct depth and form, or just a little larger.
3 Put the preform in place and ensure it

is level and that the base is fully support-ed at the bottom. Make sure it is not resting on any sharp stones. The top can be slightly below the level of the surrounding ground.

4 Refill around the sides of the preform.
5 Fill the pond with water. Allow to settle for a few days before planting up.

COLCHICUM AUTUMNALE
Autumn crocus

C. 'Waterlily'

Description: Hardy large corm which produces a posy of crocus-like flowers held by slender tubes above ground in autumn when it is without leaves. The foliage, which is of bright green, broadly oval leaves, appears in spring. Native to many countries of Europe.

Uses: It may be naturalized by a hedgerow, on the side of a ditch, in the wild garden, between shrubs or in the

border. Use in open or semi-shaded spots, not deep shade.

Colour: Mottled mauve.

Size: 10-15cm (4-6in) high and across.

Flowering time: Autumn

Relatives: C. autumnale 'Album' is an exceptionally fine pure white that tends to overshadow the type. 'Alboplenum' is a double white form. C. speciosum is more vigorous and larger with pale to pinky purple flowers. C. 'Lilac Wonder' is the most popular of the hybrids. It is vigorous and 15-20cm (6-8in) high with large clear shining pink, globe-shaped blooms freely produced. C. 'Waterlily' (pictured) has double deep pink flowers.

Cultivation: Plant purchased corms early autumn with 7-10cm (3-4in) soil over tops. Mark or remember where planted so that corms are not dug up or damaged when out of sight and leafless.

Propagation: Corms increase steadily. Lift each year or perhaps every other year as leaves turn yellow in late spring, shake apart and replant immediately giving extra space.

possible, the minimum water surface area should be 3m² (3yd²). Try to have two water depths: a shallow one around the margin about 25cm (10in) deep and a central, deeper one from 50cm–1m (20in–3ft); the deeper level will provide a bolt-hole for fish and other denizens in the depths of an ice-cold winter. At least one part of the margin should have a gently shelving side, perhaps covered with small pebbles, to enable some birds and other forms of animal life to have a way to and away from the water.

The site should be in the open, away from leaf-dropping trees, and will be most appreciated if seen from the house and patio.

Once the pond is constructed, you can begin to plant the margins. Allow a few weeks/days for the water to settle, then introduce plants into the areas of water.

Oxygenating plants are best tucked into trays or the special mesh planting containers with compost topped with gravel to prevent the compost floating all over the pond. Pieces of common fish weed (*Lagarosiphon major*) or Canadian pondweed (*Elodea canadensis*) can be weighted down into the compost and left to get on with the job. Approximately one plant per square metre/yard should serve. If the growth of any plant gets too luxuriant it can be trimmed back.

CARDAMINE PRATENSIS
Lady's smock, Cuckoo flower

C. pratensis 'Flore Pleno'

Description: Low, tufted perennial with rosettes of pinnate leaves with rounded leaflets. The leaves from the flower stems are also pinnate but with narrow segments. Attractive heads of four-petalled flowers have a light air. A widespread northern European plant found plentifully in Britain in damp sites.

Uses: Perhaps grown in the wild garden, in the open or in semi-shade.

Colour: Variable but usually pale lilac pink; white forms are plentiful.

Size: 30-45cm (12-18in) high, spread 30cm (12in).

Flowering time: Mid-spring into summer.

Relatives: The very desirable double form C. pratensis 'Flore Pleno' (pictured) has crowded heads of pale pink. Two other doubled forms are 'Edith' and 'William'. C. trifolia is an energetic but pleasing lightweight ground-covering plant with round three-part serrated leaves. In late spring it has slightly more closely packed heads of white flowers on leafless stems. Formerly listed as Cardamine species, C. pentaphyllos and C. enneaphyllos are now in Dentaria.

Cultivation: Plant established seedlings or good divisions into moist spots and allow full rein.

Propagation: Normal forms can be readily increased by sowing fresh seed. Alternatively, plants can be divided in early autumn. Double forms, being sterile, will have to be increased by division or by the taking of leaf tip cuttings in the summer.

Clay-based natural ponds In soils of sticky clay, where a spade's-depth below the surface sits layers of heavy clay, it is possible to return to the age-old way of making pools, the type that used to dot the countryside so freely. A natural depression is chosen and the top soil excavated to reveal purer layers of clay. This is puddled, that is it is worked by walking over it repeatedly until the whole surface has developed a consistent plasticity for a depth of several centimetres/inches, aiming for a thickness of about 15cm (6in). This is left as evenly graded as possible; the contours of the pool should be such that the sides slope gently inwards and the depth at the centre is around 45cm (18in). Then water is introduced.

The clay will hold the water and the whole pool lasts almost indefinitely, provided it is not allowed to dry out. Some drainage channels led from higher ground to the upper surfaces of the pool will help maintain water equilibrium.

Preforms There is now a wide choice of prefabricated pools in plastic or glass fibre, available in either formal or informal shapes. These do take some of the work out of making a pool. Remember, the smaller the pool the more difficult it is to keep the water temperatures and whole eco-system balanced. Pick a shape that has two water levels; you will want a shelf not less than about 20cm (8in) deep and wide but better 25cm (10in) deep and 30cm (12in) wide. This should encircle a generous proportion of the side.

Excavate the soil to the depth and dimension of the preform, or rather make the hole just a touch larger. Place the preform in the hole and, using a spirit level, make sure it is exactly level and that the base sits comfortably square. The base and sides of the hole can be smoothed with the addition of an even layer of material such as moist sand or wet newspapers. Make sure there are no stony projections that might cause a stress point.

When fitting the preform permanently, concentrate first on the base. When that is snug, with the top just fractionally lower than the surrounding soil of the garden, the gaps around the side can be packed with sand, washed granite dust or similar material until there are no air pockets. The pool may be filled with water and the edges disguised with grass turf, rocks, stones or gravel.

DESIGN TIP

Almost invariably a pond will turn out to be too small when you have completed it and it has had a year or so to settle in – everything has grown strongly and the water is almost lost. To start extending the pond is a hugely more difficult and less enjoyable exercise than making the original one larger to start with. 'Think of a size and double it' is a useful precept.

This inventive water garden includes attractive marginal plantings of primulas, acers and many more water-loving species

DARMERA PELTATA (SYN. PELTIPHYLLUM PELTATUM)
Umbrella plant

Description: Only species of the genus, a hardy perennial with a strong rhizomatous base. A dramatic waterside plant with horizontal, stalked leaves like umbrellas. They are rounded with spoked lobes, 15cm (6in) across. Tight heads of individual saxifrage-like flowers but packed in tight corymbs are held boldly on stout hairy stems before the leaves appear.

Uses: Makes a most effective bold foliage plant planted in very wet soil, preferably by water. Will not object to having base inundated every so often.

Colour: White or pale pink, the pure white ones given a pink cast by the anthers.

Size: 1-1.2m (3-4ft) high, spread 45-90cm (18-36in).

Flowering time: Spring.

Relatives: The most distinctive variant is *D. peltata* 'Nana', a much smaller edition.

Cultivation: Plant early autumn or early spring in a moist spot that does not dry out. Only needs to be kept free of weeds.

Propagation: Division of rhizomatous rootstock in late winter or early spring.

Liners Proper pool liners made of butyl are expensive but much longer lasting than the best PVC ones. Ordinary polythene sheeting is likely to degrade in a very few seasons and just cause disappointment and no end of work to rectify matters.

Mark out the shape of your projected pond using something that can be clearly seen, such as a hosepipe. Leave this for a few days so that you get used to the idea and can adjust the shape until you are happy with it.

Excavate a hole with a shelf as suggested on page 72 and make sure that the sides are sloping, some 20 degrees from vertical, so that there is no imminent danger of soil collapsing inwards. The deeper central part of the pool could be around 60cm (2ft) deep, a depth that will accommodate water lilies.

Measure the pool carefully before buying your expensive butyl. Remember it is not possible to make a join if you make a mistake (see page 77 for

EUPHORBIA PALUSTRIS
Marsh spurge

Description: Strong hardy perennial, a native of Germany, France and Scandinavia, forming a bush of spear-shaped, pale green leaves. It has long-lived flower heads; individual flowers are saucer- or cup-shaped.
Uses: Very much at home in wet conditions.
Colour: Lime-yellow and green.
Size: 1m (3ft) high and across.
Flowering time: Spring for several weeks.
Relatives: E. characias and E. c. subsp. wulfenii are splendid shrub-like plants with blue-green foliage and large rounded lime-coloured heads. They are for drier spots.
Cultivation: Purchase a young potted plant and establish in a permanent place. Euphorbias dislike root disturbance. Looks after itself.
Propagation: By seed which can be gathered and sown or look out for self sown seedlings and move these when they are only a few centimetres high.

a diagram of how to measure for butyl). Measure maximum length of contour, ie, down the side, along the bottom and up the other side. Repeat for the narrower pool width. With an informal shape you must allow for the greatest length and greatest width. Also allow an excess for lapping over the tops, at least some 10cm (4in) all the way round, so in all you will be adding 20cm (8in) to the measured length and width of butyl needed for pool contours.

Prepare sides and bottom of pool carefully before introducing liner. Remove any sharp projections and cover all with smooth material as suggested with preforms (above). Lay liner over the shape and gently work it into position. Weight down the edges with bricks or baulks of timber, but not so heavily as to prevent the material taking up the shape of the pool. Allow water to flow in steadily. When full, cut away surplus material but retain the 10cm (4in) flap which is then disguised as in a preform.

IRIS PSEUDACORUS
Yellow iris, Yellow flag

Description: This is a very familiar hardy wild plant in Britain and Europe in wet ground. The plants form tough dense stands of upright spear-shaped, bright green leaves and produce flowers in abundance.

Uses: For waterside or wet spots where there is plenty of space. Good in wild areas.

Colour: Rich gold.

Size: To 2m (6ft) high, spread indefinite.

Flowering time: Early to midsummer.

Wildlife: Much used by water fowl and other aquatic life.

Relatives: *I. pseudacorus* 'Variegata' (pictured) is a spectacular foliage plant in the spring as its new foliage appears, a shining picture of primrose-yellow and pale green; later the leaves become standard green. *I. laevigata, I. ensata* and *I. chrysographes* are water-loving species with narrow, upright leaves. The first grows to about 60cm-1m (2-3ft) with blue or purple summer flowers. *I. ensata* grows to the same height but has larger showy flowers from white through all shades of blue and purple to some reddish maroon ones. *I. chrysographes*, only two-thirds the height, is slimmer of leaf and flowers, but attractive in deep blue or red-purple flowers with some golden markings. *I. unguicularis* is at the opposite end of the dietary spectrum, needing warm, dry conditions that may be found at the foot of a sunny wall where it will bloom in winter months.

Cultivation: Only grow where you have plenty of space as a piece could soon fill a small pond. No problems where there is plenty of water.

Propagation: Division late winter or early spring.

BOG GARDENS

A poorly drained area of clay soil is ideal for a bog garden but so is any patch of soil that is close to the water table. If you have to artificially create bog conditions, this is best done with a perforated liner.

Excavate to about 35-40cm (14-16in) and lay the liner and hold it in position around the edge with bricks or timber. There is really no need to cover the area with anything, such as sand, as one would do if trying to protect the lining of a pool. As the liner is going to be punctured anyway a rough edge that may cause a hole is not a matter of regret. Puncture about one hole each square metre/yard. The amount of water retained will vary with rainfall; to allow some regulation of the moisture content you can provide for drainage or for topping up of the water by having a few 1-2cm (½in) holes around the edge of the liner but only some 5-8cm (2-3in) below the soil surface. If the bog garden is situated close to a pool then some of these small holes should lead to and from the top water level of the pool. Lengths of piping laid horizontally should achieve an overflow from the pond to the bog garden in times of excess pond water. Alternatively, when creating the bog garden, lead a length of plastic pipe into the bottom of the bog, punch the pipe beforehand with holes at intervals of 30-60cm (1-2ft). Leave the end of the pipe above ground, disguised by plants or stones. This allows it to be connected to a water supply to provide moisture in times of drought.

Bringing water features close to the house means

CONSTRUCTING A BOG GARDEN

For aesthetic and practical reasons bog gardens are best sited near a pond.

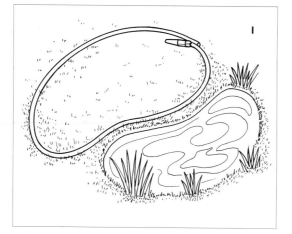

1 *Mark out the area with a hose pipe and leave this in place for a few days to ensure you are happy with the shape and position.*

2 *Dig the area to a depth of 35-40cm (14-16in). Line with heavy-duty plastic (measured as shown on page 77).*

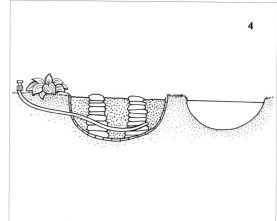

3 *Perforate the liner every metre or so to allow some of the water to drain away. Link to the pond with a length of hose if required.*

4 *Fill with garden soil mixed with plenty of humus then plant up.*

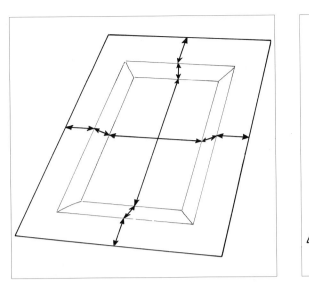

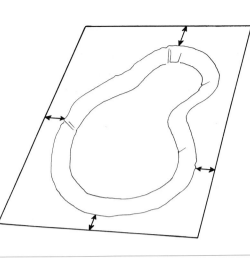

MEASURING UP FOR BUTYL LINER

Whatever the shape of your pond it is important to measure it correctly as butyl cannot be joined effectively and is not cheap to buy.

• *Measure the maximum length, including the sides.*

• *Measure the maximum width, including the sides.*

•*Allow for overlap at the top of at least 10cm (4in) on all sides. This can be disguised once the pond is complete.*

all sorts of interesting and beautiful effects can be created with contrasting forms and growth. Gravel and boulders enliven a water's edge. Walled raised beds provide enticing changes of level. Wooden decking suggests maritime associations and railway sleepers add solidity and darker backgrounds for some of the plants. Focal points such as pieces of sculpture or garden furniture are excellent in appropriate spots. Bird baths or bird tables are also suitable.

Fountains, even those of modest size, look good, sound good and produce a humid atmosphere that some plants will really adore. There can be few gardens that could not accommodate one of the tiny water-gushing features that spill water over stones or gravel. A small pump manages such features without too much outlay or upkeep.

Improving conditions

It is perfectly possible to exploit a wet site without recourse to either ponds or bog gardens, but in this case it is necessary to provide some way of getting around the garden without constantly having to tread on damp or muddy ground.

A good solution is to build up some hard landscape areas such as patios and paths, raising them above the level of the surrounding ground and constructing them on a solid hardcore base. In such situations, it is wise to be generous with the dimensions of the paths and the patio, and to be inventive with shapes; oblong or broad L-shaped patios look

LIGULARIA PRZEWALSKII

Description: One of a genus full of moisture-loving plants, this is grown for its distinctive foliage and tall narrow spires of yellow flowers. It is a clump-forming herbaceous perennial with rich green, rounded basal leaves. On the dark, almost black stems are leaves boldly and deeply cut into pointed fingers. Each stem carries a hundred daisy flowers, individually rather ragged but altogether making a distinctive and pleasing very long slender spike.

Uses: Waterside or wet areas, can also be grown in more normal soils that do not dry out.

Colour: Leaves dark green, stems maroon black, flowers rich gold.

Size: 1.2-2m (4-6ft) high depending on amount of water and soil richness, spread to about 1m (3 ft).

Flowering time: Mid- into late summer.

Relatives: *L. dentata* 'Desdemona' is a strong sturdy perennial with tough heart-shaped basal leaves, dark brownish-green above and mahogany-maroon below. Stout stems carry close bunches of large vivid golden-orange flowers.

Cultivation: Easy plants for a moist place. Best planted late winter or early spring.

Propagation: By division late summer.

more pleasing than square ones and although paths need to be functional, they are also an important part of the garden design. Normally, the closer they are to the house, the broader and more strongly defined they should be.

Mark out the area to be devoted to the path and the patio and then leave the marking in place for some days to get used to the idea and to allow any alterations to take shape in your plans. Remember that the eye follows the direction of a path and it is more pleasing to be led into the garden in an interesting exploratory way rather than on a path like a public highway. On the other hand, don't make your path full of pointless and repeated curves – anyone walking along it will be tempted to cut corners.

The making of a pathway through wet ground will entail the removal of some of the topsoil to be replaced by sharp draining hardcore. The excavated soil can be used to raise the levels of adjacent beds, which may mean that the top soil, at least, has better drainage than that underneath.

Making the most of it

There are different ranges of plants adapted to different degrees of wetness. It is usual to think of three classes: those that grow in water – the emergents; those which grow at water margins with roots in water-saturated soils – the marginals; and, finally, those closer to orthodox garden plants but which enjoy a more abundant amount of soil water, such as bog plants.

LYSICHITON AMERICANUS
Yellow skunk cabbage

Description: A large strong and thirsty plant, this species is at its most striking when, without leaves, it produces huge brilliant spathes. As the flowers fade, the leaves grow and grow, to become large rather oblong and spinach-like, perhaps 30-60cm (12-24in) long. Fully hardy.
Uses: Dramatic by stream or water, will not object to having its base inundated. Fine in bog garden.
Colour: Vivid golden-yellow spathes around greenish upright spadices.
Scent: Not a particularly alluring aroma.
Size: To 1m (3ft) high, spread 75cm (30in).
Flowering time: Early spring.
Relative: *L. camtschatcensis* is a similar water-loving plant on the same scale but with white spathes.
Cultivation: Plant at the end of winter. Easy, provided there is plenty of water at all times. Best in full sun, but can certainly be grown in light shade.
Propagation: By seed sown immediately it is harvested in summer.

In the comparatively dry Mediterranean climate, large areas of water provide welcome coolness and moisture

PLANTS IN WATER

Of the plants that grow in water, there are those that live wholly submerged, either in still or moving water and those that while their bases and growing parts are below water will produce growth above water as leaves or flowers and so make a display. In ponds and pools underwater plants are important because they may be oxygenators, producing the vital element that helps keep all other plant and animal life healthy. Any area of water must have its quota of such plants.

Water lilies are interesting and popular water plants. Their roots are well below the water's surface in deep water and all growth is initiated at this depth. Their leaves and flowers are designed to be wholly underwater until their stalks have grown long enough to reach the water surface and air. Here, the rolled up leaves are unfurled and laid flat on and supported by the water surface. Many lilies float their flowers on the surface, heavy blooms buoyed

LYTHRUM SALICARIA
Purple loosestrife

L. *salicaria* 'Firecandle'

Description: This is a hardy native of much of Europe, including Britain, and is found in the sides of wet ditches and other such sites. It is a strong herbaceous perennial that produces a series of very erect flowering stems with some small, narrowly spear-shaped leaves. Pointed-petalled flowers are in rings closely held to the stems and are so crowded as to be continuous up their length. They open up the spikes.

Uses: Reliable wetland plant. Very useful for fresh late summer colour.

Colour: Purple-red, a rich deep shade.

Size: 75cm (30in) high, spread 45cm (18in). A new plant is narrowly erect, the spread comes as it produces more growing points.

Flowering time: Midsummer until autumn.

Relatives: *L. salicaria* 'Firecandle' (pictured) is free-flowering and deep rosy red, 'Robert' is pinker. *L. virgatum* 'The Rocket' can grow 1m (3ft) tall with bold narrow columns of rosy red blossom; 'Rose Queen' is pale pink.

Cultivation: It can be grown in borders of normal soil provided it is not parched dry, but it will never be so good as in bog or waterside sites.

Propagation: Named forms have to be increased by division; best done in very early spring. Seed can be sown when ripe in autumn or in spring.

up by the water. Others raise them above water. Usually very much smaller in size, they are nonetheless dramatic held proudly aloft by their stalks.

Most emergents – plants which grow up through the water surface – hold themselves clear of the water. Zantedeschias, often called arum lilies, are fabulous examples. They use water for nourishment and protection; water keeps their tender roots free from frost and prevents predators feasting on the massive food supplies in their bulbs. But above water they take on the same forms as any land plant and, indeed, they can be grown in moist soils out of water. Grown in even very small containers, such as half barrels, they will flourish.

MARGINAL PLANTS

The second range of plants are the marginals. These are waterside plants which are happy in quite badly waterlogged soils though they do not normally grow from below water level. These are recognisable as ordinary garden plants that have mastered the trick of coping with permanent water around their roots,

Stones and sparse plants recreate the effect of a dried river bed in this Australian garden

usually extracting oxygen from the water in a similar way to underwater animal life. They have the same need for healthily aerated water: stagnant ponds give plants the same problems as they do animals.

Bog plants

The bog plants grow well in soils not particularly associated with open water but so well endowed with moisture that normal herbaceous plants would find life difficult or impossible. Some of the most spectacular of garden plants are those that thrive in wet conditions. In these sites it is perfectly possible to establish a series of plant associations that can look very dramatic in foliage for most of the year and in bloom for highlighted periods.

Strong foliage effects will be ensured by planting such items as the huge *Gunnera manicata* (page 232), royal fern (page 65), ligularias, hostas, and a selection of the less dominant rushes. Where plant sizes have to be scaled down, the gunneras can be replaced by the *Rheum palmatum atropurpureum* (page 235) and the royal fern by the broad buckler fern, *Dryopteris dilitata* (page 102), which is still very effective and bold but less than half the size.

As with most areas of garden design, a more effective wetland garden is achieved by limiting the number of types of plant and using those that are chosen more boldly. For example, a large clump of the variegated *Iris pseudacorus* 'Variegata' (page 76), with its mass of sword-like leaves piercing upwards, is very effectively contrasted with the spreading broad foliage of a wide clump of hostas like the steely-blue *H. sieboldiana* or the golden-flushed 'Zounds' – a marvellous duet.

Given enough space a generous drift of the daisy-flowered *Buphthalmum speciosum* looks tremendously opulent in leaf and flower; the same can be said for the range of ligularias. These wonderful moisture-loving foliage plants have surprising floral effects with their graceful spires of flowers over dramatic rich green foliage. They are best planted with different forms some distance apart and with contrasting foliage plants, such as astilbes to take up the ground between them.

There are plants that grow well in drier parts of the garden and will then extend themselves in moister spots. Bowles' golden sedge, *Carex elata*

NARCISSUS CYCLAMINEUS

Description: Small hardy bulb that needs moisture to live. Each bulb usually produce two or three bright green arching polished leaves and one of its distinct flowers: petals are abruptly reflexed to make a gathered point upwards; the trumpet is narrow and points demurely down towards its toes. A group is delightful, a colony breathtaking. Fully hardy.

Uses: Marvellous naturalized in not too dominant grass, between shrubs, in a rock garden corner or looking in its element in an 'alpine lawn'.

Colour: Golden yellow.

Size: 15cm (6in) high.

Flowering time: Late winter into early spring, lasts some weeks.

Relatives: The species has been one of the most potent influences in daffodil breeding and many excellent hybrids owe much to its influence. These are larger but still small enough for the compact modern garden and with smaller leaves causing less bother as they die. 'February Gold' 30cm (12in), 'Jenny' 25-30cm (10-12in) white and primrose becoming all white, 'Tête à Tête' and 'Jumblie' 15-30cm (6-12in) gold. *N. bulbocodium*, the hoop-petticoat narcissus 10-20cm (4-8in) in tones of yellow is one of the miracles of spring.

Cultivation: Bulbs should not be kept out of the ground any longer than need be. At its best in slightly acid soil that is full of humus and remains moist although of open structure. It will grow in the open or in semi-shade.

Propagation: Seed germinates readily if sown fresh, the seedlings appearing in new year. Bulbs can be lifted and divided up into separate new clumps after they have died down.

TROLLIUS EUROPAEUS
Globe flower

Description: A moisture-loving hardy herbaceous perennial happy in sun or shade. Bright green leaves are basically rounded but very divided with lobes like narrow pointed fingers. Stems carry upright flowers of petals curled over to form rounded globes. Native of all countries of northern Europe, including Britain.

Uses: A very pretty strong but graceful plant for a wet site.

Colour: Primrose-yellow.

Size: To 60cm (2ft) high, spread 45cm (18in).

Flowering time: Late spring.

Relatives: *T. europaeus* 'Canary Bird' is strong with much deeper yellow flowers.

Cultivation: No problems in wet ground; just keep clear of dominant weeds.

Propagation: By seed in summer or division early autumn.

'Aurea' (not to be confused with Bowles' golden grass, *Milium effusum* 'Aureum'), is a fine arching sedge with lime-gold leaves reaching some 40cm (16in) long. *Miscanthus sinensis* 'Zebrinus' is an upright grass, its leaves taking on a golden variegation that is more noticeable from midsummer until the frosts. It is less invasive than gardener's garters, *Phalaris arundinacea*, which, nevertheless, looks vibrant in silver, white and grey through the growing months, and can be cut down to the ground, when looking slightly tired, only to produce a second fresh crop of foliage, which can then be left as a buff-fawn mass for interest through the winter.

Through the summer months round floating lily pads make a huge contrast to neighbouring marginal plants such as irises, fern, or wide clumps of astilbes, which almost mimic ferns with their foliage but have the extra attraction of long seasons of plumey flowers in colours ranging from deep crimson through every possible shade of pink to white. The richer coloured cultivars are usually accompanied by foliage that is suffused with maroon or reddish colouring.

All these water-loving plants are usually exceedingly tough once established and the only maintenance required is to curb the territorial advances of the more extrovert among them.

Natural communities

A look at surrounding countryside will often suggest possible plant associations. Although *Iris pseudacorus* may be too large and invasive for the margins of a small pond it is attractive in bigger landscapes. The bog garden would certainly benefit early in the year from clumps of the golden king cup, *Caltha palustris* (page 97), or its very neat double form 'Flore Pleno'. Later in the season, attractive divided foliage is provided by the globe flower, *Trollius europaeus*, and colour introduced by its lemon-yellow rounded blooms.

A drift of the dainty cuckoo flower or lady's smock, *Cardamine pratensis*, a beautiful native, is a magical addition to any damp area. Beside these, ideal companions are the more exotic colours of some of the water loving primulas that, once established, will sow themselves and increase their numbers: consider the candelabra forms such as *Primula japonica* and *P. pulverulenta*.

Larger items in natural wetland communities will include alders and a variety of willows as well as rushes, bulrushes, bur-reeds and some bulbous plants such as the ransoms (*Allium ursinum*) which can run riot if introduced into the garden but can look good in wild areas.

WET AND SHADY

Pᴌᴇɴᴛʏ ᴏꜰ ᴡᴀᴛᴇʀ but too little light, a wet, shady site is not particularly stressful for plants, but nor is it a particularly rewarding one. As soon as they have coped with the problem of aerating their roots – the primary limiting factor – they have to concentrate on their need for light. Wind is often not a major problem in shade, nor is drying out from lack of water or parching in fierce sun. So here plants with diaphanous leaves are able to survive. These are plants whose foliage is designed to maximize the transmission of light deep into their translucent depths; the leaves can be flimsy and transparent as they do not need a strong structure to cope with wind stress. They are unlikely to need the protection of hair or coatings as they are not threat-ened by scorching strong sunlight. On the other hand there are some shrubs that can grow in shade or in the open that have leaves as tough as, but more attractive than, old boots. *Aucuba japonica* and laurel are a couple but so, too, are the many rhododen-drons that will be best in at least partial shade.

In such sheltered areas, frosts are tempered by the same screening that produces the shade; rainfall is slowed by the same sheltering cover. Air humidi-ty is higher, creating a further cushioning effect. There are plants such as erythroniums, trilliums and other shade lovers that will thrive here but would find it hard to keep a foothold in open, sunny spots. Some ferns that would find survival impossible in the open also manage well here.

Sheltered and partially shaded by a house and a hill, this courtyard provides a haven for hostas and a host of other plants

Do you have a wet shady site?

The ground in a wet, shady site is likely to be constantly moist. And it will be sheltered so wind may have more difficulty in getting in to dry the surface. Weed growth, of things such as nettles, docks and ground elder, is likely to flourish.

Coping with a wet and shady site

To make the area more plant-friendly, air needs to be added to the structure of the soil. And adding compost is one of the best ways of doing this. Farmyard manure must be well-rotted and ideally should have as much coarse material, such as straw, in it as possible. Coarse material traps more air in it as it is incorporated into the soil. Garden compost is also useful but lawn mowings need to be used with caution as they tend to form a solid mushy layer which sours the soil with acidity. Leaf mould is good as it is light but bulky, and so is grit which tends to keep tiny air pockets open.

As with all similar sites, the addition of compost on a regular basis is vital to continue combating the airless soil and prevent it from reverting to solid and sour. Depending on how much compost is available, add it once, twice or three times a year. A fairly straightforward course of action is to concentrate on the top few surface centimetres/inches and aim to build a freer draining topsoil which has good healthy bacterial and animal life that will break down leaf and vegetable waste. This will in turn ensure that the layer below will be improved by the increasing population of worms.

CONSIDERING DRAINAGE

Although drainage is a possibility it does have its drawbacks. It is expensive, especially over large areas and may result in the area becoming too dry. However, there is also the chance of creating ponds, bog gardens and ditches or streams, all of which provide a range of habitats for many woodland and moisture-loving plants. Before you decide on drainage consider the plants that are already growing in the area. Established trees such as alders and willows may not relish a site where the water table has been drastically lowered, and they have the

ASTILBE × ARENDSII HYBRIDS

Description: A series of hardy, summer-flowering, herbaceous perennials with attractive divided foliage and plume-like blossom. After the flowers have faded, the rusted plumes remain to add something to the scene especially in the first half of the winter.

Uses: Very good waterside or moist area plant. Can be grown away from open water in more normal soils provided they do not dry out.

Colour: White, creams, pinks or reds.

Size: From 45cm-1m (18-38in) high and across.

Flowering time: Through summer.

Varieties: 'Snowdrift' white, 'Irrlicht' 45-60cm (18-24in) high, white contrasting with very dark leaves, 'Venus' 1m (3ft) high and wide, pale pink multi-pointed plumes, 'Bressingham Beauty' 1m (3ft) high, rich pink, 'Feuer' ('Fire') 60-90cm (2-3ft) high, rather narrower plumes of dark red,

Relatives: *A. simplicifolia* pretty pink, about 38cm (15in) high. The dwarf 'Bronce Elegans' is only about 20cm (8in) high with coloured foliage and long lasting miniature pink flowers. 'Sprite' is a ferny compact plant up to 50cm (20in) but able to spread three times as wide quite quickly. Its flowers are airy feathered plumes of tiny pale pink contrasting with abundant broad leaves divided into narrow serrated leaflets. *A. tacquetii* (syn. *A.* 'Superba', pictured) has long bushy plumes of pink flowers that can easily reach 1.2m (4ft).

Cultivation: Once planted can be left for decades as it is completely trouble-free. Plant in early spring or early autumn. Clumps will appreciate a top dressing of well rotted compost in late winter.

Propagation: Seed from hybrids will give varying results. Division is straightforward in early spring or early autumn.

In Britain, *Narcissus cyclamineus* is successfully grown in Windsor Great Park, where enlightened regimes have built up good populations of this and of *N. bulbocodium* and *N. pseudonarcissus*. The thin sandy soil, on the acid side of neutral, probably has more problems with water shortage, although the daffodils normally receive plenty through the winter and early spring; springs and more permanent areas of moisture also help.

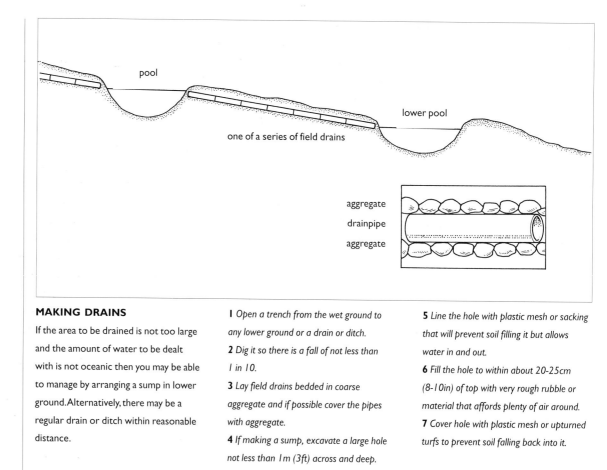

pool

lower pool

one of a series of field drains

aggregate

drainpipe

aggregate

MAKING DRAINS

If the area to be drained is not too large and the amount of water to be dealt with is not oceanic then you may be able to manage by arranging a sump in lower ground. Alternatively, there may be a regular drain or ditch within reasonable distance.

1 *Open a trench from the wet ground to any lower ground or a drain or ditch.*

2 *Dig it so there is a fall of not less than 1 in 10.*

3 *Lay field drains bedded in coarse aggregate and if possible cover the pipes with aggregate.*

4 *If making a sump, excavate a large hole not less than 1m (3ft) across and deep.*

5 *Line the hole with plastic mesh or sacking that will prevent soil filling it but allows water in and out.*

6 *Fill the hole to within about 20-25cm (8-10in) of top with very rough rubble or material that affords plenty of air around.*

7 *Cover hole with plastic mesh or upturned turfs to prevent soil falling back into it.*

somewhat annoying, and potentially disruptive habit of filling drainage pipes with their roots.

Ponds beneath trees are always plagued by fallen leaves which rot in the depths, poisoning the water, mopping up the oxygen and slowly silting up the bottom. It is impossible to cover a large pool with netting that is then to be taken away after leaf fall and the difficulty increases exponentially as the size of the pool increases. At the other end of the scale, it must be recognised that a small pool will not do a lot to drain and dry surrounding land. If you are happy with a pond that only contains a limited range of plants, however, it can be set up and then left to get on with its own affairs with only an occasional clear out of dead leaves and debris. Royal fern would look impressive in such an arrangement, with perhaps other, somewhat smaller, but still attractive ferns such as *Dryopteris dilatata* (page 102).

Using a pond as a means of draining land may help with ditches and drainage pipes leading to the water, provided the water level is lower than the ground and there is an escape to lower ground of excess water. You will need this outflow to some suitable lower level, not something that is going to be easy in a low lying site. It may well be that the surplus water of one pond may be led to one on lower ground and this is usually the most satisfactory solution. Making one or two ponds also provides surplus soil to raise the level of the surrounding ground and thereby making its surface better drained. You could incorporate an area of bog garden by a pond or between two.

Making the most of it

Even in an unpromising area there is something for ground level, above our heads and in the middle storey. Foliage in a shady site can be both luxurious and delicate, and flowers may look hauntingly luminescent, glowing gently in the shadows and stray shafts of sunshine. White foxgloves can be stunning. Aconites will look blue and mysterious. The shrubs that survive here include coloured-stemmed dogwoods such as the *Cornus alba* forms. Bog myrtle

(*Myrica gale*) is an obvious candidate but more surprisingly *Rhododendron occidentale* forms can be at home here. The red chokeberry, *Aronia arbutifolia*, with white spring flowers and red berries looks good and has the benefit of red autumnal foliage. *Vaccinium corymbosum* also has brilliant crimson autumn colour. The native guelder rose, *Viburnum opulus*, is a plant of wet and shade. It will do well in all its forms and so will the strong-growing *Spirea × vanhouttei*. There is a wealth of willows in all sizes, and perhaps a special word might be spared for the violet willow, *Salix daphnoides*, with glistening silver catkins turning to yellow and stems of violet but often with a distinctive white 'bloom'.

BULBS

Although many bulbs face rotting problems in damp soil, some still manage to produce a fine display, particularly those that take the deciduous woodland approach of flowering early before the leaf canopy closes overhead. In fact, a surprising number can manage very well in these conditions provided they are not in a continually sodden state.

Narcissus like drainage but they also like moisture. The little early-flowering species *N. cyclamineus* is found wild in very moist spots, sometimes by the sides of small streams which will periodically inundate the bulbs station. Most hybrid daffodils with *N. cyclamineus* in their breeding will also do well in wet spots.

Slightly later in the year, bluebell woods are one of Britain's national treasures, a natural phenomenon not so common on the Continent where this species, *Hyacinthoides non-scripta*, is also found. It is certainly not difficult to establish colonies in the garden. A few bulbs introduced will rapidly increase vegetatively with very little help; seed that drops will grow quickly into flowering plants, provided the ground is not harried by hoes. Alternatively, you can start your colonies by seed alone (see practical tip). This will take three or so years to show the first bloom but thereafter you could begin to worry about having too much of a good thing. Do not introduce this species, or the bolder *H. hispanica*, in those more civilized parts of the garden where you cannot cope with their invasive powers.

Snowdrops are happy with some shade and are excellent in places, such as deciduous woodland, that only become very dark for these low-growing

DICENTRA SPECTABILIS
Bleeding-heart, Lady-in-the-bath, Dutchman's breeches

Description: The largest member of a genus of about a dozen species. It is a hardy herbaceous perennial that dies completely down to be invisible through the winter. Stems, leaves and flowers give an impression of succulence; the foliage is grey-green with a glaucous sheen, and is almost fern-like as it is much cut and is held on long stems. A clump in full bloom can look very special when the arching stems are carrying generous but well spaced hanging flowers each about 2.5cm (1in) long. Growth that is too early can be damaged by frost but fresh shoots will appear from the base.

Uses: It is one of the more aristocratic border plants of spring. It will not object to gentle forcing if some of the rather

brittle fleshy-rooted plants are lifted in the late autumn and carefully potted up. Can look good between shrubs that do not overhang it.

Colour: Rich pink recurved petals and a white centre.

Size: 60-75cm (24-30in) high, spread 60cm (24in).

Flowering time: Late spring until early summer.

Relatives: *D. spectabilis* 'Alba' is a choice and pleasing contrast: pure white in bloom and paler in leaf colour. *D. eximia* is more fern-like with a mass of attractive foliage making dense ground cover up to 20cm (8in) high. Relatively short flower stems each carry a few dark near-maroon hanging flowers. *D. formosa* also has a spreading habit, but is larger with coarser leaves. Its flowers are pink or a matt-red on leafless stems.

Cultivation: Plant potted plants in early spring. (Lifted roots are cheaper and may be a good buy if they are not dried out.) Choose an open or semi-shaded spot of good soil which is moist and unlikely to dry out.

Propagation: The roots are fragile, fleshy and rather ugly. A strong plant carefully lifted in early autumn or very early spring can be divided into several bits, each with a growing point.

plants after they have completed their growing cycle. More or less the same applies to the graceful and delightful erythroniums, woodland plants from North America, with species also from Europe and Asia. *E. dens-canis* is a European, claimed as a rare native of Britain, and is a character with many different coloured party dresses. 'Pagoda' is a strong hybrid with many hanging blooms of a soft yellow shade that glows in dimly lit areas. *Leucojum aestivum*, the snowflake, can be one of the successes of a wet soil and can cope with all but very dense shade. The bulbs take a season or two to get into full swing and then are best left undisturbed, or they can be lifted and split as the leaves die back, provided they are

GROWING *NARCISSUS BULBOCODIUM* OR *N. CYCLAMINEUS* FROM SEED

Although narcissus are usually increased by bulb division, in the wild, seed is the most important factor in their spread. It is possible to follow the lead of nature, but rather than rely on chance by scattering seed in situ, it is more productive to start colonies by sowing the seed in pots and growing on the seedlings for a couple of seasons before introducing them into their permanent quarters. Pots can be sunk into the ground or placed on capillary matting under cover where they are kept more or less permanently moist. As pods of *N. bulbocodium* may have as many as a hundred viable seeds and other species almost as many, there should

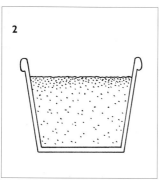

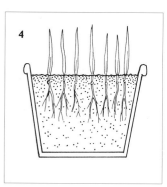

be no problem in getting large numbers quite quickly.

! *Harvest seed as soon as ripe. The narrow pods will begin to split at the tip.*
2 *Fill pots or deep trays with seed compost and moisten.*
3 *Sow seed immediately and cover.*
4 *Keep out of frost once the seedlings begin to show through.*

5 *Keep generously moist at all times.*
6 *You may choose to let the little seedlings die back in the summer by letting the soil get a little drier, but you will find that you will get better results by keeping all moist and trying to make them evergreens.*
7 *In their second year, start giving the pots/trays a regular feed with liquid fertilizer, preferably one high in potash.*

8 *Maintain the moisture régime.*
9 *In their second summer, seedlings can be planted out or pricked out into other containers and grown on.*
10 *First flowers might appear in eighteen months. In the third year they should all be blooming.*

Ferns, campion and bluebells all enjoy a relatively moist spot with shade from hot sun

replanted immediately – it is the time out of the soil that they tend to resent. It is probably best to get the large and showy clone *L. aestivum* 'Gravetye Giant'.

Bulbs to avoid in wet shady situations include tulips and those that originate in South Africa.

Among plants that use their roots for storage are the rhizomatous and the tuberous. The winter aconites, *Eranthis hyemalis*, will certainly manage in shaded areas and, in particular, in similar conditions to the snowdrops; they also get their growing done early in the year. The rhizomatous trilliums have both leaves and flowers divided into three clear sections giving them a very distinctive air. Try *T. grandiflorum*, the wake robin of the eastern part of North America; it has relatively large flowers of pure white that nod sideways above the plain shining green leaves. Plants stand 30cm (12in) high, their snowy white flowers lighting up a dark corner. There is also a more heavyweight mutant, *T. grandiflorum* 'Flore Pleno' with opulent neatly-packed double flowers.

FERNS

Shade and moisture is the brief recipe for success with very many hardy ferns. They are without rich appetites and have root systems that are intricate

but more or less restricted to the top few centimetres/inches of soil; they do not have deep tap roots which could be drowned in permanently damp soil. Where sites are overshadowed by buildings and structures such as fences and walls, ferns will flourish. They are equally effective either in beds more or less devoted to them or planted in between shrubs and other plants to give a welcome atmosphere of peace, unity and timelessness.

Some ferns are evergreen, others are deciduous, many do not make up their minds until they find out what kind of winter they are expected to face. A kind that is certainly evergreen is the hart's tongue, *Asplenium scolopendrium* (syn. *Phyllitis scolopendrium*). Familiarity with this plant will not dull our appreciation of it. It flourishes where little else will grow, and can get a toehold in the most unlikely places, provided it has some moisture. The shiny fronds are relatively narrow but can be up to 60cm (2ft) long. As they are highly lacquered, they reflect the light and look a splendid rich green throughout the year. The only maintenance needed is to occasionally

ERYTHRONIUM 'PAGODA'
Dog's tooth violet

E. 'White Beauty'

Description: A vigorous hardy hybrid with creamy white, pointed tubers each normally producing a couple of broad polished leaves with some purplish brown mottling. Leafless stems carry up to ten hanging flowers with pointed petals swinging wide and somewhat recurved, an altogether graceful pose.

Uses: Excellent for shade or semi-shade in leafy soils between shrubs or below trees. Can be grown in less exposed spots in a rock garden.

Colour: Pale sulphur-yellow.

Size: 20-35cm (8-14in) high, spread 15-20cm (6-8in).

Flowering time: Mid-spring.

Relatives: *E. tuolumnense* is the deeper yellow parent of 'Pagoda'. It has several shining flowers over plain shining green leaves. *E. revolutum* is a pink-flowered easy species with mottled foliage. *E. dens-canis* is the European species and, until recently, the one most commonly found in gardens. It is variable with flowers from white to pink, lilac, and near crimson, tinted red. The leaves are most decoratively marked in shades of brown and blue-green. There are various named clones of this species. 'White Beauty' (pictured) is an American hybrid with noticeably large flowers of pure white but for a central ring of brown.

Cultivation: Get tubers as early as possible and plant 7-10cm (3-4in) deep in a humus-rich loose leafy soil where they can be kept moist. As woodland plants they enjoy some shade.

Propagation: Stocks can be increased by lifting the plants as the leaves turn yellow some weeks after flowering. Happy tubers will normally have split to become two or three or even more. Replant these straightaway. It does them no good at all to be allowed to dry out above ground.

remove some old fronds at the rear of the display. Like many ferns, it can mutate (really the surprise is how uniform this species is) and *A. scolopendrium* 'Crispum' is one form in which the edges of the fronds are goffered, a neat waved effect that means they catch the light even more. Other forms have the fronds cut or abbreviated; these can be interesting too. It is tempting to try to make a collection, but the type and *A. s.* 'Crispum' take a lot of beating.

The lady fern, *Athyrium filix-femina*, is found worldwide. In its travels and over the aeons of time, it has produced many mutations. In the wild these may persist but do not threaten the stability of the species type. Gardeners and fern fanciers have been keen to gather up all the variations; this was done with some success by the Victorians who published the names of over 300 kinds! The type is an attractive deciduous fern with long triangular fronds, neatly cut and fresh green, their length being 50-150cm (20-60in). *A. filix-femina* 'Frizelliae' is the tatting fern, with slender mid-ribs – rachis – on to which appear to be threaded a series of small, rounded pieces of green tatting lacework. This is a variable mutation and best obtained from a fern specialist. *A. filix-femina* 'Congestum' is a tiny dwarf only around 15cm (6in) high but with perfect miniaturized fronds.

There are many, many thousands of good hardy ferns from which to choose, but do not ignore forms of the male fern, *Dryopteris affinis. D. affinis* 'Cristata The King' is a fine upright variety with frond edges and ends all very precisely crested. *Dryopteris dilatata*, the broad buckler fern, has been mentioned before as ideal for wet shaded spots. (see page 102). *D. erythrosora*, the autumn fern, is so called because new fronds unfurl in shining shades of copper, gold, orange and red. This colour is maintained for a considerable period, and by the time it fades to adult green there are likely to be new fronds unfurling to

GENTIANA ASCLEPIADEA
Willow gentian

Description: A hardy perennial that is one of the most distinctive species of a genus full of very idiosyncratic characters. It produces slender arching stems from which are displayed oval, pointed leaves in alternating pairs. The upper leaf axils bear narrow, stemless trumpets with open-pointed, flared tips: one, two or three to each axil.

Uses: Can be grown in a variety of sites, preferably damp and of good deep soil. It will do well at the side of a small stream, in the lower reaches of a rock garden or in a cool part of a mixed border.

Colour: Sky-blue with some purple inside and longitudinal green stripes. Colour can vary in depth.

Size: To 90cm (3ft) high but less in drier spots, spread to 60cm (2ft).

Flowering time: Late summer well into autumn.

Varieties: *G. asclepiadea* 'Knightshayes' is a leading form; *G. a.* var. *alba* covers the white-flowered kinds. These are usually about two-thirds the height of the coloured type and with even paler green leaves.

Cultivation: Best planted in early spring, in a moist cool spot where they can enjoy good soil, undisturbed, for a couple of years.

Propagation: Plants can be lifted after two or three seasons in the early spring or autumn, split and replanted.

HEPATICA NOBILIS

Description: Relatives of the anemones, and a particularly endearing set of plants, the hepaticas have not, so far, lent themselves to easy mass production. This hardy species is a steady, rather than rapid, grower forming a semi-evergreen low mound of rounded leaves, each clearly indented to make three lobes. Early in the year, before new foliage appears, a series of enchanting many-petalled, saucer-shaped flowers appear. These can be of a variety of colours and there are also semi-double and fully double versions. The foliage tends to be fleshy.

Uses: As one of the earliest flowers of the year it is always sure of a welcome. Good in moist rich soil in semi-shade. Excellent in light woodland conditions or between shrubs and at the front of a mixed border where it is not going to be scorched by the sun. Or choose a cool corner of a rock garden.

Colour: From pure white to lilac, pale and dark blue, purples and pinks with some reaching near carmine-red.

Size: 8-10cm (3-4in) high, spread 10-12cm (4-5in).

Flowering time: Late winter to early spring.

Relatives: *H. nobilis* 'Rubra Plena' is a double pink. *H. transsilvanica* is similar but while not much larger as a plant, its leaves and flowers are a touch bolder and bigger. It too has many colour forms.

Cultivation: Plant in moist soil rich in humus and leave undisturbed. Choose a place in semi-shade.

Propagation: By sowing seed immediately it is ripe, or by taking small rooted side shoots in early spring, or by lifting immediately after flowering, and before leaves have developed, and carefully dividing the plant with as little loss of root as possible. Replant divisions straight away and make sure they are kept moist.

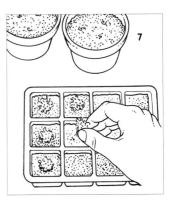

GROWING FERNS

Growing ferns from spores is not an alchemical mystery. These ancient, distinct plants can be grown just as easily from spores as other plants are grown from seed.

There are some specific essentials. The soil or other growing medium must never dry out. There must be protection from the competition of weed seeds and of the ever-present spores of mosses and other forms of life. Fern spores need time to start growing and go through the slightly complicated stages of growth before they are mature plants. Fungus and micro-organisms must be kept away. Pots or containers should be covered at all times.

1 *Fill a clean plastic pot with damp compost. (You can use garden soil.)*

2 *Select a cover for the pot, one which completely covers the top of the pot. It is possible to buy mini plastic 'cloches' in individual pot sizes, but a jam jar that fits is suitable. Alternatively, use a pot allowing ample space, 2-3cm (¾-1¼in), between the top of the compost and the pot rim, and the whole can be sealed*

with polythene or cling film. String or an elastic band will ensure the cover remains firmly attached.

3 *Either pour boiling water over the compost surface and sow spores shortly after and cover, or microwave the whole container before sowing. Microwave long enough to thoroughly sterilize the compost throughout its volume. The compost should be moist at this stage.*

4 *After a short while for cooling, remove the cover for just long enough to spread dust-like spore over surface and reseal.*

5 *Stand on capillary matting. Keep out of full sun.*

6 *Leave alone. Examine regularly. A green film over the surface signals the end of the first stage, one of the two sexual stages in the fern's life-cycle. Growths appear from the film, male and female. Sperms from the male parts swim through the film of water to fertilize the female part. Obviously, the compost must not dry out.*

7 *Small ferns will begin to grow where fertilization has been successful. Usually a complete covering of small plants can be achieved and these allowed to grow until they can be uncovered and pricked out like orthodox seedlings.*

---

maintain the attractive colour spectrum. The fronds are distinctly triangular and may be 20-50cm (8-20in) high and long.

The elegant ostrich fern, *Matteuccia struthiopteris*, is definitely deciduous. Plant one specimen in a moist place and you will soon find yourself with a wide-spreading colony. The thin black rhizomes travel just under the soil surface to establish new crowns at some distance from the parent. The fronds are upright and produced in a ring so that, on looking down to the centre, you are immediately struck by the appropriateness of its other common name, the shuttlecock fern.

The soft shield fern, *Polystichum setiferum*, must be recommended. It sends out its fronds horizontally and each is so intricately cut that the filigree effect is of a soft velvet. There are many wonderful forms, *P. setiferum* 'Pulcherrimum Bevis' is a much sought after cultivar with fantastically finely cut fronds that can measure up to some 60cm (24in) long when it is feeling at home.

Natural communities

The establishing of bulbs by seed has been mentioned. There are other plants that we may wish to encourage to spread by seed; some of these may well manage in wet shady spots. While the cowslip, *Primula veris*, is going to be more happy in the open or just on the fringes of a shady wood conditions, the primrose, *P. vulgaris*, can establish itself in shady spots and even if it dries out quite a bit through the summer will come into its own again with winter wet.

There are a range of plants that will do well in moist shady areas. Often these are woodland or edge-of-woodland plants. The wild daffodil, *Narcissus pseudonarcissus*, will grow well in the sort of semi-shade found in light woodland or the edge of woods or hedgerows. Bluebells, *Hyacinthoides non-scripta*, and wood anemones, *Anemone nemorosa*, will go from strength to strength as will wild ransoms, *Allium ursinum*, if you dare to introduce them.

A stream is an ideal
method of drainage for a
damp garden. Zantedeschias,
irises and lysichitons all
relish this wet habitat

ERANTHIS HYEMALIS
Winter aconite

Description: A hardy herbaceous perennial with a
knobbly tuberous rootstock. In the middle of the
winter, the flowers are pushed through the soil
surface and open like so many buttercups, each with a
green ruff of bracts tight around their necks. Leaves
follow and are divided and bright green.

Uses: Invaluable for colour in midwinter with flowers
that are virtually frostproof. Splendid in semi-shaded
spots below trees or between shrubs. Can be
intermixed with snowdrops which usually bloom at
the same time.

Colour: Yellow and polished.

Size: 5-10cm (2-4in) high, spread 7-10cm (3-4in).

Flowering time: Midwinter.

Relatives: *E. cilicica* is a similar plant but with leaves
usually touched with bronze and slightly firmer
flowers. Botanists sometimes consider this to be
synonymous with *E. hyemalis*. The hybrid between the
two, *E.* x *tubergenii* has a clone 'Guinea Gold' a much
stronger and bolder plant than the parents.

Cultivation: Plant from lifted clumps some six weeks
after flowering. The irregular tubers can be snapped
into several pieces: ensure there is a growing point on
each. These should be replanted immediately about
4-5cm (1½-2in) deep in leafy moist soil in semi-shaded
woodland or woodland conditions.

Propagation: Once established the species will seed
themselves about freely and, provided the small
seedlings are not hoed or otherwise destroyed, it
should be possible to create a bright carpet of yellow
flowers in winter in a relatively few seasons. *E.* 'Guinea
Gold', being sterile, can only be propagated by dividing
the tubers.

ASTRANTIA MAJOR
Masterwort

Description: A persistent perennial that steadily expands its territory by a series of thin, rooting rhizomes. It dies down completely in winter and when it resurrects itself with fresh palmate, mid-green leaves, it can look rather lightweight. However, it is very definitely a stayer and produces very erect, branching, wiry stems carrying pale coloured, unusual papery flowers of many petals that look as if they are everlasting and, indeed, can be cut and so used.

Uses: Most welcome in the border as a very reliable and long-lasting performer that can also be plundered for cut flowers.

Colour: Variable from greenish white to pink flushed white with some forms noticeably darker.

Size: 60cm (24in) high, spread will soon reach 30cm (12in), and not so long after will double this if given the chance.

Flowering time: Through summer until frosts.

Relatives: A. major 'Rubra' is a particularly rich coloured form. 'Shaggy' is free flowering with pointed petals and bracts. A. maxima is not a whole lot different, with similar leaves rather more freely produced to form a denser mass from which arise the rigid stems carrying plentiful loads of many-petalled flowers in white but tinged with pink or green or both. Blossom threatens to become permanent.

Cultivation: Very easy in most sites whether on the dry or wet side; perhaps more impressive on moister soil. Will run into other herbaceous neighbours with its narrow rhizomes; there will be a need to keep an eye on its spread. Once it has died down there may be little sign of it until rather later in spring than most herbaceous plants put in an appearance; do not overplant with some other treasure!

Propagation: By simple division early autumn or early spring.

Ferns, particularly the evergreen forms of hart's tongue, *Asplenium scolopendrium*, are ideal for these areas. An area covered with hart's tongue can look good all year round, especially if you have some of the goffered-edged ones, such as *A.s.* 'Crispum'.

ENCOURAGING SEEDING

If you are disappointed at the poor rate at which your primroses or cowslips are setting seed and spreading, there could be a good reason for this – too concentrated a population of flower forms! Like most primulas, the flowers are either pin-eyed, with a stigma prominently thrust forward more or less flush with the face of the face, or thrum-eyed, with the stigma low in the throat and having a much shorter style joining it to the ovary. In an ideally bal-

In this garden, water has been cleverly exploited to create a Japanese-style atmosphere

LOBELIA CARDINALIS
Cardinal flower

Description: This species is an erect, strong, hardy herbaceous perennial with lance-shaped, polished leaves that can be bright green but are more often heavily suffused with red to produce a dark maroon-purple. The typical lobelia-shaped red flowers are arranged as a narrow spike. One of the most vividly coloured of all garden plants.

Uses: A very showy plant especially good in a moist spot but preferably with some drainage. It can be grown in a border where it does not get dried out, perhaps surrounded by white flowers or grey-leaved plants which will help to emphasize the extraordinary colour.

Colour: Vivid rich scarlet-red – a pure pigment straight from the colour box.

Size: To 1m (3ft) high, but dependent on soil moisture content, spread 25cm (10in).

Flowering time: From mid- to late summer.

Relatives: 'Bees' Flame', richly coloured, 'Queen Victoria' with very dark foliage and stems, deep red flowers on erect but branching stems, 'Cherry Ripe' with vivid flowers that are very freely produced.

L. siphilitica is a strong growing perennial, reaching to 1m (3ft) with twin-lipped, brilliant blue flowers in late summer and autumn way above the narrow, oval leaves. This is a plant for moist soils and is happy in really heavy ones.

Cultivation: Plant early spring in a moist spot.

Propagation: Divide rootstock in early spring.

anced population, insects visiting thrum-eyed flowers will take pollen from them and are likely to deposit some on pin-eyed specimens. This encourages cross-pollination of the two types and is a clear aid to the safeguarding of genetic diversity. To hinder self-pollination, the pollen-bearing anthers of the pin-eyed flowers are low in the throat so that dropping pollen on to their own stigma is not all that easy. A group of primroses that have been planted by dividing a single large clump will be genetically identical and will be considerably less prolific in setting seed – unless surrounded by other individual clones – than a fully mixed population. A

Matteuccia struthiopteris
Ostrich fern

Description: A very hardy, spreading fern that is deciduous. Each spring more crowns of fronds appear as thin dark rhizomes range widely just under the soil surface to colonize more and more ground. Fronds are intricately cut from ground level to their tips and are arranged precisely in a cone form to make the alternative common name shuttlecock fern singularly appropriate.

Uses: One of the easiest of hardy ferns, very good for making bold stands in semi-shaded spots and very effective in moist soil. By water it can grow much taller than in somewhat drier places. Good in a wild garden. Excellent to bring coolness to more hectic colours.

Wildlife: Provides shelter for small animals and birds.

Colour: Fresh green.

Size: 45cm-over 1m (18-36in) high, spread of one crown 45cm (18in).

Flowering time: No flowers but stronger 'shuttle-cocks' will have in their centres brittle, half-length, compact, fertile fronds, somewhat brown and rusty when old.

Cultivation: Easiest of plants in moist soil. Plant pot grown specimens at any time but best in early spring. Do not hoe around settled plant otherwise you will sever the narrow running black rhizomes that will give the ever increasing number of plants.

uniform population can be made almost instantly more productive of seed by the planting of a different individual in their midst, the newcomer being pin-eyed in a thrum-eyed population or vice versa.

This is certainly a lesson to take to heart. Gardeners, always on the look out for an individual of outstanding merit, all too often concentrate on propagating one or two to the exclusion of other clones of the species. While this is a desirable course in many ways, it is not something to follow too rigidly when dealing with more natural forms of gardening and certainly not in the wild garden.

WATERLOGGED CLAY

WATERLOGGED CLAY IS likely to contain plenty of nutrients but will be lacking air in the soil, which will be almost without structure – a poreless amorphous mass. Although many gardeners complain of having a heavy clay soil, often it is actually really a comparatively good soil, with a higher proportion of clay particles than are found in a perfect loam. As mentioned on page 54, clay is formed of very fine particles, almost all of uniform minute size and with the capacity to form one solid airless mass. Perhaps the most lifeless of clay containing soils are the blue or white ones that are quarried for the manufacture of china pottery. The orange clays are almost as formidable if they are not relieved by particles of sand or non-clay materials.

Gardening on clay has a primary rule: work at all times to improve the soil structure. By physical, organic and chemical means one is constantly trying to get air in the soil and to build up humus content. If the structure is improved the rewards follow and they can be high: lush, strong, steady growth from a consistent supply of food and water.

Weeping willow is the archetypal tree of waterlogged soil, its beautiful form providing interest even when it is not in leaf

When the excess of water combined with clay is mainly a seasonal occurrence there may come times of drought when the clay dries to a solid rock-hard mass which shrinks to produce widening cracks that reach down very deep. (There is no point in sticking a hosepipe in such a crack and letting the water gush all day as the water will simply drain away.) The relatively few plants that have been successfully coping with the almost airless wet clay now find a whole new set of problems. Waterlogged clays that dry out seasonally further confine the choice of tough plants that can grow in them. If you do not feel like moving house, be prepared to undertake a long and diverse campaign to change the soil.

ALNUS CORDATA
Italian alder

A. cordata 'Ramulis Coccineis'

Description: Bold, pyramidal deciduous tree with handsome broad foliage of rich green. This Italian species is bold and dressy with large firm heart-shaped and polished leaves and big catkins followed by persistent rounded woody fruits.

Uses: Excellent specimen tree, especially in moist soil. Good for wet cold spots. Does not need to be planted in rich soil.

Colour: Rich green leaves.

Size: To 20m(60ft) high, spread 10m (30ft).

Flowering time: Late winter.

Relatives: This is probably the most distinguished species. However, *A. incana* is a yeoman for poor wet spots and has a distinctive yellow-leaved form 'Aurea' as well as 'Ramulis Coccineis' (pictured).

Cultivation: Best planted early autumn or very early spring. Thoroughly dig soil in a moist spot. Plant firmly and stake. It should grow rapidly and will need little aftercare if you have chosen a site where it can spread to its considerable size.

Propagation: Seed grows quickly into sizeable plants.

Do you have waterlogged clay?

You hardly need to be told what waterlogged clay is like if you have it. Stand on it and you can be a fixture and can certainly lose your wellingtons, so strongly does the clay take hold. After any rainfall worth measuring, the ground will develop puddles that take a long time to disappear. Drainage is poor to non-existent. Water can pour off to lower reaches.

Coping with waterlogged clay

Ways of tackling clay soils are described on pages 54-61. It is all about improving the soil structure. This is done by increasing the content of grit and humus into the clay. The other way to tackle the problem of tight compaction brought about by the tiny size of the clay particles is to treat the soil with lime. This has the effect of encouraging groups of particles to join together into super-particles, flocculating, and so clearly giving the soil a more crumbly texture. Clay soil that is roughly dug and left exposed to frost can be temporarily encouraged to form clustered particles and will be easier to work for a period. Long term there is nothing better than the boosting of the humus and grit content. This will help the soil to cope with what would normally be an excess of water and will help retain the water

through periods of drought. A mulch of compost or shredded bark will help to prevent severe cracking and drying out.

FLOODING

A few dramatic gardens have been created so that the house is surrounded by water or appears to be so. Timber decking platforms make it easy to get

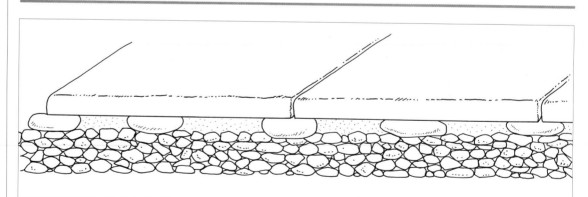

LAYING A PATH

1 Mark out path with string. Leave and amend over a period of a few days.
2 Remove turf or topsoil to a depth of 7-10cm (3-4in) and store for use in potting or elsewhere in the garden.
3 Excavate some 15cm (6in) of soil and use

where it is useful or store.
4 Lay a rough hardcore layer some 15-20cm (6-8in) deep and ram solid.
5 Spread an even layer 5-7cm (2-3in) deep of washed granite waste/grit/sand.
6 Lay paving slabs, bricks, or spread pea gravel as final layer.

7 If path is to take heavy traffic secure paving slabs in each corner and in the centre with a trowelful of cement.
8 If deciding on a cheaper pea-gravel path, lay curbs of bricks or stone to prevent stones being lost and perhaps getting on to the lawn and fouling the mower.

WILLOWS WITH COLOURED STEMS

Salix alba vitellina, bright yellow

S. a. v. 'Britzensis', orange-red

S. dapnoides, purple with whitish bloom

S. fargesii, purple-red

S. irrorata, purple with white bloom

S. matsudana 'Tortuosa', olive-green, decoratively twisted

S. purpurea, purple

CALTHA PALUSTRIS
Marsh marigold, Kingcup

Description: Strong, waterside herbaceous perennial, native to many countries including Britain, that dies down to fat crowns in the winter and quickly gets underway in spring with rounded dark green glossy leaves and lots of spring blossom looking like the buttercup's dream of the greater glory.

Uses: Streamside or wetland plant.

Colour: Rich gold polished more brightly than any of the precious metal.

Size: Variable but up to 60cm (24in) high, spread 45cm (18in).

Flowering time: Spring

Relatives: *C. palustris* 'Flore Pleno' is the magnificent sterile double form with very neat doubled blooms of gold but with a green cast over newer inner petals before they are fully expanded.

Cultivation: Given enough moisture this is a plant without awkward ways. Can be safely allowed to get on doing its own thing.

Propagation: The single form will probably increase itself by seeding. It can be divided in autumn or at the end of the winter, a procedure that will be needed for the sterile double.

---

around the outside of the house. This decking may be arranged to allow a bridge across the water to further parts of the garden where water does not hold sway. Alternatively, there can be a promontory travelling from the house through the water to the far shore. One can design an unbroken expanse or two or three separate entities and, depending on the house style and the surrounds, these water areas can be formally shaped with straight or geometrically curved margins, or informally to give them the appearance of naturally formed pools. Obviously not many houses are built where there are such readily available expanses of water but there are a few very exciting examples.

The type of vegetation that thrives in water or in wet ground bordering water is usually of a bold theatrical type, which gives ample scope for some very telling effects. Water mirrors the plant life that surrounds it, giving opportunities to produce exciting patterns with the contrast between its horizontal reflective plane and the comparatively vertical growth of the plants. The horizontal and vertical are further enhanced by the decking, pathways and retaining walls.

The proportion of the ground that is dedicated to water will naturally be one of the first considerations for practical and aesthetic considerations. The smaller the amount of ground left uncovered, the smaller the number of plants that can be grown out of water. It may not be wise to restrict normal 'dry land' gardening activities too much.

A COMPROMISE

Draining has been considered before (see pages 83-84); flooding is discussed above. But there is a third answer: just coping with the conditions is an option. This means accepting the wet state and modifying it

CORNUS ALBA
Dogwood

C. alba 'Elegantissima'

Description: Vigorous colonizing shrub, grown primarily for the colourful bark colour that is particularly useful in winter. Oval, green leaves are perfectly adequate. Flowers are small in crowded flat panicles – a secondary rather than a major claim to distinction. There are very good variegated forms (see below). Fully hardy.

Uses: Revels in very wet conditions. If space allows it can be allowed to spread over many metres; still worth a slot in smaller areas.

Colour: Red stems.

Size: 1-3m (3-10ft) high, spread as allowed.

Flowering time: Late spring.

Relatives: *C. alba* 'Elegantissima' (pictured) with bright red young winter bark and very pleasing white-edged foliage. 'Sibirica' is rather less rampant but is still an outstanding clone for the brilliance of the red young shoots, so much more fiery than the crimson-red of the type. 'Gouchaultii' varies the pattern by having leaves flushed rosy pink and edged creamy yellow. *C. stolonifera* 'Flaviramea' has rather paler leaves. It is of similar habit but with olive-yellow stems.

Cultivation: All grow easily in normal soils that do not dry out, but they do best in really moist conditions. To get the benefit of the colour of the young bark, it is best to cut back growth drastically at the end of the winter to encourage strong new growth. If you have more than one plant, half can be brought down each year to stubs of 30cm (12in).

Propagation: Probably the easiest of all shrubs to grow from winter cuttings. You can just push pieces into the ground some 30cm (12in) or so deep where you want fresh plants.

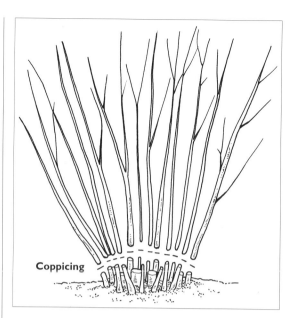

Coppicing

COPPICING AND POLLARDING

Coppicing is a system of tree or shrub management that means cutting them back virtually to ground level every year or every few years. Pollarding is the same system but this time the cutting back is to a trunk rather than to ground level.

Coppicing

1 *Plant suitable cultivars of willows or dogwoods. They can be planted very much closer than if they were going to be left to grow naturally, perhaps at spacings as close as 60cm (2ft).*

2 *Choose a moist position for the plants.*

3 *Allow young plants to grow strongly for a couple of seasons.*

4 *Cut all growth down to within a few centimetres/inches of ground*

just sufficiently to make a form of gardening possible, as well as making it possible to get from the house to the garage or public highway without being lost in a quagmire. At the very least, you will want to think about creating some outdoor spot where relaxation is possible; other considerations are clotheslines and other such utility areas. These areas may not need to be very wide or expansive, but they certainly need to be safe to walk on at all times of the year. They will have to be excavated, filled with hardcore and covered with a form of hardstanding – concrete, paving, gravel or stone.

A sensible compromise, and one that is cheaper than draining or flooding the whole garden is to produce the overall effect of a water meadow subject to flooding and sheltered by a belt of trees and shrubs. Waterlogged clay is the ideal medium to

Pollarding

level at the end of the winter.

5 *Scatter a general fertilizer around to encourage strong, fast growth.*

The willows and dogwoods propagate easily from cuttings. Cut piece of clean wood about 30-45cm (12-18in) long and push two-thirds into the ground. This can be done between autumn and the end of the winter.

Pollarding is exactly the same procedure but you allow the plants to make trunk growth of some metres and then cut back to a head. These will be larger plants and will need very much more space.

form a natural pond. Puddled clay to a depth of 15cm (6in) will hold water for centuries provided it is not allowed to dry out at any time. If the reason for the wet condition of the ground is a spring within your boundaries, there is also the option of creating a stream. A small pond will help to soak up some of the excess water and the excavated soil can be used to form areas of high ground which are somewhat better drained (see also pages 72-77).

Natural Communities

In the wild, dogwood can be found growing near or in water with the water forget-me-not (*Myosotis scorpioides*) growing among its lower parts. In the garden, we would not rush to add the meadow buttercup, *Ranunculus acris* to make a threesome –

'weeds' we have plenty of – but we could perhaps allow a place for the double form 'Flore Pleno'. This is not invasive and its pretty double button flowers shine as bright as the single ones.

On the whole, while it is possible to look to nature for ideas, gilding the lily may be required in the garden by the introduction of a few exotics that will make themselves at home there. A good way to start is to think first of the trees and shrubs that will flourish in the wet then make a stand around which smaller plants can be gathered.

Making the most of it

The plant life that grows in or near water often has an extrovert view of life: these are tough plants that have made a playground of tough situations. *Gunnera manicata*, for example, is no shrinking violet, nor are most of the others. Once construction work is completed and the area is planted, the amount of maintenance is minimal. If a healthy balance is achieved in the water, the plants in and out of it will be able to grow strongly. They will need little encouragement to flourish; the problem is more likely to be the curbing of their exuberance.

ARUNCUS AETHUSIFOLIUS

A. dioicus

Description: Strong, hardy herbaceous perennial with divided pinnate foliage that gives an overall ferny effect in dark rich green. A plant makes a rounded mass of foliage above which are borne a plentiful series of frothy plumes in the same manner as astilbes.

Uses: Persistent and reliable for a moist spot. Large enough to make an impact and able to look after itself.

Colour: Rich green foliage, creamy white blossom.

Size: 1m (3ft) high, spread 60-90cm (2-3ft).

Flowering time: Summer.

Relatives: Rather similar are the readily available *A. dioicus* (syn. *A. sylvester*, pictured) and its splendid form 'Kneiffii' with arching plumes of tiny cream flowers like exploding fireworks.

Cultivation: Trouble-free planted early spring or early autumn in moist soil. No good in dry spots.

Propagation: By division in very early spring.

PODOPHYLLUM HEXANDRUM (SYN. *P. EMODI*)
Himalayan May apple

Description: Rhizomatous herbaceous perennial producing heavily mottled, three-lobed leaves in pairs, above which are carried wide, white, six-petalled flowers, like surprised anemones, each with a central stigma as a boss surrounded by stamens. Fleshy fruits follow in summer. It is hardy, but the emerging young foliage can get caught by frost so it may be best where shrubs and trees provide protection.

Uses: Looks good in semi-shaded, woodland-type conditions where it can enjoy moisture.

Colour: Flowers usually white as snow, but can be pink. Fruits are red. Foliage is mid-green much hidden by generous heavy brown mottling.

Size: 30-45cm (12-18in) high, spread 30cm (12in).

Flowering time: Mid-spring.

Relatives: *P. peltatum*, the May apple, is a strong, spreading, rhizomatous plant with lighter palmate leaves either plain green or with some mottling, each cut into three or five deep lobes. As it emerges from the soil, the foliage looks like so many partially closed umbrellas. Next come nodding, white, cup-shaped flowers, followed by rose-pink, plum-like fruits in autumn.

Cultivation: Plant in moist peaty soil in a position with at least partial shade.

Propagation: By division end of winter, or by seed when ripe at the end of summer.

Although they like fairly good drainage, daylilies do well on moist soil in sun

USING TREES AND SHRUBS

Wet areas can be used, and considerably reduced in density by a planned deployment of trees and shrubs. A good collection of these will take up and transpire so much water that the reservoir is kept under control.

If there is the space, few things can look more splendid than a well grown weeping willow. There are several to choose from but a favourite in a large area is the yellow weeping willow, *Salix × sepulcralis* 'Chrysocoma'. As it can grow to a height of 20m (70ft) by something wider, this is not the sort of plant to introduce into a small suburban plot if you intend to give it its head. In such smaller areas an alternative is to plant a series of willows that will work efficiently in forming a screen during the growing months and transpiring quantities of water but then in the winter providing a good show from their coloured barks. There are several fine ones that can be coppiced, cut to the ground, or pollarded to allow the young bark that is highly coloured to be produced in quantity (see margin list of willows).

The dogwoods also provide coloured stems in a more shrubby form. These are natural wetland plants. The basic species is *Cornus alba* – alba meaning white for the fruits, the stems being red. Various selections have been made: 'Sibirica' is a wider growing one with rich red polished stems; 'Kesselringii' has purple-red stems and dark leaves that take on a reddish purple flush as autumn approaches; 'Spaethii' has bright red stems and foliage that is bright green enlivened by generous irregular pale yellow variegation of the margins; 'Elegantissima' has similar red stems and leaves that are variegated but with this being near white and somewhat more confined to the leaf edges.

The other dogwood species that have worthwhile and attractive coloured barks are *C. stolonifera* with the lime-yellow stems of 'Flaviramea', and *C. sanguinea* with several very good clones in burning orange-reds: those of 'Winter Beauty' are a rich flame yellow-orange at the bottom giving way to

rich pink and then red for the younger wood at the tips of the shoots.

The alders are waterside trees. The common alder, *Alnus glutinosa*, will line the banks of many streams and waterways; in the garden 'Aurea' is sometimes planted for its yellow young leaves that turn pale green by midsummer. 'Imperialis' differs from the type in having deeply cut leaves; both cultivars are slower growing than the species. The Italian alder, *A. cordata*, is a quick-growing tree of very correct, conical form and with larger, heart-shaped, polished leaves – an altogether more dressy species. It could be planted as a specimen tree though you should be warned that it can reach as high as 20m (70ft).

There are a series of trees like the Caucasian wing nut, *Pterocarya fraxinifolia*, that enjoy wet soils but need some attention paid to drainage. Caucasian wing nut can grow at least as tall as the Italian alder and wider with a spread of up to 20m (70ft). Its glossy dark green leaves are shaped like those of the ash but probably with more leaflets; the flowers are

RODGERSIA AESCULIFOLIA
Chestnut-leaved rodgersia

Astilboides tabularis

Description: Very strong, hardy rhizomatous herbaceous perennial that enjoys moist conditions. Each spring strong stems arise from which are unfurled palmate leaves looking so like those of the horse chestnut tree. Their wrinkled surfaces shine and are usually strongly flushed with pinky bronze. Overtopping these come the airy conical plumes of tiny flowers. Hardy; if leaves are well advanced they can be caught by a severe late frost, but new foliage will emerge.

Uses: One of the outstanding bog and waterside foliage plants. Can be grown in normal border where it is moist and does not get parched.

Colour: Leaves green with bronze cast. Flowers white or pink.

Size: Height varies according to site: 40cm-1m (16-36in), spread as much.

Flowering time: Midsummer.

Relatives: *R. pinnata* is similar but with the leaves divided into 5 to 9 oval leaflets. Flowerheads are a definite pink. *R. podophylla* has young leaves bronzed and then greening before again taking on a metallic copper tinge. The widespread leaflets end with several boldly indented points. *Astilboides tabularis* (syn. *Rodgersia tabularis*, pictured) has rounded, shallowly-lobed leaves.

Cultivation: Tough plants that look after themselves in moist spots.

Propagation: Chop out rooted pieces of the rhizomes at the end of the winter and plant them up immediately in their new quarters.

pale green and produced in long narrow tassels. To maintain a single-trunked specimen, keep a look out for suckers and remove them on sight; for a thicket, moving towards a grove, let all alone and just wait.

Birches we usually think of as heathland members or certainly not trees of riverbanks and wet places. *Betula nigra* is an exception, but it differs too in having rough peeling grey trunks perhaps flushed with pink and rather firmer diamond-shaped leaves.

Some poplars are not averse to having plenty of moisture around their roots, but they do tend to want some drainage. The aspen, *Populus tremula*, is the vigorous leafy tree that whispers. Its young leaves are bronzy orange in youth but take on a more serious grey-green in their mature months before turning good shades of yellow before dropping. It can make an altitude of 15m (50ft) with a spread of 10m (30ft) but there is a strait-jacketed version, 'Erecta', that is only half as wide.

The swamp cypress, *Taxodium distichum*, has been

DRYOPTERIS DILATATA
Broad buckler fern

Description: This is a moisture-loving, hardy deciduous fern. Its large triangular fronds, to 90cm (36in) long by 45cm (18in) wide, are tripinnate, much divided and intricate. Fronds may be very large and are held at spreading angles.

Uses: It makes a lovely wetland plant and can serve as a large specimen focal point by waterside where the royal fern (page 65) or huge *Gunnera manicata* (page 232) are deemed too large.

Colour: Fresh bright green.

Size: Total height and spread 1m (3ft).

Relatives: *D. dilatata* 'Grandiceps' is smaller but with crests at the end of the pinnae down each side of the frond and with a bunched tassel at its pointed end. *D. erythrosora*, the autumn fern, is much smaller at 30-45cm (12-18in) high, but has very pleasing spreading triangular fronds which in youth, and for a considerable while after, can be a shining coppery pink.

Cultivation: Plant a young, rooted specimen in spring, choosing a moist spot and allowing plenty of room for growth. Thereafter it will look after itself. The tidy minded can clear away the dead fronds at the year's end, otherwise let nature take its course.

Propagation: Best achieved by using spores like seeds to raise fresh new plants (see page 89). This is better than disturbing an established plant, though a relatively young one may be dug up and split if you can detect separate crowns and can get these away with plenty of the fibrous root.

mentioned before in passing, but should not be forgotten. It is a deciduous conifer that in full leaf is not unlike a yew, but the rich green yew-like tones turn lovely shades of golden-brown in autumn. As its common name declares, it will grow in the wettest of sites, where it can form an upright tree roughly conical in form, certainly capable of 20m (70ft) in height but only about half the width.

Willows are an obvious choice and some that are good for winter bark colour are listed above, but there are plenty of other useful species and forms in this varied genus. In the countryside, the early months of the year are made very decorative with the 'ordinary' goat willow, *Salix caprea*, transforming bare twigged shapes into a cloud of yellow with a million pussy-willow buds bursting into golden pollen fireworks. They could be included in parklands; in smaller gardens it is better to restrict oneself to the pendant form 'Kilmarnock', the Kilmarnock willow, which is sold as trunked speci-

mens about 1.2-1.5m (4-5ft) high but with dense heads of dramatically bowing branches. The plant will get a little higher with age and the head will get even more crowded with branches. At the end of the winter, the buds shed their bracts and reveal themselves first as silky silvery grey, the precursors of the golden pollen-laden powder-puffs.

Other willows worth looking at include *S. hastata* 'Wehrhahnii', a much-branched, upright shrub, with stems of dark purple to contrast with the many upright rather long catkins, all shining silver above the neat little pale green bracts. After years of looking attractive from a tiny newly-planted specimen, it will have spread to almost twice its 1m (3ft) height, which is normally the maximum. Stems later become rather a muddied yellow.

Moving away from willows, there is the guelder rose, *Viburnum opulus* (see also page 69), native to all countries of northern Europe. It is a deciduous shrub or small tree with broad, well-serrated leaves and plenty of wide panicles of white flowers in late spring to be followed by very showy bunches of glistening red fruits. 'Compactum' is a very dense neat form that restricts itself to an outside limit of 1.5m (5ft). 'Xanthocarpum' has brilliant rich golden berries.

MARGINALS

In choosing plants for the water's edge, the flowering rush, *Butomus umbellatus*, ought not to be missed. It is not a rush, despite narrow rush-like leaves and stems, and has many-flowered umbels of clear bright rose-pink flowers – the opposite to a true rush's staid statements. The water forget-me-not, *Myosotis scorpioides*, in the particularly well flowered 'Mermaid' form, is also a suitable candidate. Poking up through the shallow waters or the nearby mud it is one of those water plants that seem to belong to another plan of creation. Neat lance-shaped, cleanly-cut leaves are dark and glossy green, sculptural below the tight, crowded, poker heads of blue flowers, a shade that shines out vividly.

Among the shrubs or behind some of the herbaceous plants, teasels, *Dipsacus fullonum* could be introduced. And, in front, it is well worth trying some of those herbaceous perennials normally thought of as orthodox border plants. There are several that will manage really very well in very damp spots. The day-lilies, the *Hemerocallis*, will enjoy getting their thick, thirsty roots into the wet promise of good things. The number available now is bewildering. The best plan is to see a selection at a flower show or other display. If reading catalogue descriptions be prepared to put a mental line through adjectives such as 'indispensable', but most will be fairly accurate. Bergamots, *Monarda* forms, can be chosen in the same way. They will be in

DUCKWEED COMPOST

The continual chore of clearing duckweed and fairy fern (*Azolla*) from an over-active pond is a valuable way of collecting material for your compost heap. It is important to keep about a third of the water surface clear of plant growth for the health of the pond and also so that you can enjoy the reflections. Water plants break down quickly and their sappy juiciness will be just what is needed to mix with drier coarser autumn stems tidied from herbaceous borders and elsewhere. Fairy fern is a relative of the true ferns, but is a water plant with the capacity of fixing nitrogen from the air, an accomplishment more commonly found in the legumes. This makes the material especially useful as compost additive. *Azolla*, while often invasive, is not totally hardy and can be killed in a bad winter. A jam jar of water on a windowsill carries some safely through the winter. With the spring it can be returned to the pond to start a rapidly expanding new community.

Warning: Only put azolla into garden ponds that are completely isolated from natural water courses. In mild areas it may survive through the winter and, being vigorous, is a danger to natural plant communities.

POPULUS TREMULA
Aspen

P. tremula 'Erecta'

Description: Strong tree with young foliage tinted bronze-red becoming an adult grey-green before turning yellow for leaf fall. Fluffy male catkins are 5-10cm (2-4in) long. Rounded leaves rattle and tremble in breezes or winds.

Uses: Grows well in damp and often poor soils.

Colour: Greyish green catkins. For leaves see above.

Size: 15m (50ft) high, spread 10m (30ft).

Flowering time: Late winter.

Relatives: *P. tremula* 'Erecta' is very narrow and upright in habit.

Cultivation: Grows best in moist good loam but can cope in waterlogged clay and will need little if any maintenance.

Propagation: Not as ready to root from hardwood cuttings as many poplars, but nevertheless this can be done. Softwood cuttings will also take.

bloom with rounded heads of 'nettle' flowers on erect stems for many weeks through the summer. Both day lilies and bergamots want plenty of light to excel. Candelabra primulas like marginal spots and will seed around with a little encouragement.

GROUND COVER
To the front of any wet area, plant as ground cover some *Polygonum affine*. There are various forms of this creeping knotweed, which is evergreen in the sense that it may retain some green leaves but normally allows them to rust to an orange shade and they then persist through the winter. Blooming is an extensive festival from midsummer through until winter, when lots of spikes of pinky red flowers approximately 20cm (8in) high are boldly displayed above the foliage.

Some ground-covering plants such as this polygonum can sometimes try to cover more ground than you want. It is not difficult to trim back the excess by slicing off portions with a spade. It may help to define the area you have given a plant by using rocks or even logs.

There are other plants that will cover wet ground. Large-leaved ivies will manage (see page 39). *Rodgersia* species are excellent and will make a real feature; *R. aesculifolia* is the one with magnificent leaves rather like those of a horse chestnut. In wet areas the plants can grow 60-90cm (2-3ft) or more. Groups of hostas will look marvellous through the growing months.

OTHER DIFFIC

SOIL CONDITIONS and the amount of sun or shade your garden enjoys are the main factors determining what plants you can grow and what problems you might face in their cultivation. However, there are also a few more minor difficulties that have to be considered and overcome. For example, otherwise splendid sites can be rendered very difficult by high winds. This particular problem is given some attention in this section. There are things that can be done to alleviate the effects of wind across and in gardens, and there are plants that manage in such fraught spots. Also covered in this section are the problems of new gardens or houses built on old industrial sites, where a multitude of sins and trouble lies buried under a compacted surface. These are something that can be tackled if approached sensibly and methodically. Although they may be daunting at the beginning, any difficulties will lessen quickly and a decent régime can soon be established.

Eschscholtzia californica, California poppy, is ideal for using as a stop gap until more permanent planting is arranged. The strain shown here is Dalli

ANIMAL LIFE

My own particular cross-to-bear concerns animal life. My garden is surrounded by farmland, with racehorses given the freedom of bordering fields. They have necks like giraffes and stomachs that seem to be able to digest anything, especially those plants growing our side of the boundary fences.

The other threats to our plants are smaller in stature but nevertheless do their bit towards undermining the garden's well-being. We have voles like some people have aphids – in parts the ground looks like a piece of Swiss cheese. We also have extremely industrious moles. The only effective and

ANEMONE BLANDA
Windflower

Description: In the spring when this little anemone is in flower and in leaf it looks dainty and fragile. It does not look a toughie but is a persistent and strong grower in the right place, its neat divided foliage and many-petalled flowers looking excitingly fresh early in the year. Fully hardy.

Uses: It can be naturalized at woodland edges or in sites that mimic these conditions, and will quickly spread between and below shrubs.

Colour: Perhaps the most appealing of the colour variants are the blue ones. 'Atrocaerulea' is the name given to the best clones, brilliant deep sky blues with contrasting white centres formed of a boss of stamens. There are also white and pink forms.

Size: About 7cm (3in) high, spread is indefinite.

Relative: *A. apennina* looks very similar but differs in its hidden parts; the rootstock of this is a narrow spreading rhizome much like that of the native windflower *A. nemorosa* (page 35).

Cultivation: Plant the lumpy rhizomes in autumn in loose-textured, leafy soils.

Propagation: Flowers can seed and spread that way or the rhizomes can be lifted a few weeks after flowering and broken into pieces and replanted.

105

Animal pests, such as moles, are something nearly every gardener has to cope with at some time or another. Remedies vary and can be more or less effective, sometimes it is best to try to live with the pest, just limiting, as far as possible, the damage it does

reasonable method of dealing with these fellows is by trapping. Noises, camphor tablets and holly twigs are all futile, and as for the anti-mole smokes, our moles do not seem to be sensitive non-smokers. I have bought traps but cannot summon up the necessary hardness of heart to install them so we are currently trying a season of living in a state of peaceful coexistence.

KEEPING WITHIN CAPABILITIES

There is, of course, the ever-present restriction of our own capabilities. We should never make the garden our master. Certainly it is not ideal to have an increasing load of gardening as working lives get more demanding or when energies are ebbing as retirement approaches. Those with mobility problems – and most of us will face these to a greater or

MAHONIA AQUIFOLIUM 'SMARAGD'
Oregon grape

Description: This is a low-growing, rugged shrub which gives splendid evergreen cover of broad, flat, pinnate leaves, dark green and glossy. In spring each twig is topped by tight fists of crowded flowers. Plants spread by suckering and will make a persistent dense cover. Fully hardy.

Uses: Excellent ground cover. Can provide some shelter for more gentle things.

Colour: Flowers golden, leaves bronze when young.

Size: 75cm (30in) high, but spread over 1.5m (5ft).

Relatives: *M.* x *wagneri* 'Moseri' is a more discrete grower, rarely spreading by suckering. It forms neat plants of evergreen foliage that is coloured in wonderful warm tones of orange, red and bronze throughout the year.

Cultivation: Easy in most soils. Will look after itself.

Propagation: Sever one of the rooted suckers and replant in fresh site.

lesser extent at some time or another – are best advised to have their garden designed to meet their requirements fairly precisely. If a wheelchair is needed or you have problems bending, beds may well have to be raised to a more sensible height. Such beds need to be just so wide that all parts of them can be reached from one side or another. In such situations, there is a powerful case for reliable ground cover for lower areas, and shrubs could well come into their own around the boundaries as well as elsewhere. Open areas where grass might be considered could be better paved to save upkeep and to make access easier. Do not use gravel or shredded bark on areas where it is necessary to wheel a chair or if any family member is unstable on their feet and could find the loose surface difficult.

WINDY SITES

In sites that are in exposed positions, it can be quite difficult to establish a reasonable, ornamental garden. Wind can cause a lot of damage, both superficial and more permanently harmful. The most obvious problem is broken stems or branches of trees, shrubs and herbaceous plants. Strong winds can tear foliage from plants or they can burn up leaf areas by forcing a rate of transpiration in excess of any possible rate of replacement. Where they are planted, tall conifer hedges or screens can be scorched to the windward side causing severe disfigurement or even death. In winter some evergreens are going to be at risk as there is likely to be more wind and this combined with cold or freezing weather can 'burn' the foliage; water cannot be brought quickly enough from roots to the leaves. In particularly severe cases evergreen hedges can be browned all down one side. Fortunately this scorching is usually overgrown fairly quickly through the following growing season. More severe damage can be caused to trees with shallow roots. They may be blown over.

The physical effects of the wind go beyond that of motion damage. In dry periods when wind is prolonged, soil surfaces can become parched, and cushioning humid layers close to the ground, which

E. 'Apple Blossom'

ESCALLONIA RUBRA VAR. MACRANTHA
Escallonia

Description: Evergreen compact shrub that is very wind resistant. Serrated leaves are polished dark green and measure 2-8cm (1-3in) long; they make a dense cover. Richly coloured tubular flowers in long lasting bunches are borne at stem ends. It is South American and is best sheltered in very cold areas.

Uses: Good in a mixed planting, especially useful for screening or hedging. In cold climates can be pruned to grow up a wall.

Colour: Crimson-pink.

Size: According to site and locality, 1.8-3m (6-10ft) high and wide.

Flowering time: From early summer into autumn.

Relatives: Many good hybrids exist: 'Apple Blossom' (pictured) is pale pink; 'Donard Seedling' has pink buds that open to white flowers; 'Iveyi' has dark green leaves with contrasting pure white blossom; 'Crimson Spire' is a particularly strong thrusting upright grower with deep red blossom.

Cultivation: Best in sunshine in healthy well-drained soils.

Propagation: Easily propagated by cuttings in midsummer or by layers.

protect some plants, will be stripped away. In this situation, smaller plants with less reserves can be severely hit. Particularly vulnerable to damage and death are newly planted seedlings that have yet to establish a strong root system with main roots and root hairs in balance with the leafy growth above.

When wind is combined with other conditions, such as hail and extreme cold, its effect will be exacerbated. Seaside gardens are particularly vulnerable to wind; not only are they likely to be unprotected on the seaward side, but also any wind from that

***EUCALYPTUS PAUCIFLORA*
SUBSP. *NIPHOPHILA***
Snow gum

E. gunnii

Description: Quick-growing, attractive tree, erect but with some branches bending. Evergreen, spear-shaped, flat leaves of tough texture hang like mobiles from the twigs. The trunk is jigsaw-patterned with flaking bark of different colour shades of grey, buff, brown and green. Small powder-puff flowers. Fully hardy.
Uses: For specimen or as a group for difficult dryish ground.
Colour: Adult foliage silvery grey-green sometimes with a thin pencilled rim of red, young foliage orange-red tinted. Flowers cream.
Scent: Eucalyptus scent from crushed foliage.
Size: Can reach 10m (30ft) high, spread

4-5m (12-15ft).
Flowering time: Spring.
Relatives: *E. pauciflora* has more polished, greener foliage. *E. gunnii* (pictured) tends to shoot up to the heavens and needs restraining. By coppicing every two or three seasons one can ensure a fountain of stems with the attractive, round, silver shilling leaves so beloved by flower arrangers. Adult foliage is similar to that of *E. p. niphophila*.
Cultivation: If possible raise your own from seed and plant out when knee-high. If using nursery stock, pick young specimens that have not got roots circling the pot. Pot-bound specimens take a long time to get going and are never as successful as ones with roots just ready to explore the new soil. Pick a sunny site with well-drained soil. If you can steel yourself cut the whole down to a short stump after a year. This allows the plant extra time to expand its root system. Young specimens can make such a lot of top growth that they are liable to get blown down. Adult specimens can be kept small by periodically cutting them to the base.

Propagation: Sow dust-like seed at the end of the winter under glass, prick out seedlings and repot frequently until ready to plant out. Seed germinates freely and seedlings grow rapidly.

direction will carry with it corrosive salt. Moorland areas, being of high altitude, will also be more prone to strong winds and low-growing moorland vegetation offers little defence; indeed it is the wind that ensures it remains close to the ground.

Within built-up areas, while the force of the wind at ground level may be partially dissipated by buildings and other screening constructions, such as fences and walls, it can also be channelled between such buildings to create a wind tunnel effect that in turn leads to difficult growing conditions.

A substantial evergreen hedge acts as a tough wind screen in this exposed Scottish garden, enabling more sensitive plants to thrive within its shelter

HEBE PINGUIFOLIA 'PAGEI'
Disc-leaved hebe

Description: A prostrate evergreen shrub with tough, oval, concave leaves making wide ground cover and decorated with rounded spikes of flowers held just above the foliage for several weeks. A tough native of New Zealand, it is much hardier than many of the taller hybrids.

Uses: Useful rock garden plant but also good at the front of a border or planting of mixed shrubs, or in a raised bed.

Colour: Very glaucous silvery grey leaves and pure white flowers.

Size: 15-30cm (6-12in) high, spread 75cm-1m (30-36in).

Flowering time: Late spring or early summer.

Relatives: *H. canterburiensis* is not so dwarf but makes a compact bush of bright green leaves, tightly stacked along each stem. It covers itself with white blossom in early summer. Height and spread 30-90cm (1-3ft).

Cultivation: Easy in an open site in well-drained not too rich soil.

Propagation: Easy by summer cuttings or layers.

Do you have a windy site

Although almost everyone might, if asked, say that their garden suffers from the wind, those people who genuinely have severe wind problems are all too well aware of how difficult it can make gardening. In this case, it means more than a little draught, more like regular and constant exposure to gales.

Coastal sites are obviously more prone to wind and can be damaged by salt spray. In extremely windy areas trees are wind 'pruned' with the better growth on the lee side and often with the mature trees leaning away from the prevailing wind. Even in less extreme situations, some gardens get more than their fair share of wind, and this may be noticed not only by the amount of leaf and twig growth blown off through the year, but by the desiccating effect on foliage and flowers. Blooms can be bruised and brought to an end earlier than in more sheltered spots. Even daffodils 'tossing their heads in sprightly dance' are also likely to be rubbing against each other with the result that tissue is damaged and flowers are more quickly brought to their end.

In windy gardens newly planted seedlings, and even more mature plants, bedded out may take longer to get established unless given some extra protection from the drying and battering elements. Soils too may be dried more quickly.

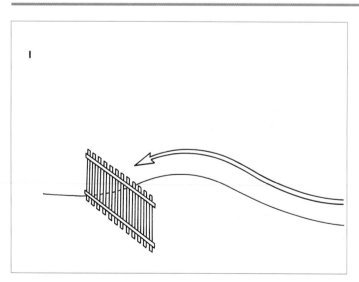

IDEAS FOR WIND BREAKING

1 *If you have the space, bring in an earth-moving machine and build a sloped bank which will send the force of low wind upwards. A quite modestly low solid wall will act in a similar way. A major solid wall can cause unwanted turbulence on the sheltered side of the* wall with the wind twisting down with considerable force in a downdraught.

2 *Install paling fence to height of approximately 1.2m (4ft).*

3 *Plant a first line of trees.*

4 *Plant a second line of trees or shrubs.*

5 *Plant an inner band of shrubs.*

Coping with a windy site

Obviously the first priority is to lessen the impact of wind: shelter must be created. It is not an impossible task – some world-famous gardens have been created close to the coast in windy spots. Examples include Caerhays Castle in Cornwall, Overbecks Garden in Devon and the University of Liverpool Botanic Gardens at Ness. In these you can be sure that shelter was the first thing to be established by means of tree and shrub planting. As the windbreak has grown up and been improved over the years, planting within has been begun in earnest.

Windbreaks of living or inanimate materials can be decorative and lend a real sense of privacy. They can vary from a substantial band of trees that will make a fairly dense uniform wall to a staggered screen that consists of varying colours, forms and textures. If living material is what you choose as a screen, remember that the aim is to break the force of the wind and to begin a filtering process. The approach should be to try to ameliorate the wind effects by a process of attrition. The first barrier blunts the strength, a second one lessens it and a third layer can reduce what had once been a strong wind to a zephyr or a gale to a manageable wind. The main brunt may be borne by outer plantings or a fence on the windward side and then a series of other bands of plants will reinforce the effect until the main centre of the garden is well sheltered. Windbreaks may take up a considerable part of the garden, and by their nature may need to be quite dominant, so they must be considered for looks as well as for practical shelter.

FENCES

It may pay to erect a fence or wall to start the defences. Normally the best bet is to avoid over-solid constructions. The popular interwoven fences made of strips of larch or pine can cause problems. They provide total wind resistance and so stresses on them and their fixings are great. When winds build up and arrive at such an obstacle they cannot just stop dead, they tend to flow over the obstacle and be channelled with even more force on the plant life beyond. A picket fence, either of split chestnut palings or cheap sawn lengths, is more effective. It will break the initial wind force and can

LIMONIUM SINUATUM
Sea lavender, statice

Description: While this is really a perennial, it is normally grown as an annual and has angled, winged stems and lobed, waved leaves. The firm sprays of the flowers are used extensively in dried arrangements. Half hardy.

Uses: Useful filler in borders but mainly grown for the flower stems which are cut fresh and dried.

Colour: Mauve, blue, pink, yellow.

Size: To 45cm (18in) high, spread 40cm (16in).

Flowering time: Summer into autumn.

Relatives: *L. platyphyllum* (syn. *L. latifolium*) is a perennial forming a clump of large tough, spreading leaves above which, in contrasting style, it produces a rounded mass of tiny mauve-blue flowers in many branched sprays, a light and airy effect. There are several named cultivars, all good.

Cultivation: Sow late winter under cover, prick out and then plant out in mid-spring. Harvest stems for drying when flowers are freshly opened.

Propagation: Seed.

SAVING MONEY

Young tree specimens are cheap, as are the more common species, which have the added benefit of being common (and therefore readily available at local garden centres) because they are popular and being popular because they survive in your area. Bare-rooted plants are also cheaper. Remember they are best set in position in late autumn or late winter.

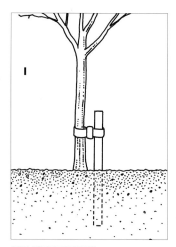

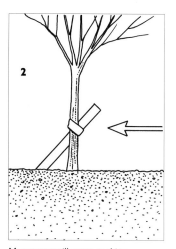

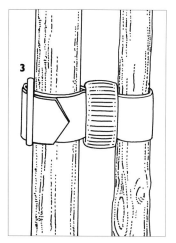

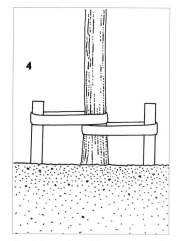

STAKING TREES
IN WINDY SPOTS

Newly planted trees may well need support for two or three years. The well established and recommended practice is to use a short stake or stakes to secure the tree close to the base. The thinking is that this will enable the tree to build up its own strength in the trunk. It is important that the base is maintained so securely that there is no movement.

Movement will cause rocking and lead to the making of a hole in the soil around the trunk, which could then fill with water and cause rotting or death.

1 Use one or more stakes. Use strong stakes that have been treated with preservative and ensure that they are driven very securely into the ground. This may well be best done before the tree is planted into the hole.

2 A single stake is driven in at an angle of 45°, pointing towards the direction of the prevailing wind.
3 The trunk is attached by means of a rubber or plastic tree-support, or something similar – not narrow string, binder-twine or other material that could bite into the bark.
4 An improvement on this method for very windy places is to have two stakes driven in upright, equidistant from the tree, with one on the windward side.

Attach heavy duty rubber supports to the two stakes and around the tree trunk so that they pull equally strongly in both directions.

* Larger specimens may be secured with three posts driven in at angles pointing away from the tree and 'guy-ropes' led to the tree trunk to which they are attached with rubber or wide plastic supports.

be used as very workmanlike protection for the embryo shelter of plants.

CHOOSING THE RIGHT PLANTS

Although the initial choice will be directed towards evergreens for their ability to provide year-round defence, it is best to include some deciduous specimens in the screen as well.

Winds do the most damage when the plants are at a vulnerable stage – spring or early summer. Fortunately, the worst wind is normally experienced in winter when deciduous trees and plants offer less resistance to wind and are thus less subject to damage. Evergreens, which will be putting up a fight all year round, should be of the type to produce strong, deep roots, and not liable to be blown clean out of the ground as can happen to some of the shallower-rooting conifers and eucalyptus.

A sensible plan is to look around at local wild plants first and also to established gardens that face similar conditions. From these it should be easy to

make a list of the trees and shrubs that appear to have been successful. These may include native species such as yew, *Taxus baccata*, Scots pine, *Pinus sylvestris*, and holly, *Ilex aquifolium*. When making your list take care to observe the habit of these species to ensure that they will suit your needs. For example, Scots pines are excellent in their youth when their branches are close to the ground but as the years pass and they begin to make their dramatic sky-high silhouettes, the sheltering at lower levels will have to be taken over by other plants.

Making the most of it

PINES

Some of the hardiest and relatively quick-growing species for the first lines of defence are the pines *Pinus pinaster* and *P. sylvestris*. *P. pinaster* is especially good for positions close to the sea where salt-laden winds can cause leaf burning on other kinds. Better in very cold areas is the Austrian pine, *P. nigra*, an exceptionally tough leafy species. It makes dense dark growth that is resistant to wind. Ultimately a huge tree of up to 25m (80ft) with a rounded, spreading crown, it will serve well for many years before it reaches these exalted heights. Other pines also in the top bracket are *P. cembra, P. contorta, P. leucodermis, P. muricata, P. radiata, P. thunbergii.*

LEYLANDII

For very quick growth and thick cover consider × *Cupressocyparis leylandii* or some of its cultivars. It is fashionable to talk down these very robust plants, so very popular for hedging. But in this situation try to be objective. Even if they are too readily chosen for hedges, grow too quickly and need such regular cutting, a few planted among other plants as a screen and windbreak will serve very well. A mix of the standard rich greens and the yellow forms such as 'Castlewellan', 'Gold Rider' or 'Robinson's Gold' will give very quick and deep shelter. Some consideration needs to be given to their rooting. It is sensible to cut back young specimens quite strongly until you are assured that their root systems are very thoroughly in place, then you can stand back. However, remember these are trees that can reach about 7m (22ft) in seven years and are ultimately 25m (80ft) tall.

LAWSON'S CYPRESS

While *Chamaecyparis lawsoniana* is not so fast growing as leylandii, it is quite quick, some cultivars more so than others. One of the best screening kind is the bright 'Green Hedger' which is well clothed with leafy branches to ground level. Left to its own devices it makes a rather slender conical shape. Also attractive is the lovely colour of 'Pembury Blue' but this cultivar is a much slower grower. 'Green Pillar' is narrow in habit with the outline of a slender lozenge; most others are triangular with the shortest side parallel to the ground. Most plant centres carry stock of several cultivars and, if you don't want a uniform wall-type effect, it is a good idea to choose several to give varying colours.

OTHER CONIFERS AND EVERGREENS

Some spruces make excellent windbreaks. *Picea asperata* looks opulent with its stems thick with bright sparkling blue-green needles. *P. sitchensis*, the Sitka

OLEARIA × HAASTII
Daisy bush

Description: A sturdy, erect, evergreen bush with lots of hard, tough, oval, dark green leaves, which are glossy above and white felted below. The foliage is almost lost under the abundant floral display – lots of wide posies of daisies for many weeks in the summer. A New Zealander and probably the hardiest of the genus.

Uses: As a specimen bush, in mixed plantings or for an internal hedge.

Colour: White flowers with yellow centres.

Scent: Warm pleasing scent.

Size: 1.2-2.5m (4-9ft) high and spread nearly as much.

Flowering time: Mid- and late summer.

Relatives: *O.* × *macrodonta* is a larger shrub or small tree with holly-like foliage that makes a handsome mass clear of which are held many large heads of scented, closely-packed, white daisy flowers. Hardy in milder areas but best in a sheltered spot in cooler ones.

Cultivation: Plant in sun with good drainage.

Propagation: Cuttings in midsummer, or layers.

spruce, has tremendous vigour and can manage well in exposed, windy sites. It is a deep green colour and makes a roughly conical shape. Eventual size depends on the site. A 40m (130ft) height is not out

LINUM PERENNE
Flax

Description: There is a whole assortment of flaxes in a wide variety of colours and ranging from annuals to shrubs. This hardy native of Germany, France and Britain is a very upright herbaceous perennial with many slender wiry stems with narrow, grassy leaves and a good succession of round faced, funnel-shaped blossoms looking upward – typical flax flowers.

Uses: This is a charming accommodating plant ideal for a sunny border or rock garden.

Colour: Frank clear blue.

Size: 30cm (12in) high, spread 15cm (6in).

Flowering time: Early and midsummer.

Relatives: *L. narbonense* forms a clump of erect stems with narrow grey-green leaves and has lots of flowers in shades of blue through spring and summer.
A perennial but does not last for ever; allow seedlings to develop to take place in event of a sudden demise.

Cultivation: Plant in an open well-drained site. Rear plants for replacements.

Propagation: By seed.

of the question in wet spots, but the top measurement could be less than half this in dry soils.

Yew, *Taxus baccata*, is much quicker-growing than is normally thought and makes good thick dark cover. If the species is too dark for your liking, there are cultivars that have some yellow in the leaves to produce a lighter effect, for example, the Aurea group. Remember all parts of yew are poisonous to humans and farm animals.

Common holly, *Ilex aquifolium*, is also much quicker-growing than tradition would have it, espe-

cially once it has had the chance to get its roots established. As a shrub or small tree *Euonymus japonicus* is an old-time yeoman available in many named forms of which 'Latifolius Albomarginatus' is one of the best with the creamy white margin variegation of its leaves.

Careful planting, combined with clever hard landscaping, gives this difficult seaside site its natural charm. The unusual, pale yellow plant rearing up from the rock (left) is navel wort (*Umbilicus rupestris*)

DECIDUOUS TREES

Willows and poplars are useful. Most forms of apples and pears stand up to wind. *Sorbus* species such as the rowan or mountain ash can spend a lifetime being buffeted by wind but the whitebeams are good as well. In damp or wet soils alders as well as willows are good choices. Beech, lime, ash and Norway maple (*Acer platanoides*) are some more reliable windproof trees. The field maple, *Acer campestre*, is always an attractive tree with a rounded clouded form and with lobed leaves that take on good autumn colours. The common hawthorns and other

The film maker Derek Jarman created this beautiful and dramatic garden on the south east coast of Britain. It is planted on pebbles and exposed to all extremes of weather

related thorns are less tall than some trees listed here, but they are second to none in hardiness and wind resistance. For quick growth on poor soils the birches are easy, *Betula pendula*, the silver birch, being as good as any. They do not provide a very dense wall against the wind but will help to diffuse its strength.

Other familiar trees of the countryside can be relied upon. The hawthorns, *Crataegus monogyna* and *C. laevigata* (syn. *C. oxyacantha*), are both among the hardiest of small trees well able to maintain themselves in the face of winds. Grown to maturity, they make wonderful flowering specimens and are again colourful with their fruit from autumn into winter. If they were rare exotics gardeners might vie with each other in growing them.

SHRUBS

Evergreens that head the queue for the windy terraces are *Brachyglottis* 'Sunshine' (syn. *Senecio*), *Elaeagnus macrophylla* and *E. pungens*, Escallonias such as *E.* 'Iveyi' and *Olearia × macrodonta* 'Major' and some relatives. Deciduous toughies include the silvery-leaved *Elaeagnus* 'Quicksilver' and the oleaster, *E. angustifolia*, with its little sweet-scented yellow flowers and yellow fruits. Some roses are prepared

to weather wind. These are those like *R. rugosa* (see page 125), which is upright and produces a thicket of stout strong stems. There are larger species such as *R. wilsonii* which can make a huge rounded dome some 3m (10ft) high and two or three times as wide. It would stop a tank and will put its armoured back up against any wind. In summer it smothers itself with large white, single flowers. Other stalwarts of exposed sites are the tamarisks, *Tamarix ramosissima* and *T. tetrandra*, which are particularly useful in exposed coastal spots. The tamarisks are open-branched, vigorous shrubs with long-reaching branches and feathery foliage. They have lots of plumes of smoky pink flowers, individually tiny, but making a pleasing contribution from summer into early autumn. Other shrubs useful in coastal and other very open sites are the *Olearia* forms often called the daisy bushes, the *Hebe* species and hybrids, *Escallonia*, *Buddleja*, the blue-green foliaged *Bupleurum fruticosum* and the silvery tree purslane, *Atriplex halimus*. Of course, all the heathers, brooms and gorses are plants of wild, open areas and will be well able to help build a community of wind-resistant plants. The winter-flowering *Erica carnea* cultivars are ideal to start with as they give such welcome colour through the dull months. For extra height choose some of the *E. arborea* forms. They can grow up to, or over, head height and not only provide foliage and flower but the blossom is a magnet for bees, and humans can enjoy its warm scent. A range of *Cistus* forms will vary the display and will be excellent where wind and dry conditions combine.

HERBACEOUS PLANTS

These could be headed by some of the tough grasses that one might see at the seaside, the marrams. But there are more surprising plants. The green hellebore, *Helleborus foetidus*, seems able to take lots of punishment without too much wear and tear. Sea holly, *Eryngium maritimum*, expects to have the wind at its back, but others of the genus manage well enough too. Try *E.* × *tripartitum* and *E.* × *oliverianum*. These silvery-leaved thistle relatives are very decorative in the garden and are worth using to make a feature. A group will look good for weeks or months. *E. giganteum* is the plant well known as 'Miss Willmott's Ghost', due to reports that Miss Willmott, an eminent gardener of early this century, dropped seeds of this plant when visiting other gardens. It is no difficulty to get a good store of seed as the plants are very prolific. Although it is only a biennial, once established it will reproduce itself by self-sowing each year so that it is as permanent as any of its perennial relatives. It is certainly one of the most spectacular, with metallic multipointed leaves and large flowerheads collared with vivid silvery blue, fiercely pointed bracts below the tight cone of mauve flowers. Some of the lower mound-forming anthemis are windproof, but so are less obvious candidates such as the *Kniphofias*. The red-hot pokers, *Kniphofia* species and hybrids, have large rosettes of pointed leaves looking almost like an informal yucca, although there are some diminutive forms with delicate, thin leaves. The plants are best left undisturbed in good soil which does not dry out. Different cultivars bloom in succession from mid-summer well into autumn. Also worth cultivating are the beautiful *Agapanthus* forms, which are either bright blue- or white-flowered and some with heads of up to a hundred bell-like blooms on stems some 1m (3ft) high. They are at their best in the second half of the summer. Established plants can be wonderful in warm, open spots and be in bloom for many weeks.

SORBUS AUCUPARIA
Rowan, Mountain ash

Description: This familiar deciduous, small tree hardly needs describing, but there are many forms. In youth a rather sparse plant, it improves with age and veteran specimens can be real characters. The pinnate foliage has up to 15 leaflets of fresh green with good autumn colours. Wide clusters of blossom are followed by bright autumn fruits. Very hardy.

Uses: Good permanent tree for normal or moist soils.

Colour: Cream flowers, orange-red fruits.

Size: 9m(30ft) or more high, spread 6m (18ft). Rather upright in youth becoming more widespread.

Flowering time: Late spring.

Relatives: *S. aucuparia* 'Fructu Luteo' is a golden-berried form, a wide-spreading tree eventually. *S. aucuparia* 'Sheerwater Seedling', by contrast, is a somewhat corsetted, erect tree which will rarely outdo a spread of 4m (12ft) despite considerable height – 10m (30ft).

Cultivation: Best in sun or light shade with fertile, well-drained but moist soil. Will grow in difficult situations, as witness the wild specimens holding their own in cracks in rockfaces. Fireblight is a threat in some parts.

Propagation: The species grows quickly from seed; forms are increased by grafting or by cuttings.

CALAMITOUS CONDITIONS

THE PLANET Earth is a very fertile place, there being only one or two areas that are totally devoid of plants. Parts of Antarctica with soil that is permanently frozen to a depth of nearly 1km (about ½ mile) are plantless; where active volcanoes create high ground temperatures, plants are absent for a

This coastal garden makes use of tough, native plants such as *Crambe maritima*, which flourishes beside the sea and has a strong architectural form

time but they rapidly recolonize when ash and debris cools. Shifting desert sands may hinder the growth of plants, but when stabilized and after rainfall, they are home to a miraculous flora which quickly grows and blossoms. Your garden, however difficult, comes a long way after these environments.

However bad the conditions, within reason,

there are plants that can survive and in time a varied community is built up. The worst situation a gardener is likely to have to face is the kind of debris and destruction that builders leave behind on a new housing site – compacted ground with lots of hard rubbish on top and concealed below the 'top soil'.

Do you have a disaster area?

Most disaster areas are man-made. Perhaps most daunting might be where houses have been built over areas which were formerly industrial sites. Occasionally large areas of concrete are left below ground. It is worth ensuring that there is an adequate depth of soil over concrete or compacted rubble; at least 30cm (12in) of reasonable soil is needed to start a garden. If you have purchased a newly-built home you can be almost guaranteed to have a minor disaster area for a garden. Builders have a way with soil. For them it is a surface to drive on, reshape, and stand buildings on. They parch it, waterlog it, compress it, turn it over, and push it all over the place. In the process nearly every scrap of natural structure is choked out of it. Slag heaps of former coal mines having been levelled and built on will provide a rootrun that is at first less than nutritious. However, it is usually well-drained and with a reasonable cover of soil can support plant growth. Most plants have a wide system of roots and these tend to specialize to an extent. Often those roots nearer the surface are busy collecting rich nutrient supplies, whereas the deeper ones are imbibing water with lesser quantities of soluble chemicals.

Natural communities

If a patch of ground is left bare, without any human attention, a series of plant communities will take over in succession. First come the almost microscopic forms of life: algae, lichen and mosses. Next come the first flowering plants which may be things like groundsel and some grasses. Later, larger-leaved herbaceous plants join with the grasses in forming a lively cover in damp and shady areas. Ferns may come along too. Thereafter, the first shrubs and trees will get a toehold and eventually a woodland cover is established, its character depending on the soil type.

Coping with calamitous conditions

In real disaster areas, two or three points need to be firmly borne in mind in order to make progress. The first is that it is the *ground* that you are tending. Devote most of your efforts towards improving soil structure and health. Garner all forms of organic material and either introduce them directly to the top soil or compost them before doing so. Building up the precious top few centimetres/inches so that they become rich in humus and open in structure is vital. Soil organisms – worms and other small and microscopic creatures – will become more plentiful and help to incorporate the goodness into the whole soil. Grit is also a great benefit in heavier soils.

The second point is that you must choose your first permanent plants from among species that are the toughest of the tough.

The third point is that some kind of show is needed to give you optimism for the future and cover the desolation at least for a time. This show is easily provided by the modest flowers that children often enjoy – quick-growing undemanding annuals. A blinding sheet of colour is rapidly produced with generous plantings of things such as eschscholzia via a packet of seeds. In California eschscholzias can colonize huge stretches of ground and make a dazzling, dramatic sweep of colour. In the garden, the usual colours are ranges of brilliant oranges, but

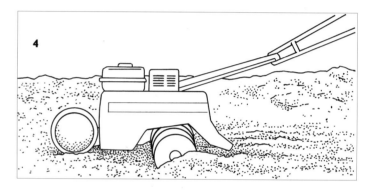

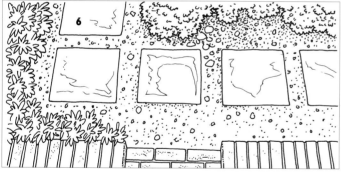

TACKLING CALAMITOUS CONDITIONS

Even if your site seems impossible, by following the steps below you can gradually improve it – and your situation. You may be surprised at how well it turns over!

1 *Remove mineral rubbish: bricks, concrete, metal, wood. (Bricks and rubble may be saved to use as hardcore under paths, patios and so on.)*

2 *Spray all tough weeds with systemic weedkiller. (Docks, nettles, bindweed, ground-elder.)*

3 *Test soil for pH levels (see page 57). You can have soil more fully sampled by professionals. This can be done by the Royal Horticultural Society. Ministry of Agriculture advisers will be able to suggest other testing agencies and let you know the fees charged.*

4 *Work over soil with rotovator or by digging. If possible incorporate compost or humus while doing this.*

5 *Spend one season sowing green manures and digging the resulting crops in when they have reached a full leafy stage.*

6 *Make paths and paved areas such as patios and use the good soil from such sites to bulk up the soil of growing areas.*

7 *If conditions are extreme consider building some raised beds and filling them with soil and compost that you have made or acquired elsewhere. Hanging baskets and other containers can augment raised beds.*

8 *If all else fails, perhaps where the ground is little more than concrete or rubble, the whole area can be converted into a patio with raised beds and other features such as ponds, sculptures, and trees growing in half-tubs or other large containers.*

RUBUS TRICOLOR

R. thibetanus

Description: A real toughie, but quite a dashing one; an extraordinary low-scrambling bramble that is handsomely evergreen with pointed, serrated, and textured leaves of a glistening green and stems gingery with hair. It grows quickly to provide dense ground cover. The flowers are like small single roses, just a sprinkle of them tucked in among the foliage. Unquestionably hardy.

Uses: Ground cover that can become impenetrable. Great for covering difficult sloping banks and rough places with poor soil.

Wildlife: Birds and small animals find plenty of cover.

Colour: Foliage rich green, flowers white, fruits like red raspberries.

Size: To 60cm (2ft) high, spread will quickly reach 3m (10ft).

Flowering time: Midsummer.

Relatives: *R. biflorus* and *R. thibetanus* (pictured) are two species grown for their winter stems which glisten silvery white. Totally without any thorns, *R. deliciosus* is a strong deciduous shrub with late spring blossom or large pure white flowers, easily the showiest of the genus and the reason for its name, which does not, as one might think, refer to the fruits as these are of little consequence and have no taste.

Cultivation: Needs little care once planted. As stems root where they touch the ground, the plant can leapfrog over the space and the main job is keeping its exuberance under control. Grows on most soils including impoverished ones. Will be happy in some shade as well as in full sun.

Propagation: Detach rooted pieces.

there are also creams and pinks. Once introduced they will self-seed and appear year after year so long as the soil is clear of other vegetation. One garden had had a patch that had been used for many years for burning rubbish. All the humus had been burnt out of the soil which was left an almost lifeless, ashy grit. Here an odd seedling eschscholzia germinated and soon the area was colonized and two or three generations of plants were produced each growing season for several years; there are still plants growing there now, many years later, when most of the ground has been reclaimed.

GREEN MANURING

Begin to rebuild a healthy structure in the soil by introducing as much humus-rich material as possible and then growing crops of 'green manure'. Green manuring involves planting quick-growers like mustard or red clover which also have root formations that help improve the soil. Green manures need to be used in conjunction with other composts and humus material, but they are especially useful for improving the structure of 'thin' soils such as sand or silt.

Clover and other leguminous plants such as peas, beans and lupins have nodules on their roots that are able to grab free nitrogen from the air in soil and employ it in forming plant tissue. The nodules are full of bacteria that do the actual 'fixing' of free nitrogen. When leguminous plants are dug back into the soil as green manure, the nitrogen products become available to other plants.

Once they have grown to a certain stage, they are turned into the soil to rot – leaves, stems, roots, flowers and all. If you are patient, this can repeated two or three times to build up the soil's humus content and hugely increase the number and activity of worms and other useful animal life. Allow yourself as long as a year if possible to restructure the soil by growing a series of plant crops to rotovate or dig in. Look for those that make fast sappy growth but think also of the roots that these plants produce. The work of the roots and their subsequent rotting into the soil is as important as the top growth.

It may well be that there is only a certain area of ground that needs to be treated to the green manure regime for an extended period. There may be other parts where you can begin the work towards making

GREEN MANURE PLANTS

Borago officinalis (borage)

Lolium perenne (rye-grass)

Sinalpis alba (mustard)

S. arvensis (charlock)

Symphytum officinale (comfrey)

Trifolium pratense (Red clover)

Trifolium spp.

Also:

Leguminous plants such as peas, beans and lupins

Grasses, various strong leafy ones

ROSA 'RAMBLING RECTOR'

Description: One of a number of rambler roses introduced at the beginning of the twentieth century and still very popular. A strong grower with a thick pattern of branches forming a tall spreading shrub which is very generously loaded with large sprays of small flowers. Fully hardy.
Uses: Makes a fine specimen against a tree, up a pillar, over a substantial pergola or allowed to make its own shape.
Colour: Flowers pure white, hips orange-red.
Scent: Good strong warm perfume.
Size: 6m (20ft) high, spread more.
Flowering time: Summer.
Relatives: 'Seagull', white, slightly larger flowers with golden stamens. 'Wedding Day', a prodigy of strength with large sprays of flowers, buff-apricot in bud, opening creamy and soon becoming pure white.
Cultivation: Plant where it will have enough room. Probably best in sunlight or in light shade.
Propagation: By layers or cuttings.

an attractive garden sooner. However, you need not be ashamed of the even growth of green manure crops. They are certainly worthwhile and you can be sure that the plants you introduce the following season have a very much better chance of getting away to a good start.

Making the most of it

FERNS

All ferns are surprisingly shallow-rooted plants and can therefore take advantage of many sites that others will find inauspicious. The hart's tongue fern, *Asplenium scolopendrium*, is one such. Provided there is moisture it seems to be able to spread a network of dark roots over a wide shallow area and begin to produce its splendid evergreen fronds. The male fern, *Dryopteris filix-mas*, is another tough character that will soon get a foothold and can florish in wide varieties of sites, both moist and relatively dry. It is a species that has mutated to good effect (see margin page 123 for names).

Ferns spread by the production of very fine dust-like spores in astronomic numbers. The air is full of these at times and any suitable spot will soon have its quota scattered on it to try to colonize. There are some small kinds that can get a foothold in hardly discernible cracks of wall (see page 180 and 182).

OTHER PLANTS

Many other early colonizers are prepared to reproduce in similar vast numbers and among flowering plants large crops of seed are produced. Wastage is huge because the plant needs to spread its bets with such poor odds. A single poppy seedhead can contain thousands of seeds. If these fall on broken soil they are likely to germinate readily and produce a further generation for the following season. However, if conditions are unfavourable the seed has the ability to lie dormant for a long period, waiting for a time when the soil is disturbed so that it can germinate and grow. There are recorded instances of at least an 80-year interval between seed falling and germinating!

Buddleja, Gorse and Broom Following the Second World War Blitz of London, when huge tracts of land were reduced to piles of rubble, one of the most surprising things was how quickly some plants established themselves in really very unpromising sites. Willow herb became a frequent sight with its abundant pinky red flowers producing yet more fleecy seed to blow about. But the real success plant was *Buddleja davidii*, which started to grow everywhere, sometimes at ground level, but often on broken walls, and sometimes high up on the sides of the remaining buildings. In difficult gardens it is well worth pleasing the butterflies by introducing *Buddleja davidii* forms such as the dark violet 'Black Knight', 'Empire Blue' or the Nanho Series, which are supposed to be dwarf but are only fractionally less tall and wide than their relatives. *B. globosa* grows as strongly as any form and is prolific, with round heads of deep orange. Just as quick to grow and produce good cover and colour in difficult soils and conditions are all the brooms. *Cytisus scoparius* is the common wild broom, which is brilliant, and there are no end of different-coloured hybrids. The double gorse, *Ulex europaeus* 'Flore Pleno', is a wonderful shrub in any garden but will be doubly welcome in calamitous conditions where it will soon establish an intricate mass of green spines and lots of golden blossom. The other broom genus is *Genista* with many excellent easy garden plants. Difficult terrain presents an opportunity to grow *G. hispanica*.

Lupins Long ago I had a largish patch of garden that needed quick covering. It was done with speed and great economy by sowing seed of the tree lupin, *Lupinus arboreus*. While the standard flower colour is a creamy yellow, I was surprised at the range of colour we managed to find. There were plenty of whites and golden specimens but we also had a range of mauve and pinky flowered specimens and bicolour forms. This is not a long-lived plant but individuals grow rapidly to make substantial wide bushes, and seed is produced very freely so that regeneration is no problem. Eventually the lupins were cleared but it was a pleasing interlude and it is an experiment well worth copying if you are faced with poor soil and bad conditions.

There are also some tough, quick-growing shrubs such as the evergreen *Rubus tricolor* (page 121) and the decorative forms of elder. If you need a lot of plants the *Rubus* will soon produce plenty of rooted layers, and cuttings of the elders root rapidly. Hazels and dogwoods are also suitable.

Among the brawny perennials you can certainly shortlist *Acanthus mollis*, *Rodgersia* species, *Aster amellus*, for dwarf colour, and *A. ericoides* and *A. umbellatus* as taller ones. There are other tall asters that grow easily in rough conditions and are not prone to mildew disease.

SAMBUCUS NIGRA
Elder

S. nigra 'Guincho Purple'

Description: This rapidly growing bush-tree can only be used in the largest of gardens perhaps as part of a mixed planting or in a mixed hedgerow. It seeds and can colonize large tracts, becoming a pestilential weed if given the chance . However, there are some attractive forms which are best used by cutting them down frequently to enjoy the fresh young foliage. Flowers are the familiar wide plates of blossom, the fruits are drooping bunches of shining juice-filled balloons. Too hardy.

Uses: Informal hedging or shrubberies. The cultivars are fine foliage plants.

Colour: Creamy white flowers, purple-black fruit.

Scent: Flowers have that pleasing, but difficult to define, perfume that is given also to elderflower cordials.

Size: 6m (20ft) high and wide, coppiced plants will reach about half this.

Flowering time: Early summer.

Relatives: *S. nigra* 'Aurea' has the typical pinnate foliage but in a rich golden yellow. 'Guincho Purple' (pictured) has very rich purple foliage with darker stems and flowerheads. f. *laciniata* is a rich green colour with each leaflet much cut, giving a ferny appearance.

Cultivation: Grows best in fertile, moist soils, but is not demanding. To get the best results from the cultivars, either cut the bushes almost to the ground in the winter, or prune out all the old wood.

Propagation: The easiest way is to take hardwood cuttings about 40cm (16in) long and insert two thirds into gritty soil, or even just where you want the new plants to grow!

SOLVING EVER

S ECTIONS ONE TO three covered the extremes of situations that are found in gardens. Fortunately most of us do not have gardens that are entirely made up of insurmountable problems – normally they are just next door's cat and the children! This is not to say that there are not difficult corners that can be a challenge for plants. Sometimes difficulties are created by our own actions – patios, paths and other dry surfaces can alter the balance of soil life and the distribution of moisture – sometimes it is the presence of something unalterable – a tree with a preservation order or a tall building next door that develops problem areas.

Work load

The secret of enjoyable gardening is that the garden should need just that amount of work which is pleasurable, and certainly should never threaten to make you into its slave. There is truth in the maxim that one should never take on more than one's partner can cope with. However, it is simple to agree that the work load should never be too onerous; what is more easily overlooked is the human condition: we age, we change our ambitions and we alter our responsibilities. It is, therefore, vital that we adjust the garden to our changing needs, perhaps making it more labour-saving as the years tick by. This does not mean that it becomes more boring; it may mean fewer annual bedding plants but it can also mean more glorious shrubs to vie with self-sufficient naturalized bulbs and strong herbaceous plants in providing the ever changing pictures of colour, form and texture.

Several chapters in this section deal with cutting down on maintenance. Some consideration is given to the 'hardworking' garden, which may be overrun by children or animals and is expected to be used as additional living space for the household. The problems of scale are tackled in two chapters: how to maintain a large garden with minimum labour is considered, as is the endeavour to make the very most of the too often very small space of a modern

Brick edging is used here to highlight the move from the formal lawn to the more natural woodland area

garden. Ways of making the most of lawns and open areas are also looked at.

AMBITION AND FAILURE

Perhaps the greatest danger facing the gardener is enthusiasm and a lack of restraint. Just as it is all too easy to walk through a garden centre and pick up a plant that was not on the shopping list, so it is too easy to plan masterpieces that have no basis in reality.

ROSA RUGOSA

Description: A shrub rose of bushy upright growth which spreads wider than its height. Bristly stems branch but are sturdily erect rather than arching. Leaves are fresh green, lined with impressed veins. Single flowers are large, up to 10cm (4in) across, with noticeable bosses of stamens; large bulbous hips like tomatoes follow in the autumn and look decorative for a long time. Fully hardy.

Uses: In shrubbery or border as a specimen, very handy as a screening and barrier plant and not infrequently pressed into service as an informal hedging plant which should prove fairly stock- and childproof.

Colours: Purple pink with pale stamens.

Scent: Crushed leaves have fresh scent, flowers are fully perfumed.

Size: 1-2m (3-6ft) high and across.

Flowering time: Summer into autumn in succession.

Relatives: *R. rugosa* 'Alba' is pure white. There are many fine hybrids with other rose types. *R.* 'Mrs Anthony Waterer' is a dense shrub with good rich foliage and well doubled flowers of rich crimson and rich scent. Height and spread 1.5m (5ft).

Cultivation: Easy on most soils that are not completely sodden all the time; mercifully free of rose diseases. Occasional pruning of older or broken wood may be necessary but is probably not needed.

Propagation: By seed or softwood summer cuttings.

ALCEA OFFICINALIS HYBRIDS
Marsh mallow

Description: A tall, downy herbaceous perennial, related to the hollyhock, with heart-shaped leaves soft with down and stems reaching chest-high with hollyhock-type flowers. Native to Germany, France and Britain.

Uses: Bold strong plant for any kind of soil especially if it is wet. Grows well by the seaside and manages in salty soils.

Colour: Pale pinks, purples, yellows and white.

Size: 1-1.2m (3-4ft) high, spread half this.

Flowering time: Late summer to early autumn.

Relatives: *A. rosea* is better known as the hollyhock.

Cultivation: Once planted in a wet spot will look after itself.

Propagation: By seed, which it will probably manage itself.

It is a common thing to become enthused by a planting in a public garden, a park, or just in a next door plot, and to feel the desire to reproduce it almost regardless of whether it fits in with the present or hoped for ambience of our own site. And, of course, gardeners should be on the look-out for good ideas and good plants, that is the way to learn, but restraint is needed and an acceptance that if we give in to temptation, surely forgivable once in a while, we must also be prepared for the extra work and occasional failure that may result. Restraint need not lead to dullness, unusual elements can be introduced and vivid colour can be used to lend emphasis to the whole. Sometimes the exotic touch acts as punctuation; sometimes the unusual focal point highlights the whole surroundings.

This section does not try to minimize the opportunities for experiment. What is aimed at is to exploit facets, to create interesting associations of plants with the idea of providing solutions and ideas for identifiable areas in the garden. These solutions and ideas do put an emphasis on a minimum of repetitious work, but not at the expense of interest. No garden is free of some work, but we can design for less.

The aim is also to help gardeners avoid making mistakes – forest trees in a tiny suburban garden, shrubs that need continuous careful pruning. And the aim is achieved by the same philosophy that runs through the whole book: plants have to be matched to their environments. Size is one of the most important factors. In a small garden it may mean choosing smaller or dwarfer forms of plants, the compact golden rods, rather than the old-fashioned tall ones, the dwarf delphiniums rather than those that would take their blueness to the blue skies above, the smaller rhododendrons of the *R. yakushimanum* blood rather than the larger old favourites like 'Pink Pearl', which can grow to 4m (12ft) high and through. On the other hand it would be a mistake to have everything miniaturized.

Design and restraint

In taking up some of the ideas suggested in this book the first step is always the same – look at the garden. Consider all its aspects. Decide whether it is small enough to be cultivated thoroughly all over, or whether it is too large to be intensively managed.

Gardening is the art of juxtaposition. One plant looks great; it looks the greater by being placed by a contrasting one of totally different habit, colour, or foliage type.

BIG GARDENS

The boundaries of big gardens, especially those furthest from the house, can be planted informally with trees and shrubs that will look after themselves and dominate their environment restricting weed

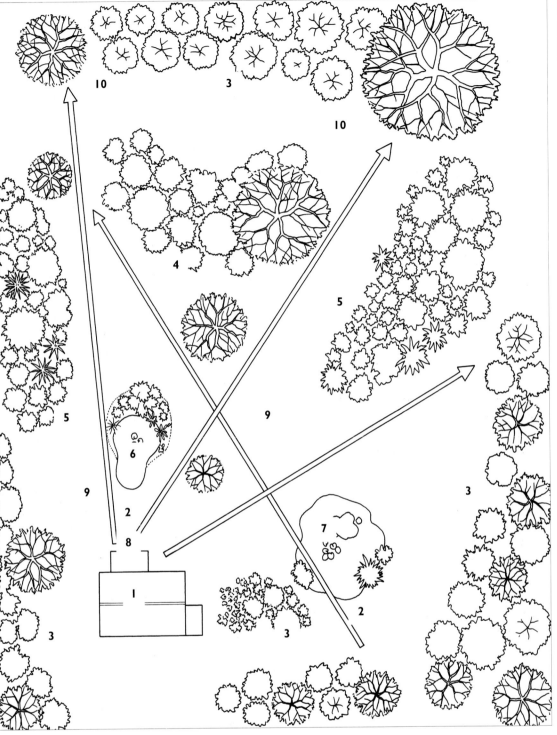

**DESIGN FOR A
LARGE GARDEN**

The basic idea is to provide a
unified plan giving a sense of space and
privacy, plenty of interest but not too
much labour.

1. *House*

2. *Vistas*

3. *Screens of trees and shrubs*

4. *Shrubbery*

5. *Herbaceous or mixed borders*

6. *Pond with bog garden*

7. *Pond or herbaceous border*

8. *Patio or conservatory*

9. *Close-mown lawns near house*

10. *Grass less closely mown
away from house*

JUNIPERUS × *PFITZERIANA* '**AUREA**'

Description: Evergreen, prostrate conifer of a bright colour and making a dense weedproof cover of thick foliage. Spreading strongly horizontally to form a flat-topped layered shrub with branch ends tending to arch downwards.

Uses: Can be called upon to serve in many places except in deep shade. Will manage well in poor soil and in fairly dry places as well as moister spots. Makes deep ground cover and can drape large rocks, walls, banks or awkward low protuberances such as tree stumps.

Colour: Golden, particularly bright new growth, green in depths of branches.

Scent: Brushing the foliage releases a resinous scent.

Size: After a decade or more can be 2m (6ft) high, spread 5m (15ft).

Relatives: *J.* x *pfitzeriana* is a similar flat-topped shrub with grey-green foliage.

Cultivation: Easy. Cut away broken or dead bits.

Propagation: By cuttings of current wood taken in autumn or winter.

growth. Most of the ground level at distant parts of the garden can be put down to ground cover plants, of which the most obvious are less formal grasses. If you prefer to have a well-kempt look, then perhaps make tree and shrub plantings in the character of a small arboretum with the grass kept down by an efficient grass mower. Here you are not aiming at a close lawn-type sward, so the cutting will not be a scalping job and will only need doing a relatively few times each season.

The simple garden plan suggested here for a large garden illustrates some of the points that ought to be considered with labour-saving being a primary concern. It is meant as an *aide-mémoire* rather than a particular plan.

ROOMS IN GARDENS

There is a common tendency to design a garden as a series of smaller gardens or outdoor rooms: a well known example of this is Hidcote Manor in Gloucestershire. Such an approach can be useful where the scale is large and there is a need for intimacy, it is less sensible in small modern gardens where it is the illusion of greater space that is really

SORBUS VILMORINII

Description: One of the daintiest and best of an interesting and beautiful genus; a perfect, fully hardy deciduous shrub or small tree. The pinnate leaves are made up of as many as 31 neat little oval, gently serrated leaflets. The effect is of a ferny lightness. Small flowers in open

clusters some 8cm (3in) across are followed by round fruits that persist well into the winter months.

Uses: As a specimen plant, especially for a small garden.

Colour: Creamy white blossom, rosy fruits that pale with age to blush-pink then white.

Size: Eventually 6m (20ft) tall and wide.

Flowering time: Early summer. Fruiting from early to mid-autumn well into the winter.

Relatives: Mostly single-trunked trees, such as the rowans – splendid but not so dainty.

Cultivation: Grows well in an open position in most soils except those squelching with water.

Propagation: Take greenwood cuttings in early summer, or plant seed in autumn.

A dramatic effect is created in this very dry patio garden using well-placed cacti and minimalist decoration

LILIUM MARTAGON
Martagon lily

L. martagon var. *album*

Description: A strong, persistent bulb that has strong erect stems with distinct whorls of clean cut leaves. Flowerheads are narrow pyramids of hanging blooms with petals curled back. Can easily have over fifty flowers to a stem. Very hardy, it grows wild in Siberia and in many areas down to Balkans and across western Europe.

Uses: Naturalize in rough grass, in light woodland, at the back of borders and almost anywhere. Not a pot plant. One of the lilies that is happy in limy soils as well as acid ones.

Colour: Warm pink-mauve with darker spots, but colouring varies (see Relatives).

Size: 1-2m (3-6ft) high, spread of one plant only 30cm (12in), plant in groups or allow to increase.

Flowering time: Early summer.

Relatives: *L. martagon* var. *album*

(pictured) has white flowers, with some forms having some small dark dots. Var.*cattaniae* has very rich deep maroon flowers with a polished finish.

Cultivation: Plant bulbs with 10cm (4in) of soil over them in a well-drained spot. Bulbs can be lifted every two years some five weeks or so after flowering, carefully divided and replanted immediately. Warning: bulbs purchased from dealers may not put in an appearance above soil for the whole of the first season. They will be rooting below ground and will start work upstairs the following year. So be patient and take care not to dig them up. There are gardens with colonies that have been flourishing for up to a hundred years. These will have increased their spread by self-sowing seeds.

Propagation: Fresh seed germinates freely after a while. The seedlings will take up to seven years to flower.

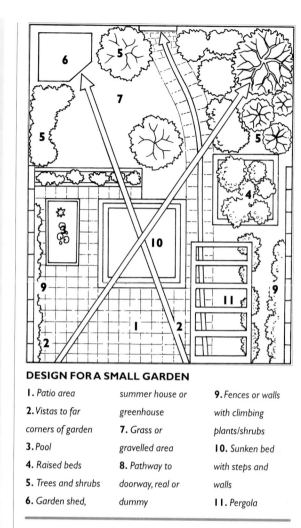

DESIGN FOR A SMALL GARDEN

1. *Patio area*

2. *Vistas to far corners of garden*

3. *Pool*

4. *Raised beds*

5. *Trees and shrubs*

6. *Garden shed,*

summer house or greenhouse

7. *Grass or gravelled area*

8. *Pathway to doorway, real or dummy*

9. *Fences or walls with climbing plants/shrubs*

10. *Sunken bed with steps and walls*

11. *Pergola*

required. A compromise is to create a unified whole with a series of areas that have differing atmospheres, and to be successful this will require care as plants or landscaping need to be positioned to suggest mystery, to entice the eye, to lead the foot from one part of the garden; as far as possible moving from one area to another needs to open up individual mini-vistas. Ideas can be quite simple – a pool may dominant one area, a bower another and a third can suggest a wild garden – but the transition from one to the other should not be totally abrupt, although it may be physically defined. Excellent physical separators include a low interior hedge, even of quite short length, a half screen of trellis overgrown with roses and clematis, or a clump of shrubs. Focal points created by specimen trees or shrubs, or by artifacts such as a large pot, a sundial or a bird bath help concentrate the eye and produce different centres of interest.

The plan shown suggests some of the features that you may wish to incorporate in a smaller garden. The basic idea is to try to create a unified whole but give plenty of suggestions of intimacy, hidden areas and surprise while also trying to give an impression of greater space.

COPPICING

It is important to have the occasional very bold plant highlighting the remainder by its size and character. This can be done without planting something that has to be continually hacked back to keep within unnatural limits. Some, such as the fine foliage plant, *Melianthus major*, can be cut back at the very beginning of spring if the winter has not already done the job. It is really a shrub of some 2m (6ft) high, but can be coppiced to get good strong growth with the wonderful silver-green pinnate foliage so precisely veined and serrated that it borders on the artificial. The golden-leaved elders, *Sambucus canadensis* 'Aurea', *S. nigra* 'Aurea' or *S. racemosa* 'Plumosa Aurea' can all be coppiced in what may seem a drastic manner; the result certainly justifies the means, a wonderful fountain of golden yellow, perhaps especially effective in 'Plumosa Aurea' which has bronze-tinged young leaves, very finely cut. The purple-black hazels are also the better for this treatment once they have got established. These are *Corylus avellana* 'Fuscorubra' and the larger leaved *C. maxima* 'Purpurea'. Their leaves get much larger, darker and more polished following coppicing. It is not difficult cutting these bushes down once a year, and you end up with splendid pea-sticks or supports for taller herbaceous plants.

Even the modest golden privet will produce wonderful new growth with super foliage all gleaming in freshly minted gold. For a talking point you could try the same with *Paulownia tomentosa* and possibly manage leaves looking like umbrellas up to a staggering 1m (3ft) across.

Natural communities

In this section, it is less a case of looking at natural plant associations, those were dealt with in section one. Here, horizons are broadened: the plants may come from anywhere – the Alps, South Africa, Asia, California or Britain and can be planted cheek by

PRUNUS SUBHIRTELLA 'AUTUMNALIS'
Winter-flowering cherry

Description: Small deciduous tree with a wide-spreading, somewhat flat top and ends of branches tending to arch downwards. Neat, serrated foliage is mid-green but takes on good autumn colours. It may start opening flurries of blossom in autumn and continue to do so in the milder weather throughout the winter until spring. Individual blooms are smallish, 1-2cm (½in) across, smaller in colder weather. Fully hardy.

Uses: An obvious choice for its winter interest and beauty. Not too large a tree for most smaller gardens.

Colour: Flowers white in winter but may be flushed pale pink in autumn and spring.

Size: 8m (25ft) high and across after many years.

Relatives: *P. subhirtella* 'Autumnalis Rosea' is pink.

Cultivation: Grows well in most soils that are not waterlogged.

Propagation: Grafted commercially. It is possible to air-layer slender branches.

jowl – just so long as they get along together and enhance each other's qualities. Expediency is the watchword.

PLANTS FOR COPPICING

Ailanthus altissima

Corylus avellana 'Aurea'

C. avellana 'Fuscorubra'

C. maxima 'Purpurea'

Eucalyptus in variety

Paulownia tomentosa

Rhus glabra

R. typhina

R. typhina 'Laciniata'

Rubus biflorus cockburnianus

R. thibetanus

Sambucus canadensis 'Aurea'

S. canadensis 'Maxima'

S. nigra 'Aurea'

S. nigra 'Guincho Purple'

S. racemosa 'Plumosa Aurea'

HARDWORKING GARDENS

Tremendous demands are placed on the areas around the outside of our houses; growing plants for enjoyment is only one of the activities that are likely to take place in the garden. Unfortunately the requirements of plants are often in conflict with other uses of the same space. Few will survive many rugby scrums even if they only consist of two 8-year-olds. Dog runs, vehicle maintenance, washing drying, camps in the undergrowth, bikes, trikes and go-carts, teenage parties and barbecues, all put pressure on the space and are almost inevitably going to become too closely involved with the plants, however accidentally. Plant life enjoys peace; the only benefit plants are likely to derive from a meeting with animal life is when it is the gardener's caring hand. The smaller the garden, the greater the problem.

Yet despite the fact that there will be conflict, few of us would dispute the importance of having some plants around the place and most people, even those who do not call themselves gardeners, like to have at least a little in the way of vegetative ornamentation in their patch.

Generally, the environment of buildings cannot avoid being hard: offices, shops, paths, roads or steps, all are constructed of tough, usually angular materials. Plants are vital for softening the effect; used in this context they are not a superfluous luxury. As well as being decorative, there are carefully designed plantings that are intended specifically to buffer us from inhuman environments: trees, shrubs and planted earth banks are used to shield us from noise and dirt pollution. By thinking about how and where we plant, we can make schools, offices and factories more pleasing places to work, and at home we can help to create a private Eden, a place of peace and privacy.

Considering the options

A private garden goes through various phases of use; priorities changing as the family grows up and children leave home. Each phase needs to be considered and planned for.

A home which has children living in it, or frequently visiting it, needs a playing area. A lawn is probably the best answer as an all-purpose surface for play and relaxation as well as for providing a framework to the rest of the garden. In the absence of children, and in smaller gardens, a gravelled area can be attractive, utilitarian and less labour-intensive. (Lawns and Alternative Open Areas, page 186, fully considers a wide range of alternatives to lawns.)

A children's playing area may well be used as a clothes' drying spot, with the ground being paved, gravelled or well covered with shredded bark. The grade of bark used in public amenity areas, such as children's playgrounds to provide soft landings, is the largest of the three sizes normally produced, the smallest being sometimes listed as 'powdered', and

the medium-sized, which is probably the most popular for garden-bed use, is of pieces predominantly about 2.5cm (1in) across and called by some large manufacturers 'pulverized'.

There certainly need to be some hard surfaces where children can play and adults take their ease. Pathways used by young children will be far more serviceable if they are made of level paving rather than gravel or bark.

Plants close to a youngster's favourite playing areas are best selected for their long-suffering and hardy characteristics as well as their child-friendliness. Low hedges or screens of one of the smaller-leaved laurels are a good choice. Shrubs such as *Viburnum tinus*, privets and *Euonymus fortunei* cultivars are also likely to cope better than most. Thymes, heathers and creeping ground-cover plants such as periwinkles, or on a smaller scale *Erigeron karvinskianus (E. mucronatus)* are likely to survive better than more delicate items.

ALCHEMILLA MOLLIS
Lady's mantle

Description: Tough herbaceous perennial with very attractive foliage and loose frothy sprays of blossom. The rounded leaves have up to nine rounded outward-curving lobes. They are soft green, made lighter by the cover of fine hairs that hold water in the centre of each leaf like a polished jewel. The leaves appear in spring, by midsummer there is a mound of foliage, above this the many flower stems hold their galaxies of tiny stars. Completely hardy.

Uses: A useful and hardworking auxiliary in the border in both dry and wet soil. Can be used as a ground coverer and is a constant stand-by for the flower arranger.

Colour: Fresh grey-green foliage, limey yellow flowers that die to rusty brown.

Size: Height and spread 50cm (20in).

Flowering time: Midsummer.

Relatives: *A. conjucta* is smaller with pleasing foliage, this time with leaves so indented as to be star-shaped. They are bright green but with some hairs, especially at the margins, which glisten silver. Loose bunches of lime-coloured flowers have outsize outer calyces. Cut when fresh, these stems can be dried for winter décor. *A. alpina* (Alpine lady's mantle) forms smaller mounds, 15cm (6in) high. It can be grown on the rock garden where it will manage well enough with dryish soils.

Cultivation: Grows in all but stagnant boggy soils. Is happy in full sun or in partial shade. With winter the leaves die off but can persist in fawny brown colours. If you want to tidy these, they are best cut off, as pulling may bring parts of the crown away.

Propagation: Usually plants produce a bevy of self-sown seedlings. It is not worth the trouble of dividing clumps. The problem may be to contain the number rather than to increase them.

Making a hardworking garden

A hardworking garden needs maximum performance from all its constituents, with the least input of work. This applies to the infrastructure as well as the planting schemes.

HARD LANDSCAPING

Hard landscaping is necessary to get around the garden in good weather and foul. For a multipurpose garden, this means having sensible and attractive looking paths and standing areas that are free of water in the rainiest times. Brick, imitation

Full use is made of all the available space in this small Mediterranean garden. A pond provides a focal point around which low-growing bulbs and lavender are planted. Pots are used for tender plants

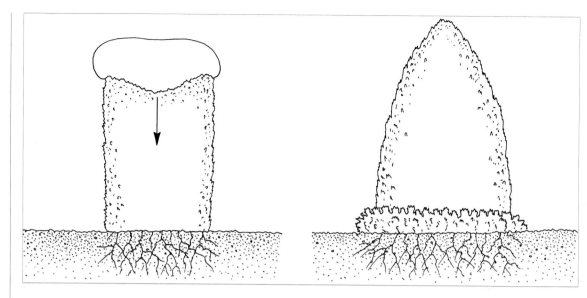

HEDGE SHAPES

The profile of a hedge should be such that the bottom is clearly wider than the top. Thus the bottom twigs get their share of light and will remain healthy and the hedge is somewhat less prone to weather damage by wind or lodged snow on the top.

BORAGO OFFICINALIS
Borage

Description: Hardy annual herb that grows rapidly to form a large clump with oval leaves, stems and flower buds all bristly. It has lots of multi-flowered sprays.

Uses: Large herb for filling space; a focal point from late summer. Young leaves can be plucked and used in iced or hot drinks, chopped they can be used in salads or in soups.

Colour: Bright gentian-blue flowers, often turning pink-red on dying.

Size: 90cm (3ft) high, spread 30-40cm (12-16in).

Flowering time: Second half of summer well into autumn.

Cultivation: Easy, tough annual, best in well worked soils in a sunny position.

Propagation: Sow seed under cover in spring, plant out young plants when easy to handle. If they are allowed to seed, they can produce their own crop of seedlings.

York stone or gravel laid over free-draining hardcore should serve.

A patio area, for the children to play, for relaxing, alfresco dining or for entertaining, adds a further dimension to the garden. Plan it with the main use in mind – a play area does not want obstacles to trip up toddlers, a grown-up's retreat can have semi-permanent containers and even one or two paving stones missed out for planting up.

A patio is often seen as an essential adjunct of house or garden. It should be of as generous a size as practical. It needs to be able to house chairs, table and toys easily. An oblong or L-shaped one is usually much more visually attractive than a square one. If one or more sides are bounded by low walls these can be utilized by children and others as seating accommodation and a variety of other uses.

A pool adjoining or close to the patio area may be an attractive feature for grown-up families, the dangers with young children being obvious. However, a little forward planning can be done. A sand bed made with brick sides and concrete can be converted to a pool when the children have given up buckets and spades. The concrete pool should have a base slightly sloping to a drainage hole which can take surplus rain water away quickly. This can be bunged up when the conversion to a pond takes place.

A small summer house/garden shed/play house or even a sheltered arbour could be incorporated into the garden design and stationed not too far from the house. This may be a godsend for children to play in when the weather is not being cooperative. Some garden sheds made of wood can be very attractive and are made more so when flanked by trellis and climbing plants. Play houses get outgrown quickly, the children are likely to be as happy with a shed that houses the patio furniture over the winter.

DISGUISES

Fuel tanks, rubbish bins, garden sheds and compost areas all need disguising. Painting may help to soften the impact of some of these awkward items but colours should be chosen carefully. Green is often imagined to, but rarely does, disguise items we would prefer to fade into the background. Drabs, shades of brown, tans, greys, many with some green in their make-up, are usually more effective. More important are their tonal values, how light or dark they are. If the tones match or are close to those of the surrounds there is a better chance of the object receding into the background.

It could be better to cover unsightly objects with suitable plants. There is a wealth of climbers and scrambling plants, all prepared to do the job. However, plantings do not quickly obscure the warning red of gas bottles or the white of large fuel tanks. In this case plan some simple, sensibly coloured screening structure which can then be

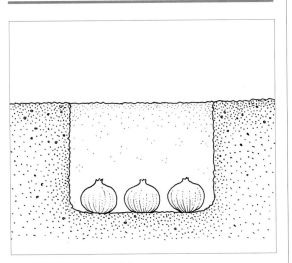

PLANTING DAFFODILS

When planting daffodils do not leave bulbs too shallow, this will encourage them to split up into lots of small bulbs which are able to produce leaves but have not the resources to form flowers. Plant your bulbs in holes that are at least three times the depth of the bulb, measuring from base to nose-tip.

AQUILEGIA VULGARIS
Columbine,
Granny's bonnets

Description: This herbaceous perennial is the wild blue aquilegia of much of Europe including Britain. The true species is a pleasing plant with short spurs but in the garden it is the hybrid series that are favoured, the strains closest to the species are dominated by dark blue, slightly mauve pinks and white. The more sophisticated hybrids are to be found in a wide variety of colours. If you want to maintain a colour strain careful self- or cross-pollination of similar flowers needs to be undertaken as the genus is noted for its permissive attitude towards interbreeding. The classy grey-green foliage is divided and, with the older leaves removed, always looks attractive.

Uses: Can be used in the border as a feature or as a filling plant between larger items. It can be used more informally and allowed to naturalize.

Colour: Basically rich blues and lilac pinks but includes albinos.

Size: To 1m (3ft) high in bloom, but with foliage about half this, spread 50cm (20in).

Flowering time: Early summer.

Relatives: One of the most distinct forms is A. *vulgaris* 'Nora Barlow' with curious doubled fussy short-spurred flowers in red but with cream or pale green petal tips.

Cultivation: Plant as young pot plants or sow seed in pots or in situ. Young seedlings can be moved more successfully than large plants. Specimens will last a few years and will normally produce a welter of self-sown seedlings.

Propagation: By seed sown when ripe or when convenient. To maintain colour lines self-pollinate good specimens, tag the flowers and use only this seed.

used as a plant support. Allow plenty of room for necessary replenishment and maintenance work. Pick your screening plants with care: think about their round the year appearance and the amount of work involved in keeping them tidy. The Russian vine, *Polygonum baldschuanicum*, is famed for its speed of growth and can be beautiful when covered with frothy creamy flowers alive with bees, but its aspirations do not end when it has comfortably obliterated your tool shed.

When erecting any structure to be used for plant support, ensure that it will be able to cope with not only the weight of climbing plants but the stress caused when wind pushes against the whole, a great multiple sail area of foliage and stems. Snow may be another hazard. The material of the structure is best if strong enough to support the plants without too much need for regular maintenance. Using pressure-treated timber of good quality should ensure a 20–30-year life even without recoating. Rotting is most likely in the topsoil level where there is the greatest concentration of soil bacteria. Posts held by metal holders or concrete should last.

LAWNS AND PLANTS

While it is not vital to restrict the lawn shape to an oblong, make sure that it is easy to mow and to keep edges tidy. This will mean avoiding planting too many trees or small beds within the grassed area. A lawn that has to act as a football stadium must be made of tough grasses. No point in trying to create a bowling green of miniature fine grasses. Choose mixes that are recommended for hard wear, such as the leafy strains of rye-grass which hold their own and still look green.

For the hardworking garden, major planting schemes may be planned to last for a decade or more. Plant types need to be balanced and year-round effect needs to be considered. It is easy to choose shrubs and trees that can provide two high-lighted periods of interest – in flower and fruit, or giving a blaze of autumn colour. And there is a substantial shortlist of shrubs and small trees together with bulbs and herbaceous plants that once planted will need little attention. In a hardworking garden, the soil should be covered with plant life or heavily mulched to a depth 8-10cm (3-4in) with material such as shredded bark that once placed in position can last for three seasons. This means that weeding and watering is kept to a minimum. No staking of plants is envisaged.

Choosing the plants

Plants must give maximum effect for minimum effort. There are so many calls on time and energy that the garden as far as possible has to look after itself. Bold hardy plants are ideal. Forget annual bedding schemes, they mean work. Avoid the sort of

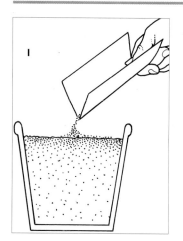

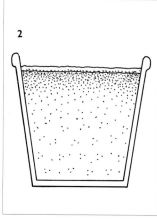

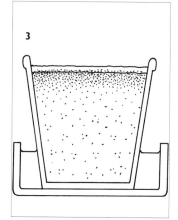

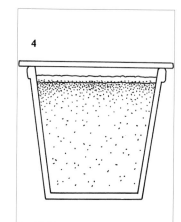

SEED SOWING IN VERMICULITE

1 Sow seed on vermiculite or perlite in small pots.

2 Cover with a thin layer of vermiculite.

3 Stand the pots on capillary matting or place them in a saucer to soak up plenty of water. (Don't leave them knee-deep in water for too long.)

4 Cover the pots with clingfilm or a sheet of glass or perspex.

Vermiculite has masses of advantages over ordinary compost when it comes to raising seedlings. The conditions are just about perfect for most seeds. The vermiculite takes up the right amount of water from below while still keeping enough air around the roots. Its surface does not sprout bitter cress or go mouldy. It does not even grow moss as quickly as ordinary composts, so seed that takes a year or more to germinate has

all the time it needs. There is no need for watering from above and so no disturbing the seed. When the seeds germinate damping-off is less likely in this sterile medium with its enclosed air. The young seedlings can be moved when still only with cotyledon leaves or more easily when the first true leaf is showing. It is easy to lift them individually from the lightweight granular material without breaking tender young roots or disturbing

remaining seeds. Prick out into open-structured compost.

Vermiculite can be left in its pack for years without deteriorating, whereas composts lose their freshness and go sour after one season at the most. If you have been tempted to use old compost and have achieved only poor germination, the compost may well be to blame. Discard old compost on a garden border, where it will condition the soil, and try vermiculite.

bush roses that need annual pruning and repeated spraying to be kept healthy and give good results. And don't go for the fast-growing option without careful consideration: leylandii will make a quick good hedge, but to remain within bounds it needs someone standing over it with the power clippers to ensure that it does not start reaching for the sky.

TREES

Trees give a sense of permanence. Almonds look lovely in bloom early in the year but are quite ordinary out of flower, so choose instead an ornamental cherry or apple. Flowering cherries are wonderful in bloom, can look very respectable throughout the year, and will dress themselves with overall colour in autumn before dropping leaves. Popular *Prunus* 'Kanzan' can be hugely prolific with rich pink blossom, but its form is less pleasing than some: it grows upward like an umbrella blown inside out. Eschew the candyfloss allure of 'Kanzan' and opt for kinds such as *P. × yedoensis*, the Yoshino cherry, a round headed tree with spreading and bending branches carrying plentiful crops of pink buds that open a paler shade or become near white in early spring before the dark foliage in unfurled. Thinking of winter effect, *P. subhirtella* 'Autumnalis' is well-named. This spreading rather flat-topped tree has arching branches that decorate themselves with flurries of smallish white or pink-flushed blossom from late autumn in mild intervals, through until spring. Its autumn foliage is reasonably colourful.

Among the ornamental apples are those with dark purple leaves and rosy red blossom and crops of crab apples in the autumn. *Malus* 'Profusion' is one such beauty, making a mature tree some 8m (25ft) high and wide, but attractive from being planted as a stripling. *M. floribunda* is magic each spring. It makes a spreading rounded small tree with an intricate pattern of branches. In spring the red buds begin to open to display pale pink flowers, an irresistible mix. Then the leaves are a clean green and autumn brings a crop of miniature yellow fruits.

HEDGES

Hedges are the first consideration. Avoid leylandii, privet and, on a smaller scale, *Lonicera nitida*. Choose instead evergreens such as holly or yew which you can get away with cutting only once a year. Both are

BUDDLEJA DAVIDII
Butterfly bush

B. davidii 'White Bouquet'

Description: One of the fastest-growing shrubs and exceptionally easy. It colonized war time bomb sites and can be seen growing on buildings where there would appear to be no possibility of life or nourishment. Long, dark green leaves with a grey cast, partially due to the rough surface, white-felted below. Long, pointed, and arching panicles of small crowded flowers in various colours. Deciduous but may hold on to youngest smallest leaves into winter. Unquestionably hardy.

Uses: Will rapidly fill a sunny spot. See Wildlife.

Wildlife: Probably the most famous of butterfly plants. Also attracts bees and less glamorous insects.

Colour: Mauves, purples, crimsons and white (see Relatives).

Scent: Sweet scent.

Size: To 5m (15ft) high and across, but can be pruned back to somewhat lesser dimensions.

Flowering time: Midsummer into autumn.

Relatives: *B. davidii* 'Black Knight' dark violet-purple flowers; 'Dartmoor' reddish purple; 'White Bouquet' (pictured), white. *B. alternifolia* has narrow grey-green leaves and slender falling stems enwreathed with clusters of perfumed lilac flowers. *B. fallowiana* has arching stems and foliage that is noticeably silvery especially when young. Old leaves become dark green. Fragrant flower panicles are 20-40cm (8-16in) long and lilac or white. It is slightly more tender than other species.

Cultivation: Allow plenty of space. Soon established and then should be cut back ruthlessly at the end of winter. The new growth will produce the better blossoms. If seed is allowed to drop you may find you have lots of seedlings but these may not be as good as the original named form.

Propagation: Easily propagated from prunings thrust into preferably gritty soil. Use pieces as thick as a pencil and approximately 30cm (12in) long, inserting two thirds into the ground.

excellent long-term hedges with rich colouring and able to form an impenetrable barrier. Remember that all parts of yew are poisonous. A very good evergreen alternative is *Viburnum tinus* (page 250), trimmed once a year in spring. It will provide a dense mass of dark green and usually a continuous show of blossom from late autumn through to spring. A large number of plants can be produced by layering. Beech hedges, while not truly evergreen, will, if kept clipped, retain a cover of dead brown leaves looking warm through the winter. You get a better effect with two clippings a year.

DIGITALIS PURPUREA
Foxglove

D. x *mertonensis*

Description: Biennial hardy plant forming rosettes of rough, grey, pointed leaves in the first year and then sending up the familiar one-sided spikes of tubular flowers with spotted mouths. There are strong strains such as the Excelsior hybrids which produce tall spires with flowers all round the stem. A native to most parts of Europe.

Uses: Groups at the back of a border; it may be naturalized between shrubs, by hedges or in woodland-type conditions.

Wildlife: Attracts bees and other flying insects.

Colour: Purple-red or white, and multicolours in white, creams, pinks, purples and reds.

Size: 1-1.5m (3-5ft) high, spread 60cm (2ft).

Flowering time: Summer.

Relatives: *D. lanata* is a very attractive short-lived perennial with deep green, textured leaves and well packed erect spikes of narrowish cream flowers sometimes lightly marked purple.

D. x *mertonensis* (pictured) is a perennial hybrid which reproduces from seed without much variation. It has tapering columns of large flowers above a rosette of rich grey-green leaves, the flowers are an interesting warm raspberry-red but with coppery tones.

Cultivation: Sow seed where you want plants or in pots and prick out. Do not plant closer than 40cm (16in) apart. If you want to maintain particular colour strains, eliminate unwanted colour forms immediately they come into bloom, otherwise insects will cross-pollinate. In semi-shade or light woodland conditions colonies of white foxgloves look most effective; best pull out all other colours within short insect flight of the whites. Mark any especially good white forms and then scatter their seed in preference to others.

Propagation: See above.

White busy lizzies are used to lighten this cool ivy-clad screen

SHRUBS

For interest all the year round, select a good mixture of evergreen and deciduous shrubs. In borders and shrubberies include evergreens such as flowering *Berberis darwinii* (page 146) and *B.* × *stenophylla*. For year-round effect but especially for some winter colour include *Eleagnus pungens* 'Maculata' with its vivid golden-variegated foliage. Consider, too, some of the dwarfer conifers such as *Thuja occidentalis* 'Rheingold', which makes a neat rounded cone of golden-green foliage that becomes decidedly tinged with orange-brown in winter. For coloured winter bark effects choose *Cornus* species see page 98.

The viburnum genus contains both evergreen and deciduous shrubs that require minimum attention. Some of many include the evergreens, *V.* × *burkwoodii*, *V.* 'Anne Russell', *V.* 'Park Farm Hybrid', *V.* × *carlcephalum*, *V. carlesii*, *V. davidii*, *V. rhytidophyllum* and ever-faithful *V. tinus*. Deciduous kinds will include the *V. farreri* types and the *V.* × *bodnantense*

GERANIUM MACRORRHIZUM
Hardy geranium

G. macrorrhizum 'Spessart'

Description: Very strong, hardy herbaceous perennial with globe-trotting proclivities. Handsome, semi-evergreen foliage – rich green and rounded and divided – makes a dense ground cover. Takes on red tints in autumn. Strongly coloured flowers for weeks.

Uses: Excellent ground cover that will defeat normal weeds.

Wildlife: Shelter for ground eating birds and other small animal life.

Colour: Shrieking magenta.

Scent: Leaves are sharply aromatic if bruised.

Size: 30-40cm (12-16in) high, spread 60cm (24in).

Flowering time: Late spring to midsummer.

Relatives: A number of forms have been named, including 'Ingwersen's Variety' and 'Spessart' (pictured). *G. macrorrhizum* 'Album' is a fine contrasting form with large white flowers.

Cultivation: Will grow well in any but sodden land. A few plants will cover a wide patch.

Propagation: By seed raised in pots and seedlings planted out when of handy size. An alternative method is cuttings of semi-ripe stems in summer.

HARD-WORKING SHRUBS FOR FOLIAGE AND EFFECT

Brachyglottis 'Sunshine'

Caryopteris forms

Cistus spp.

Choisya ternata

C. ternata 'Sundance'

Cotinus coggygria forms

Cotoneaster franchetii

C. horizontalis

C. lacteus

C. x *watereri*

Cytisus spp. and forms

Elaeagnus pungens 'Maculata'

Genista spp.

Rhus glabra 'Laciniata'

R. hirta (R. typhina)

Rosa rugosa forms

Rosa English Rose types

Skimmia japonica

Spiraea japonica 'Fire Light'

S. x *vanhouttei*

clones. Deciduous spiraeas such as *S.* 'Arguta', bridal wreath, are smothered with white blossom in spring, *S.* × *vanhouttei* may be a little later and is as generous, with many round dense clusters of white flowers. Forsythias grow quickly and provide lots of early colour. Although one is supposed to prune away a proportion of the flowered wood each spring, not many of us manage to do this and the bushes continue to bloom magnificently. The foliage is a little boring so the position should not be too prominent

LONICERA PERICLYMENUM
Common honeysuckle

L. periclymenum 'Graham Thomas'

Description: Very hardy, strong deciduous climber with oval, mid-green leaves with grey under-surfaces. The fast-growing stems twine themselves round each other or a support and become woody with age. The species is variable in flower colour and timing.

Uses: Can help to mask unsightly buildings or dead tree stumps, will intertwine into trees and shrubs giving them a second season of interest. Can drape a fence to become a virtual hedge, or can be grown up trellis against walls, on pergolas or, chocolate-box picture style, around the house door.

Wildlife: Attracts moths and other flying insects such as small beetles and, unfortunately, aphids.

Colour: From palish creams and yellows with pinks to very deep dark purples with reddish pink and orange-tinted golds.

Scent: Sweet perfume.

Size: Height and spread easily up to 8m (25ft) given the chance and support.

Flowering time: Early to late summer according to clone.

Relatives: *L. periclymenum* 'Serotina', Late Dutch honeysuckle, is a particularly rich-coloured kind in dark purple-red and pinky gold shades. 'Graham Thomas' (pictured) has flowers opening white and becoming a slightly buff-yellow. *L.* x *heckrottii* 'Gold Flame' is rich pinky gold with orange throat and some suffusion. *L. japonica* 'Halliana' is evergreen with highly scented white flowers in summer and autumn, the flowers becoming pale yellow. *L. tragophylla* has blue-green, rounded foliage and large clusters of bright yellow flowers in early summer.

Cultivation: Easy on all drained soils in sun or all but very deep shade. Best planted with a definite support to which it can attach itself. Maintenance can be minimal, perhaps restricted to removing such deadwood as you can manage, or you can cut out flowered pieces to encourage fresh growth. Can be clipped to keep all within sensible bounds.

Propagation: Easiest by hardwood cuttings taken in autumn, up to 25cm (10in) long and three quarters plunged into gritty soil.

(see margin list page 139, for more shrubs).

If you must have roses, restrict yourself to those that really need little or no pruning and are not subject to mildew and black spot diseases. Species such as the robust *Rosa rugosa* will thrive on neglect. Tough roses that will cope with poor soils and conditions include the Alba roses, *R.* 'Frühlingsgold', *R.* × *cantabrigiensis*, *R. eglanteria*, *R.* 'Paulii' and *R. pimpinellifolia*. For climbing roses you could choose many of the ramblers and such favourites as 'Cécile Brünner Climbing', 'Constance Spry', 'Leverkusen', 'Madame Alfred Carrière' and 'Maigold'.

It is sensible to pick some shrubs that have persistent berries; the pyracanthas can be colourful in fruit from autumn until spring when they will please yet again with frothy white blossom.

HERBACEOUS PERENNIALS

There are those herbaceous plants that, although once planted can be left to their own devices, may take a while to get going. These include the late-flowering *Anemone* × *hybrida* series. Drifts of these with elegant flowers in pink and white will require little attention apart from keeping clear of weeds — something that can usually be achieved by generous

bark-mulching. Monkshoods, *Aconitum* forms, are similarly long-lived and trouble free. This genus is poisonous and should not be near young children. The elephants' ears, *Bergenia* forms, are really tough and their large evergreen leaves ensure no awkward holes through the winter. The foliage can take on reddish hues and the bold spikes of flowers in rich rosy pinks and reds may start opening before spring really arrives.

GROUND COVERING

Ground covering plants help stifle weed growth and provide interest. Some are outstanding foliage plants such as the rodgersias (page 101) and the huge selection of hostas (page 247).

BULBS

Some of the hardier bulbs are really wonderful value. Daffodils, snowdrops and bluebells will come without fail each year, increasing in numbers and really giving our spirits a welcome lift. Choose from among the smaller daffodils for naturalizing as they look more in keeping and do better. *Narcissus cyclamineus* hybrids are early to bloom, persistent in flower, look dainty and have smallish leaves that die down early. Pick kinds such as 'Tête-à-Tête', with one or two golden flowers to a 15cm (6in) stem, 'Jumblie', a sister to the last but with longer crowns and petals reflexing more, 'February Gold', which blooms in early spring and stands about 25cm (10in) high, and 'Jenny', of similar height but with swept back white petals and trumpets of pale primrose fading to white.

LUNARIA ANNUA
Honesty, Silver dollar

Description: Biennial with serrated rough textured grey green leaves making a mound in the first year. The flower stems quickly rise up the following season and will provide several weeks of abundant bright blossom before starting to produce flat round seedpods. Individual flowers are of four petals, a simple design, but there are myriads of them able to provide an enchanted area. Then come the seedpods which when ripened delight children – and others – rubbing off the two outer coverings to reveal the shining silvery white circle of membrane.

Uses: Very useful in difficult semi-shaded spots – often dry – where very little else will survive. Here it can naturalize and maintain its territory year after year by copiously self-seeding. Dried seed-pods can be a long-lasting indoor decoration.

Colour: Violet-magenta shades, also white.

Size: 75-90cm (30-36in) high, spread of an individual 30-45cm (12-18in).

Flowering time: Summer.

Relatives: *L. rediviva* (Perennial honesty) is a smaller plant with lilac or white flowers.

Cultivation: Grow from seed and thin to about 25cm (10in) apart when the first true leaves appear. Choose a well-drained spot preferably with a touch of shade. The first plants will soon establish a right to permanent residence.

Propagation: Seed germinates very easily. It can be sown where you want plants.

This low hurdle-fence in the herb garden of Buster Ancient Farm, Hampshire, is a very good way of providing interest and introducing a change of tempo

SMALL GARDENS

IT IS THE very smallness of most new modern gardens that presents their greatest challenge. Making the most of small spaces requires thought and careful planning. Although it may seem best to go for everything in miniature, so that as much as possible can be crammed into the available space, this can produce a feeling of clutter. It is better to try to create an illusion of greater space; sometimes less is more. The same principle applies to the perimeter of the garden. Privacy is valuable and should be increased where possible, but to form heavy barriers all round a small plot may mean ending with little more than a feeling of claustrophobia. Success is measured by the extent to which the opportunities are maximized while the problems are minimized.

While there are the occasional very large scale problems – the local factory or an electricity pylon – which will be very difficult to overcome, most of the time, such is the density of house building to space available, it is simply our own property and that next door which are the most intrusive objects to be hidden from view.

Framework and infrastructure

The plan most likely to succeed is one that ensures that all parts of the garden are contributing something throughout the whole year. Out go beds of dahlias that will be empty of colour for more than half the year; a traditional herbaceous border is a non-starter – it takes time to get going in the spring, is at its best midsummer and soon collapses into an 'after the party' tiredness in the autumn. Of course, your choice depends also on the use you make of the garden. If you do not use it during certain times of the year then you can afford to stack the plants of other seasons more heavily.

Any plantings that blur the definite borders of the site will give it a chance to look greater than it is. Walls and fences can be stark and may serve to emphasize the small dimensions of a plot, on the other hand they can form a useful framework but, whatever, are much the better for being half dis-

guised by abundant plant growth. Clothed with creeping evergreens, such as interesting forms of ivy, they will be rendered more informal and more lively, and in front of this further plantings of shrubs, both deciduous and evergreen, will improve the scene: with skilful choice you could suggest a woodland edge or an interesting thicket. A gate or door in the wall, even if it is never opened because the wall behind is solid, will suggest space beyond, and appearance is all.

Hedges in small gardens

To some extent choices for hedges depend on the character of the property. The more formal the building the more correct and in keeping the clipped hedge and neat paths. It could be that the front garden is given over to a stricter more formal plan than at the back of the house. Formality may be extended to the extent of introducing a knot garden and having clipped shrubs climbing the house walls.

Hedges can grow strongly above ground and take up more breadth than planned; the same thing will be happening below ground with a network of greedy rooting grabbing all the sustenance. It is very easy for a hedge to take 1m (3ft) width of airspace and to influence a much wider width of the soil below. A slimline model that will do the same job of providing shelter and a lively backcloth is needed. The answer could be to run up a lightweight but sturdy fence of chain-link, trellis, or wood and cover this with evergreen climbers. Large-leaved evergreen ivies such as *Hedera colchica* 'Dentata Variegata', *H. c.* 'Sulphur Heart' (syn. 'Paddy's Pride') or *H. caneriensis* 'Gloire de Marengo' will clothe the support quickly and provide something that is half-screen, half-hedge.

These ivies are all enlivened with bright bold variegation, but our screen-hedge could be further enlivened by allowing other climbers to clamber in among and over the ivy. Clematis (see page 174) might be added and so too might be such exotics as the tuberous-rooted *Tropaeolum tuberosum*, with its

CREATING ILLUSORY SPACE

The eye is open to suggestion and is readily deceived by carefully placed screens and walls with windows and openings producing illusions of space in places beyond. One or more partial screens, formed by trellis or other material and jutting out towards the centre of the garden can be used to support climbers and other plants thus suggesting a sense of mystery in the hidden garden beyond. What is around the corner? Paths and other main parts of the infrastructure, will lead the eye into the garden and the distance. Diagonal lines of vista will make the garden feel longer than if they are taken directly down the centre. The illusion of greater length is enhanced by paths, pergolas or screens getting somewhat narrower towards the far end.

Brick walls, wooden decking and pots full of nicotiana, abutilon and succulents combine to create a comfortable and restful retreat in this city garden

ALLIUM SCHOENOPRASUM
Chives

A. schoenoprasum 'Forescate'

Description: Hardy bulbous or tufted perennial, its erect cylindrical dark green leaves forming neat clumps on top of which the flowers are borne as tight heads not unlike thrift (page 12).

Uses: Culinary for flavouring. Edging of borders or herb garden. Containers.

Colour: Pinky mauve.

Scent: Flowers lightly scented, crushed leaves have a chive/onion aroma.

Size: Dependent on clone, up to 30cm (12in) or more, the neatest are half this.

Flowering time: Early to midsummer.

Relatives: A. schoenoprasum var. sibiricum (Giant Chive) is larger leaved with rosy violet flowers. 'Forescate' (pictured) is rosy pink, 'Frulau' is a dwarf early flowering form.

Cultivation: Grows easily and enjoys, but does not need, chalk.

Propagation: Division of clumps early spring.

lobed nasturtium leaves and cup-shaped, flame-coloured spurred flowers. You could add the annual *Thunbergia alata*, black-eyed Susan, with round orange-gold flat flowers startlingly centred with staring dark brown centres.

WALLS AS GARDENS

Walls are the most under-used part of many if not most gardens. This is a shame. They are an ideal habitat for many attractive climbing plants. They are special places because of the shelter and warmth they can offer plants: it is possible to have climbers all the way up to the bedroom windows, there are also micro-climates at the wall bases that are much more inviting than the open garden for a range of plants. Wall plants are at eye-level and so more easily appreciated than those that we must bend down to study. Plants also add to the general attractiveness of the property and can be used to mask unsightly features. Finally, fully or partially clothing the walls helps to unify the garden and house.

Self-clinging climbers include the wide range of

ivies and the three forms of climbing hydrangea of which *H. anomala petiolaris* is the most often seen. There are also two similar related plants: *Schizophragma hydrangeoides* and *S. integrifolium.* Perhaps rather more familiar are the very ornamental vines, commonly but incorrectly grouped together as Virginia creepers. *Parthenocissus henryana* is one of the most decorative of these, its leaves divided into five leaflets with nearly-white veins showing clearly in the rich green or bronzed day to day colourings that become brilliant in autumn. *P. tricuspidata* 'Veitchii' has large leaves like an opulent ivy. They are green through the year, but turn every fiery shade in autumn.

Evergreen climbers can be useful to avoid an undressed appearance through the winter. Apart from the ivies, there are several evergreen clematis including the white-flowered *C. armandii* and *C. cirrhosa* with bell-like cream flowers. These and the evergreen honeysuckle *Lonicera japonica* are useful interest plants; the most popular form of the honeysuckle being *L. japonica* 'Aureoreticulata' with oval

POLEMONIUM CAERULEUM
Jacob's ladder

Description: A hardy, clump-forming herbaceous perennial with a very fresh look. The bright green pinnate leaves have over two dozen narrow oval leaflets and the upright hollow stems bear outward-looking open cup-shaped flowers with frank appeal.
Uses: Useful, quite long-lived plant for healthy well-drained soils in full sun or only light shade.
Colour: Bright blue with a hint of lavender.
Size: 45-60cm (18-24in) high, spread similar.
Flowering time: Summer.
Relatives: *P. carneum* is similar but pale lilac or pink in bloom; 'Apricot Delight' is unusual in tones of peach and apricot. *P. reptans* 'Lambrook Manor' is similar.
Cultivation: Easy. Plant early spring or early autumn. Can be tidied after flowering by cutting away flowering stems. This will preclude the appearance of a large family of self-sown seedlings.
Propagation: Easy from seed. This may be a better way of keeping stock fresh than dividing old plants which tend to ride high out of the soil.

leaves most clearly and decoratively marked by bright golden veining.

Not all walls are equally easy to clothe. The one on the shady side of the house is often left solely to the ivies. These will do well, but it is also worth adding some of the attractive large-flowered clematis hybrids such as the old favourite 'Nelly Moser';

BERBERIS DARWINII

B. x lologensis 'Apricot Queen'

Description: Evergreen shrub with glossy, mini-holly leaves. A rounded cloud-shaped bush which is transformed in blossom with every twig having its generous quota of rounded rich coloured, clustered flowers. Fully hardy.

Uses: A specimen bush or in a mixed border or shrubbery; can also be used to form a very good decorative hedge.

Colour: Lustrous dark green foliage, flaming orange-gold flowers.

Size: 3m (10ft) high, spread almost as much.

Flowering time: Mid- and late spring.

Relatives: *B. x lologensis* 'Apricot Queen' (pictured) is a very prolific, strong bush with arching stems of many crowded bunches of rich apricot-orange blossom. *B. x stenophylla* hybrids form upright hummocks of dark narrow foliage on arching stems enwreathed with round, golden orange flowers.

Cultivation: Easy in all but very waterlogged soils and although normally grown in full sun will not object to partial shade.

Propagation: The species by seed or cuttings. The hybrids by soft or semi-ripe summer cuttings.

out of the sun, the blooms do not lose colour. For early bloom, one of the *C. montana* cultivars will look good, *C. montana* f. *grandiflora* is larger than the type and has a mass of ivory buds and white flowers in spring; the foliage is green but opens with a purple-bronze cast. The golden hop, *Humulus lupulus*

'Aureus', with its limey yellow foliage can look well. *Schizophragma integrifolium* is another good choice. Its flowerheads are organized very like those of the climbing hydrangeas, with small fertile inner flowers and much larger showy sterile ones around the outside, but the outer ones are leaf-shaped unlike the round 'petalled' ones of the hydrangeas. Another unusual plant which will not mind the 'cold shoulder' treatment of a shaded wall is *Berberidopsis corallina*, the coral plant. This is an evergreen with rambling long-reaching stems and plenty of neat heart-shaped leaves and it has a long season from summer into autumn for the series of hanging globe-shaped flowers in brilliant coral-red. Its stems need tying in to trellis or other supports.

Side view

MAKING A SMALL ROCK GARDEN

1 *Choose a position in the open, well clear of trees or heavy shade. Preferably find a spot away from unnatural features such as fences and buildings.*

2 *Prepare the site to form a small outcrop appearance. Excavate soil to give a rise and dip, perhaps arranging for two high points, one much more prominent than the other, with an intervening valley.*

3 *Ensure there is good drainage. Drainage is of major importance – rock plants demand it.*

4 *The soil mix should approach as close as possible, by volume, 2 good loam, 1 leaf mould or similar form of humus, and 1 part grit or wash coarse sand.*

5 *Use rocks that are as large as possible: sandstone, limestone, slate or tufa. Arrange the pieces to appear as if they belong to one unified*

Plants for the base of a shady wall The base of a shady wall is not the site for every aspiring garden plant but there are some that will be happy here, including herbaceous plants such as *Galium odoratum*, the sweet woodruff, which makes thick ground cover and has its tiny starry white flowers in summer. It manages well in alkaline soils. Bolder effects are achieved with a clump of *Acanthus mollis* with its robust and large divided, shiny black-green leaves and unusual spikes of hooded flowers. And there is ground-elder. No, not the normal weed, but the variegated form, *Ageopodium podograria* 'Variegatum', which can be managed quite easily and makes a bright carpet of foliage that is so strongly variegated creamy white it will light up a dark corner. Other herbaceous plants could include

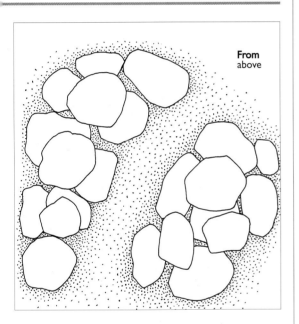

From above

piece pushing out of the ground. Strata lines or the main outline of the rocks should be parallel. Bury the backend of each rock at least one-third into the soil.

6 *Choose a 'key' or large stone, place it in position, then build backwards, adding the soil mix as you proceed.*

7 *Choose your rock plants and introduce them but do not plant too close; some remain small but others will spread widely.*

8 *Finish off the rock garden with a layer of rock chippings, grit or small stones.*

9 *It may be a good idea to isolate the rock garden by having an informal York stone or rock path to one side and a strip of gravel as a 'cordon sanitaire' around other areas so that grass or other plants do not invade easily.*

HELLEBORUS ORIENTALIS HYBRIDS
Lenten roses

H. foetidus

Description: Strong herbaceous perennials with an evergreen aspect and variously coloured blooms very early in the year. Dark green palmate leaves surround bunches of nodding bowl-shaped flowers that last for many weeks.

Uses: Best in semi-shade, but can be grown in a variety of sites and will cope with various soil types.

Colour: Basic colours range from pure white, creams, primrose-yellows, whites-flushed green, pure greens, pale to deep pinks, mauves to purples and various near black shades. Flowers may be uniform colour shades or can be spotted or very decoratively marked with dark maroon or purple-black. There are some with one colour on the outside and another inside. The dark ones may be further enhanced by a plum-like bloom.

Size: Varies but up to about 45cm (18in) high and wide.

Flowering time: Winter and early spring.

Relatives: There are named forms and seedling strains. Try to see the flowering plant before buying and so avoid inferior narrow-petalled and wishy-washy coloured ones. *H. foetidus* (pictured) and *H. argutifolius* are evergreen species useful as foliage plants and with masses of green winter and spring blossom.

Cultivation: Plant in deep humus-rich soil if possible, preferably in semi-shade. Plants are best left undisturbed. Check encroaching weed or larger plants. Early winter may be a time to cut away and dispose of all old leaves; this stops leaf fungus troubles and makes the flowering heads very much more accessible.

Propagation: Early spring, before new leaf growth, lift and divide chosen plants. Cut away any flower or old leaves and replant immediately. Save seed from good colour forms and sow immediately, prick seedlings out into pots or permanent spots when the first true leaf is fully developed.

some of the spurges, hostas and the lower-growing comfreys such as *Symphytum grandiflorum* with white flowers that are a brownish red in bud. The foam flower, *Tiarella cordifolia*, *Waldsteinia ternata* with yellow buttercup or potentilla-like flowers, and the Pick-a-back plant, *Tolmiea menziesii*, are others to try. Shrubs could include some of the hydrangeas if the soil is reasonably moist. *Skimmia japonica* could be used and is best in somewhat acid soils. Real toughies are the cherry laurels such as the tidy *Prunus laurocerasus* 'Otto Luyken'. Again *Euonymus fortunei* in its many forms will serve well in difficult conditions, and you could include *Mahonia*, too.

RUDBECKIA FULGIDA VAR. *DEAMII*

Description: This form is a strong, hardy herbaceous perennial growing strongly from soil level to form an erect but spreading plant of many stems with narrow, pointed, mid-green, hairy leaves and galaxies of blossom like large daisies for many weeks.

Uses: Excellent border plant, can be grown between shrubs.

Colour: Very rich gold daisies with almost black central cones.

Size: 1m (3ft) high, spread almost as much.

Flowering time: Late summer through the autumn.

Relatives: *R. fulgida* 'Goldsturm' is a ridiculously generous bloomer with countless narrow petalled flowers. It stands about 75cm (30in) high and about 45cm (18in) wide.

Cultivation: Strong rhizomatous roots enjoy moist soil and will spread to form a colony. After three or four years the centre of the patch could begin to be less active; the plants can be lifted, split and replanted every few seasons.

Propagation: Divide rootstock early spring.

Standard wisterias provide height in a tiny half-walled garden. (Another view of this Mediterranean garden can be seen on page 32)

Plants for the base of a sunny wall Sunny walls are home to all sorts of pleasant things including climbing and rambling roses, the climbing solanum, *S. jasminoides*, wisterias and passion flowers, as well as clematis hybrids and species, with their toes tucked into cooler shaded spots. Honeysuckles and grapevines, either productive ones or ornamentals such as *Vitis vinifera* 'Purpurea', further widen the choice. Perhaps also there is a spot for the relative of the kiwi fruit, *Actinidia kolomikta*, with its hydrangea-like leaves of plain green or splashed creamy white or wholly pink as if they had been dipped into paint pots.

Plants to have at the foot of the sunny wall include the showy South African bulbs *Nerine bowdenii*, *Amaryllis bella-donna* and maybe some of the little gladioli together with the Algerian iris, *Iris unguicularis* for winter bloom.

PERGOLAS AND PILLARS

The successful garden is about all three dimensions, all of which must be exploited in a small plot. Pergolas and pergola walkways with a central area enlivened by pillars of wood, metal, stone or plastic are ideal for filling the air. Energetic climbers can be allowed to clamber up the pillars and swarm across cross beams or loops of rope or chain linking uprights for a lighter effect. Shrubs that like a bit of borrowed backbone can be trained up some of the pillars: pyracanthas or ceanothus are suitable. Less manipulation is required by plants that form their own perfectly natural columns. There are the pillar-forming junipers such as 'Skyrocket', all very upwardly mobile and skinny as a supermodel. Then there are fastigiate growers which mean that even in a small plot there can be trees. *Prunus* 'Spire' is aptly named. It is a collection of tightly bound branches narrowly clustered and erect with plenty of pink blossom in spring and with colourful autumn foliage. *P.* 'Amanogawa' is larger with pale pink blossom, a tight column in youth but with middle-age spread taking some effect later.

Steps cutting down to a lower level rather than a simple slope can add to an illusion of space, within reason. A raised bed placed at a distance not only allows the cultivation of a wider range of plants but again emphasizes the third dimension.

ALPINES

Small plants have the benefit that many can be crowded into a small space, satisfying the gardener's urge for accumulation. Rock garden plants are so diverse that within a few square metres no end of interest can be created. A properly designed rock garden looks splendid and, to get the best effect, is best placed in as natural a spot as possible, not crowded in by house, walls, fences or pergolas. If your garden is full of man-made infrastructures then it is better to add another in the form of a raised bed to complement the surroundings and accommodate the alpines. Build the sides to some 40cm (16in) or

YUCCA FILAMENTOSA
Adam's needle

Description: A fully hardy, formidable architectural foliage plant with long spiky evergreen leaves in dark steely grey-green. A shrub but with rosettes of the leaves looking more like a fantasy giant grass.
The leaves have armed points and their margins are marked with finespun curling threads. A reliable bloomer with tall narrow panicles of larger rounded or tulip-shaped hanging bells that last for many weeks.
Uses: At all times a focal point, a piece of living sculpture.
Colour: Dark foliage, creamy white flowers.
Size: To 2m (6ft) high, spread 1.5m (5ft).
Flowering time: Midsummer until autumn.
Relatives: Other species are less hardy. *Y. filamentosa* 'Bright Edge' has pale gold leaf margins, 'Variegata' is similar perhaps a little paler. Both are worthwhile.
Cultivation: Full sun and well-drained soil. Little maintenance unless you want to cut away dying leaves – taking care not to get spiked by leaf ends.
Propagation: Root cuttings in winter.

149

Greys and whites emphasize the coolness of this tranquil courtyard garden

SALIX RETICULATA
Net-leaved willow

Description: An alpine willow that is entirely prostrate and has very handsome round leaves that are rich dark green, glossy and have a neat network of impressed veins. There are male and female forms; the males with upright catkins and the females with narrower ones. Sturdy stems spread across the soil surface rooting where they can. Fully hardy.
Uses: Most attractive in lower, damper reaches of a rock garden, in troughs or at the edge of low beds of small plants. Can drape low rocks and fall over wall edges.
Colour: Rich green foliage. Catkins; male, pale golden; females, pinky red.
Size: Only 5-8cm (2-3in) high, spread 25cm (10in) or more.
Flowering time: Spring.
Relatives: *S. herbacea* is even smaller with narrow branches at or even below soil surface, tiny rounded leaves and tiny powderpuff catkins. *S. x boydii* is an unusual upright small shrub with firm grey branches and close-clasped, round, tough grey leaves. It will take years to get to 15-25cm (6-10in) high.
Cultivation and care: Likes a peaty moist soil and a cool spot.
Propagation: By removing rooted pieces.

so high and fill it with drainage and suitable soil. A suitable soil mixture is healthy loam or garden soil, humus, as leaf mould or peat, and grit in a ratio of 2:1:1. Scree plants and those demanding very open soil and fast drainage may be tucked into a mix of 2 parts grit to 1 each of loam and leaf mould.

The really small garden

Sometimes space is very restricted: a garden of only a few square metres/yards. There is no need to forgo the pleasure of a lively garden scene. One of the most successful gardens near our home is very small indeed. The owners can cross the garden from the house in three steps, and it is not that much longer. Nevertheless, for much of the year it is full of life and colour, so much so that people are always pausing to admire it.

The plan for this garden is simple and could be adopted by many others. Two raised beds were built up to a height of about 45cm (18in). The remaining floor space was covered with imitation York stone. The walls of the house were painted white as was the tall end garden wall and the half wall opposite. Strong supports were installed for hanging baskets, for windowboxes and for a couple of semi-circular cradles, which were twice or three times as large as the biggest of the baskets. Two half tubs were included for permanent tree-cum-shrubs. Some other sensible-sized containers were bought. The raised beds were planted with a number of medium-sized shrubs, some deciduous and some evergreen. Trellis was fixed to the tallest garden wall, and various climbers, such as honeysuckles, clematis and a rambling rose, were given their head. Some of the larger containers standing on the paving or raised on a couple of bricks were mainly filled with evergreen shrubs and plants but room was left for the addition of some annuals that could add a touch of more vibrant colour in the summer. In the summer this 'courtyard' garden looks its most lively, colourwise, but bulbs and items such as winter pansies help to keep it looking attractive through the winter and the winter-flowered jasmine pegged back to the wall also helps.

While the effectiveness of this small garden is dependent on the baskets and containers, these are not so numerous as to look messy. By picking good quality, simple containers of a generous size, rather than trying to make the effect with a multitude of small ones, the picture is very unified. The garden can get hot in the summer, so the larger containers

are very much easier to keep watered and the plants are more likely to be happy.

With a small yard or garden area there may be an even greater temptation than normal to organize the space as an outside room. It is vital to make use of all the space and it may well be worth covering the whole or a considerable proportion of the area with a pergola-type structure so that the airspace above your head can be used. The beams can be clothed with a variety of climbing plants. Or restrict yourself to vines and watch the grapes developing! The walls can also be covered with flowering climbers, with some evergreens included, to help the whole thing look alive throughout the year.

Extra liveliness can be added by including water. It is quite easy to construct a wall-mounted feature, such as the popular lion's head, to allow a trickle of water to fall on to a basin filled with rounded boulders, the water being recycled by a small pump. Garden centres can supply all the artifacts you need to install such a feature.

LIRIOPE MUSCARI
Lilytuft

Description: Evergreen, frost hardy perennial that looks bulbous but makes do with thick fleshy rhizomes. This species spreads to make a clump of dark green leaves like straps. Tight spikes of rounded flowers look almost artificial and last almost as long.

Uses: Ground cover and for late season blossom.

Colour: Violet flowers, leaf colour from dark green to purple suffused darker, almost black.

Size: 20-30cm (8-12in) high, spread 45cm (18in).

Flowering time: Late autumn.

Relatives: *L. muscari* 'Majestic' is a good strong form with glossy dark foliage and lots of flowers. 'Monroe White' is white flowered with paler leaves. *L. spicata* is similar with grassy leaves and paler lilac or lavender blossom.

Cultivation: Plant in spring in fertile soil in a light spot.

Propagation: By division in early spring.

LARGE GARDENS, LESS LABOUR

A LARGE GARDEN is both a blessing and potential problem – there is the space to produce something breathtakingly beautiful and there is the space to produce something backbreakingly difficult to maintain. However, with thought, sensi- ble planning and bold design, it should be possible to enjoy most of the possibilities without becoming a slave or landing in the bankruptcy court.

For gardens that are less labour intensive, shrubs and trees are the dominant plantings. Following a

The sweeping plantings of foxgloves, lupins and delphiniums in this cottage garden are a colourful way of filling a large space

good selection of these are the very dramatic large herbaceous plants such as the giant gunnera, royal ferns, the strongest inulas and ligularias, sweeps of rodgersias, and stands of bamboos along with plants that can hold their own in grass such as paeonies and many bulbous plants. The aim is to create a multi-faceted semi-wilderness of many types of plants that can be given their head or managed with the lightest of reins.

One of the best things about large gardens is that plantings can be really big. In fact, plants must be made to work for a living. There is the room to plant

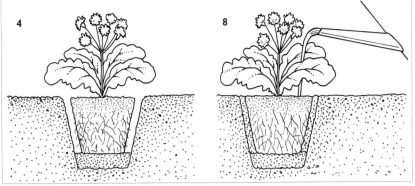

GOOD PLANTING TECHNIQUES

1 *Deeply cultivate the soil to a width much greater than the plant to be installed.*

2 *Ensure drainage is good.*

3 *Encourage good soil structure by adding generous quantities of humus. In heavy soils try also to add lots of grit and rough material which will help keep the soil open.*

4 *Make a generous hole for the plant. Dig over the bottom of the hole and incorporate humus.*

5 *Water the plant thoroughly before installing it. In*

most cases, the soil level of the former container-ized plant should match that of its new position.

6 *Backfill around the plant and firm in.*

7 *Scatter a light dressing of general fertilizer around plant and tickle it into soil surface.*

8 *Water in thoroughly.*

9 *Protect the plant from encroaching weed by covering the surrounding area with either a water permeable plastic membrane hidden by a thin layer of soil/grit, or a 8-10cm- (3-4in-) layer of shredded bark.*

strong plants boldly. Wide areas can be planned to imitate natural communities, similar to those created in the wild, and then these can be allowed to be self-regulating. With careful forethought, the work load will get less as the large get larger and come to dominate their station more fully. The garden will improve as the years pass allowing the gardener to sit back and enjoy the fruits of their labour without a pang of conscience.

Coping with a large garden

Large gardens are more easily managed if the plants can grow happily without the need for regular watering and feeding. Their health relies on good soil conditions and careful planting.

IMPROVING CONDITIONS

Soils are improved by better structure which means plenty of air and humus leading to improved drainage. While very ill-drained soils will have proper drainage plans executed, most soils can be improved by continual mulching and encouraging the natural organic life of the soil.

BOLD FOLIAGE PLANTS

Acanthus spp.

Aralia elata, variegated forms

Arundinaria spp.

Astilboides tabularis

Fatsia japonica

Gunnera manicata

Iris pseudacorus 'Variegata'

Ligularia spp.

Liriodendron tulipifera

Lysichiton spp.

Osmunda regalis

Podophyllum spp.

Rheum palmatum 'Atropurpureum'

Rhododendron, various large-leaved kinds

Rodgersia spp.

Yucca filamentosa

HYACINTHOIDES NON-SCRIPTA
Bluebells

H. hispanica

Description: Hardy native bulb of Germany, France and Britain. The arched one-sided flower stems have narrow tube-like flowers with recurved pointed tips.

Uses: One of the easiest of naturalizing bulbs. Can be grown in woodland conditions, between shrubs or in grass in wild gardens. Introduced into the border it can be so invasive as to be a nuisance.

Colour: Blue is the standard but white and pink sports are not uncommon.

Scent: Pleasing almost sharp perfume.

Size: To 20-40cm (8-16in) high, spread of one plant 10-20cm (4-8in).

Flowering time: Spring.

Relatives: *H. hispanica*, Spanish bluebell (pictured), is a bolder plant with erect stems carrying much wider, more open bell-shaped flowers all round the stems. If grown in proximity the two species will interbreed, eventually giving a full range of intermediate flowers.

Cultivation: Plant in early autumn only where you are willing to allow for dramatic increase.

Propagation: Bulbs give rise to numerous progeny of all shapes. They are capable of producing stolons with bulbs forming at the ends. Seed germinates freely with seedlings growing quickly to flowering size in damp soils.

Wildflowers have been allowed to take over in this meadow area, which is made accessible by a neatly mown grass path

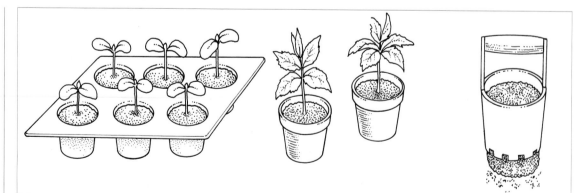

ESTABLISHING A MEADOW

Make a more floriferous meadow, more quickly, by introducing well grown plants rather than relying on scattered seed. To make planting easier grow on plug plants or seedlings raised under cover in pots that are close to the size of the type of bulb planters that take out a soil plug.

MULCHING

A generous cover of a weed free mulch helps to maintain large areas in good order with little extra need for maintenance. Shredded bark spread to a depth of 10cm (4in) will certainly last three seasons and will continue to have a beneficial effect even after that. It may have a slight inhibiting effect on plant growth by preoccupying the bacteria that work to release nitrogen in the soil, but if you establish routines to make plenty of good compost from rotted vegetation then this material, applied around the plants, certainly helps stimulate growth. To minimize work, consider allowing fallen autumn leaves to stay where they are, rather than sweeping them up, and let nature do the rest. They could even be

EUPHORBIA GRIFFITHII 'FIREGLOW'

Description: From a diverse genus, this is a hardy perennial that takes on the look of a bush with neatly-cut, lance-shaped leaves of rich green from a series of upright stems that initially push through the soil surface like so many asparagus shoots. Stems end as wide-flowering heads made more noticeable and colourful by the showy saucer-shaped bracts which last for a good number of weeks. At the end of the growing season the bushy plants die back to the rootstock which expands steadily just below soil surface.

Uses: Good in a border, could be used in a heather garden or between shrubs.

Colour: Flowering heads are glowing orange, fading to the green of the plant.

Size: 60-90cm (2-3ft) high, spread of young plant 50cm (20in).

Flowering time: Mid- and late spring.

Relatives: *E. characias* looks like a shrub with long, oval, grey-green leaves and long-lasting, rounded heads of lime-coloured flowers with dark eyes.

Cultivation: Grows strongly and spreads in fertile, well-drained soils.

Propagation: By seed or very early spring division.

PLANTS FOR A FLOWERING MEADOW

Anchusa arvensis, bugloss

Cardamine pratensis, lady's smock

Fritillaria meleagris, snake's-head fritillary

Galanthus nivalis, snowdrop

Genista tinctoria, dyer's greenwood

Leucanthemum vulgare, ox-eye daisy

Linaria vulgaris, common toadflax

Lychnis flos-cuculi, ragged robin

Malva moschata

M. moschata alba, musk mallow

Narcissus pseudonarcissus, wild daffodil

Primula veris, cowslip

P. vulgaris, primrose

Succisa pratensis, devil's bit scabious

Symphytum officinale, comfrey

Viola odorata, sweet violet

V. tricolor, wild pansy

V. riviniana, common dog violet

All the vetches such as *Vicia cracca*, tufted vetch

spread over other parts of the garden where they will rot down to provide a healthy leaf mould mulch. In more cultivated areas a mesh membrane can be laid on the soil to prevent weed germination, the mesh being covered with a mulch. Gravel can be a useful and attractive mulch in many areas, perhaps especially so near the house, by paths and by rock garden features.

Planting plans

Bedding plans dependent on plants raised annually are the complete antithesis of what is needed. Plants will be in groups not standing as individuals: shrubs in threes or fives; herbaceous plants in tens or more. The shapes of plantings and beds must not be fussy; informal shapes rather than regular blocks succeed better in large areas. Formality is allowed near the house where it can be appreciated. Here clipped tall hedges and even knot gardens or herbaceous borders bounded by box hedges are not out of place. But they should be planned so that powered trimmers can be run over them easily to maintain the spit and polished look, so do not plant any awkward shrubs or plants nearby or have any projecting superstructures around. Make sure that you can walk around easily carrying tools and trailing electric cable.

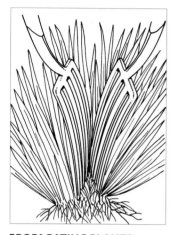 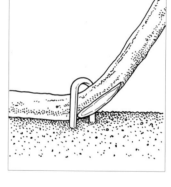 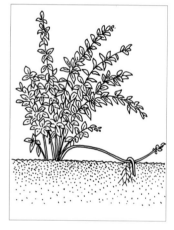

PROPAGATING PLANTS

Herbaceous plants

Most of these are readily increased by division in early autumn or early spring including *Aconitum, Agapanthus, Aster, Astilbe, Doronicum, Epimedium,* some *Geranium, Helenium, Heliopsis, Hosta, Ligularia, Monarda, Polygonum, Rodgersia, Rudbeckia, Solidago, Symphytum, Thalictrum* and *Trollius.*

1 *Lift clumps.*
2 *The basal rootstock is broken into a number of parts by easing them apart using two forks, back to back.*
3 *If you have a surplus, discard the centre of the clump; the more lively pieces will be on the outsides of clumps.*
4 *Replant divisions in new positions immediately. Water in thoroughly.*

Bulbs

These are best lifted and bulbs split just as the foliage is failing, that is becoming limp and perhaps turning yellow. Snowdrops, daffodils, lilies and most bulbs can be safely handled this way. Tulips can be treated in the same manner, but some gardeners prefer to lift them and store the cleaned bulbs until late autumn to replant.

1 *Lift clumps, remove leaves, shake free of soil.*
2 *Pull bulbs apart, discard damaged ones and replant the remainder immediately.*

Shrubs

Those with large gardens will want the easiest and most trouble-free way of propagating their shrubs. Many can be layered. If this job is done in the early autumn there should be strong rooted layers of most types ready to be severed from their parent and moved to new quarters after twelve months. A good rate of increase can be achieved easily this way. Some shrubs that respond readily include *Amelanchier, Andromeda, Aucuba, Cassiope, Chaenomeles, Chionanthus, Corylopsis, Cotinus, Disanthus, Elaeagnus, Erica, Forsythia, Fothergilla, Hydrangea, Ilex, Kalmia, Laurus, Magnolia, Osmanthus, Skimmia* and *Syringa.*

1 *Select branches that can be brought easily to ground level.*
2 *Cut a small thin sliver of bark from a section of lively wood, or graze it.*
3 *Dust the wound with rooting hormone.*
4 *Peg the branch into the soil. If need be, improve this rooting soil by adding grit and peat.*
5 *Sever from the main plant after about a year when the growing layer is clearly independent.*
6 *Lift carefully with the roots kept as intact as possible and replant in new quarters. Shrubs that do not have branches that can be easily brought to ground level may be propagated by air-layering (see page 195).*

Wherever possible, shrubs and trees will be of kinds that are unlikely to need pruning, or only the very minimum. Shrubberies can be left to their own devices after a few years if strong growers are planted and the whole planting is given a generous mulch of shredded bark to keep weeds at bay until the bushes themselves provide weed-suppressing cover.

Herbaceous and other plants will be those able to maintain themselves for decades without attention. Those of a shorter lifespan should be kinds that can maintain themselves by normal spread and self-sowing. Plants that will more or less look after themselves include most shrubs that do not require regular pruning. Herbaceous plants include *Acanthus* species, *Aconitum* species, *Anemone hybrida* forms, *Euphorbia*, *Geranium* species, *Helleborus* species and hybrids, *Rodgersia* species and *Yucca filamentosa*.

Making the most of it

Choosing trees and shrubs for the contrast in forms as well as colours helps to make the garden lively throughout the year. Combine shapes, including cloud-shaped trees with weeping ones or next to fastigiate types. Position deciduous trees and shrubs near evergreens, so that they emphasize each other's forms. The silhouetted tracery of the empty branches in winter complements the more defined shape of the evergreens. Vary the greens and have blue-greens and limey greens to add interest. Some conifers take on rusty tones in winter; pick these for the warmth they will bring to the scene. The rich purple-leaved shrubs and trees such as the copper beeches, the deep purple-black *Prunus cerasifera* 'Nigra' and smoke bushes, *Cotinus coggygria* forms such as 'Royal Purple' are all tempting. They look splendid, but need a 'Handle with care' label. One or two as focal points can enliven the whole but too many can be heavy and oppressive.

On acid soils there are the hordes of rhododendrons from which to choose. On other soils there are the stalwarts such as *Viburnum tinus* (page 250), *V. davidii*, *Prunus laurocerasus* (laurel) and *Aucuba japonica* (page 32) to hold the fort while others get established. Below these it is easy to naturalize bulbs for spring and autumn display, together with *Lilium martagon* (page 130), a lily that will grow on most soils, for summertime.

HELIANTHUS × MULTIFLORUS
Perennial sunflower

Description: Herbaceous perennial bred from the lemony species *H. decapetalus*, with a strong, fully hardy rhizomatous rootstock which expands just below the soil surface to create wide clumps of upright stems. Tough, ovate leaves smooth on the upper surface are very rough below. Basal and lower ones can be 15cm (6in) long and at least two thirds as wide, upper ones down to half the length and narrow. Sunflowers are 5-12cm (2-5in) across on erect branched stems.

Uses: An amenable plant to make a bold patch in any border scheme and not afraid of wet soil that is not permanently sodden. Can be used in a wild garden.

Wildlife: Birds will visit seedheads.

Colour: Golden.

Size: 1.5-1.8m (5-6ft) high, spread initially 60cm (2ft).

Flowering time: Late summer and early autumn.

Relatives: *H.* 'Loddon Gold' is another tall plant but with fully double flowers in rich gold each about 10cm (4in) across.

Cultivation: If planted in moist spots in good soil there is no stopping them. Their height may benefit from some informal support. An established clump will look more impressive if the weaker stems are cut out. Responds well to an annual mulch of compost.

Propagation: Division in early spring.

GROUND COVER PLANTS

Ajuga reptans
Bergenia forms
Cistus forms
Cotoneaster dammeri
C. horizontalis
Epimedium forms
Erica, various
Euonymus fortunei forms
Euphorbia amygdaloides var. robbiae
Hedera forms, ivies
Hosta
Houttuynia cordata 'Chameleon'
Lamium forms
Tanacetum densum
Thymus forms
Tiarella cordifolia
Vinca forms

LAMIUM GALEOBDOLON
Yellow archangel

Description: A hardy native of much of Europe, including Britain. Oval leaves and lots of dead-nettle flowers over a long period.

Uses: Ground cover in sun or shade. An auxiliary plant to use in less formal spots especially in well-drained ones that remain rather damp, such as ditch sides.
Colour: Yellow flowers.
Size: 20-30cm (10-12in) high, spread as allowed.
Flowering time: In succession through summer.
Relatives: *L. galeobdolon* 'Florentinum' (syn. *L. g.* 'Variegatum') is as easy and rampant as the type but has its green leaves much overworked in silver.
Cultivation: Easy if not allowed to dry out; care is a matter of making sure larger plants do not overwhelm it (unlikely), and just checking the extent of its territorial advance.
Propagation: By detaching rooted pieces in late winter.

Flowering meadows

Grassland, away from the more carefully groomed sward by the house, can be mown only once or twice a year, its informality going well with the groups of shrubs and trees that dominate here. A flowering meadow would be effective in such a site, the grass acting as a backcloth for the myriad meadow plants that are at their height in the spring but not without colour through the summer and into the autumn. With the autumn, the whole can be cropped and cleared to compost heaps. Through the growing periods pathways can be kept mown perhaps every ten days or so to make the meadow accessible.

Plant associations

A very happy, easy-care association on a bankside and elsewhere is the triumvirate composed of spring bulbs such as snowdrops, hellebores, especially of the *H. orientalis* type, and primroses. Other bulbs that could be added are small daffodils, such as *Narcisssus pseudonarcissus*, the golden Tenby daffodil, *N. obvallaris* and all the hybrids of *N. cyclamineus*.

Trees and grass grow
unrestrained in this
wilderness area

ROMNEYA COULTERI
California tree poppy

Description: Woody-based, hardy herbaceous perennial. The sight of the enormous pure white satiny poppies, their perfect gold centres as bright as the sun and with a slight scent, is one of the joys of summer. Sculptural glaucous leaves on smooth grey stems help excuse the rather short flower season, one that can be even briefer in bad weather.

Uses: Space filler; when happy this plant will aggressively invade surrounding territory, but you need to get the situation right as it is fussy about getting started.

Colour: White with golden boss of stamens in the centre. Blue-grey leaves and stems.

Scent: Slight.

Size: Height and spread up to 2.1 m (7ft), but this depends on situation and age; it will look good at half the dimensions.

Flowering time: Late summer to mid-autumn.

Relatives: *R. coulteri* 'White Cloud' is a scarce, bushy, strong cultivar with a longer flowering season.

Cultivation: Needs a warm sunny spot in deep well-drained soil. Slow to establish but once happy can spread rapidly. Does not move well, avoid root disturbance.

Propagation: By seed sown in autumn or by root cuttings in late winter. Sow seed one or two to a pot and plant out seedlings without disturbing the root-ball. Take only a limited number of root cuttings for fear of disturbing the plant. Pieces 4-5cm (2in) long and about 5mm thick, placed in pots of open compost, with their tops just below surface, and kept moist, not wet, should produce leaf buds and develop into small plants. Again plant with as little disturbance as possible into permanent site.

None of these have huge masses of foliage; they are discrete in dying down. Groups of *Pulmonaria* hybrids in the same spot will increase interest with their early blue, pink and white flowers and often very attractive spotted foliage. An odd clump or two of the early dwarf doronicums in brilliant gold will create focal points.

RHODODENDRONS AND LILIES

On acid soils it seems entirely suitable that rhododendrons should play a part and their natural allies are the heathers and camellias, but when their flowering is over their dark foliage is an ideal backcloth for groups of lilies which will revel in similar soil conditions. You might choose to grow bold groups of *Lilium regale* or use some of the fine trumpet hybrids such as 'Pink Perfection', 'Golden Splendour', 'African Queen', in salmon-orange shades, or very dark pink purples like 'Damson' or 'Midnight'. The Asiatic hybrids such as orange 'Enchantment' and the hundreds of its multi-coloured relatives are easy to grow and establish and if lifted and respaced every three years are simple to manage. The new range of hybrids bred between this series and the lovely Easter lily, *L. longiflorum*, look set to make a very important place for themselves in all gardens. They are large and attractive, and grow so easily and increase so prodigiously that everyone is bound to want them: they are currently mainly sold as mixed colours, but some are now being separated out and named; 'Rodeo' is a strong, sturdy plant with bright pink flowers.

HEATHERS

Heathers have been popular for decades. They are colourful for months and manage their own affairs so well that they are a gift in small and large gardens alike. Their growth inhibits most weeds if one starts with clean ground. On alkaline soils there are the many forms of *Erica carnea* and the hybrid series *E. × darleyensis* to provide plenty of choice; on acid soils these kinds and all others can be grown. The natural associated plants with heathers are conifers such as junipers and a range of the dwarf and slow-growing types. Silver birches too are part of the heathland picture, together with brooms and gorses. To add variety naturalize bluebells and a range of small bulbs between the heathers.

FERNS

The hardy ferns that were so popular in Victorian times have staged a considerable comeback. The range of these in both size and form is very considerable. There are kinds that can manage fully in the open, like bracken does on our hillsides, but there are more that enjoy shade or part shade, normally easy enough to find. Ferns associate well with hellebores, snowdrops and a range of other plants, including the up and coming grasses that seem to become more important year by year. Some of the

LAVANDULA STOECHAS
French lavender

Description: This is the Mediterranean shrub with the traditional lavender foliage, habit and scent but with darker flowers made decorative by upward-pointing conspicuous bracts. It is frost hardy.

Uses: Leaves give year-round scent. Can be used like *L. angustifolia* forms for hedges, border plants or even bonsai.

Wildlife: Small copper butterflies make a perfect colour combination with the lavender. Bees, hoverflies and other insects add to the throng.

Colour: Dark lavender-blue and pinky purple flowers above dusky green foliage.

Size: 1m (3ft) high and across.

Flowering time: Early summer until autumn.

Relatives: *L. angustifolia* is the traditional, hardy and reliable lavender. 'Munstead' and 'Hidcote' are compact forms of it with silvery grey foliage and lots of bright flowers; 'Hidcote' normally being more dwarf at under 60cm (2ft) high. There are seedlings on the market masquerading under cultivar names.

Cultivation: Easy in sunny well-drained soil.

Propagation: Semi-ripe cuttings. Seed may provide a somewhat varied set of plants; seedlings grow quickly and you could select your own clones.

larger grasses may afford some shade for ferns. They certainly make an interesting contrast in form and most can be planted boldly without requiring much further maintenance.

GROUND COVER

Ground that is well covered with plant life is not likely to be easily invaded by weeds. The better the cover, the less the work. Ground cover simply needs to be matched to soil type and situation, but be careful with choice, some ground cover plants are not deliriously exciting to look at: to cover the ground may be admirable but we ask for rather more. Below and between shrubs and trees in the darkest places it is necessary to fall back on some of the more interesting ivies in combination with periwinkles and the splendid spurge *Euphorbia amygdaloides* var. *robbiae* (page 40). Over very rough ground *Rubus tricolor* can make a dense low cover of dark polished evergreen foliage, a match for almost every weed. In more civilized areas a little more picking and choosing is possible (see margin for suggestions).

THE RAMPANT ROCKERY

A small rock garden full of small often tricky specimens involves too much work, but a large garden can be an ideal setting for a bold rock garden that depends considerably on its rock and construction for much of its long-term appeal. The larger the rocks the better the effect – and the worse the effect on the bank balance. However, once installed they are there for the rest of time. And a large rock garden need not be planted with huge numbers of plants. Try just a few strong growing kinds, perhaps some ferns and grasses, among the rocks.

For once, easy rampant plants can be used. The standbys such as aubrieta, arabis and alyssum create a pattern of mauve, white and yellow. Miniature bulbs that are ideal in such a site include *N. bulbocodium*, the hoop-petticoat narcissus, especially now that a very strong-growing free-flowering strain is being marketed under the name 'Golden Bells'. There are many easy and strong geraniums, useful for covering the ground, 'Mavis Simpson' is one. Some of the strong but dwarfer spurges, *Euphorbia* species, and low shrubs such as some of the hebes like *H. pinguifolia* 'Pagei' with grey evergreen foliage are also effective (see margin for strong rock plants).

ROCK GARDEN PLANTS

Ajuga reptans

Alyssum

Anthemis cinerea

A. montana

Arabis

Aubrieta

Campanula cochleariifolia

C. garganica

Cyclamen hederifolium

Dryas octopetala

Erica

Erigeron karvinskianus

Genista lydia

G. sagittalis

Geranium sanguineum var. *striatum*

Helianthemum

Iberis sempervirens

Phlox adsurgens

P. subulata

Pulsatilla vulgaris

Salix reticulata

Saxifraga, mossy kinds and others

Sedum

Sempervivum

Thymus serpyllum

PATHS, PAVING AND STEPS

FEW PARTS OF the garden are more important than paths and paved areas. Obviously it is important to be able to get out into the garden in all weathers, to walk about and to transport one's equipment perhaps using a wheelbarrow. The part played by such hard landscaping in the overall design of the garden is almost impossible to exaggerate. The strong lines of paths can convert even a fairly mediocre garden into one that pleases. A carefully placed area of paving can provide an important focal point for activity and relaxation. It is important to ensure that the most is made of all these structures. Do not rush their design or construction.

These well disguised steps nevertheless lead the eye effectively into the heights of this rock garden

162

Paths

Paths must look good, be safe and lead somewhere. They form some of the strongest lines in the garden design and are almost impossible to disguise. Their form depends on the character of the property and the type of garden you are creating. A brick house suggests a brick path. A meandering, crazy paved one should not be the first choice for a strictly formal design. Brick-edged paths of imitation York stone are right for a more complex layout, whereas

PARAHEBE CATARRACTAE

Description: An evergreen subshrub with slender spreading and arching stems carrying pointed, oval leaves with discrete serration. It has rather an easy loose demeanour and lots of open sprays of open trumpet-shaped, small flowers with or just clear of the foliage. Fully hardy.

Uses: Delightful in a rock garden or rock beds, or maybe beside pathways.

Colour: Flowers are basically white but are heavily lined or suffused with lilac-purple.

Size: Height and spread 30cm (12in), usually wider than tall.

Flowering time: From midsummer well into autumn.

Relatives: Various clones have been propagated and named. 'Delight' is a particularly good one. There are also pink-flushed and white ones.

Cultivation: Best in good light conditions in drained gritty soil high in humus and acid not alkaline.

Propagation: By cuttings of semi-ripe wood in early summer.

THYMES

T. x *citriodorus* (lemon-scented thyme)

T. x *citriodorus* 'Aureus' (golden-leaved thyme)

T. x *citriodorus* 'Silver Queen'

T. serpyllum var. *coccineus*

T. serpyllum 'Pink Chintz'

T. serpyllum 'Snowdrift'

T. vulgaris (culinary thyme)

T. vulgaris 'Silver Posie'

in some situations a path of gravel enclosed by curbs or bricks can look more effective.

Whatever is chosen the foundations must be sound and the path should be dry and quick-drying. Rainfall will wet it but a well-drained foundation will ensure it soon dries off. Heavy use, in the form of constant wheelbarrow traffic, should be allowed for. In such a case, 15cm (6in) of rammed hardcore, topped by 4-5cm (1½-2in) of washed sand or granite dust will make an excellent base for the brick or stone path surface. Where traffic is lighter it may

Neat box hedges are clipped level with the steps in this split level garden, increasing the upward emphasis and formality

PLANTING IN PAVING

Squeezing a rootball into a narrow crack does little good to the plant or your patience. It is easy enough to propagate your own purpose-designed crack-filling plants with rootballs that slip easily into the gaps between paving stones. Naturally, when laying the paving, it is sensible to leave gaps of some 1-2cm (½-¾in) between stones where you want to put plants, rather than butting them hard up against each other.

Thyme is a good candidate for this technique. One good plant could provide hundreds of new ones in a season.

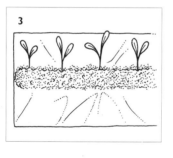

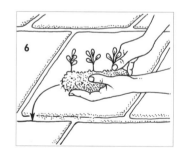

1 Cut a strip of polythene roughly 13cm (5in) wide and as long as you feel you can easily handle – 25-45cm (10-18in) is good.

2 Mix good potting compost with half as much again of grit and spread a line of this evenly along the upper half of the polythene strip.

3 Take cuttings approximately 3-5cm (1-2in) long from the thyme plant and lay them about 2cm (¾in) apart along the line of compost. Cover with a relatively thin layer of extra compost.

4 Fold the bottom half of the polythene to cover the cuttings and then roll from one end of the strip to form something like a Swiss roll. Use a large elastic band to keep all in place.

5 Stand the roll with the cuttings facing upwards. Keep it damp but not sodden for a few weeks.

6 Thyme cuttings may well have starter roots when first taken; certainly they will root quickly, other plants may take longer. Once rooted the roll can be undone. Now you can slide the linear-rooted plants into your empty cracks, as densely or thinly as you require.

7 Work in a little extra grit or gritty compost to leave cracks filled, water and when settled top up with compost where needed. Keep moist until plants are well established.

AUBRIETA DELTOIDEA

Description: Well-known, evergreen, carpeting perennial, the best of a dozen or so species found from Sicily across to Turkey. It has many spreading thin stems and wedge-shaped or spathulate, sticky leaves made a grey-green by short bristles. Growth is smothered with masses of single four-petalled flowers; selected forms have semi- or fully doubled blooms. Fully hardy.

Uses: For larger rock gardens, rock beds and raised borders. Exceptionally valuable for draping down from the top or halfway down a wall. Much used as a front of border plant and ideal for softening path edges. Can manage in dry soils if given an early start to get roots deep.

Wildlife: Bees and other insects visit flowers.

Colour: Various, white to pinks, mauves and darker shades with greater or lesser amounts of blue in the pigments. Some effective maroon to crimson kinds.

Scent: Faint.

Size: 8cm (3in) high, spread 30-45cm (12-18in).

Flowering time: Spring.

Relatives: Do not grow any of the inferior colours or poorer seedlings. Select from potted flowering kinds on display, or choose only the really worthwhile ones from a modern good seed strain.

Cultivation: Plant in well-drained soil in a sunny site. New plants should be well watered in but, after becoming established, will manage in even quite dry spots. After flowering the seedheads can be sheared off; older plants can be kept tidy and encouraged to produce healthy new growth by being cut back after flowering, particularly restricting or removing older low layers of stems.

Propagation: By seed, selecting the best colours. Good forms by green cuttings early summer and semi-ripe ones somewhat later.

PLANTS FOR PATHS AND PAVED AREAS

Look to these genera:

Acaena

Antennaria

Anthemis

Arabis

Arenaria

Cotula

Cymbalaria

Dianthus

Erinus

Erysimum

Euphorbia

Frankenia

Globularia

Gypsophila

Helichrysum

Hieracium

Iberis

Linaria

Lithodora

Lychnis

Mentha

Minuartia

Oenothera

Papaver

Polygonum

Saxifraga

Sedum

Sempervivum

Thymus

suffice to strip the top few centimetres and replace them with washed sand or grit before placing paving stones. The stones of a patio or important path can be anchored by a trowelful of mortar at each corner, and at the centre of large slabs.

The patio

One of the most important parts of many gardens is the patio. It is the space where house meets garden and vice versa. Here we can rest from labour, take ease and admire our handiwork – and the miracles of creation. To be comfortable, the patio needs to be a good size, to take as much garden furniture as is required and still allow free movement around it. It also needs to the right shape – an oblong or L-shaped form is more pleasing than a square. If you have enough room for a spacious patio, it is a nice idea to leave one or two spots without paving stones where plants can be allowed to grow. Even if not, it is often possible to grow some plants in the cracks

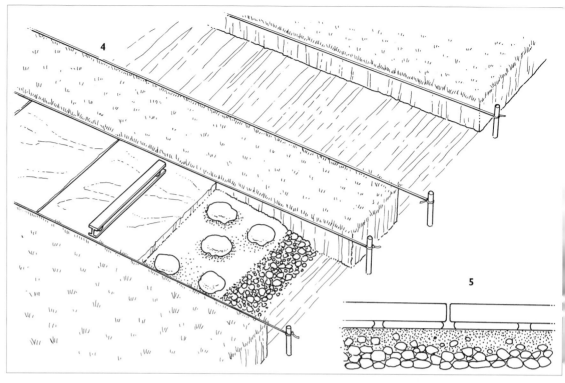

LAYING PAVING STONES

1 Mark out area to be paved with string and leave for a few days to see that it does not need adjustment.

2 If area needs extra draining arrange this now. Field drainage pipes can be laid towards lower ground or a substantial soak-away.

3 Strip topsoil/turf and store for future use.

Excavate some 10cm (4in) of soil and replace with hardcore, finishing with a layer of sharp, washed sand or grit-dust. Compress evenly.

4 Select your choice of paving stones. Imitation York stone is very good. Avoid very highly coloured stones unless they are exactly what you want for a special place.

The normal flat public utility paving stone can look a little plain.

5 Using a spirit level lay your stones and secure them with a trowelful of mortar at each corner and at the centre. If a pathway is going to bear really very heavy traffic the amount of mortar below the stones can be increased.

between stones. Limit their numbers as you still want a bit of stone showing, but here and there they are very effective. Thymes are the obvious candidates for such a site; pretty and sweet-smelling, they do not object to being trodden on one bit.

Steps

A gift to the garden designer, steps have plenty of work to do in a garden. Most obviously, they allow access from one part to another; visually they are a note of a change of level; they are also ideal for bedecking with plants in pots or in the nearby soil.

Whether the steps are to be made of stone, brick or wood, it is an idea to make up a dummy set before going ahead with the real thing. The height and breadth of each step should be comfortable to

move up and down. The width is best generous, unless the steps are to lead to some secret place, a hidden garden.

Plants

The patio and other paved areas can be vibrant with colour through the summer with ground-based containers and hanging baskets spilling over with every colour of the rainbow. The winter is not so well served, but the look of a stage swept bare can be avoided by strategically positioning some evergreen shrubs growing in pots. An expensive, shaped box specimen can be ideal, but equally effective and a real budget item is golden privet. Grown in a container, well fed and neatly clipped, it can glow with gold through the winter. Other evergreens to con-

CAMPANULA PORTENSCHLAGIANA (SYN. C. MURALIS)
Wall bellflower

C. poscharskyana

Description: Rumbustious, sprinting prostrate perennial quite extraordinarily beautiful when it is smothered with countless five-pointed open bells. Foliage forms low mats of tiny ivy leaves. Very hardy.
Uses: Only plant where its invasive habit is not going to threaten other plans. It will thrive in the cracks between large paving stones and can colonize a wall, either a relatively informal 'dry' one or one in which the mortar is capable of surviving invasion.
Colour: Vivid violet-blue.
Size: 15cm (6in) high, spread to the seaside!
Flowering time: Summer.
Relatives: The genus is a large one, bursting with good things, both exuberant spreaders and very discrete small choice alpines such as *C. zoysii* with pinched bottle-shaped flowers and a spread not exceeding 10cm (4in). 'Birch Hybrid' makes a splendid show on a 30cm- (12in-) wide plant only 15cm (6in) high. *C. poscharskyana* (pictured) has star-shaped blue flowers and more lax growth.
Cultivation: Easier to grow than bindweed.
Propagation: By division.

sider are among the huge range of conifers. Here the range extends from the small dwarfs to those that make considerable specimens but can still be managed in a large pot or other container. Some of the *Chamaecyparis lawsoniana* cultivars are suitable and × *Cupressocyparis leylandii* 'Castlewellan' gives a bold mass of yellow. It can be clipped as tightly or as loosely as you wish. The shiny evergreen *Prunus laurocerasus* 'Otto Luyken', with branches fanning out sideways, can be very effective. So, too, can almost all the holly cultivars.

Standing in carefully chosen spots on the patio or on pathways or corners a bold earthenware or other container can look good on is own, the bolder the better. Other artifacts can be used including sculp-

HYPERICUM OLYMPICUM

Description: Deciduous woody plant of erect and gently spreading habit making a subshrub of easy temperament. Small, oval, greyish leaves are crowded neatly on the erect stems which are topped by terminal bunches of upward-looking bright flowers each up to 5cm (2in) across, stars formed of five oblong petals. Fully hardy.
Uses: Warm dry spots where fussier things might find the rather arid life difficult. Small ones may find a niche in rock garden or rock beds.
Colour: Golden.
Size: Depending on the clone 15-40cm (6-16in) high, spread 15-25cm (6-10in).
Flowering time: Many weeks through summer.
Relatives: *H. olympicum* 'Citrinum' is eye-catching with its shining pale lemon flowers.
Cultivation: Plant in spring in well-drained soil. Sunny spot. Minimum maintenance needed.
Propagation: By seed or summer cuttings.

LITHODORA DIFFUSA (SYN. LITHOSPERMUM DIFFUSUM)

Description: On the borderline between an evergreen perennial and a low prostrate shrub. Thin hairy stems scramble over the soil surface well clothed with thick, small, spear-shaped leaves looking a dull matt shade of dark green because of their covering of short hairs. It has many small, almost stemless, flowers, tubular opening to a star outline. Fully hardy.

Uses: Grows in peaty acid soils, so use in a peat bed or a humus-rich spot in the lower reaches of the rock garden.

Colour: Vivid gentian-blue with a hint of a red line down the centre of each petal.

Size: 15cm (6in) high and, with age, up to double this, spread 30cm (12in) or more but then usually trimmed back.

Flowering time: Early summer; and it is rarely without some flowers through into the autumn.

Relatives: The most usually offered clone is *L. diffusa* 'Heavenly Blue' closely followed by the similarly rich-coloured 'Grace Ward'.

Cultivation: Acid conditions are needed. Carefully install plants from pots, they do not like root disturbance. Moist soils are appreciated. Plants are kept tidy by trimming back in autumn or early spring.

Propagation: By semi-ripe cuttings in summer.

BUILDING A SIMPLE PATIO

1 *Mark out the patio form using pegs and string. Normally this will be close to one entrance/exit of the house, but could be at some distance from it if shelter and sunshine demand. Leave marked area for a period to see whether it receives all the sun you want or for one reason or another needs adjustment. There will be some garden sites where it will be best to have the patio on two levels; if so then it normally looks best to have them of clearly different sizes.*

2 *Measure up the area and work out the amount of paving or other material needed. You will need a solid floor or paving stones where you are planning to seat and eat; some economy could be made by using pea gravel for other defined parts.*

3 *Lay stones as suggested in 'laying paving stones', page 166. If using stones of the same size it is more effective to arrange these so that in each direction there is a broken line of cracks. There are stones of different sizes but of modular forms that can mean that the pattern can be varied and this can look very good. Imitation York stone is very much easier to lay than the genuine article as the base side is exactly level.*

4 *If laying stone close to the house walls, ensure a slight fall away from the house to take excess rain water away. Make sure that you never build up above the damp course.*

5 *The completed patio will look much better if it has clearly defined edges. These could be low walls useful for sitting on or for planting up if they have a hollow centre. A simple curb of stone or bricks could give the finishing touch.*

ture, bird baths, sundials or garden seats, but other not so obvious items can also be effective. Tree stumps, weather-beaten posts, old farm or garden tools can sit their time out in retirement. Do not create a glorified rubbish dump, but the suggestion of former life passing is not without charm.

Pergolas and screens (see pages 142-48) help improve the mystery, design and utility of your garden. Baskets hanging from the pergolas can help to make this an exciting place. A large pot of lilies can transform an area – a splash of colour, and possibly scent, on a paved spot or sitting by a path.

These bricks are laid in a series of gentle curves to soften the line of the path. Groundcover and overhanging plants increase the effect

FENCES AND HEDGES

Fences and hedges: both provide screening from outside and in, and give shelter. They also define boundaries and create a sense of privacy. But hedges take a lot more room to do their job than fences, and they can be greedy with soil nutrients and available water. They also require work to keep them tidy and within bounds. The best thing is to match hedge, screen or fence to the situation.

What for?

Begin by being clear about the task for the barrier: defining boundaries, increasing privacy, excluding animals, children, casual burglars. Or is it to create some shelter from wind or hide the dustbins? Interior screens can be trellis or little fences, but a small hedge may be less intrusive.

A white fence provides a perfect backdrop for this red and orange rose

PROS AND CONS:
HEDGES V FENCES OR WALLS

A fence is put up quickly; a hedge can have a much longer life. A hedge is more likely to be easier on the eye and may repay our time and energy in keeping it tidy with fresh lively colour and a more natural effect. The colour and life of the hedge is likely to be a far better backcloth for plants growing nearby. While a fence can block wind, it may create turbulence, especially if it is a solid overlapping design. A hedge will break the force of the wind more effectively by filtering it. In gardens where space is at a premium, the fence scores in taking up so little

LATHYRUS SYLVESTRIS
Narrow-leaved everlasting pea

Description: Herbaceous, fully hardy climbing perennial with narrow leaves and lots of tendrils to help it get up and over whatever support it can find and then in summer and early autumn provide posies of blossom, four to a dozen in each bunch. Native of all countries of northern Europe including Britain.
Uses: Looks good clambering over hedges, informal walls or through shrubs. Will grow in light woodland conditions.
Colour: Rosy pink, usually marked with purple and green.
Size: To 2m (6ft) high.
Flowering time: Summer and early autumn.
Cultivation: Best in fertile well-drained soil, not in too deep shade. Tidy up by cutting away dead vines at end of season.
Propagation: By seed sown in early spring.

room, especially as a hedge not only absorbs considerable airspace but has roots below that can be very extensive.

Compromises can be made. The wooden fence can be disguised by being overgrown with creepers, perhaps evergreen ones, to present a wall of living foliage – a virtual-hedge. This can also be done with a chain link fence, the plant growth now creating a hedge-like look and providing some of the wind-breaking and sheltering qualities that the chain-link alone failed to do. Another great advantage of this,

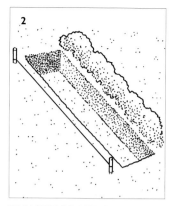

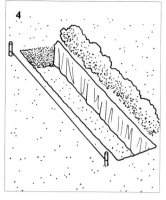

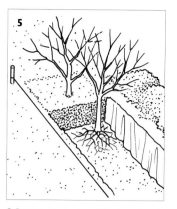

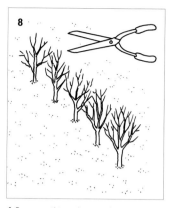

PLANTING A HEDGE

Choose your plants depending on whether it is a boundary hedge or an interior decorative one. Interior ones could be made of lavender, box, *Berberis thunbergii* f. *atropurpurea* forms or *Lonicera nitida* and can be groomed to a relatively small size. For a boundary hedge, most robust species, ones that will make a good screen and act as a barrier, are usually best. Usually an evergreen hedge is

the more serviceable boundary one, but beech is popular as it retains its rusted leaves as a closely clipped hedge and so has an 'evergreen' effect.

1 *Choose your hedging plant. Consider rate of growth and the consequent amount of trimming needed.*
2 *Mark the line of the hedge and excavate a wide trench one spit deep, 20-25cm (8-10in).*

3 *Dig over the bottom of the trench and incorporate humus material.*
4 *If you are concerned about greedy hedge roots taking too much out of the ground on the garden site, excavate a little deeper this side of the trench and line the garden side with a strip of thick grade polythene to within a few centimetres of the surface.*
5 *Place the hedge plants at intervals along the side of the trench. See margin for recommended distances.*

6 *Return soil into the trench around the plants so that the soil level is the same as the original soil level of plants. Plant firmly.*
7 *Water thoroughly. Keep weed-free.*
8 *Trim gently if needed. Thereafter try to establish a hedge profile that means that the sides go in a little as they rise, the top of the hedge being narrower than the bottom.*

ILEX AQUIFOLIUM '**J. C. VAN TOL**'

I. aquifolium 'Golden Queen'

Description: One of the best of hollies with dark foliage that is less spiny than many and grows densely. It is a good berrier and has the distinction of not requiring male hollies around to produce its rich red fruits. This makes it a

good choice for the smaller garden. Very hardy.

Uses: Specimen or as a hedge.
Wildlife: A nesting site for birds. Fieldfares and other thrushes will sometimes gather to enjoy the berries.
Colour: Dark green foliage, red fruits.
Size: To 6m (20ft) high, spread 4m (12ft).
Flowering time: Insignificant flowers, early spring.
Relatives: Many good kinds. The variegated ones such as 'Argentea Marginata', 'Golden van Tol' and 'Golden Queen' (pictured) are excellent.
Cultivation: Plant in well-drained soil. They take a year to settle and then grow faster every season. Can be pruned to shape.
Propagation: By layers or semi-ripe cuttings from late summer until winter.

especially in confined spaces, is that such climbing cover is not nearly as greedy on airspace or root-space as a full hedge.

Inside the garden a quick screen of trellis held by securely installed posts is often the answer where the aim is to create hidden areas in the garden or mask unsightly 'work' areas. The trellis work will be a help for rambler roses, clematis and all other manner of climbing or scrambling plants.

Hedging plants

There are the two options: evergreen or deciduous; there is also a mixture of both. A closely clipped beech hedge retains a good cover of brown foliage through the winter, or deciduous flowering plants, such as *Rosa rugosa*, are marvellous for spring and summer colour. Evergreens are unbeatable for year-round effect. Choosing between conifers or other evergreens is the only task. Appearance is the first consideration but then choice may well be mainly governed by two further factors – quickness of growth and cost.

SPEED

Rapid growth favours × *Cupressocyparis leylandii* and privet (*Ligustrum*). Cost, too, favours these two plants, but there are other considerations. Quick-growing hedges need more trimming and the hedge is going to last for many years, so the extra cost of a rather better plant adds up to very little if considered as so much per year. An initially more expensive plant may require a lot less effort to keep trim and time saved is wealth saved in the form of energy and tool use.

EVERGREEN CONTENDERS

Ilex aquifolium forms (holly)

Makes an impenetrable barrier, is a rich shining colour and although a little slow to start can be kept in good order with one major trim each year.

Taxus baccata (yew)

An excellent barrier, rich colour and relatively easy to trim. Not quite as bright as holly and both berries and leaves are poisonous. Grows well after getting established in the first year. Trim once or possibly twice a year. Dense surface roots.

Chamaecyparis lawsoniana

Makes a dense hedge and responds surprisingly well to regular trimming. Depending on how fine a finish you want, you can manage on two trims a year but could go over it half a dozen times. 'Green Hedger' is a bright green clone of uniform growth.

Thuja plicata

Another conifer that responds well to cutting and can make a dense hedge with a pleasing resinous smell that makes trimming a happy olfactory experience. Bright green colour in summer, can take on bronzy hue in the colder months.

× *Cupressocyparis leylandii*

Quickly established. If regularly trimmed it can form a dense hedge and be kept down to reasonable limits, but you must expect to cut it several times a year. There are bright yellow forms such as 'Castlewellan'. Has a lot of roots.

Prunus laurocerasus and *P. lusitanica* (laurel, Portuguese laurel)

PANDOREA JASMINOIDES
Bower vine

Description: Australian twining evergreen climber with dark green leaves divided into five to nine narrow leaflets and loose clusters of funnel-shaped flowers with round, five-petalled faces. Tender, min. temp. 5°C (41°F).

Uses: Greenhouse climber; wall plant in milder areas to grow up through other plants.

Colour: White flowers may be blushed lightest pink but with rich crimson pink throats.

Size: To 5m (15ft) high.

Flowering time: Summer; late winter to summer under cover.

Relatives: There is a completely white form *P. jasminoides* 'Alba'.

Cultivation: Needs sunshine and a fertile soil. Prune after flowering to restrain growth. Keep frost free over winter when it will need only very moderate watering.

Propagation: By seed or cuttings of semi-ripe shoots in summer.

Large-leaved laurel, *Prunus laurocerasus*, and some much narrower cultivars will make an impressive shining screen. One major cut a year should suffice. The darker-leaved *P. lusitanica* can be pruned to shape but may look as well on a slightly easier rein.

Pyracantha (Firethorn)

The *Pyracantha* forms can provide foliage, evergreen dark foliage, creamy blossom, and lots of persistent

BOUNDARY HEDGES WITH PLANTING DISTANCES

Carpinus betulus, hornbeam
45-60cm (18-24in)

Chamaecyparis lawsoniana forms 60cm (24in)

Cupressocyparis leylandii 75cm (30in)

Fagus sylvatica forms 30-60cm (12-24in)

Ilex aquifolium, holly 45cm (18in)

Taxus baccata, yew 60cm (24in)

Thuja plicata 'Fastigiata' 60cm (24in)

**MAINLY
DECORATIVE HEDGES
WITH PLANTING
DISTANCES**

Berberis x *stenophylla*
60cm (24in)

B. thunbergii forms
45cm (18in)

Buxus sempervirens, box
30cm (12in)

Cotoneaster lacteus
45cm (18in)

C. simonsii
45cm (18in)

Escallonia
45cm (18in)

Euonymus japonicus
45cm (18in)

Erica
30cm (12in)

Lavandula
30cm (12in)

Ligustrum, privet
30cm (12in)

Prunus cerasifera
45cm (18in)

P. x *cistena*
45cm (18in)

Pyracantha
45cm (18in)

Rosa rugosa, and others
60cm (24in)

Trimmed hedges are the
neat backbone in this
informally planted garden

CLEMATIS MONTANA

C. montana 'Elizabeth'

Description: A very robust, deciduous climber,
popular for its huge crops of four-petalled flowers as
well as for its good-natured habits. Lobed, tripartite
foliage looks pleasing.

Uses: Will clamber up almost anything.

Colour: White.

Scent: Rather fleeting.

Size: Height almost indefinite up to 8-12m (25-40ft),
spread usually less but can be trained.

Flowering time: Late spring.

Relatives: *C. montana* var. *rubens* is pale pink.
'Elizabeth' (pictured) is a rather fuller flower in soft
pink with clearly spaced petals. Sweetly scented.
'Tetrarose' has much larger leaves and flowers 6-7cm
(2 ½-3in) wide, at least half as large again as the type.

Cultivation: Easy with their toes in the shade and
their faces in the sun. If pruning is needed do this after
flowering to encourage fresh wood and allow it time
to ripen before winter.

Propagation: By layers of softwood or semi-ripe
cuttings in summer.

berries together with a goodly sprinkling of spines to
back up the defensive aspect. Prune back a little in
autumn to expose ripening berries and remove old
berried shoots in spring to make way for new
growth.

Other decorative evergreens are more useful as
interior hedges or screens, see margin, left, for suggestions.

DECIDUOUS CONTENDERS

Some of the other top contenders for honours in the
hedging stakes, are *Prunus cerasifera* 'Pissardii', hornbeam (*Carpinus betulus*) and beech (*Fagus sylvatica*).
The prunus has pale pink flowers which fade to
white before the dark leaves appear. Beech is excellent on lime soils and in sunny spots. Its pale green
spring leaves are a delight and it often retains some

Passiflora caerulea
Common or blue passion flower

Description: Very upwardly mobile climber with tendrils; evergreen or semi-evergreen in colder districts or bleaker winters. It has palmate leaves of 5-7 narrow leaflets and plenty of blossom when established in a sunny site. Flowers are in plentiful succession, each bloom being 7-10cm (3-4in) across. Sepals and petals point outwards from a central corona with many narrow filaments radiating outwards and coloured in three concentric rings. After a good summer, produces crops of oval fruits. Hardier than most species; it will normally be fully hardy on walls in warmer areas.

Uses: Climber for trellis or similar support by walls and happy to clamber through other plants.

Colour: Leaves dark green. Flowers varying shades but usually white or pale pink, maybe flushed pale green. Filaments are purple at their bases, white for a central zone and with longer ends of mauve-blue.

Scent: Faint scent.

Size: To 10m (30ft) in areas where it is not pruned by frosts, spread as directed.

Flowering time: Summer, more particularly midsummer well into autumn when flowers and fruits can mingle.

Relatives: Best known variant is *P. caerulea* 'Constance Elliott' with ivory white blooms probably wider petalled than the standard.

Cultivation: Likes fertile, well-drained soils in sun but will be quite happy in semi-shade. May need water in times of rapid growth and activity. Stems are best discretely supported. Pruning in spring will be to remove any dead frosted pieces and to thin crowded parts by bringing straying laterals back to spurs that are likely to give flowers.

Propagation: Not difficult either from seed in spring or semi-ripe cuttings in summer.

rust-brown autumn leaves through the winter. Copper beeches can be impressive but make sure you are happy with so much of so dark a colour. Its winter dead foliage is the same as the common kind – warm brown. Hornbeam is similar with a slightly less polished and narrower leaf. The dead leaves hang on as tightly on well clipped specimens. It grows well in all soils.

WALLS AND BANKS

WALLS AND BANKS bring our attention to the vertical. We are forced to look up to view the sheer or sloping surfaces: a third dimension. On a basic level, vertical constructions provide a frame for the garden but they can be a lot more. By fully exploiting the potential of these planes we inestimably increase the richness of our garden design.

Walls and banks can be gardens in themselves: they can be the habitat of small clinging plants and they can be the support of climbers. In uncertain climates less hardy shrubs and plants can nestle in their shelter and comparative warmth. Walls and banks may make boundaries and help to maintain privacy and produce seclusion. They can hem in or, with some creative flair, they can draw the sky into the garden.

When plant-clothed, house walls form a marriage between house and garden. Walls can be sleek with formality, perhaps dressed by a crisp covering of ivy or some sharply pruned shrubs – pyracanthas, ceanothus or euonymus – or they can be informally associated with jostling shrubs and, if freestanding, capped by houseleeks, valerian and wallflowers.

Banks are often best treated as a separate element in the garden design and given a different treatment to the surrounds. They give the chance to grow a variety of shrubs and other plants that will be happier here, and their height and fall enables the display of some plants in a more rewarding manner. A part-shaded bank may be the ideal site for a collection of Lenten roses (*Helleborus orientalis* hybrids), their shy downward-posed blooms the easier seen and admired.

The conditions for plant growth near walls and on banksides can be dramatically different from those just a step or two away. Walls facing the sun will gather and reflect heat to make the microclimate there much warmer throughout the year. Very often a wall will mean that the ground at its foot is very much drier than in the open, the soil can be sheltered from rainfall and the wall itself can leach out some of the moisture. On the other hand, some walls facing the prevalent wind that brings rain may

induce a greater soil water content than the norm though the soil may still be warmer.

Banks facing the sun will be warmer than level ground below; ground falling away from the sun will be that much cooler. The banks themselves being sloped will facilitate the running off of surplus rainwater and will, in all probability, drain much more

White and yellow flowers lead the eye gently up this sloping garden

rapidly than the level ground; obviously the top of the bank is likely to hold a very different amount of moisture than the lower bankside where the bank is of any reasonable size.

Types of wall

A new wall of strong brick with cement mortar does not allow much growth on it. The best way to exploit such a wall is probably to use its shelter and warmth to encourage those shrubs, climbers and plants that need an extra bit of shelter, something to

AURINIA SAXATILIS (SYN. *ALYSSUM SAXATILE*) Gold dust

A. saxatilis var. *citrina*

Description: Evergreen hardy perennial with rather woody stems forming wide mounds of oval grey-green hairy leaves all of which are lost under a mass of spikes of clustered flowers in spring.
Uses: For the bolder rock garden, for growing in or down walls, for raised beds, for the front of borders.
Colour: Brilliant and rather sharp rich yellow.
Scent: Light musky fragrance.
Size: 22cm (9in) high, spread 30-45cm (12-18in).
Flowering time: Spring.
Relatives: *A. saxatilis* 'Compacta' is less sprawling; var. *citrina* (pictured) is a paler but rich lemon-yellow.
Cultivation: Plant young seedlings in permanent quarters and leave undisturbed. Straggly pieces can be cut back to keep tidy. Not a long-lived plant.
Propagation: Seed in early autumn or early spring.

temper the wind. Older walls with crumbly lime mortar, however, can be a home for many plants. A stone wall built dry or with soil is an ideal spot for many alpine plants and other scrambling hardy characters. Walls built to hold and contain banksides will allow a wide range of plants to be grown in them or to cascade down them. Or walls may be built specifically with hollow centres to hold com-

ARABIS CAUCASICA (SYN. *A. ALBIDA*, *A. ALPINA* SUBSP. *CAUCASICA*)
Rock cress

Description: Low-growing evergreen forming mats of oval mid-green leaves in many rosettes. Covered in simple four petalled flowers for weeks. Fully hardy.

Uses: For larger rock garden, raised beds, in or falling down containing walls.

Colour: Usually white but can be palish pink.

Scent: Surprising sweet scent.

Size: 15cm (6in) high, spread 30cm (12in) or more if not checked.

Flowering time: Late spring into summer.

Varieties: *A. caucasica rosea* is pink; there are several other named pink cultivars. 'Flore Pleno' is a showy double white.

Cultivation: Very easy in sun and with good drainage. After flowering may be trimmed back to keep tidy and help new growth.

Propagation: Like mustard and cress from fresh seed. Special clones by softwood cuttings in early summer.

Stonecrop and flint are effective partners on this wall

PLANNING WALLS FOR PLANTING

For those with a neat frame of mind, the wall bonded with mortar can be built incorporating clay pots as building proceeds; once all is finished, these can either be pulled out and replaced with soil, or to be left *in situ*. If to be left in place the pots will be more useful with their bottoms knocked out and placed with their rims fractionally behind the face of the wall and at an angle so that water falling on the wall is encouraged to run back towards the roots. The advantage of such a wall is that it can be built completely upright and is a little smarter for positioning close to the house or other permanent buildings. It should be a double sided wall with a gap in the middle for compost so that the top may be planted and those plants in the sides may have a home for exploring roots. The gap between the two sides ought to be 20cm (8in) or more; if less it will be difficult to keep the internal compost or soil moist to any sensible degree. Get any wider than a 20cm (8cm) gap and it might be an idea to consider a full-scale raised bed which may be as wide as you like so long as you can reach the middle easily from each side.

ARTEMISIA SCHMIDTIANA
Wormwood

Description: A low-growing perennial with creeping stems, making a cushion of ferny foliage with deeply cut filigree silver leaves. It is an outstanding, more or less evergreen, foliage plant; the flowers are poor things, anaemic yellow bits in meagre rounded heads. Frost hardy.

Uses: Excellent for rock gardens, in open sunny spots, or for growing on a bankside or a wall.

Colour: Sterling-silver foliage.

Size: 8-25cm (3-10in) high, spread 60cm (24in).

Flowering time: Summer.

Relatives: *A. schmidtiana* 'Nana' is similar but much more compact: height 8cm (3in), spread 20-25cm (8-10in).

Cultivation: Grow in an open sunny spot and give a gritty soil enriched with plenty of peat or other humus. If need be it can be given a barber's light touch in the spring.

Propagation: Division, taking off rooted pieces.

WALL PLANTS

Arabis

Asperula

Aubrieta

Campanula

Erigeron

Genista

Helianthemum

Iberis

Onosma

Origanum

Potentilla

Saponaria

Saxifraga

Sedum

Sempervivum

Thymus

Verbascum

Veronica

post and with the explicit idea that the addition of a range of plants will make them a special feature.

BUILDING WALLS

A wall made by a gardener for his plants will be distinctly different from the professional builder's smart effort stuck together with impervious cement mortar. Although a gardener's wall may be virtually as solid, with most of the courses of brick or stone held together with cement mortar, there will be plenty of gaps left for plants. Alternatively, the wall can be 'dry', without mortar, and with compost or soil used in its place, making many ideal pockets for plants.

Retaining walls

Sloping ground may be retained as such with shrubs, bulbs and strong herbaceous plants planted through grass or a mulch of shredded bark. Alternatively, the ground can be terraced with the upper level held in place by a retaining wall. Build the retaining wall dry or only partly mortared, or use railway sleepers or logs, and you have created a fine foil for specimens planted to tumble down from the top or perch in the wall itself. The whole face of the wall needs to be tilting backwards to help maintain security and to encourage rainfall to penetrate from the face. Courses of stones or bricks should be laid on a firm foundation in the soil with each course covering the breaks in the layer below.

On or in the wall

Some plants almost demand a wall to grow well. The gorgeously coloured lewisias – species as well as

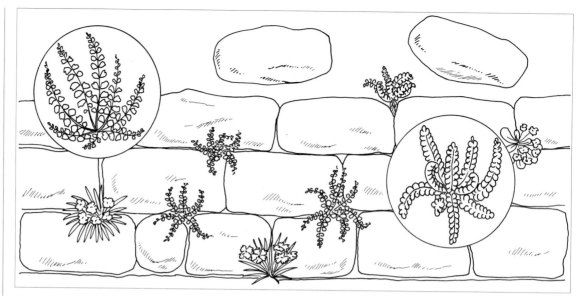

FERNS IN WALLS

Asplenium ruta-muraria, *A. ceterach* (above, right) and
A. trichomanes (above, left) are naturally plants of limestone
areas, but the limy mortar of old walls means that they have long
since sallied forth and are now found in all parts. Try to have a little lime in the walls where you want to establish them.

These little ferns are as tough as old boots once they have made
themselves at home, but it is not always easy to get them going.

They do best in narrow crevices and cracks on a wall, but getting
a pot grown specimen into such places is next to impossible.
Plant your specimens as you build your wall or try to get a
specialist nursery to sell you a few tiny specimens that you may
be able to work into small places. The alternative is to gather
spores and gently blow these on to suitable places on your wall
and hope that nature will take its course. (See page 89 for details
about rearing ferns from spores.)

CYTISUS BATTANDIERI
Moroccan broom,
Pineapple broom

Description: The most distinctive
species of the genus, this is a more or
less evergreen frost hardy bush with
tripartite leaves 5-8cm (2-3in) long and
silvery grey above, nearer white below.
Large tight bunches of flowers, plenty of
them, for a prolonged period.

Uses: In the open in warm spots but
loves a sheltered wall especially in an
angle where it can enjoy basking in the
sun.

Colour: Bright yellow over silvery
green foliage.

Scent: Unusually like pineapples!

Size: 5m (15ft) high, spread 4m (12ft).

Flowering time: Early to midsummer.

Relatives: All other cytisus species and
hybrids are very much smaller.

Cultivation: Plant in well-drained soil
in a sunny spot. Give some support in
early years. Trim off awkward branches.
It remains healthy for a good number
of seasons but is not one of the longest-
living shrubs.

Propagation: By seed, by air or ground
layers, by cuttings of semi-ripe wood
towards late summer.

the hybrids – find a wall an ideal habitat. Here, they
can be grown with their crowns facing outwards
from their vertical homes so any water that lands on
them will drain off, reducing the chance of rot.
More modestly, the wild ivy-leaved toadflax,
Cymbalaria muralis, is happy to grow along a wall, if
you are happy to let it, and it will surprise you with
its winking eyes of bloom most months of the year.
The daisy *Erigeron karvinskianus* (syn. *E. mucronatus*) is
another candidate: time its progress as it runs along
the wall by seed and runner opening masses of white
daisy flowers, which fade to pink or purple. Better
still have a community of plants take over the wall.

ON THE SUNNY SIDE

The sunny side of the wall is going to be extraordinarily hot at times and may get very dry. Plants
introduced here should be placed in position in the
autumn or late winter so that they can get their
roots well into the soil that is kept cool at the back
of the stones or bricks. It follows that there must be
soil in the interior of the wall so that the roots do not

CEANOTHUS 'GLOIRE DE VERSAILLES'
California lilac

Description: One of many evergreen hybrid ceanothus, this one being a fast growing bush with bright green leaves and large rounded racemes of crowded tiny flowers. Fully hardy although appreciating some wall shelter, it comes into its own later than many flowering shrubs and is very showy for a long period.

Uses: By or up a wall or in a mixed planting of shrubs.

Colour: Light blue.

Size: 1.8m (6ft) high, spread 1.5m (5ft).

Flowering time: Midsummer into early autumn.

Relatives: *C.* 'Blue Mound', height 1.5m (5ft), spread 2m (6ft), late spring, dark blue. 'Italian Skies', height 1.5m (5ft), spread 3m (10ft), late spring, rich blue. *C. arboreus* 'Trewithen Blue', height 6m (20ft), spread 8m (25ft), spring-early summer, rich blue.

Cultivation: All ceanothus are the better for some protection, full sun and a drained soil. Good on light soils. Water well when planting and keep moist while they establish, thereafter they can cope well with long periods of drought. Cut away dead wood at the end of winter. Shrubs can be pruned hard to encourage close growth to walls or other supports.

Propagation: Cuttings of semi-ripe wood in summer.

reach back to find an airy space. The soil packed into the wall should be high in humus. It will help if the stones are placed at a slight angle so that any rainfall tends to soak back into the heart of the wall and will not be totally deflected off.

Those plants that are adapted to manage the conditions can look their best on a sunny wall: encrusted saxifrages look properly encrusted and are in sympathy with their stony surroundings; sedums will be succulent but not grossly so; sempervivums gather their initmate but extended family to themselves defiant of their spartan fare – growth is tight, flesh is firm, rosettes are packed together. In fact, these plants are very much 'in character'; probably in a dryish wall made or modified for them. (Sempervivums are also happy on the shady side, see below.)

An old wall can support and supplement the simple beauty of plants such as *Erysimum cheiri*, the wild wallflower, which might look a lost and awkward guest in a border beside more flamboyant garden-bred descendants. Introduce the wild wallflower as tiny seedlings or as scattered seed worked into tiny crevices. Then it is there for decades, self-seeding down the sunny wall side with long-lasting, round headed displays of whorls of yellow flowers topped by the tight top of dark russet buds waiting to carry on a succession for months. When a colony has established there will be veteran plants and all ages down to young seedlings, which helps to spread the flowering period so that it is unusual for such a site not to have some blossom, even in the winter. On dark days it is shining bright, on bright days it is smilingly cheerful.

ON THE SHADY SIDE

The sun does not beat down directly on the shady side of the wall, but nevertheless the site is an extreme one, and water is going to be severely rationed at times. Again, the soil in the wall should be high in humus to retain moisture and provide a healthy rootrun.

If you are starting from scratch, the building of the wall should be such that it ensures that rainfall is encouraged to penetrate into the centre. It helps if the top of the wall is formed of narrower upright stones that allow plenty of access for water into the centre of the wall and to the roots below. The roots

LIMNANTHES SEED

If you collect your own seed of limnanthes, do not sow it immediately. This is one of relatively few plants that germinate better after drying out thoroughly, it manages better than most in a seed packet!

of alpine and wall plants can grow to extraordinary lengths.

The shady side of a wall can be the perfect site for some of the delightful little ferns that have made the leap from their natural habitats on rocky hillsides to man-made wall sites. One such little fern is the little dark green wall rue (*Asplenium ruta-muraria*), which grows only some 5cm (2in) high with little tough fronds halfway between a lichen and French parsley! Quite distinct and looking more like a fern viewed through the wrong end of a telescope is the maidenhair spleenwort (*Asplenium trichomanes*), its tough narrow black fern radii with precisely placed pairs of fresh green pinna, almost square and almost like a double string of beads graded down to the smallest at the pointed tip. These are evergreen little fellows and once established stand a good chance of colonizing a shady wall, especially if it is just slightly damp. Undisturbed walls can end up with hundreds of plants, the progeny from spilt spores.

As a foliage contrast, encourage navelwort (*Umbilicus rupestris*), a strange outer-space type plant producing perfectly round fleshy leaves with the likeness of a navel in the centre of each. There are a few slightly more heart-shaped leaves on the 15cm (6in) flower stems with their attractive spikes of nodding bells, greenish ivory-white or slightly blushed pink. Children love its unusual appearance, a magic fairy plant if there ever was one. It certainly makes a change from its relatives, the sempervivums. A native to many rocky places through Europe and Asia, it will grow more freely on the shaded side of a wall than on the sunny side.

The houseleeks (*Sempervivum* spp.) will grow on the sunny or shaded side of a wall, anywhere they are not overshadowed by other plants. Folklore suggests that they are a protection against lightning, but I don't suggest you take this up with your house insurance agents. *Sempervivum tectorum* is the true houseleek but it has many cultivars with differing amounts of dark purple and red shading to the main parts of the leaves or to their tips or margins. You could spend a lifetime collecting the different species and forms: there are many hundreds. Hybridists are introducing new ones each season, especially those working in America. The sizes range from giants such as 'Commander Hay' with rosettes up to 15cm (6in) across, to the tiny

ERINUS ALPINUS
Fairy foxglove

Description: A low semi-evergreen short-lived perennial thought of as an alpine from the hills, but often found in lowland situations. Small soft oval leaves are in rosettes and scattered up stems which bear a succession of small bright two-lipped flowers. Fully hardy, it is a member of the Scrophulariaceae, the family that includes the proper foxgloves.

Uses: Rock gardens, rock- and raised beds, and walls. It loves to self-sow itself in crumbling mortar of old walls and similar spots.

Colour: Rich bright pink is the norm but there are a few dark ones bordering on purple.

Size: Only 5-8cm (2-3in) high and across.

Flowering time: Late spring and summer.

Relatives: *E. alpinus albus* is a common pretty white mutation. Various colour forms have been named at different times.

Cultivation: Easy in a light position given fast drainage.

Propagation: Will seed itself freely where it is happy. Seed can be saved and sown in pots to be planted out later.

rosettes of the smaller forms of the cobweb house-leek (*S. arachnoideum*) which have gossamer hairs running from tip to tip of each minute leaf. Here is another fun plant that will amuse children as well as grown-ups.

THUGS AND WALLS

A warning. There are plants which like walls and banks but which can get out of control and be a pestilential nuisance in the garden proper. These plants can help clothe a wall attractively and so should be used, but ensure that they stay where they are put.

One dangerously rampant plant is *Cerastium tomentosum* perhaps even better known as snow-in-summer, such a charming name. It is the white flowered plant with silvery white hairy oval leaves that has overrun countless rockeries and caused the faint-hearted to sell up and move. On the top of a wall or draped down a side, it can look quite splendid, but it must not be allowed to touch base, nor must pieces be allowed to fall in any part of the garden proper. The common stonecrop, *Sedum acre*, is another example of a useful wall plant that can be a pest if bits fall below onto the fat land. I like to see a little of the herb Robert, *Geranium robertianum*, on a wall where the rather spartan diet will keep the plant somewhat in check and encourage the red flushing of the foliage and stems, but it needs to be kept in check so that it does not seed all over the garden. The same might be said of valerian, *Centranthus ruber*.

Rather in the same league as snow-in-summer for tough extrovert behaviour are a number of rampant low-growing campanulas. *C. portenschlagiana* has already been mentioned (see page 167), but there are many others, *C. poscharskyana* is another rampant but low growing kind with myriads of blue bells. Also spreading easily is *C. garganica* with its star-shaped flowers, usually a uniform pale lavender but some with white eyes. These campanulas will grow in sun but can be even more abandoned in behaviour in walls with a little shade.

Plants for banks

The pretty stitchworts (*Stellaria* spp.) of our hedgerows are relatives of the *Cerastium*. A natural

HEDERA CANARIENSIS
Canary Island ivy

H. colchica 'Dentata Variegata'

Description: One of the large-leaved ivies; a species that grows rapidly to form wide self-clinging plants with plenty of tough evergreen leaves, roughly triangular and rich in colour. Can be caught by frost but soon recovers.

Uses: Like most ivies this manages well in dry spots once established; as it enjoys some shelter it is ideal for a shady wall or to grow up a tree trunk or other support in shade, although it is perfectly happy in the open light.

Colour: Rich green with leaf stems a maroon red.

Wildlife: Can give shelter to nesting birds and will foster insect life.

Size: Approximately 6m (20ft) high and across.

Relatives: *H. canariensis* 'Gloire de Marengo' has long been exploited as a pot plant but is good outside, the leaves are variegated cream and have silver-grey patches over dark green. Another excellent large-leaved kind is *H. colchica* 'Dentata Variegata' (pictured) with drooping leaves of rich green generously and irregularly variegated in creamy yellow. There are hundreds of good cultivars of the common ivy, *H. helix*. They manage well enough in dry shady spots, though here their colours may not be quite so bright. 'Goldheart' is popular with very pointed leaves, a basic polished dark green but with a large portion of the centre of each shining gold; they are very firmly ironed flat to their support.

Cultivation: Newly planted specimens need to be watered until the roots have got well away. The new plant will start growing much quicker if it is securely fixed to the wall or other support it is supposed to climb.

Propagation: By layers, or by cuttings in midsummer.

hedge or bankside will be nicely enhanced by them. They clamber upwards in a seemly way with pleasing light green narrow foliage and elegant white flowers on thread-thin stems. On the bankside, especially lower down in moister spots, you may allow *Limnanthes douglasii* (meadowfoam or poached egg plant) to naturalize itself. (See plant profile, page 233.)

Banks are ideal sites for many plants that look effective in a colony. Snowdrops, crocuses, daffodils and some of the lily species such as *L. martagon* look good here. And there are some plants that may be better appreciated with the lift that the bank can give them, for example early in the year the nodding flowers of Lenten roses, *Helleborus orientalis* hybrids.

Some plants, like these lewisias, are happiest on a well-drained, sunny wall

CENTRANTHUS RUBER
Valerian

Description: Herbaceous perennial which forms loose clumps that die down to an overwintering rootstock. Polished pointed leaves and branched rounded heads of small flowers for a very long period. It grows wild in Germany, France and Britain.
Uses: Will colonize areas of very poor soil, broken walls and very exposed spots. Particularly good in alkaline soil.
Wildlife: Visited by various flying insects.
Colour: Pink, reddish pink and white.
Size: 60-90cm (2-3ft) high, spread 45-60cm (18-24in).
Flowering time: Very prolonged, may be from late spring until well into autumn.
Cultivation: Needs sunny spot and little else.
Propagation: By seed. Will self-seed.

Plants for beside walls

There are different categories of wall plants. Most obvious are the climbers that are self-clinging, the useful ivies, Virginia creeper (*Parthenocissus quinquefolia*) and *Hydrangea petiolaris*. Then there are those with tendrils like the vines, and those like clematis with leaf stems that wrap themselves round any possible support. Numerous clambering kinds, like honeysuckles, support themselves by twisting around other plants or supports. Some are less obviously adapted, such as the rambling roses and many long reaching shrubs that in nature make their way by leaning on stronger neighbours.

A large number of shrubs are more easily grown by a wall, for support or for warmth. Pyracanthas and ceanothus hybrids are popular examples, but there are others that do not necessarily need to be so precisely trained to a wall; *Garrya elliptica*, with its winter catkins, is well worth a privileged spot as is wintersweet (*Chimonanthus praecox*).

The base of the wall may be a very special microclimate. The soil is likely to be dryish and warm and the wall will add to the warmth and result in the plants being well ripened through the summer months and not too sodden through the winter. Here are perfect spots for the winter-flowering Algerian iris (*I. unguicularis*), for the South African bulbs, *Nerine bowdenii* and *Amaryllis bella-donna* and perhaps for some of the small-flowered gladioli species and hybrids that are on the borderline of hardiness.

TRAINING SHRUBS AGAINST WALLS
Many wall shrubs will need some support to keep tidy against the wall. While it may be possible to use masonry nails and attach main branches to these using tree-ties, a more thorough job can be done by arranging a series of horizontal wires at 25cm (10in) intervals attached each end to strong masonry eyelet nails that allow wires to be attached and strained

against them. Alternatively, trellis can be fixed to the wall and shrubs trained up this. The best method is to very securely fix strong wooden battens to the wall and to mount the trellis onto the battens so that it can be removed carefully if you want to reach the wall behind for maintenance or any other reason (see page 234).

Shrubs such as the spring-flowering *Chaenomeles*, *Jasminum*, *Forsythia suspensa* and many others will benefit from a rather severe pruning régime so that branches are kept close to the wall to benefit the more from the warmth. *Euonymus*, *Ceanothus* and *Pyracantha* forms will be helped by trellis and need to be pruned hard but not quite so hard as the ones mentioned in the previous sentence. *Garrya elliptica*, *Magnolia grandiflora* and *Camellia* hybrids may be initially given some support but will later probably manage well enough on their own. As the base of a house wall is likely to be a very dry area, the addition of plenty of humus material before planting any shrubs, bulbs or other items is recommended. If planting climbers or other shrubs it is best to plant with the rootstock pointing away from the wall but leading the upper growth directly to the wall. Give new plants plenty of water until they are established.

NERINE BOWDENII

Description: In Britain and similar climates, the only hardy member of this bulbous South African genus. Bright green leaves grow through spring into summer; they are long, narrow and strap-shaped. In autumn, it blooms without foliage, producing 6-12 flowers on long stems. They are trumpet-shaped with recurving ends. The bulbs have long necks.

Uses: Excellent bright fresh colour in the autumn. Bulbs flourish against walls in awkward dryish warm spots. Can be grown in containers such as pots and left for many years undisturbed.

Colour: Sparkling rich pink.

Size: 30-60cm (12-24in) high, spread 15-20cm (6-8in).

Flowering time: Autumn.

Relatives: Various clones such as 'Mark Fenwick' have been named; these are usually just a fraction larger and bolder in bloom. *N. bowdenii* 'Alba' covers white forms, sometimes with a light pink blush. Other species and the many fine hybrids are not hardy.

Cultivation: Plant bulbs with noses just level or just under the soil surface. Choose a well-drained warm spot. Leave undisturbed until, after many years, the clumps get overcrowded. Bulbs may take a season or so to feel really at home but thereafter get better year by year.

Propagation: Division, end of summer or early spring.

LAWNS AND OTHER OPEN AREAS

OPEN AREAS ARE important in a garden. They add the feeling of space, they provide vistas and views, they tempt us in to enjoy the garden's delights, they are our space among the plants: careful thought must be given to their provision.

In temperate parts of the world, the standard response to the need for open areas in the garden is to establish lawn. But it is not the only answer and if you inherit a garden without a lawn or if you feel you have too much lawn, there are other solutions that work well and can be just as pleasing, if not more so, than a green sward. It is sensible to take time to look at the alternatives and weigh up the costs in terms of its establishment and upkeep.

Pros and cons of the lawn

A good lawn can do many things for a garden. Its gentle shades of green form the restful foil for the rainbow colours of flowers, bringing the most gaudy effects under control. The surface is reasonably soft for walking and playing on, it is firm enough for sitting, for picnicking, for afternoon tea in the shade and for sun bathing. A large patch is an ideal area for games or simply for a peaceful stroll.

Against all this attractiveness should be placed the disadvantages of green stuff that grows: the cost of purchase and maintenance of cutting equipment and the time involved in taking care of the grass. Oddly enough, the smaller the area, the more difficult it is to keep in very good order because it will suffer more wear and tear.

COSTS OF A LAWN

When adding up costs don't forget to take the following into account:

1 *Preparation of ground for turfing or seeding – time and labour.*
2 *Seed or turf – costs.*
3 *Sowing seed, and subsequent care, laying turf – time and labour.*
4 *Mowing machine – costs.*
5 *Machine storage – costs and organization.*
6 *Mowing – time and labour (number of hours x number of times a year).*
7 *Other upkeep – spiking, moss and weed killing, fertilizing – time and costs.*

CHAMAEMELUM NOBILE
(SYN. *ANTHEMIS NOBILIS*)
Chamomile

Description: Energetic, ground-covering, evergreen perennial. Bright green much-divided ferny foliage is rather sharply but pleasantly aromatic when crushed. Daisy flowers. Fully hardy.
Uses: Sometimes this invasive low plant is used to make a 'lawn', sometimes, but more rarely, this is successful. The smaller the area the more likely you are to achieve a reasonable cover (see margin on page 193 for how to make a chamomile lawn). Dried flowers were once used to make a drink to reduce fever.
Colour: Daisies with white ray florets and yellow disc centres.
Scent: Leaves pleasingly scented when crushed, flowers slight musty aroma.
Size: 10cm (4in) high, spread 45cm (18in).
Flowering time: Late spring and summer.
Relatives: C. nobile 'Treneague' is a more compact non-flowering form that is better adapted to lawn-making. C. nobile 'Flore Pleno' has very neat, attractive, fully-double button flowers more prolifically than the type and for many weeks. Pretty, less invasive plant for edges of border or elsewhere.
Cultivation: Wants sun and a drained soil. Plant rooted pieces 20cm (8in) apart in a border or raised bed, but thicker for lawn.
Propagation: By rooted pieces detached in spring.

LAWN EDGES

Good edges make the lawn. Ideally all grass should have a mowing strip set alongside it, a barrier to stop the incursion of grass into beds, thus saving the time and trouble of constant edging.

In this cottage garden, foxgloves, cow parsley, and other self-seeders have made effective fillers for a wide open space

AZORELLA TRIFURCATA (SYN. *BOLAX GLEBARIA*)

Description: Like a compact saxifrage, this fully hardy perennial has tiny tough, leathery, much-divided leaves forming rounded tight humps on which stemless bunches of little flowers are occasionally displayed.

Uses: Usually an alpine-house dweller but a possible rock garden plant, perhaps chosen to grow out of a piece of the soft tufa rock.

Colour: Blue-green foliage, flowers are yellow.

Size: Only 2.5cm (1in) high, spread 10-15cm (4-6in).

Relatives: *A. trifurcata* 'Nana' is even smaller.

Cultivation: In perfectly drained soil in full light.

Propagation: By division in early spring.

Encouraging wildflowers to take over a grassy site has created an informal, low-maintenance meadow

There is an equation to be solved. Is the input of money and labour involved in maintaining a healthy and attractive lawn going to be balanced by the enjoyment and use it affords? (See box Costs of a lawn, page 187.)

Lawns are hard work. How many flower beds in your garden would receive the same attention? Two or three hours of it, every week during the high season? Of course, mowing is a different sort of labour, a routine that can be carried out without much thought and it could be that you enjoy this mindlessness once in a while. There is also the opportunity to delegate the work to idle teenagers or less-skilled minions.

Lawns as an attitude of mind

Having said all this against lawns, it is possible to have a perfectly good open grassy area without being enslaved. It is no good in the long run getting obsessed with growing a perfect carpet of green. I suggest relaxing a little. Do some lateral thinking. Forget the bowling green and think more of the idealized meadowland, a miniature hayfield that need be cut only a few times through the year.

MAKING A MEADOW

It is no good simply letting your existing lawn grow. Often the only thing that is encouraged is a weedy mass with docks and nettles instead of a bright collection of buttercups, daisies, primroses, cowslips, bird's foot trefoils, snake's-head fritillaries, vetches, bedstraws, bugle, cranesbills and knapweeds. It is best to start with a clean canvas, an area free of the worst perennial weeds. If starting on untamed ground, begin by applying a systemic weedkiller (glyphosate will normally clear weeds in one appli-

MALUS '**PROFUSION**'
Ornamental crab apple

M. 'John Downie'

Description: Small deciduous, spreading tree with purple young foliage becoming dark green. It has bountiful all-covering blossom in bunches of cup-shaped blooms, followed in the late summer and autumn by crab apples. Fully hardy.

Uses: Decorative specimen tree.

Colour: Crimson-pink flowers, dark crimson-purple fruits.

Size: To 8m (25ft) high, spread 7m (22ft).

Flowering time: Late spring.

Relatives: *M.* 'Golden Hornet' is a more upright tree with green foliage, white flowers and very heavy crops of golden fruits that persist through the autumn into winter. M. 'John Downie' (pictured) has white flowers from pale pink buds, followed by orange and red fruit.

Cultivation: Having thoroughly cultivated the ground and made a generous hole for the containerized tree, dig over the hole's bottom and position tree, with stake if necessary, ensuring that it is neither deeper or shallower than when in the pot when the fertilized topsoil is returned. Firm and water. Further maintenance is minimal.

Propagation: Grafting or budding on apple stock. You could try air-layering (see page 195).

HAYFIELD FLOWERS

Achillea millefolium

Agrimonia eupatoria

Alchemilla vulgaris

Bellis perennis

Cardamine pratensis

Chamaemelum nobile

Cirsium arvense, and other thistles

Galium palustre, and other bedstraws

Geranium pratense

G. sanguineum

Hieracium umbellatum, and other hawkweeds

Lathyrus pratensis, and other vetches

Leucanthemum vulgare

Origanum vulgare

Plantago major, and other plantains

Primula veris

Primula vulgaris

Ranunculus acris, and other buttercups

Taraxacum vulgaria

Trifolium pratense, and other clovers

NARCISSUS PSEUDONARCISSUS
Wild daffodil, Lent lily

Description: Hardy bulb with flowers with pointed petals and serrated trumpets. Being small and early they will not cause much problem with foliage after flowering.

Uses: A delightful naturalizing bulb. It resents constant disturbance so it should not be used like the larger hybrids in the border. Plant in grass, between shrubs, by hedges, in ditch sides and in light woodland conditions.

Wildlife: Can attract some of the earlier flying insects including small beetles.

Colour: Petals are normally pale cream, trumpets are usually rich buttery yellow. Colour varies.

Scent: Very light.

Size: 15-30cm (6-12in) high, dependent on clone and position, spread dependent on size of clump.

Flowering time: Early, towards mid-spring.

Relatives: *N. obvallaris*, the Tenby daffodil, is slightly taller but is bolder with wider petalled and trumpeted blooms of uniform rich gold. Naturalize in all the positions suggested above or grow at the bases of specimen trees or shrubs.

Cultivation: Plant early autumn with 8-10cm (3-4in) soil over bulbs. It will not do much the first season; thereafter, it will improve year on year to give greater quantities of bloom.

Propagation: Increases in the wild by steady division, but more widely by scattering seed that takes some years to form flowering size bulbs. When garden clumps have become crowded, lift as soon as foliage begins to turn yellow with age, split bulbs up and replant immediately in groups.

AMELANCHIER LAMARCKII
Snowy mespilus

Description: Deciduous, hardy shrub of upright form with many branches, smothered with blossom in spring. Serrated, oval, pointed leaves unfurl bronzy red when the flowers are out. They mature to dark green but take on brilliant orange and red shades in autumn. Can make a small tree after many years.

Uses: Popular for its easy-going nature and very free-flowering habit, the autumn colour is a welcome bonus.

Colour: White flowers.

Size: Eventually up to about 5m (15ft) high, but to about 3m (10ft) in six or seven seasons, spread two thirds of height.

Flowering time: Spring.

Relatives: *A. canadensis*, also white-flowered, makes a dense shrub or small tree up to 6m (20ft) high.

Cultivation: Best in moist, well-drained soil that is neutral or slightly acid. In sun or semi-shade.

Propagation: Easiest by layering low branches in autumn or early spring. Alternatively try air-layering. See margin.

cation if used when they are in full growth). After ten days or so the ground can be worked and left to allow any further weed seed to germinate. With a further digging over, this weed will be eliminated. You can now sow a mix of fine grasses to which can be added a 'hayfield mix' of wild flowers. Do not sow the grasses as heavily as recommended for a lawn, a fifth to a tenth of the amount will suffice. You can add mature plants that have been raised from seed or propagated by divisions.

Clumps of cowslips or primroses can be lifted in early autumn or very early spring and split into many small lively bits. You may find it easier to do this by washing off soil with a hosepipe jet of water. Discard older pieces and plant up divisions into permanent quarters making sure they are firmly secured and are not poking above the surface.

A piece of existing lawn can be left unmowed and allowed to become a hayfield, but only if it is free of potential troublemakers. These can be killed off by spot spray weeding. Any weed on the borderline of acceptability may be just kept in check by preventing its spread, especially by stopping seeding. You will succeed best if the ground is not too rich and has not been heavily dosed with fertilizers. This is one reason why it helps to start out on this venture by removing the top layer of turf and so immediately reducing fertility.

Alternative surfaces

Alternatives to lawns fall into two basic categories: soft surfacing with plants or shredded bark and hard surfacing with paving, gravel and so on.

BARK

Bark is an attractive background to many plants. The very largest grade bark is acceptable in large-scale plans and in wilder places; in more civilized areas medium-sized bark is preferable, the very smallest grade is often too fine. Birds enjoy rooting around in bark and will move quantities of it onto any open areas or grass if they are alongside. To avoid this go a little easy when applying it close to the grass or organize a paved or bricked strip from which the bark can be swept back onto the border.

PAVING

Paving has a great deal to be said in its favour. The most important factors are the increased accessibility of the garden and the absolute minimum of upkeep needed once properly installed. The appearance of paving is, of course, distinct from that of a lawn. However, while lawns may look good for much of the time if cared for, there are going to be times particularly in dry summers when they may be reduced to a parched or patchy expanse just at the time when they are most used. Paving does not suffer this problem although on hot summer days the sun's glare on the stone surface can create a forbidding heat.

Where paving meets borders or beds, plants falling across the margin soften the edges and add an effective contrast of living growth with the inanimate. Where plants fall over the lawn edge they make mowing more difficult and tend to kill off patches of grass.

PRETTYING CONCRETE

Concrete can be made more pleasing by incorporating attractive coloured even-sized stones in the aggregate used for its making. By brushing and washing the surface of the laid concrete before it is wholly dry, the pattern of these stones will be revealed to give an effective colour and texture to the whole.

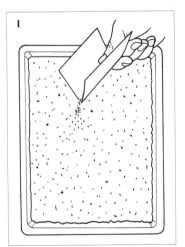
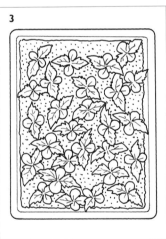
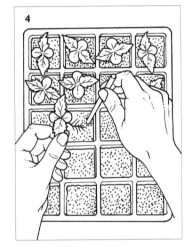

RAISING MATURE PLANTS FOR MEADOWS

It is safer to introduce well-grown plants of a number of chosen kinds than to trust to nature by scattering seed. Your established plants will then provide plenty of seed for further colonization.

1 Sow seed in pots or trays, either in late winter or when they are harvested, if you have saved your own.
2 Keep moist and covered with glass, plastic/cling film.
3 Place in a cool greenhouse, cold frame, conservatory or kitchen windowsill until seed begins to germinate.
4 Prick off seedlings when they have fully grown their first true leaf. Use trays, preferably modules.
5 Grow on until plants have filled their module/pot.
6 Plant out before plants get too root-bound.
7 Plant in groups but not necessarily too close together. They will increase size and number naturally.
8 Water in after planting.

MEMBRANES OR NOT

Where gravel surrounds plants, seed that falls can find the cool moist soil below a surprisingly good place to germinate. You may find yourself with progeny to use elsewhere or to give away.

A membrane below the gravel makes it more difficult to free seedlings without losing the roots; if you want extra plants you could leave some membrane-free areas. You may be able to free small seedlings from the top gravel and the membrane, but if they are worth the retrieving, they can be lifted by cutting

away the membrane together with the seedlings. They can then be removed individually without trying to get rid of all the membrane. The membrane hole

can be made good by laying a fresh piece to cover the area and covering this with gravel. No one but you will know.

FRITILLARIA MELEAGRIS
Snake's-head fritillary

Description: The best known of the smaller fritillaries and a joy when it gets going well. It has thin grass-like foliage and slender stems from which are hung large, square-shouldered flowers often with the chequered patterning that gives this elfin plant its common name. Hardy.
Uses: A pretty addition to a low moist rock garden niche or, better still, for naturalizing in light grass that is not mown until the flowers are well past and seedheads have come to maturity.

Could also be grown in a heather garden or associated with hellebores, snowdrops, anemones and hepaticas – plants that enjoy similar cool somewhat moist conditions.
Colour: Usually matt purple-mauve, but variable with darker tones, light pinks and relatively frequent pure whites.
Size: 20-30cm (8-12in) high, spread only 5-8cm (2-3in).
Flowering time: Mid- to late spring.
Varieties: Specialist growers may offer a number of named clones, but usually bulbs are offered in mixed colours. (Often the larger, paler bulbs are the white forms.)
Cultivation: The bulbs are best in the ground, so purchase early and plant straightaway in fertile well-drained soil that is likely to remain moist. Best in the open but can manage light shade.
Propagation: Bulbs will divide, but seed is produced prolifically and germinates freely if sown fresh outside or in trays; it will take three or four years to reach flowering size.

CHOOSING PAVING

The choice for paving is between prefabricated stones or concrete laid within defined margins. Never go for the cheap option of a poorly-concreted path or patio. Every single time you look at it you will regret that you did not spend more effort and money, and it will be with you a long while. Well-laid concrete, on the other hand, has several attractions: it can be cheaper than paving, it can be made to any shape and it is permanent. When laying it, cracks can be left for creeping plants and there will be fewer unfilled crevices for weeds to find. With care, the surface can be slip-proof, perhaps looking better than some of the less attractive paving stones and certainly less liable to become slippery.

Both paving stones and concrete are laid on a hardcore base which will tend to act as a drain for part of the surrounding ground.

Paving stones vary tremendously in appearance and quality. There is a vast choice of both shape and colour. Man-made materials predominate; the days are gone when a garden of any pretension would be paved with genuine York stone. Few want the expense of using this rare material now and from a conservation point of view it is best discouraged. However, the best of the imitations are so close to the original that the difference in weathered appearance cannot possibly justify the huge difference in price. The artificial stones, often made from moulds created from original York stone, have another advantage for the do-it-yourself gardener. They are of more or less uniform thickness and all have flat bases that can be laid on to a bed of grit or coarse sand with little trouble to get a uniform flat secure finish.

There are times during the year, such as in frosty weather, when the lawn is no place to tread, but paving is still serviceable. Paving provides a place for garden furniture at all times, no sinking into soft soil there.

GRAVEL

A run of hot dry summers has resulted in there being more and more interest in laying down gravel as a working surface in places where before grass may have been *de rigueur*. There may be some danger of the popularity of gravel getting out of hand; it is not the answer to every problem but it certainly deals with a great many. In the right place and used sensibly it can be a great help for some tough garden problems.

Gravel has many advantages. It is easy to lay. If the area is clear of serious weed before gravel is put down then there is likely to be only very minor weed problems afterwards, so long as the layer is sufficiently deep. The weed-suffocating effect will be enhanced if a mesh membrane is laid down before the gravel is applied. Gravel is easy to walk on at all times and also aids surface drainage.

Many plants can be planted within gravel or top-dressed with it to give enhanced performance and gravel sets off many plants very well. The stones act as a mulch which keeps the soil surface cool and moist. The soil organisms are likely to work as well or better under a layer of gravel, reaching to the very surface of the soil without risk of discovery or drying out.

Gravel also prevents the soil surface compacting in a solid layer when rain falls and leads the rain into it in a way that ensures it is more likely to be absorbed evenly.

The above considerations apart, the most important factor for most people is its appearance. There is a wide range of gravel stones and rock chippings, so many that it is difficult to make a choice. Consider existing colours in your garden and the colours of any buildings or other structures. Granite gravel is likely to be of a uniform colour and can look rather dead. Some Cotswold and other rock chippings can look aggressively bright yellow or gold, although some of the initial brightness can be discounted as the material will weather and algae and moss growth will soften it. Graded pea gravel is possibly the most acceptable choice. It is made up of small rounded pebbles of varying colours, the balance of which will vary.

Many small plants seem to relish the gravel and membrane culture. We introduced thymes, *Thymus serpyllum* cultivars, to such an area and found that

ERICA CARNEA VARIETIES
Winter-flowering heather

E. carnea 'Vivellii'

Description: Low-growing, evergreen, ground-covering shrubs with needle-narrow leaves and bell-shaped small flowers. Very hardy.

Uses: For winter colour, for ground-cover, for easy-care gardens. For a heather garden in all soils.

Wildlife: Early bees and flying insects come visiting the flowers whenever the weather allows.

Colour: Foliage usually dark green but may be as dark as almost black to golden and yellow. Flowers range from pure white through innumerable shades of pink to dark crimson.

Size: 15-30cm (6-12in) high, spread to 1m (3ft).

Flowering time: Cultivars to cover from mid-autumn to early spring. Some bloom for months.

Relatives: Huge number of cultivars: 'December Red' and 'Vivellii' (pictured) are two rich coloured ones. 'Springwood White' and 'Cecilia M. Beale' are good whites. 'Westwood Yellow' has splendid yellow foliage and 'Foxhollow' is golden in summer but brightly flushed with orange in winter.

Cultivation: Plant deeply in an open spot in well-drained soil and top-dress as the plants grow. A haircut after flowering will keep older ones tidy and lively. Tolerates lime.

Propagation: Easy by layers or cuttings early summer.

MAKING A CHAMOMILE LAWN

It is recommended that the non-flowering compact form, *Chamaemelum nobile* 'Treneague', is used. You may find it sensible to purchase some plants and spend a season propagating these by division and cuttings so that you build up your own stock for planting and are not spending an undue amount on the initial planting. While seedlings can be used, these will be flowering kinds and will consequently take more looking after. The flower-heads need removing and this tends to spoil the effect.

1 *Define the area to be treated, probably best not too large an area.*
2 *Cultivate soil, fertilize and rake flat.*
3 *Using pot-grown plants, rooted cuttings or divisions, plant the area distancing plants about 15cm (6in) apart. If you are prepared to wait a little longer for an all-over green effect, the plants could be up to twice as widely spaced.*
4 *The lawn is kept neat by mowing with rotary cutter, strimmer or clippers. Do not try to get too close to the ground.*

Tulips and other bulbs have been naturalized in this spring meadow

LIRIODENDRON TULIPIFERA '*FASTIGIATUM*'
Fastigiate tulip tree

Description: If you have the space, and the years to spare, try the type, *Liriodendron tulipifera*. It grows to 30m (100ft) and about half as wide! It is a deciduous giant but is attractive as a youngster with its unique leaves, wide and lobed and looking as if the children have been at them with a pair of scissors to cut off their tips. Flowers are borne more freely on older specimens, large upward-facing tulips with showy yellow stamens. 'Fastigiatum' makes an upward reaching column that is more easily accommodated in normal-sized gardens. It will start blooming as a youngish plant. Fully hardy.

Uses: Specimen tree in a lawn or elsewhere.

Colour: Foliage rich green, golden in autumn. Flowers mix of pale green, white and pale orange.

Size: Eventually very high, but only half the width of the type, making a narrow pyramid.

Flowering time: Midsummer.

Relatives: *L. tulipifera* 'Aureomarginatum' has leaves irregularly splashed around the edges with yellow.

Cultivation: Best in neutral or slightly acid soil which is well-drained, and in a sunlit or lightly shaded spot.

Propagation: Grafting on to stock of type or air-layers (see opposite).

AIR-LAYERING

The main advantages of this method of propagation are that virtually any shrub or tree can be treated without the necessity of getting a piece pegged to the ground and that the layer can be left in position indefinitely.

1 *Select the branch to be air-layered. Choose ripe young wood of the previous year. Remove any leaves along a length up to 15cm (6in).*
2 *Open a small slit using a sharp blade and moving towards the branch tip. The cut needs to be about 4cm (1 ½in) long. Alternatively, slice off a tiny sliver of the young bark, or graze it.*
3 *Treat the cut wood with hormone rooting powder.*
4 *Cut a piece of polythene twice as long as the area of cut wood and about 30cm (12in) wide. Secure one end to below the treated area.*
5 *Wrap the treated area with a couple of handfuls full of wet moss or similar material, such as peat or compost, and secure this all around the layer using the polythene to make sure it is airtight. The moss must remain moist for the wood to start rooting. Secure the top end of the polythene to result in a long balloon around the treated part of the layer.*
6 *Leave the wrap in position for one growing season by which time the layer should be well rooted.*
7 *Open the wrap and, if the layer is well rooted, sever the layer from the parent shrub/tree.*
8 *Pot up or plant in nursery area to grow on a further year before placing in permanent quarters.*

the year after planting there was a widespread generation of seedlings making their own way in the world very successfully – varying slightly in colour and with some having variegated foliage. The sedums also found conditions much to their liking; we allowed them just as much room as was decent without it looking like a takeover bid. Others that managed well were the coloured-leaved *Ajuga reptans* forms. These include 'Burgundy Glow', 'Catlin's Giant', and 'Multicolor' in various purple shades. The tiny carpeting Corsican mint, *Mentha requienii* and *Globularia* in neat rounded clumps are worth trying. In our site, silvery-leaved *Anthemis* almost ran riot.

CONTAINERS

GROWING PLANTS in containers is an artificial method of culture and is considered successful when a large amount of plant growth is supported by a minimum of growing medium. It only works for the plant if all its necessities of life are provided: light, moisture and food heading the list.

Why use containers?

There are several advantages to containers. Unless very large, they are easy to move and so can be brought in succession into the most vital parts of the patio or garden as they come into their own; tender

This hot, dry garden has been enhanced by containers — both planted and empty

plants can be moved into warmer quarters in the winter. Containers also allow gardeners to accommodate plants that demand certain soil conditions. Acid lovers can be grown by gardeners on alkaline soils and vice versa.

Large containers are a way of growing some plants that would otherwise be altogether too much of a good thing; containers keep them within bounds and such discipline may lead shy-to-bloom kinds to be more prolific. Fruit trees can be made more productive. A fig is better grown in a large pot

A. americana 'Marginata'

Description: Mexican native with huge, fleshy, spiked leaves up to 1.5m (5ft) long. They emerge so tightly packed from the central rosette that each leaf has a permanent textured imprint of the silhouette of its neighbour on the outside. After many years, but unlikely as long as the hundred years of its common name, an incredible stem reaches up to as much as 10m (33ft) with clustered plates of flowers. Min. temp. 5°C (41°F).

Colour: Leaves are blue-green, or have variegated margins, flowers creamy white.

Size: 2m (6ft) high.

Relatives: A. americana 'Variegata' has a clear, creamy-white edge to the leaves. 'Marginata' (pictured) has wide creamy-yellow leaf-edges.

Cultivation: Well-drained soil in full sun. Unhappy with high rainfall.

Propagation: By seed or offsets in summer.

AGAVE AMERICANA
Century plant

CHOOSING CONTAINERS

When choosing bear in mind several points:
1 *Larger pots are more easily managed as growing environments.*
2 *Very large ones may be too heavy to move once in place.*
3 *There should always be as much depth for growing medium as possible, 20cm (8in) at least if possible.*
4 *The shape should be attractive but usually the plainer, bolder forms are more pleasing. Too much decoration detracts from the plants.*
5 *There should be adequate provision for drainage, or you should be able to manufacture drainage holes without threatening the integrity of the whole.*
6 *If you choose earthenware or terracotta, try to ensure they are as frostproof as possible – a guarantee is given with some ranges.*

AEONIUM ARBOREUM

A. *arboreum* 'Zwartkop'

Description: A succulent looking like a house leek on stilts. It comes from desert areas of Morocco. Bright flowers in tight oval heads about 10cm (4in) long. Min. temp. 10°C (50°F).
Colour: Flowers yellow, leaves bright shining green.
Size: To 60cm (2ft) high, spread perhaps 1m (3ft).

Flowering time: End of winter up to late spring.
Relatives: A. *arboreum* 'Atropurpureum' has rich purple red foliage, 'Zwartkop' (pictured) has narrow, dark purple, almost black leaves.
Cultivation: Well-drained soil in sun or light shade.
Propagation: Stem cuttings in spring or early summer.

which restricts its roots, so that it remains a manageable size, and encourages it to exert its energy in producing fruit.

Containers are movable, so it is possible to grow more tender plants that can be wheeled under cover for the worst of the winter; slightly exotic species become a real possibility. Some of the citrus fruits could be grown outside in the good weather and then just be kept frost-free over winter. The spectacular fleshy agaves are also good for introducing a tropical or desert-like touch on the patio or in a corner of the garden so long as they are protected for the cold months.

Starting out

WHAT CONTAINER?

Containers range from pots used for plants on display in the garden or on the patio, and include jardinières, bowls and other artifacts up to the size of troughs. The range of containers on offer in the larger garden centres and elsewhere is daunting, but there are ways to narrow down your choice.

A small pot is just a small pot; it is not usually worth considering as a container as it cannot be used for a semi-permanent display outside and special arrangements would have to be made to keep it moist. A pot size of 20cm (8in) diameter is large

WATERING SYSTEMS

The simplest form is a 'reservoir' within the container which can be topped up periodically. It can be as simple as an upturned plastic bottle with the bottom cut off and the sides punctured and then sunk into the container so that the bottle can be filled with water, which then percolates through the compost.
It ensures that water is getting to the base. Often a container can look well watered when really only the top crust is wet.

TRICKLE SYSTEMS

1 *The most successful small-scale system is one based on the trickle idea. Pipes of relatively narrow gauge, perhaps 1cm (½in) in diameter, are led to the containers. At each container there is a T-junction with a small nozzle at the end.*
2 *The nozzles unscrew to give an increasing frequency of drip.*
3 *The pipes are connected either to a permanent waterpipe, via a non-return valve, or to a hosepipe that serves the same purpose but which is connected to the mains supply also via a non-return valve. (It is against the law not to have such valves fitted.)*
4 *The mains supply can be turned on for as long as it takes for the nozzles to water their containers. You will need to fine tune the nozzles: the ones nearest to the mains supply will have to be more closely tightened than those at the far end of the run.*
5 *A refinement for a major installation is a time clock that regulates the flow to the nozzles.*

enough to use for special duties. The larger the pot, the easier it is to maintain a healthy growing medium.

The material that the container is made of will govern part of the life and management of the whole when planted up. Moisture in a pot may trickle out of the drainage hole and be evaporated from the compost surface, but in pots of porous material it will also be lost through the sides of the container. Clay is the most porous material, terracotta is fairly porous as is stoneware; glazed ceramics and plastics are not porous. Wood is porous but not to a great extent.

COMPOSTS

Potting composts are available in several different mixes. They can also be made up by gardeners. With a very finite amount of growing medium in any container it is important to make sure that it is as useful as possible to the plants that are growing in it. It should be a friendly medium for roots and a good anchorage. It should be able to provide a balanced supply of the foods – not necessarily the same balance that might be needed by plants in the open garden. And it must be watered easily and moisture-retentive.

John Innes composts – No. 1, No. 2 and No. 3 – are soil-based potting mediums that were specially developed by the John Innes Institution, Merton, Cambridgeshire, in the second half of the 1930s and introduced widely in the following two decades. When they were introduced, they brought sense to earlier chaos in the potting compost world. The composts are made of healthy sterilized loam, fibrous peat and sharp sand or grit in the ratio 7:3:2, by bulk. To this is added a John Innes base fertilizer made of 2 parts hoof and horn, 2 parts superphosphate of lime, 1 part sulphate of potash. The numbered composts have one, two or three doses of fertilizer (hence the numbers) plus 28g (1oz) of ground chalk to every 50kg (1cwt) of compost, 112g (4oz) being one dose of the base fertilizer per 50kg (1cwt).

Peat-based composts are very largely peat but have added minerals to support healthy plant growth. They are clean and easy to use. Their disadvantages are that once dried out they can be very difficult to get wet again and being light they will not

TRACHYCARPUS FORTUNEI
Chusan palm, Fan palm

Description: One of the hardiest of Asian palms. Its huge leaves, 1.2m (4ft) across, are crimped fans held from the single stem. Trunks are rough and hairy. Mature specimens will produce crowds of creamy, tiny flowers in downward curving panicles 60cm (2ft) long. Frost hardy to -5°C (23°F), will manage well outside in a warm spot, sheltered from winds.
Colour: Creamy flowers.
Scent: Flowers are scented.
Flowering time: Early summer.
Cultivation: Give full sun, shelter, and well-drained soil. No wind.
Propagation: By seed in autumn or spring.

give so much stability to pots when plants are being blown by the wind. They are available commercially or can be made up. A suggested compost mix is, by volume, equal parts of coconut fibre, composted bark and grit or coarse sharp sand. For every 9 gallons or 34 litres of such a mix there should be additives of 140g (5oz) dolomite lime, 56g (2oz) blood, fish and bone, 56g (2oz) bonemeal, 28g (1oz) hoof and horn.

Whatever compost is used, the water retention quality is hugely enhanced by the use of gels that swell up to form a soft jelly-like material when water is added. The water stored in the 'jelly' can be used by plant roots and compost as the need arises and is less easily drained or evaporated.

WATER-RETAINING GELS

Add the gels to the compost mix, add water, and allow the gel to swell for at least an hour before placing any of the compost in a container. It is easy to allow gel to take up water in a bucket before adding it to composts. If it is added dry and the compost used immediately, once it is watered in the container the whole lot will begin to expand over the top.

PHORMIUM TENAX
New Zealand flax

Description: Evergreen perennial with arching sword-shaped leaves. A plant can make a sculptural focal point. Stout, dramatic, leaning stems carry tight handfuls of dull red flowers. Frost hardy to -5°C (23°F).

Colour: Dark green leaves, there are many coloured variegations, red flowers.

Size: To 2m (6ft) high and spread.

Flowering time : Summer.

Relatives: *P. tenax* 'Dazzler' is 2m (6ft) high with dark striped leaves in red, purple and bronze. 'Bronze Baby' has burgundy-coloured leaves, this time in a 'miniature' 1m (3ft) height. 'Yellow Wave' is brilliant in yellow and green, also around 1m (3ft) tall.

Cultivation: Well-drained soil in full sun, may need extra moisture in hot weather. In its native New Zealand it is often found close to water.

Propagation: By division in spring.

Management

A town house with only a paved area outside will depend heavily on containers and may have a large collection. Usually it is wise to have a limited number of good large containers rather than a proliferation of small ones. Individual pots can be placed strategically or may be grouped. If you plan to have abundant potted plants, it is a good idea to arrange a spot out of general view where the containers are filled, planted and able to grow into readiness for their stage appearance.

WATERING

Watering is always a prime concern. Try to organize matters so that you can get water easily wherever you need it. A trickle drip irrigation system, where it is possible to hide much of the unsightly piping will certainly lessen the labour. Hard water tends to deposit limescale which blocks nozzles, so such systems are likely to be more successful in soft water

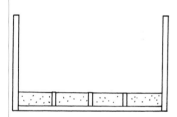

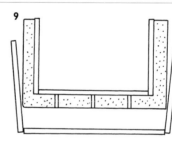

MAKING A TROUGH OF 'HYPERTUFA'

1 Decide on dimensions. Depth should be at least 15cm (6in) but would be better at 20cm (8in). A useful overall exterior size might be: length 60-75cm (24-30in), width 38-45cm (15-18in), depth 15-20cm (6-8in).

2 Make a wooden mould of the chosen exterior dimensions. Ideally the sides should be joined with brass screws that can be unscrewed after use. (There is no need for a base to this mould. It will be standing on flat soil or sand when in operation.)

3 Make a second mould allowing for a gap of 5cm (2in) all the way around and for the base, ie the width at the top will be 10cm (4in) less than the exterior mould. Try to make this second mould slightly narrower and less long at the base than the top. (This will make it easier to remove the mould after use, something that can be further eased by securing a piece of wood across the top of the inner mould to act as a handle.)

4 Make four plugs that can be stood inside the exterior mould some 10cm (4in) from each corner. These plugs will be 5cm (2in) high and will support the interior mould. After completion of the job the plugs will be knocked out leaving four drainage holes.

5 Mix the 'hypertufa' dry: 2 parts sifted moist sphagnum peat, 1 part clean sharp sand or washed fine grit and 1 part cement. Mix thoroughly and gradually add water until the mix is sloppy but not runny.

6 Cover the base of the inner mould to the height of the 5cm (2in) plugs.

7 Lower in the inner mould and work in hypertufa evenly around the sides. Make sure no air holes are left. Continue until the top is reached.

8 Leave the whole for three or four days covered with damp sacking or a loose polythene sheet.

9 Carefully remove the outer mould. Gently rub away any exposed sharp edges of the trough.

10 After a further two or three days remove the inner mould and again dull any sharp edges.

11 Leave another week for further drying and then knock out the drainage plugs.

12 Install the trough in its permanent quarters raised on bricks or stones to prevent slug-snail access.

13 Fill with compost and plant up.

areas or where water is treated before use.

Another way of ensuring adequate water reaches the plants is by grouping containers together on a single tray which should then be covered with gravel. When water is introduced into the tray it will percolate up into the pots.

FEEDING

The potting compost will provide enough food for the plants to last them for a few weeks after planting, thereafter with them growing ever bigger and making more demands on the limited amount of growing materials, the containers will be the better for a regular feed. This is probably best given as a liquid every week or ten days. Use one that doubles as a foliar feed so that the goodness is absorbed by leaves as well as roots. Most container plants are there for their flowering ability so use a fertilizer that is high in potash (K) and phosphate (P) and low in nitrogen (N), which is good at encouraging leaf growth. Tomato fertilizer often proves useful, but you can check the levels of N, P and K as shown on the outside of any fertilizer mix.

WINTER PROTECTION

In colder areas some permanent container plants are taken under cover for the winter mainly to avoid hard frosts. Plants in containers are more than usually liable to frost damage in very severe weather as the frost can not only penetrate the soil block from the top but from the sides also. Examples of plants that may be moved into a cool greenhouse or conservatory over winter include fuchsias, especially standards, the cordylines and even *Agapanthus*.

Enthusiasts for citrus fruits in containers may follow suit, but some large specimens are too large and heavy to move. These may be protected by giving them extra protection *in situ*. In times past, this was done by wrapping specimens with jute sacking. Now you sometimes see shrubs wrapped up in polythene sheeting, but this is not the best of materials as it catches every bit of wind, and condensation inside can start various fungus troubles. The answer is horticultural fleece. This allows the plants to breathe but secures a stable atmosphere of air around it that is kept significantly warmer than if left to the elements.

DIASCIA BARBERAE HYBRIDS
Twinspur

Description: Becoming more popular season by season and deservedly so; these plants are very generous with pastel-coloured, tubular flowers. Frost hardy to -8°C (18°F).

Colour: Pinks, mauves, purples and salmon shades.

Size: 8-40cm(3-16in) high, 15-60cm (6-24in) wide.

Flowering time: Prolonged period through summer and autumn.

Relatives: Among the many cultivars is 'Ruby Field', with white-lipped salmon flowers; it is compact and forms mats of wiry stems with heart-shaped pale leaves. 'Salmon Supreme' is a large plant with larger flowers that are rather paler.

Cultivation: Plant in warm spots in well-drained soils. Tidy by cutting back old stems in early spring.

Propagation: By softwood cuttings in late spring or semi-ripe ones in summer. Always overwinter a few under cover as insurance against really severe weather killing parent plants.

POTTING ON

The idea is not to let the plants suffer any check in growth and to end up with specimens hardened off ready for planting.

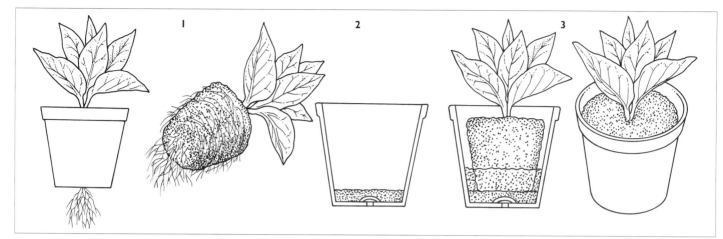

REPOTTING

Try not to allow plants to get hopelessly root-bound, ie a thick band of roots circling the extremities of the pot.

1 Knock the plant out of pot and, unless it is a well-known hater of any root disturbance, work out a little of the soil around the outside of the pot and a little off the top surface.

2 Take a pot the next size up but not one hugely larger than the original. Place fresh compost in the base so that the plant, when it sits upon it, will come to a level just some 1cm (½in) below the pot rim.

3 Add fresh compost all around the empty sides of the pot, working evenly until reaching the top.

4 Add a little fresh compost to the top surface.

5 Stand the pot in water until the changed colour of the soil surface indicates that the whole is thoroughly watered.

6 Finish off the top of the pot with fine chippings or gravel if you wish. Stand the pot in its proper place.

FELICIA AMELLOIDES

Blue marguerite, Blue daisy

Description: Bright, green, long, oval leaves, and a long succession of long-petalled, elegant daisies. Frost tender, min. temp. 3–5°C (37–41°F).
Uses: Great in containers, large hanging baskets and raised beds as well as in borders.
Colour: Clear pure blue, with yellow centre discs. Leaves green or green with cream variegation.
Size: 45cm (18in) high and wide.

Flowering time: Late spring through into autumn.
Relatives: F. amelloides 'Santa Anita' is a fine large-flowered clone with 'Santa Anita Variegated' having the cream marked foliage.
Cultivation: Good drainage and full sun.
Propagation: Take softwood cuttings in summer or early autumn and overwinter under glass.

Prick out seedlings into pots or modules when they have their first true leaf fully expanded. Handle them gently with the roots carefully disentangled and distributed through the potting compost. Position them in good light with just enough warmth to keep plants growing healthily, and keep them moist but airy at all times. Too much heat and lack of light will result in tall 'drawn' plants that are going to be vulnerable to diseases and other troubles. Water plants with potash-high fertilizer once a week and move them into their final containers before they get root-bound.

Making the most of containers

The choice of plants for containers is a matter of individual preference but do not ignore the most obvious choices, often sold as 'container plants' in garden centres. They are colourful, have a very long season of bloom and are able to cope with occasional shortages of moisture. If you do not want

LILIUM REGALE
Regal lily

Description: Wonderful hardy lily from China discovered and introduced by Ernest 'Chinese' Wilson at the beginning of the century. Large bulbs, tough stems with many narrow, purpled, dark leaves. Huge purple-maroon buds open to wide trumpets. Very hardy.

Uses: Wonderful in border, glorious in large containers.

Wildlife: Attracts bees and other flying insects.

Colour: Maroon buds, large white trumpets with golden centres.

Scent: A huge outstanding perfume.

Size: 50cm-2m (20in-6ft) high.

Flowering time: Midsummer.

Relatives: *L. regale* 'Album' has flowers white in bud, and the leaves are greener.

Cultivation: Grows strongly in deep soils. Bulbs should have at least 10cm (4in) of soil over their tops. Growing points emerge quite early; if hard frosts threaten, these growing points should be carefully protected, as they can be killed.

Propagation: By division of the bulbs, by scaling or by seed. Fresh seed will germinate freely and, if well grown, can be brought to blooming in under two years.

Wooden decking and foliage plants in pots have been combined to create a restful patio garden

Pots on columns provide
strong focal points in this
informal 'rock garden'

BRUGMANSIA SUAVEOLENS
(**SYN.** ***DATURA SUAVEOLENS***)
Angel's trumpets

Description: A simple shrub with wide, oval, pointed
leaves 15-30cm (6-12in) long and sturdy stems. In
summer it drapes itself with extravagantly long,
hanging trumpets, each measuring 20cm (8in) or so
long. Tender, min. temp. 7°C (45°F).

Colour: White flowers, but there are other kinds
with pink or yellow flowers.

Scent: Heavily scented at night.

Size: Dependent on age and management, up to 5m
(15ft).

Flowering time: Summer into autumn.

Cultivation: Normally grown in large containers in
full sun using good, open-structured soil. Can be
grown under glass full time or wheeled out onto the
patio or elsewhere for the growing and flowering
months.

Propagation: By summer cuttings, or seed sown in
early spring.

shrieking reds and oranges there are plenty of good
whites and pale pinks to use.

The new breed of hybrid diascias fill containers
well and will cascade over the sides. 'Hopley's
Apricot' has become a firm favourite, but 'Lilac
Belle' and 'Salmon Supreme' are still among the
leaders. They look that bit classier than some of the
other bedding/container plants of the past.

Large earthenware containers filled with different hostas never fail to please and their foliage helps

VERBENA × HYBRIDA

V. x hybrida 'Sandy Scarlet'

Description: Scrambling plant with soft, serrated, narrow leaves and clustered heads of tubular flowers in many bright and pastel shades. Half hardy.

Uses: A most accommodating plant for containers, hanging baskets, window boxes and raised beds.

Colour: Reds, pinks, blues, mauves, purples, salmons, white and bicolours.

Size: 20cm (8in) high, spread 40cm (16in).

Flowering time: Summer into autumn.

Relatives: .'Amethyst' is blue with white eyes. Derby Series has a full colour range. 'Carousel' has petals striped with purple and white. 'Dwarf Jewels' is more compact in lots of vivid colours. 'Sandy Scarlet' (pictured) is dazzling scarlet-red.

Cultivation: Sow seed end of winter. Prick out and grow on to plant out in mid-spring. Use balanced compost with good drainage and grow in full light.

Propagation: Apart from seed, stem cuttings can be taken in late summer or early autumn and the plants overwintered under glass out of frost.

damp down the excesses of other more colourful extroverts. It is sometimes useful to have one or two containers devoted mainly to foliage plants, maybe only a shaped box or a bay tree.

If the children are giving a hand they will be hap-pier with quicker results. Nasturtiums grow considerably day-by-day and they can be very bright and enjoyable. Morning glory is marvellous twining its way upwards and surprising with its blue trumpets.

More permanent plants such as as *Agapanthus*,

CORDYLINE AUSTRALIS
Cabbage tree

C. australis 'Variegata'

Description: Sparsely-branched tree from New Zealand with rosetted bunches of sword-shaped leaves 30-90cm (12-36in) long. Young plants look like very formal yuccas and make splendid container specimens. As they age the stem-trunk expands until the rosette of leaves is hoisted high up and the whole thing begins to look more like a kind of palm.
When mature there can be rather rigid sprays of flowers flung out sideways, interesting rather than breathtaking. Borderline frost hardy, min. temp. around 0°C (32°F).
Colour: Green leaves, lime and white flowers.
Scent: Flowers are perfumed.
Size: Normally grown as young plants 1-1.5m (3-5ft) high but capable of going up with a single stem to 15m (50ft) in the wild.
Relatives: 'Purpurea' has reddish purple leaves and those of 'Variegata' (pictured) are white-edged.
Cultivation: Normally grown as large container plants, but may be used in the open garden in warm spots with good drainage. In sun or light shade.
Propagation: By suckers in spring. By seed.

Lilium regale, cordylines, yuccas or fruit trees can also be considered.

COLOURS

You may decide on having certain colours to brighten particular sites. A specimen of the golden hop, *Humulus lupulus* 'Aureus' climbing up a wigwam of canes or trellis will provide lovely limey golden foliage through the growing months. At the base you could plant a group of small daffodils such as 'February Gold' or 'Tête à Tête' to give early yellow sunshine. The yellow theme can be extended by planting *Lysimachia nummularia* 'Aurea', yellow-leaved creeping Jenny, to cover the soil surface and cascade down the sides of the pot.

One could go for a cooler silvery look using plants such as *Helichrysum*, trailing *Plectranthus coleoides* 'Marginatus' and silvery-leaved *Anthemis punctata* ssp. *cupaniana* perhaps with white geraniums, lobelias and petunias.

Even the richest of colours, the fuchsias, red geraniums, petunias and busy lizzies look all the more vivid with white- and blue-flowered neighbours. If you want to try something in these cooler colours in containers or even at the edge of the border, you could be pleased with the effect of *Laurentia axillaris* in blue or white forms, narrow-petalled flowers like a thousand bursting stars.

TENDER PLANTS

Among the tender plants suitable for containers are all the non-hardy ferns, which look so good grown by themselves in pots or in mixed communities in other containers. The bright-leaved *Coleus blumei* and variegated *Ficus* forms will certainly be attractive and need frost-free conditions. The large-leaved *Stephanotis floribunda* looks well in containers but will need winter protection, as will such old favourites as *Gardenia jasminoides* and the scented-leaved *Pelargoniums* (geraniums), which may look more like the hardy true geraniums with their cut foliage but are very soft-hearted.

ALPINES

A well planted trough garden can be a delight, especially in the spring. Try to find or make a trough with a depth of 20cm (8in) if possible, ones with only 10-12cm (4-5in) are in constant danger of drying out or becoming unduly hot. The plants want as cool a rootrun as possible and they need to be moist without being sodden. Ensure good drainage holes that will not get blocked.

Alpines like an open-structured soil with good drainage. A good mix is healthy loam or good topsoil, humus, such as leaf mould or coarse peat, and grit or washed sharp sand, in the ratio 2:1:1 by volume. Plant up with your choice of small plants, perhaps a mixture including a dwarf conifer, some plants that have good evergreen qualities through the year and other flowering specimens that are not too rampant.

BOLD PLANTS

Alpines appeal partially because of their very smallness, but they need to be presented boldly to have a real impact. A successful garden creates a picture in which both container and plants make their contribution. There are many container plants that are more telling if they are used boldly, some of these being primarily foliage plants.

Cordyline australis (see page 206), *Phormium tenax* (see page 200), *Trachycarpus fortunei* (see page 199) and the *Yucca filamentosa* are four examples of statuesque or sculptural plants that are ideal for making an impact in containers. They are hardy in most areas; to avoid any damage they can be wheeled under cover for the worst of the winter.

There are several yuccas available commercially, but *Y. filamentosa* is by far the hardiest and is the one often found growing in the open garden. Its pointed dark leaves point up and out to make a dramatic focal point. In most summers any reasonable sized plant will produce one or more tall stems of large creamy hanging bells. 'Bright Edge' and 'Variegata' are forms with the leaf edges painted creamy white. In pots these variegated forms are possibly more decorative, they tend to be slightly less massive in size than the standard kind that in the open can reach a formidable 2m (6ft) high and as wide but will be constrained to less in a pot.

Some succulent plants can be effective in containers; they help to give a tinge of the tropics. None are more impressive than *Agave americana* (see page 197) which hails from Mexico and has naturalized around the Mediterranean and the shoreline of Portugal. Young specimens look great, but the

AGAPANTHUS HYBRIDS

Description: Strong herbaceous perennials with arching strap-like, long leaves that give them the look of bulbous plants, but they grow from thick fleshy roots. Tall leafless stems carry as many as a hundred trumpet-shaped flowers in an umbel! Remarkably hardy, South African native.

Uses: Important border plant and can be quite wonderful in a large container.

Colour: Various shades of blue and white.

Size: 60cm-1.2m (2-4ft) high, spread 50cm (20in).

Flowering time: Most bloom late summer into autumn.

Relatives: 'Ben Hope' and 'Loch Hope' are capable of 1.2m (4ft) high, and have crowded umbels of rich dark blue bells. Most often offered are Headbourne Hybrids, a set of strong-growing good blues. 'Bressingham White' and *A. campanulatus* var. *albidus* make a contrast with pure white blossom.

Cultivation: Grow in sunny spots in good soils that have plenty of moisture but are open-structured to give plenty of air and free drainage.

Propagation: By division of the clumps in early spring.

plants can grow to 2m (6ft). The most impressive are the variegated forms.

CONTAINER PLANTS FOR WILDLIFE

To encourage wildlife with container plants concentrate on those that will provide nectar. These include some low-growing rock plants such as

A courtyard garden
enhanced by potted plants

ARGYRANTHEMUM FRUTESCENS HYBRIDS
Paris daisy, Marguerite

A. frutescens 'Jamaica Primrose'

Description: A bushy perennial with soft blue-green serrated leaves and sprawling stems and then a long succession of daisy flowers through summer and autumn. Half hardy.

Uses: A container plant *par excellence*, but also a great standby in borders where its free and long-lasting flower production always wins it huge praise. If you have the patience you can restrict growth to a single stem and over several seasons establish a standard perhaps 60-90cm (2-3ft) high – it will certainly be a focal point on the patio or anywhere.

Colour: White, yellows, pinks, salmon and near red.

Size: According to cultivar, height and spread about 1m (3ft).

Flowering time: Through summer into autumn.

Relatives: *A. frutescens*, the original marguerite, has rich green divided leaves and open white daisy flowers with golden centres. Perhaps the most famous and still an excellent kind is 'Jamaica Primrose' (pictured) with crowds of soft yellow daisies. 'Mary Wootton' is pink with a double pin-cushion centre.

Cultivation: Plant out in spring in sunny well-drained soil. In mild winters and warmer areas plants will survive the winter, but it is wise to have some protected stock.

Propagation: Basal cuttings in spring, stem tip cuttings later in the year to provide small plants to overwinter under cover.

Alyssum and *Iberis* (candytuft), together with other familiar annuals such as *Matthiola bicornis* (night-scented stock), *Nicotiana*, and *Calendula officinalis* (pot marigold). The herbs should not be forgotten. Thymes of all sorts bring bees and other insects; sages, rosemary and lavender are favourite stopping points, too. Early in the year, a potful of crocuses will be heavily visited by the earliest insects. If you are particularly interested in helping insects it would not be difficult to grow some of the dwarf *Aster amellus* cultivars in pots or other containers. They will be decorated with flowers and butterflies in the autumn. If you pot up a large *Sedum spectabile* (ice plant) this has the same irresistible lure for butterflies as the buddlejas that are too big and rangy to containerize.

The seasons

Spring comes early with bulbs grown under cool glass to bring them forward a few weeks without real forcing. When in bud and ready to open they can be wheeled to strategic positions for display. All the normal gamut of bulbs can be deployed: the sturdy early-flowering daffodils, tulips both early and later kinds, crocuses, scillas, and perhaps hyacinths.

Summer can be crowded with all the traditional container plants: geraniums (*Pelargoniums*), verbenas, busy lizzies and petunias. And there is the chance to experiment with the seedsmen's novelties. Lilies are probably the best and easiest bulbs for pots. They can be chosen to open in succession for months. Later in the summer, the stately agapanthus come into bloom, brilliant blue with up to a hundred flowers on tall stems.

With autumn, *Nerine bowdenii* can be relied upon. It is happy to grow in the same pot for a decade. *Amaryllis bella-donna* too grows well in large pots and looks very exciting with its large pink trumpets. On a smaller scale there are colchicums and autumn-flowering crocuses.

Winter is not without its own pleasures. The much publicized winter pansies earn a place, their vivid shades can be brought under control by restricting one colour to a container. Containers of shrubs, bays, trained box, conifers, camellias, and trained ivies are all worth bringing into prominence for winter.

HANGING BASKETS

Hanging baskets and
window boxes are a
traditional feature of
canal barges

FEW ASPECTS OF gardening have enjoyed the popularity that hanging baskets have experienced over the last decade or so. Commerce has not been slow to exploit this renewed interest. There is now a wider choice of better baskets, and linings, composts, fertilizers and watering needs have been given a lot of attention so that the gardener is very well served with many excellent products. Above all, there is now such a wide choice of suitable plants, raised and bred specifically for baskets, that

Hanging baskets and window boxes are a traditional feature of canal barges

a comparison with what was available only a relatively few years ago is quite remarkable. Looking back, the range available to gardeners seems to have been quite meagre.

Classic hanging baskets are flourishing balls of flowers and foliage rejoicing in the summer sun. Baskets planted in a more modern way often have loads of trailing plants, giving a larger impact. Cascading petunias and trailing geraniums, as well as improvements in other traditional plants, are responsible for part of this trend.

Some very effective baskets can be created using a single cultivar or plant type. The cascade petunias are a good example of an ideal plant to use. Children and adults will get a kick out of a simple basket devoted solely to nasturtiums that are allowed to trail as far as they may; the limited amount of food will ensure that there is plenty of the bright flowers, not an overabundance of the disc-like leaves.

It is little wonder that hanging baskets are so popular, they give everyone a chance to expand their gardening activities and transform a place that otherwise might be barren of life. There are many people who live in homes without a plot of open ground, but they can produce their own gardens in miniature through hanging baskets, and enjoy the solace and beauty this affords.

Making the most of it

A well designed basket that is well looked after is a joy to all who view it. A poorly done one, the result of misunderstanding the techniques involved, can be disappointing. Sensible planning, a careful selection of plants, composts and all the components all add up to more chances of success.

Despite the attractions of hanging baskets, they are a tough environment for the plant, there are few worse. Large amounts of plant growth are dependent on very small quantities of rooting medium. The plants spend their life up in the air, totally at the mercy of the elements: they are subject to every breath of wind and every ray of sunshine. The rates of evaporation and transpiration from the foliage are exceptionally high.

Lack of water is always going to be the major stress factor for plants growing in baskets. The smaller the basket, the worse such problems are going to be. Use as large a basket as is practical. Remember it must be easy to handle and install. All fitments from which baskets are hanging must be as safe as a very safe house. A basket that is filled up with compost, plants and water is very heavy. Make sure that you allow for all this weight, it is something that will increase rather than decrease after the basket is first hung.

POSITIONING

Baskets are there to be enjoyed so they must be on view. It is a good idea to site some so that they are visible from inside the house as well as some to simply decorate the house. There should be many suitable places around the house walls and in the gardens, including pergolas and other independent structures.

TIP

After lining the basket with foam or moss, add a piece of polythene over the base to form an invisible saucer helping to retain water.

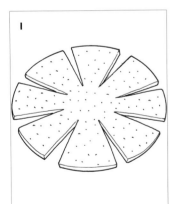

PLANTING UP A HANGING BASKET

1 *Choose as large a basket as is practical. Purchase a foam liner.*

2 *Place basket on top of a bucket or empty flower pot under cover where it can remain until ready for hanging up.*

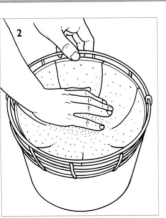

3 *Take water-resistant gel and, following the packet instructions, work into the compost (either soilless or soil-based with high humus content) to be used for basket. Thoroughly water and leave for at least a couple of hours.*

4 *Fill the basket two-thirds full of the*

compost.

5 *Slot in a number of plants through the sides of the basket where slits in the foam liner allow, or add your own slits using a sharp knife.*

6 *Fill remainder of basket with the compost and plant up the top.*

7 *Water basket thoroughly and cover the compost surface with gravel or fine shredded bark to contain moisture and make watering easier.*

8 *Grow on under frost-proof cover until fear of frosts recedes and the basket may be hung out.*

PLANTS FOR WINDY SITES

Asplenium scolopendrium, hart's-tongue fern

Calendula officinalis, marigold

Gazania

Geranium endressii

Hedera forms, ivy (page 183)

Lamium maculatum forms, deadnettle (page 43)

Myosotis, forget-me-nots

Viola forms (page 246)

TROPAEOLUM MAJUS
Nasturtium

Description: The well-known, annual climber. Its rapid growth and large orbicular leaves together with its abundant flowers make it a favourite of children, the not so young and caterpillars! Half hardy.

Uses: A most useful trailer for hanging baskets, but also a first class plant to cover an ugly bankside until something more permanent can be managed. Might also be used to drape piles of hardcore or other eyesores that are not going to be cleared for a season. Leaves and flowers sometimes used in salads, flowers sometimes accompany kippers!

Colour: Very varied, bright oranges and reds predominate but plenty of creams, yellows and flame shades.

Size: Usually to 20cm (8in) high, spread of most rampant strains, when grown in the ground, up to several metres. In hanging baskets, the fall can be over 1m (3ft).

Flowering time: Prolonged, from early summer until early autumn.

Varieties: Each seedsman will have several strains, some dwarf and non-running, others with double flowers. (See page 236 for perennial *T. speciosum*.)

Cultivation and propagation: Sow seed in early spring. Watch out for caterpillars.

WINDY SITES

The plant choice is more limited if the basket is to go in a windy, not too sunny spot. Wind dramatically increases the difficulties hanging-basket plants face due to increased transpiration, but there are plants that seem to be able to withstand a little more than a breeze (see margin list, left).

SUNLESS SITES

Places where there is no sun are even more difficult than windy ones to furnish with a hanging basket. Most hanging basket plants are ones that expect sunshine and need to enjoy good helpings of light to flower, in shady areas the amount of bloom could be disappointing.

However, shady area baskets can depend on plants such as ivies for trailing and background effect and they can be bright with young well-flowered forgét-me-nots and *Viola hederacea* with its blue-violet flowers on periscope stalks. A lightening effect can be introduced with silver-leaved deadnettle, *Lamium maculatum* 'White Nancy'. Its pale plum-coloured blossom will aid the colour scheme and the purple hint can be emphasized by adding some of the darker-leaved sedums (see magin list: Plants for semi-shaded baskets, page 213).

Plants for full shade are more limited. Ferns of the *Adiantum* genus could be added to the hart's tongues (*Asplenium scolopendrium*) suggested for windy spots, the many variegated ivies will be splendid, together with various forms of the deadnettles, *Lamium maculatum*, especially those with lots of light silvery variegation. Creeping jenny, *Lysimachia nummularia*, and forms of the low growing bugle, *Ajuga reptans*, will also serve well.

Seasonal baskets

Obviously, the main focus is on the summer-flowering baskets, ones that will be enjoyed when we are most active outside. But other seasons need not be forgotten. Spring is easily enlivened by adding snowdrops, scillas or small daffodils, but it is the long winter months when the need for colour is felt most keenly, a touch then is worth a carnival in summer. Winter pansies planted together with crocuses can liven up late autumn and winter baskets that are overflowing with trailing ivies. Or a perma-

ANTHEMIS TINCTORIA
Yellow chamomile

A. tinctoria 'E. C. Buxton'

Description: Makes an evergreen clump of cut, rather wavy-edged, fresh green leaves. It is covered through summer with a glut of bright daisies. Fully hardy.

Uses: Excellent border plant, can be tucked into warm corners to mirror the sunshine. Very effective in large containers, especially those on the ground.

Colour: Mid- to golden yellow daisies.

Size: 1m (3ft) high and wide.

Flowering time: From midsummer well into autumn.

Relatives: *A. tinctoria* 'E. C. Buxton' (pictured) is easily the most popular cultivar – robust, very prolific with paler lemon flowers and golden central discs.

Cultivation: As soon as the flowering display begins to look tired, cut back strongly to encourage plenty of basal growth so that the clump goes into the winter with a healthy green low mound of foliage.

Propagation: By basal cuttings, sometimes they will have bits of root already, taken early spring or early autumn.

nent basket of perennials could be the answer. The only limit is your imagination and willingness to experiment.

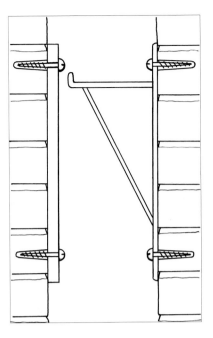

SUPPORTS FOR HANGING BASKETS

* Remember baskets are heavy. Either attach brackets directly to the wall (above, far right) or to a plate fixed to the wall (above, right).
* Make sure that wherever the baskets are hung they can be easily watered, ie, they can be reached easily with a watering can, with an extension from a water pump or by lowering the basket by pulley.
* If possible utilize a pergola or some strong permanent overhead structure.

SUMMER BASKETS

Each summer basket is expected to do splendid duty. So the plants are chosen for their long period of bloom and, of course, for their drought-resistance. The back bone of the display can be made by geraniums, especially the hanging or cascade types with bidens, diascia, impatiens, Gazania, osteospermum and tagetes all worth featuring strongly. While simple classic basket plants such as lobelia can look enchanting for many weeks, they may well fail before the end of the display life of the basket (see margin list).

PERENNIAL BASKETS

A set of stalwarts to see the year round might include some toughs such as the grey-leaved evergreen *Hebe pinguifolia* (page 110), the silvery-leaved forms of *Lamium maculatum*, an excellent all-rounder already starring several times in this chapter, together with the succulent very classy, silver-grey *Euphorbia myrsinites*. Apart from the all-purpose ivies, touches of excitement can be added by using forms

PLANTS FOR SEMI-SHADED BASKETS
Cyclamen coum (page 38)
C. hederifolium
Myosotis forms
Sedum forms
Tropaeolum majus, nasturtium (page 212)
T. peregrinum, Canary creeper
Viola hederacea
Waldsteinia ternata

Eyecatching, sweet-shop colours have been used in this hanging garden

of *Helianthemum*, the sprawling coral gem, *Lotus berth-elotii*, with various sedum forms and perhaps the yellow-leaved creeping Jenny, *Lysimachia nummularia* 'Aurea'.

CONSIDERING FOLIAGE

Most of the flowering plants have good foliage but it is often hidden under a floral exuberance. A more balanced and perhaps more restful effect can be achieved by using a few foliage plants as fillers or in their own right. It is worth considering creating bas-

PLECTRANTHUS FORSTERI 'MARGINATUS'

Description: An evergreen, trailing foliage plant with rounded, soft leaves. This variegated form has toothed-edged white-margined leaves. Tender, min. temp. 10°C (50°F).

Uses: One of the most popular plants for hanging baskets.

Scent: Leaves smell of lemon-mint when crushed.

Colour: Grey-green leaves, white or pink flowers.

Size: Only 6cm (2 ½in) high, but the trails may measure well over 1m (3ft).

Relatives: Look out for the bushy *P. coleoides* 'Variegatus' and for *P. madagascariensis* 'Variegated Mintleaf'.

Cultivation: Just keep moist in sun or semi-shade. Overwinter under cover.

Propagation: Stem cuttings, division in spring, or by detaching rooted pieces.

PELARGONIUM HYBRIDS
Geraniums

Description: Evergreen perennials, some with soft hairy leaves and some with polished foliage, all, or almost all, with very prominent flowers. Frost tender, min. temp. 2°C (36°F).

Uses: Traditional zonal types are fine for bedding, for raised beds, and large containers; the regals with their dramatic, rich colours are for the conservatory and such up-stage spots; ivy-leaved and cascade types are tailor-made for hanging baskets; scented-leaved kinds are pleasant as pot plants or as members of a mixed community in low containers perhaps on the patio.

Wildlife: The regals make wonderful host plants for whitefly and lots of other naughties.

Colour: White, oranges, reds, purples and pinks.

Size: Dependent on types. Cascade type will reach up 30cm (12in) or more and spread twice as wide while trailing down perhaps 60cm (24in) or more.

Flowering time: From late spring until mid-autumn.

Varieties: Choose cascade types for hanging baskets. 'Sophie Koniger' is glowing pale pink enriched with deep raspberry centres. 'Rote-mini' is a rather small but hugely prolific scarlet-crimson. 'Ville de Dresden' is white with a pink blush.

Cultivation: Plant up in hanging baskets under cover in early to mid-spring. Place in position when frosts are past.
They will manage without huge amounts of water and feeding but should not be subjected to drought and hunger.
Avoid too much nitrogen in feeds.

Propagation: Easy from softwood cuttings taken in the second half of the growing season and kept out of frost through winter.

kets devoted entirely to foliage plants. Foliage is colourful in its own way and has interest in form and texture. The performance of many cannot be faulted, including *Plectranthus australis* , which will trail for ever with its polished firm green leaves, and the popular *P. coleoides* 'Variegatus', which has grey-green leaves with their serrated edges painted creamy white and is a bushy and falling perennial. *Helichrysum petiolare* is a South African native, and should be considered for a foliage basket. It is a scrambling climbing shrub and is very attractive with its grey felted rounded leaves and silvery shoots. A tender perennial, it is best grown as an annual. 'Limelight' (syn. 'Aurea') is a version with limey coloured leaves that complement warmer

BIDENS FERULIFOLIA
Tickseed, Bur marigold

Description: Perennial with finely cut leaves and a continuous display of five-petalled stars. Scrambling mass of light, fresh green, ferny foliage above which the flowers are carried for many weeks. Frost hardy.

Uses: Popular hanging basket and container plant.

Colour: Brilliant yellow.

Size: To 1m (3ft) high, spread 1.2m (4ft).

Flowering time: Second half of summer into autumn a continuous succession.

Relatives: *B. ferulifolia* 'Golden Eye' is a prostrate tumbling form.

Cultivation: Well-drained soil in full sun.

Propagation: Summer cuttings.

colours. The yellow-leaved form of creeping Jenny, *Lysimachia nummularia* 'Aurea' is, again, a useful choice as are the wormwoods, which are all foliage plants. *Artemisia schmidtiana* is possibly the best in baskets. It is semi-evergreen with very finely divided, silvery foliage.

Practicalities

Choose the largest basket that it is reasonable to work with, but remember that the weight increase is huge between a 25cm (10in) and a 30cm (12in) or 35cm (14in) basket. There are smaller baskets around 20cm (8in) diameter, but these are normally too small to be practical.

Traditionally baskets were lined with moss. This is now generally frowned upon because of the ecological damage done to the environment from which the moss is gathered. Instead, use one of the purpose-made spongy plastic foam liners that fit perfectly into the basket and perform their functions well. They are split several times down the sides to fit into the concave basket and these slits allow plants to be squeezed in the sides as well as on the top. The spongy material is water-retentive but also allows drainage.

Plant summer baskets during spring. Crowd them with plants, water them and then stand them on empty pots or buckets under glass to grow on until the fear of frosts is past and the community of plants have got really settled. They should then be decorative for perhaps four months or more.

WATERING

The biggest problem, the major stress area, is water. Plants use lots of water in airy situations, and this is compounded by the fact that the limited amount of growing medium can only hold a limited amount of water at any one time. The better the plants flourish, the quicker the rate of water loss. On rainy days less water will be used, transpiration and evaporation will be vastly less, but just because it is raining does not mean that the growing medium is receiving enough water as the thick growth of plants is probably deflecting it all, duck's-back-wise. It is vital to arrange matters so that watering is efficient and the plants get all they need. There are several approaches to the problem: choose one, or more, that suits you.

Nearly ideal is a piped water supply to each basket, with the amount of water going into the growing medium being governed by individual nozzles. A trickle system works on a similar set up but needs careful adjustment so that just the right amount of water is supplied. Avoid the constant drip, drip and the miniature waterfall effect. Another solution is to arrange for the link up to the mains water supply to be a tap that can be turned on for a limited period each day. Large scale installations around some public buildings are watered in this manner and the watering period is governed by a timeswitch, but this has few real benefits for the gardener except during days of absence. It is most efficient to turn a tap on when it is wanted and off when everything is sensibly watered.

Alternatively, you can make use of one of the many gadgets on sale in garden centres. These include a long lance with a turned head so that high baskets can be reached easily and the water allowed

PETUNIA HYBRIDS

Description: There are many trailing kinds with wide closely clasped leaves of pale green and a glorious profusion of huge wide open, rounded flowers. Half hardy.
Uses: For baskets, window boxes, raised beds and other positions where the falling stems loaded with flowers can be displayed for months.
Colour: White through pinks to mauves, reddish purples and darker shades. Almost all have striking dark centres and darker delicate veining.
Size: 20cm (8in) high, spread 30-45cm (12-18in), overall trailing length 75cm (30in).
Flowering time: Summer until mid-autumn.
Varieties: The Surfinias have captured a huge market: they are available in many colours.
Cultivation: Grow seedlings under warm protection until frosts are past. A good watering will bring growth of rather upright plants down to begin their trailing habit.
Propagation: From seed under glass in early spring.

to flow from the mains supply or be pumped up by hand from a portable water reservoir.

Life can be made much easier by fixing high baskets on a pulley system so that they may be lowered when necessary to be properly filled at a comfortable level. This would also allow them to be half dunked into a container full of water to make sure they are fully soaked before being hauled back to their place of duty. Another wheeze for baskets in awkward places is to place a number of ice cubes on the basket surface. The water is absorbed as they slowly melt, rather than running off the side if the basket is given a good dose of water all at once.

In times of stress we may congratulate ourselves on having added water-retaining gels to the compost before planting up the baskets (see page 217), but it's too late if you did not add it with the compost. The gel will form an emergency reservoir which will see many plants over a time of stress.

Human fallibility being what it is, there will be times when the baskets do not receive their ration of water. The result of this is that the plants will begin to wilt. Some will start doing this earlier and more drastically than others. Fuchsias and lobelias are particularly vulnerable. Given a thorough soaking all is likely to come to again but not without having the flowering display disrupted to a greater or lesser extent, it could be a few weeks before the loss is made good.

PLANNING FOR DROUGHT

Plants vary greatly in their ability to withstand drought. Those whose native home is dry and difficult will have learnt to cope and will have drought-proof qualifications of exceptional merit. Many of these are narrow-leaved plants that quickly batten down the hatches against water loss, and others are familiar members of communities that expect to meet droughts every so often. Some are really very attractive and excellent for containers; the list in the margin is headed by *Bidens ferulifolia* which has ferny foliage and bright yellow flowers.

Other drought-tolerant plants which may wilt but which will perk up again after a good drink are listed in the margin on page 219: Plants that recover well from neglect. Diascias are becoming more popular year by year. They are particularly good in this respect. Surprisingly enough the succulent

PLANTS FOR FLOWERING BASKETS

Anagallis monelli, blue, 20cm (8in)
Antirrhinum pendula multiflora 'Chinese Lanterns', cascading
Asarina purpusii, purple, trailing
Brachyscome, swan river daisy, white, blue or purple, 25cm (10in)
Campanula carpatica, white or blue, 15cm (6in)
C. cashmeriana, lilac-blue, trailing
Fuchsia
Geraniums
Godetia, mixed colours, 30cm (12in)
Impatiens, busy lizzie, 20cm (8in)
Laurentia axillaris, white or blue, 25cm (10in)
Lobelia
Petunia

TRAILING PLANTS

Lobelia
Bidens
trailing *Pelargoniums*
Tropaeolum majus (nasturtiums)
Verbena
Brachyscome iberidiflora

PLANTS FOR THE TOP

Petunias
Fuchsias
Pelargoniums
Helichrysum

A classic hanging basket with, among others, pelargoniums, lobelia, petunias and ageratums

IMPATIENS HYBRIDS
Busy lizzy

Description: Much-improved plants in many different strains. Grown as annuals with shiny, pointed leaves and succulent, brittle stems. The low mound of growth is completely covered with a continual supply of large showy flat flowers. Borderline of frost hardy.

Uses: For hanging baskets and mixed containers or to fill containers on their own.

Colour: White through pinks and apricots to scarlets and mauves, burgundies and crimsons. Often colours are enlivened with richer painted eyes.

Size: 30cm (12in) high and wide on average.

Flowering time: Early summer through into autumn.

Varieties: Too numerous to list.

Cultivation: Sow in early spring under glass and plant out at the end of spring. Enjoys moisture but should not be permanently sodden.

Propagation: Seed. Cuttings can be taken of good forms in summer.

impatiens, which indisputably likes plenty to drink, can suffer the indignities of wilt and is quite ready to stand up again once it has drunk its fill. Nasturtiums too, will put up with thirst.

FEEDING

The basket starts life with a balanced amount of feed in the compost that is used. It helps if some slow-release fertilizer capsules are also added along

BRACHYSCOME IBERIDIFOLIA
Swan river daisy

Description: Cheerful annual with needle-thin foliage lost underneath lots of daisy flowers. Half hardy.

Uses: In containers, raised beds and borders.

Colour: White and every shade of pink to purple and the traditional blue.

Size: 45cm (18in) high and wide.

Flowering time: Through summer into early autumn.

Relatives: *B. iberidifolia* 'Blue Star' is an excellent blue. 'Purple Splendour' is a really rich shade.

Cultivation: Pick a sunny sheltered spot with fertile open soil. Nip out tops of young plants to encourage the bushy habit.

Propagation: Sow seed under glass in late winter or early spring. Can be raised outside in its flowering site by sowing later.

with the plants and these will be working for most of the life of the plants. It does no harm at all however to supplement these existing sources with a soluble foliar feed every 10 days or so. One that is high in potash is likely to be useful; there are plenty of specially formulated feeds for baskets. Remember that the plants are growing in a tiny amount of compost compared to their size; they are likely to be very hungry.

PLANTS TO WITHSTAND DROUGHT

Bidens ferulifolia (page 216)

Cheiranthus cheiri, wallflowers (page 20)

Dianthus forms, pinks

Hedera forms, ivies (page 183)

Lobularia maritima, sweet alyssum

Origanum forms (page 18)

Oxalis forms

Pelargonium forms, geraniums (page 215)

Portulaca afra

Thymus, thymes (page 245)

PLANTS THAT RECOVER WELL FROM NEGLECT

Brachyscome iberidifolia

Convolvulus sabatius

Diascia integerrima

D. barberae (page 201)

Felicia (page 202)

Gazania

Heliotropium

Impatiens, busy lizzies (page 218)

Osteospermum (page 31)

Tagetes, French and African marigolds

Tropaeolum, nasturtiums (p212)

Verbena, provided they are mildew-resistant ones such as 'Sissinghurst' (page 205)

CONSERVATORIES

ADDING A CONSERVATORY extends the home and should be a new room for normal family activities in the most welcoming environment of the house. It may help with heating bills, gleaning free heat from the sun and, in cooler times, sheltering the warmer hub of the house from the extremes outside. If craftily designed, it may function as a natural form of air-conditioning by helping to provide your house with cooling air movements in the hottest weather through careful ventilation arrangements.

A well designed and equipped conservatory can be the most wonderful room in a house, welcoming at all times of day, at all times of the year. Sadly, it is all too common for conservatories to be badly managed so that they deteriorate solely into a winter refuge from poor weather; they are often allowed either to get so hot as to be uninhabitable in warm weather or so damp as to be uninviting in cold weather. Successful summer shade creates the condensation of the cool months, a dank, dripping environment and a constant reproach. However, it is possible to enjoy the benefits of a conservatory and avoid the pitfalls with a little bit of care.

Conservatories for plants

Conservatories may be designed for both people and plants. It is worth considering exactly what you want, some designs allow greater flexibility in providing for varying plant needs. The plantperson's conservatory can be used to provide benign environments for plants that are not able to manage so easily elsewhere: either arid or humid conditions can be exaggerated. It can be useful as a scent factory or a place of continual aromatherapy, where the perfumes that so many flowers and plants produce is captured in an enclosed space rather than being quickly dissipated as happens when they are grown outside. It also offers the opportunity to grow many plants that are too tender to grow outside and to extend the growing and flowering periods of others.

CATHARANTHUS ROSEUS
Madagascan periwinkle

Description: Spreading evergreen shrub that will need some trimming as it ages to keep it tidy. Flat, open, five-petalled blooms are freely produced over a long period. It is frost tender min. temp. 5-7°C (41-45°F).

Uses: Pot plant under glass. Young plants taken from under glass to provide bedding specimens.

Colour: White to rosy pink.

Size: 30-60cm high, spread several times this given the space and time.

Flowering time: Early spring to mid-autumn and in winter under warm glass.

Cultivation: Normally grown in pots of open-structured soil and placed in a light airy spot. Keep warm. Cut back straggly stems in early spring to give more groomed, erect appearance.

Propagation: By cuttings in summer or seed in spring.

Conservatory design factors

Two factors above all others will decide upon the success or failure of a conservatory – its ventilation and its shading.

To enjoy your conservatory in all weathers – and surely the whole object of having one – insulation should be included in the design along with ventilation and shading. The glass needs to be double-glazed to cut down on the heat loss and the structural materials should not transmit heat too readily. If you do not protect against heat loss, the fluctuations in temperature can cause terrible condensation problems. Lines of drips will trace the path of overhead structural members over the floor space, furniture and, of course, plants. Damage will be caused to furniture and the compost of plants can become water-sodden, ready to encourage fungus and other diseases.

A cleverly designed conservatory with brick walls and glass roof

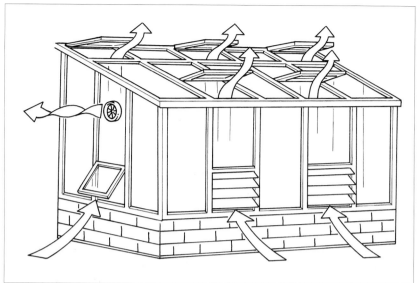

VENTILATION SYSTEMS

It is far better to err on the side of making provision for excessive ventilation rather than to limit it. In the past the principle adopted was to have a low vent for the intake of cool air and high roof ones to let out the rising warmer air. This involved manual adjustments, but there were some ingenious devices which meant that turning a wheel at a convenient height would operate a series of these vents. Manual systems are perfectly acceptable in homes where there is likely to be someone around most of the time. Busy owners going out to work are likely to want to rely on an automatic system. This may be a total system comprising roof vent openers, louvre openers in the sides and an extractor fan, all governed by a thermostat; such a system is driven by electricity. However, there can be a compromise which would rely on cool air vents being left open low down and having

a generous number of roof vents. The roof vents could be governed by a thermostat and electrically controlled, but need not be. Instead, they may be like many automatic greenhouse vent openers, which are triggered and operated by the expansion of wax in a tube. This happens when the air reaches quite a high temperature, around 16°C (61°F). These are adjustable to some extent and can then be left for the whole season without attention. Of course, this leaves no provision for the forced entry of cool air, but this will not be necessary in most cases.

Ventilation systems can be purchased and installed from large garden centres or good DIY stores. Instructions should be followed carefully and if you are installing an electrical system be especially careful and either have it installed by an electrician or after installation get an electrician to give your work a thorough check.

MATERIALS

Wood is a poor transmitter of heat and aluminium is a good one, but it need not have too bad an effect in modern conservatories as there is usually a thermal insulating barrier incorporated into it during manufacture. Plastic also works well but as a sole structural material it is not, at present, totally satisfactory and can age badly. There are clever laminated and double-walled plastic sheet materials

that are lightweight, effective and relatively cheap. They are often used in roofs and have fairly good heat insulation properties. Used knowledgeably they can be useful but they are not as clear as glass and their strong parallel lines need to be carefully assessed for use – they might be fine on the roof but intrusive in the side walls. For enjoying a clear sight of sky or a view, glass is unbeatable. It should be strong enough – thick, toughened or laminated – to

reasons for the success of greenhouses and other similar structures. Beware that cost cutting with plastic can mean less efficient heating. You pays your money and takes your choice.

There are other factors when choosing between plastic and glass. In sunshine plastics have brief lives when compared with glass. Also scratches build up on plastic severely impairing its efficiency, light is blocked and the roughened surface gathers dirt and disease inexorably. Plastic also suffers from static electricity, attracting more dirt particles, something

Pelargoniums, ivy and jasmine revel in the protected environment of this conservatory

CLIVIA MINIATA
River lily

Description: One of the three species that make up this South African genus which hovers between being a bulb and a tufted rhizome. It is one of the most reliable of pot plants under glass, a real toughie with handsome, broad, dark green straps of leaves, erect and then arching. Above this, open rounded umbels of large flowers, ten to perhaps two dozen on each stem. They are six-petalled, open funnel-shaped and brilliantly coloured. Tender, min. temp. 10°C (50°F).

Uses: Pot plant for greenhouse or conservatory but can be brought into the living room when in blossom or placed outside in summer.

Colour: Bright scarlet orange with a golden throat.

Size: 35-40cm (14-16in) high, spread 30-60cm (12-24in).

Flowering time: Spring, summer or autumn.

Relatives: C. miniata 'Aurea' is yellow with a richer centre. C. nobilis has less erect flowers in flame-golden-orange shades. C. x cyrtanthiflora hybrids are golden orange, apricot and salmon shades.

Cultivation: Use good quality John Innes compost, pot firmly and start into growth with minimum of water. They require plenty of water and warmth in full growth but when at rest in winter months need only sufficient heat to keep well clear of frost levels and enough water to keep compost from becoming a dust-bowl. Start a plant in a 12cm (5in) pot and only graduate to a 25cm (10in) one when it absolutely demands more room. They tend to bloom better if left undisturbed except for a top dressing of good compost at the winter's end.

Propagation: Detach offsets from the sides and grow on in a 12cm (5in) pot for one or two seasons. These divisions may take two or three seasons to establish an equilibrium that allows them to start producing bloom.

cope with its own weight together with the pressures of wind and possible snow loads – plan for the maximum you are likely to experience ever.

Another important thing to note about plastic glazing materials is that they do not produce the same physical effects as standard glass. Glass makes the heat gain by allowing the sun's energy through but not permitting it to bounce straight back out again. This 'greenhouse effect' is one of the main

A WATER FEATURE

In large conservatories it may be possible to incorporate a small pond. This is not something that can be unreservedly recommended as the water temperature fluctuates considerably and keeping a healthy ecological balance may prove very difficult. It would, of course, have the beneficial effect of providing welcome humidity for the plants though. A more practical suggestion for a water feature is to organize a small fountain or a bubbling reservoir where the water is allowed to flow over boulders, and returns to a cache below to be recirculated around the system by a pump. One can enjoy the sound of moving water, have the benefit of added humidity and have a visually attractive feature and one which may very well suit some neighbouring plants such as moisture-loving ferns.

that sheet glass will not do. Cleaning plastic can mean increasing the electrical charge so that you are left with a potentially more dirty item after moving away.

My own preference is for a conservatory with a low brick-wall base. This gives a useful low ledge but more importantly in the winter it helps to conserve heat and tends to make the temperature fluctuation less extreme.

VENTILATION

If you are commissioning a new conservatory, insist that at least one tenth of the roof area is openable: a proportion that is greater than is normally offered. There will be some days when any lack of roof ventilation will be very much regretted. A simple arrangement of vents low in the walls of the conservatory together with roof vents that can be opened to different degrees will allow warm air to rise, a more or less natural ventilation system. It may also be worthwhile to incorporate some high vents through into the house to help with warming the interior and perhaps bringing some of the flower scent through.

There are simple automatic vent-openers governed by a thermostat so that at a certain temperature pistons are activated to open the windows or vents. They are usually highly effective and

HIBISCUS ROSA-SINENSIS

H. syriacus 'Lady Stanley'

Description: A rounded evergreen shrub with plenty of polished, oval, pointed leaves rather unevenly serrated in their upper halves. Large flowers shaped like wide funnels, measure at least 10cm (4in) wide. Frost tender, min. temp. 10-13°C (50-55°F).

Uses: For growing in large containers, or in borders under glass, or in the open in warm areas.

Colour: Rosy pink with a red prominent stamen column.

Size: 1.5-3m (5-10ft) high and wide depending on age and growth allowed.

Flowering time: Flowers most numerous in summer but a shrub is rarely without some blossom in spring or autumn.

Relatives: Many named cultivars. *H. rosa-sinensis* 'The President' is shocking pink with a magenta centre contrasting with yellow anthers. *H. syriacus* is deciduous and hardy with many coloured forms, such as 'Lady Stanley' (pictured) a double, white.

Cultivation: All like plenty of light and sunshine. In growth they can take lots of water but can be kept dryish when less active. A humus-rich drained compost or soil suits.

Propagation: Seed sown in spring can provide sizeable plants quite quickly, offspring's flower colour will vary. Good percentages of semi-ripe cuttings taken in summer will root. Air layering is reliable.

reliable, taking charge of your conservatory whether you are there or not. These systems must be easy to disconnect so that if there are problems such as extraordinarily high winds you can batten down the hatches.

SHADING

Probably the most effective blinds are those that are incorporated on the outside of the conservatory and which stop all heat or light entering, but these are usually excessively expensive and are, of course, subject to the wear and tear of the elements. Internal blinds combined with effective ventilation should cope well, but it is important that the ventilation system is sound.

WATER SYSTEMS

Water will be needed for the plants. A tap and pot sink will be invaluable if you can fit them into your design without spoiling the effect.

Making the most of it

The conservatory can be very hot in the summer and really cool in the winter unless quite a bit of extra heating is installed. However, it is unlikely to be without some heating so frost-tender plants will be safe. The summer time will certainly be a period when an attempt at creating a lush leafy – almost jungle-like – environment is worthwhile. The shade will be welcome, the exuberance of the growth stimulating. The best way to achieve a really interesting effect is to have a mixture of plants, climbers, potted trees and herbaceous plants all together but arranged not only at floor level but at various levels. Hanging containers are effective, some fixed high to the sides and others halfway down.

Watering needs to be considered. Arrange trickle irrigation, or make sure that you have the type of watering cans and pumps that mean all can be dealt with easily. Each container is best topped off with a layer of shredded bark or pebbles to act as a mulch, containing water and maintaining some coolness at the roots. While plants such as cacti and succulents may manage in smallish pots, most conservatory dwellers will be best in fairly generous-sized containers so that they have a large reservoir of moisture and a store of food.

SHADED AREAS

A shaded area of the conservatory is ideal for growing shade-loving plants, provided certain conditions are met. Shade-lovers are likely to be sensitive to the sun, so should not be exposed to too much light otherwise they may burn to a crisp. They are also lovers of coolness so ventilation is a must, and in times of prolonged heat, when all the vents are open but the conservatory is still hot, a system of forced airflow will be needed. A fan is the only answer.

Assuming that your shady conditions are under control, the following is a list of some of the plants you might try. None are hardy outside, and most benefit from quite high humidity. Plants that do not require high humidity include *Caladium, Howea, Hypoestes, Sansevieria, Schefflera* and *Thunbergia*.

Caladiums are tuberous plants with the typical arrow-shaped leaves of the arum family. While species are usually green-leaved, the kinds most usually grown are variously coloured: 'Candidum' has white leaves with green veins, 'Pink Beauty' is a

PLANTS FOR SHADED AREAS

Adiantum forms
Bromeliads, all
Codiaeum
Cryptanthus
Dieffenbachia
Kohleria
Mandevilla
Maranta
Neoregelia
Peperomia
Saintpaulia
Sinningia
Spathiphyllum
Stephanotis
Streptocarpus
Syngonium
Tradescantia

JASMINUM OFFICINALE
Common jasmine,
Jessamine

Description: An old established garden species originally from Arabia, India and China, this is a vigorous twisting climber with attractive dark pinnate leaves of 7-9 pointed, oval leaflets. It produces its five-petalled starry flowers over an extended season. Frost hardy -5°C (23°F).

Uses: Up pergolas, trellis and wherever climbing plants can be grown in sunshine. While familiar as a plant outside, it can be very good in conservatories.
Colour: Pink-flushed buds, pure white flowers.
Scent: One of the great perfume plants.
Size: To 12m (40ft) high and wide.
Flowering time: Through summer deep into autumn.
Wildlife: Can attract flying insects including some moths.
Cultivars: *J. officinale.* 'Argenteovariegatum' differs only in having leaves precisely pencil-margined in white, a worthwhile kind.
Cultivation: Use a few ties to keep it in place so that the most can be made of its foliage and bloom. An easy plant in all soils save the most sodden. Maintenance is a matter of monitoring its spread and curtailing it where necessary.
Propagation: Easy from cuttings.

MYRTUS COMMUNIS
Myrtle

Description: Tough evergreen shrub with polished, narrowly oval, pointed leaves in abundance. This dark lustrous foliage is aromatic if crushed. Wide sprays of rounded flowers are produced at stem ends for a prolonged period, followed by berries. Exceptionally hardy.

Uses: With its strong branching system and massed foliage it is a windproof plant

that can be used as effective shelter or screen. While this is not normally thought of as a conservatory plant, it is especially good in some of the cooler ones and in shady spots.

Colour: Buds pink, flowers white. Berries dark purple close to black.

Scent: Fragrant blossom, scented bruised leaves.

Size: To 3 or even 5m (10-15ft), spread just a little less.

Flowering time: Mid-spring possibly to midsummer.

Relatives: There is a pleasing double-flowered form and the more compact, smaller-leaved *M. communis* subsp. *tarentina* with a height and spread of about 2m (6ft) is also attractive. It has white berries and is at least as useful as a hedging plant in milder districts.

Cultivation: Full sun, fertile, well-drained soil and some shelter in cold areas.

Propagation: By layers or semi-ripe cuttings in summer.

of tiny, dull red flowers in summer and autumn. Thunbergias come as annual or perennial, twisting climbers, and need support. The most popular is the annual *T. alata*, black-eyed Susan (see page 227). Flat round flowers of five orange-gold petals are centred by very dark brown centres.

PLANTS FOR SUNNIER AREAS

These include some favourite conservatory plants such as the *Bougainvillea* species and hybrids together with the well-known shrub *Hibiscus rosa-sinensis*, and the winter-cherry *Solanum capsicastrum*. The climbing bougainvillea scrambling over other plants or up pergolas and the like is a familiar sight of many a Mediteranean home. Their flowers are often scarlet or crimson but also orange or white.

dark-leaved form with long-stalked leaves much mottled and marked with mauve-pink. Howeas are palms with slender stems but very long feathery leaves. They need lots of moisture in the summer but little through the winter – more or less the régime for most conservatory plants. Hypoestes may sound like a medical condition, but they are really evergreen shrubs with attractive foliage; *H. phyllostachya* is the sub-shrub better known as the Polka-dot plant propagated for the houseplant trade. It can grow to 75cm (30in) high and wide. *Sanseveria trifasciata* is one of a series of fleshy-leaved plants, grown for their foliage, this species being the one possessing the common name mother-in-law's tongue. The scheffleras are evergreen trees with handsome foliage. *S. actinophylla* is the Queensland umbrella tree, the umbrella simile being derived from the big, spreading, oval leaflets, 5–16 of them radiating from a central point. It has largish sprays

Like a tropical rainforest, this conservatory is filled with lush foliage plants

While some forms of *Hibiscus* are perfectly hardy, such as the blue, white or red forms of *H. syriacus*, the popular conservatory deciduous shrub *H. rosa-sinensis* is, like several other species, frost tender. *H. rosa-sinensis* has glossy oval leaves with irregular serrations and a wealth of open funnel-shaped, crimson flowers each some 10cm (4in) wide, most generously in summer, but also willing to fly the flag in spring and autumn. The winter-cherry, *Solanum capsicastrum*, is really too well known to need description. It is really a perennial sub-shrub but is almost invariably grown as an annual. Commercially it is still produced in some quantity for the Christmas trade, at which time it is decorated with green, golden, orange and red, large, round 'cherries'.

THUNBERGIA ALATA
Black-eyed Susan

Description: South African annual that grows strongly as a twining climber and has pointed, heart-shaped leaves with some moderate serration. Very flat-faced flowers have five petals making a circle. Usual bright colour made more dramatic by very dark centres. Tender, min. temp. 7-10°C (45-50°F).

Uses: Showy summer and autumn flowers as a climber over artificial support or other plants.

Colour: Rich burnt orange with purple reverse and a dark brown 'eye'. Size: To 3m (10ft) high, spread usually much less.

Flowering time: Early summer until early autumn.

Varieties and relatives: *T. alata* 'Alba', white with dark eye; *aurantiaca* is particularly deep orange. There are some paler yellow forms without a dark eye and at least one variant, *T. a. fryeri*, with pale yellow flowers with a wide centre.

Cultivation and propagation: Raise by seed under glass late winter. Grow on in individual pots until planted out into fertile soil in a warm spot after fear of frost. Thin outgrowths if necessary, lead to support and, where needed, tie in. Will manage with a little light shade.

PLANTS FOR SUNNY CONSERVATORIES

Ananas

Billbergia

Bougainvillea

Campanula isophylla

Capsicum

Chlorophytum

Clivia

Coleus

Crasssula

Cyrtanthus

Echeveria

Euphorbia pulcherrima

Gerbera

Hibiscus rosa-sinensis

Hippeastrum

Jasminum

Justicia

Kalanchoë

Nerine

Opuntia

Pelargonium

Senecio

Solanum

Streptocarpus

Veltheimia

ZERO-MAINTENANCE
GARDENS

A GARDEN THAT requires 'no' maintenance should be the culmination of all the ideas in this book.

Is it possible to arrange a really effective garden that requires almost no maintenance? There is a chance. Using the techniques recommended, choosing the right plants for the right places, and the correct mix of these plants, a stable environment can be established. An environment of plant communities that enjoy living together, where plants thrive in each other's company and serve to enhance each other, perhaps mingling and twining together, blending their colours, scents, foliage, fruits, sizes, textures, growth patterns and habits. Maybe not exactly, but as near as can be, the garden of Eden (before the Fall) – all harmony and delight.

Once the garden is created, some, maybe many, of the techniques used in its creation can be forgotten, no longer needed on a regular basis. Soil does not need to be moved in great mountainous loads; that has been done. Now it is better to encourage its health with mulching and maintaining good drainage. All permanent features have been installed. New ones can be added – a pond once the children are older perhaps – but they will have been planned for in the early stages, 'pencilled in' on the original design.

The evolving garden

Most forms of plastic art, sculpture, ceramics, architecture or painting, are static objects, once finished, they are finished. A garden is different, it evolves with time. Even the almost-no-maintenance garden will change with the years – the plants will grow and mature, small plants will become large clumps, some will die, some will do better than expected, some worse. Change must be planned for.

It can't be said too often that it is best – and more likely to meet with success – to work with nature,

Informal planting cuts down on the need for strict maintenance regimes

not against it. Very heavy clay soils can be vastly improved over the years but they are more than likely to remain generally rather heavy and this needs to be taken into account and exploited. Water features may be much easier to organize on such soils than on very sandy, water-hungry, fast-draining ones.

REDUCING WORK

For really low maintenance, jobs must be simplified and techniques standardized. Thus for seed sowing think about using vermiculite or perlite; the germinating seed does not need complicated composts or fertilizers until the seedlings are surprisingly well advanced. To germinate, most seed needs only appropriate temperature levels, air and water.

Pruning is an operation which can obey the Parkinson law that work takes up the amount of time available. If you know what you are hoping to achieve, pruning need not take a long time. One form is hedge trimming done with a power trimmer. Relatively recent research has proven that bush roses will bloom as well if pruned with such a tool rather than with careful secateur-work. Early spring-flowering shrubs such as forsythias perform better with much of the flowering wood removed

BERGENIA CORDIFOLIA
Elephant's ears

B. 'Abendglut'

Description: Tough (from Siberia), evergreen perennial with a strong rhizomatous rootstock at soil level and large round leaves on stalks. These are bold and shiny and tend to be lightly puckered with crimped margins. Clusters of flowers, gathered in a posy, are held upright on stout stems. Individually the flowers look more gentle than the butch plant.

Uses: Tough cover over rough ground. May be used in front of or between shrubs, in borders, beds and awkward corners. A plant to use boldly; almost indestructible.
Colour: Clear light rosy pink flowers, rich green leaves but older ones can take on a purplish red cast in winter, much more pronounced in some clones than others.
Size: To 45cm (18in) high, spread 60cm (2ft).
Flowering time: Late winter-early spring.
Relatives: *B. cordifolia* 'Purpurea' has richer coloured flowers and foliage that is far more suffused with purplish red at most times. *B.* 'Abendglut' (pictured) is about two thirds the size, with neatly serrated leaves, crimped at the edges and dark green, much suffused red. Clusters of flowers are pinky red.
Cultivation: Very tough and easy. Keep lively by dividing every 2, 3 or 4 years.
Propagation: By division in early spring.

Well-defined edging and
heavy gravel mulching will
reduce work in this rock
garden

after blooming. This encourages fresh wood which supports next year's blossom. However, bushes that are not pruned at all still look very colourful! Fruit trees and others needing some thinning can benefit from air being let into the centre.

Remove branches that grow across the centre – this is one of the main rules of most shrub and tree pruning. It is usually much more efficient and easy to remove one or two largish pieces rather than fiddling around taking a lot of twigs away.

Work is minimized if no weeds are grown. Open soil without plants can be sprayed with a pre-emergent weedkiller that will inhibit weed germination and is effective for months if the soil surface is not moved. The use of shredded bark will do more than just suppress weeds, which it does efficiently. It will keep the soil below moist and cool, and allow the rainfall to penetrate without forming a cap; it also encourages a good soil structure and life right up to the surface.

The total systemic weedkillers based on glyphosate are ideal to clear uncultivated ground, and take ten to fifteen days to effect a complete kill. Paths can be kept clear of weed using a proprietary killer which will be a cocktail of chemicals, some contact, and translocated killers and others that will remain active for several months.

The labour of keeping grass tidy can be reduced dramatically and the whole lawn given a permanent face-lift if its edges are marked with permanent materials such as stone or bricks. In the greenhouse, tidiness and efficiency can be increased by a decrease in the number of different pot sizes employed. Think about using square ones that pack together more easily on benches when in use and can be kept in less space when stored.

Brachyglottis 'Sunshine' (syn *Senecio* 'Sunshine')

Description: Hardy, everygreen, spreading shrub, one of the Dunedin Hybrids Group, with rounded, oval, tough leaves covered with hairs that make them glisten grey or silver. The undersurfaces are white felted. Many bunches of bright daisies in summer.

Uses: One of the most useful of shrubs in places with poor soils and in seaside sites, always provided it has plenty of light. Resistant to drought once established.

Colour: Silver-grey foliage, white young stems and bright golden flowers.

Size: 75cm (30in) high, spread 1.5m (5ft).

Flowering time: Early to midsummer.

Relatives: *B. monroi* is a tough evergreen with dark green, slightly greyed leaves with white undersides and neat wavy-edges. Bright yellow daisy flowers in summer. Somewhat more compact and upright than 'Sunshine'. Good windbreak, especially in seaside gardens.

Cultivation: Easy in all soils with drainage. Can be cut back if over-large or getting a little untidy.

Propagation: Easy by cuttings through growing months.

APPROPRIATE TOOLS

Every garden demands some maintenance. The work involved can be drastically reduced if the tools needed are well chosen and well looked after. Good tools make a pleasure of many otherwise mundane jobs. It is the quality not the quantity of tools that counts. Each garden will demand its own set. I have a stainless steel spade that is in frequent use, over ten years old and the successor to one that lasted much longer before being lost in a house move. The stainless steel ensures that it is simplicity to keep clean and that it cuts through the soil sharply without much adhering to it. The time it has saved me over the years must be huge. Similarly, I have a stainless hand fork and trowel that seem like an extension of the arm and hand when in use. Again, they are years old and in perfect order despite almost daily employment.

Power tools are excellent in limited numbers. If you have sufficient grass to justify a sit-on mower, make mowing efficient by having curved edges that can be easily negotiated and grassed pathways of

Chimonanthus praecox
Wintersweet

Description: Rather spare, upright, deciduous shrub with rough, richly coloured, polished leaves. Unusual flowers with outer sepals and petals almost translucent but with darker coloured smaller central ones.

Uses: Grown for highly perfumed winter blossom. Usually sited by a wall to help its somewhat weak backbone in early years but more importantly to provide floral display with frost protection. It makes sense to have the perfume close to the house.

Colour: Limey yellow with centres of dark maroon.

Scent: One of the most sweetly and heavily scented of flowering shrubs.

Size: 2.5m (8ft) high but more against wall, spread 3m (10ft).

Flowering time: Mid- to late winter.

Relatives: *C. praecox* 'Luteus' has brighter yellow flowers; 'Grandiflorus' has somewhat larger blooms.

Cultivation: Plant in a warm, sheltered position near a wall with plenty of humus in the soil.

Propagation: By seed sown when ripe. Cultivars by air layers or semi-ripe summer cuttings.

GUNNERA MANICATA

Description: Perhaps the most theatrical and imposing of all garden foliage plants. From a strong rootstock which expands year by year, curious rugby-football flowering heads arise, ginger-coloured and of many-branched florets, just clear of the ground. Then bristly stems rise up and huge leaves are unfurled, large enough to shelter under in a rain shower! The sheer size of the leaves is fantastic but their shining rich green colours and rounded form and structure back up the impression of strength. Although strong and hardy, new small plants need protection through their first winter.

Uses: Hugely impressive waterside plant where you can afford the space.

Wildlife: Ducks and other waterfowl can shelter in the clumps.

Colour: Ginger flowers, stems rough with ginger hairs.

Size: 2m (6ft) high, spread 2.5m (8ft).

Flowering time: Spring.

Relatives: *G. magellanica* has rounded, serrated leaves, bronze tinged in youth, bright green later. It is a carpeter only about 7cm (3in) high but spreading at least 30cm (12in).

Cultivation: Pot-grown plants should be established in early spring if possible and given the chance to get well rooted before the winter. Protect crowns from frost; dead leaves, extra bracken or other loose vegetation will do. After flowering, spikes can be removed to save every scrap of plant's energy for the production of the huge leaves.

Propagation: By seed from the red fruits that follow flowers, or by carefully detaching parts of the rootstock in late summer and getting them rooted in position before winter.

either one or two mower widths. A petrol-driven edger with a solid blade is helpful to keep lawn edges in order. They are hand-held but run on a small wheel and are easy to use. A shredder, allowing prunings and trimmings to be shredded and composted, is quite useful but can be managed without. When I bought a vacuum collector of fallen leaves and litter, I felt somewhat guilty thinking it to be an indulgence. It quickly proved one of the most useful weapons in the arsenal. It helps to keep the drive tidy and various places where leaves fall and detritus lodges. It runs over the driveway without picking up the gravel. The suction mode fills a sensible-sized bag with the leaves. The blowing mode enables one to remove leaves, and similar detritus, and blow them on to the border where they can rot down as a mulch. An electric hedge trimmer is also very useful. Wind up the cable on a reel manufactured for hosepipes.

Tool storage Having the right tools is the first step. Knowing where they are and being able to get them quickly is another. They need space and to be kept dry, cleaned and in good order.

The mixed – very mixed – border

Pure herbaceous borders are an extreme rarity in a no-maintenance garden. It is rather a mix of shrubs, herbaceous plants, ground cover and bulbs. Shrubs give permanent shape among the seasonal perennials, and trees lend some shade. Below and between these major plants ground-covering, weed-suppressing energetic carpeters are planted to help keep all in order. There are a few ideas for herbaceous plants that are low maintenance and much can be learned from them.

WILLIAM ROBINSON AND NEW GERMAN GARDENING CONCEPTS

The great gardener and writer William Robinson (1839–1936) was a man who knew his own mind and was not afraid of expressing it. His *The English Garden* was first published in 1883 and went through very many editions. He had ideas. Although he was sensible enough to be able to change and modify these, he was never able to hide his distaste for very formal Victorian bedding. This was not gardening to him. He wrote about growing plants naturally and to some extent tried to follow out his own precepts. Sweeps of plants both native 'weeds' and cultivated dandies, such as peonies, lilies, phloxes, primulas and hollyhocks, were planted and expected to manage on their own. With peonies he picked a good hardy plant, this being a genus that, planted in the wild garden, will continue to grow despite neglect, provided it has sunlight and the normal necessities of life. Some of his natural associations come very close to the concept of garden design now being expounded in Germany and other European countries.

Herbaceous plantings in broad sweeps, choosing plants that stand a good chance of looking after themselves through the growing months, is an idea that is gaining popularity with many gardeners all over the world since it has been demonstrated very successfully by German garden designers in gardens such as Westpark in Munich. The ideas are not dissimilar to those preached by William Robinson.

The basis of the philosophy is a healthy respect for the individual characters of plants and the realization that large collections of one kind of plant are better than single specimens or twos or threes. So groups of one plant are grown alongside – and blending with – contrasting types in wide ranging drifts. Grasses feature strongly. The plants chosen are usually those that will thrive in the open. Dot plants are almost unknown. Consideration is given to the colours of flowers but as much or more importance is placed on the characters of the plants in their groups. Careful planning is done to try to effect clearly observable changes of character as the seasons pass. The plantings are thought of as semi-permanent. When cold weather comes the plants are left substantially alone; tidying is done at the end of the winter and the cycle of growth is allowed to repeat itself.

Bulbs can be planted in bold groups and many left for decades. Daffodils planted with at least 12cm (5in) of soil over them should prosper without any extra aid. Lilies such as *L. martagon*, *L. pardalinum* and *L. lancifolium* should carry on for ever without further lifting. There are gardens where the martagon lily has flourished for a century. Peonies will do the same and will grow strongly for decades in cultivat-

LIMNANTHES DOUGLASII
Meadow foam, Poached-egg plant

Description: A fully hardy annual from California and Southern Oregon with upward-facing, saucer flowers, 2.5cm (1in) wide. Soft and sappy, it has divided light green foliage.

Uses: Lower reaches of a large rock garden, front of borders or almost any spot where its propensity to rapidly colonize can be allowed or kept in check.

Colour: Each petal bright yellow with a white notched tip.

Size: Height 15cm (6in), spread 10cm (4in).

Flowering time: Through summer from early to late.

Cultivation: Easy in sunny spot in normal to moist soil. It readily colonizes rich soils, especially ones that do not dry out and can cope with really moist spots.

Relatives: In the wild there are all white, all yellow and pink-tinted ones but these are not commonly seen in cultivation.

Propagation: By seed sown *in situ* in spring.

ed soil or even in grass. The bolder *Inulas* such as *I. hookeri* look impressive in leaf and in bloom with large yellow daisy flowers with narrow petals. *Achillea ptarmica* 'The Pearl' makes tight clumps of erect, slender stems with narrow leaves and brilliant white double flowers, while *A.* 'Moonshine' and others form wider heads of mustard-yellow accompanied by grey ferny foliage.

In damper sites groups of ferns such as *Osmunda regalis* or *Dryopteris dilatata* look effective. In similar areas, you can also grow the splendid foliage plants

PLANTING GROUND COVER

Particularly good ground cover plants include hostas for damp or normal conditions, and *Houttuynia cordata* 'Chameleon' for its bright foliage, useful in rather moist soils. *Lamium maculatum* silver-leaved forms are very good for dry spots, *Tiarella cordifolia* is useful in most places, together with *Epimedium* forms and shrubby things such as heathers and low-growing *Cotoneasters* such as *C. dammeri* and *C. horizontalis.*

1 *Define the area to be covered.*
2 *Thoroughly eliminate all perennial weed.*
3 *Cultivate soil and add humus if needed.*
4 *Select suitable plants for the area, taking into consideration soil moisture content and sun/shade factors.*
5 *Plant each selected kind in groups usually about 30cm (12in) apart so that they will grow quickly into each other.*

LYCHNIS FLOS-JOVIS
Campion

L. flos-cuculi

Description: Herbaceous perennial that forms clumps of grey-green soft foliage and branching upright and spreading stems with many campion flowers.

Uses: Good border plant, the white hairy foliage and stems forming a complement to the flower colour. Can be grown in wild gardens and less formal sites such as banksides and hedge bottoms.

Colour: Deep pink.

Size: Height and spread 45cm (18in).

Flowering time: Mid- to late summer.

Relatives: *L. flos-jovis* 'Alba' is pure white. *L. flos-cuculi* (Ragged Robin, pictured) has pale pink flowers with feathery petals. It is best in a wild garden.

Cultivation: Easy in open sunny sites in well-drained soils.

Propagation: By seed in autumn when ripe or in spring.

such as those of the *Rodgersia* clan. Other foliage plants can also look good. These include the hostas which will do well in normal soil, as well as the damp ones so often recommended. *Acanthus*, once planted, is there for ever, looking lush, strong and splendid in leaf and noble in flower.

Traditional low maintenance plants

IN PRAISE OF HEATHERS

There is much to be said for the sadly rejected and neglected heathers. One of the original arguments in their favour was that they were labour-saving. They grow easily. You can have collections of the lime-tolerant kinds on any soil; those with acid soils can employ every species. They smother weeds and, once planted, will last for a good number of years, especially if they are clipped back – a light haircut – to encourage fresh growth.

All these advantages have been ignored in recent years and heathers have come to be regarded as *passé*. This is something that should be disputed. Granted, planned as a monoculture, a coloured carpet of varieties of similar height, then the idea could be unexciting. But there are so many to choose from that even a monoculture could work well. There are those that hardly get a few centimetres/inches off the ground and others that grow 2m (6ft) or more, high. Combine this huge range of sizes with the varying colours of foliage and flower and then add a few dwarf conifers, companions of heathers of old, and the picture is marvellously enriched. The other obvious member of this plant association will be the silver birches as found on heathlands.

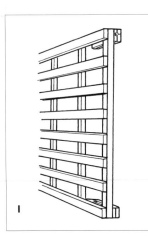

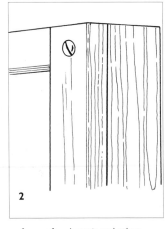

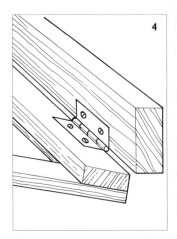

WALL PLANTS

As far as possible use wall-hugging shrubs rather than trellis, especially against awkward walls. Then you do not have to worry about maintenance of the trellis, and the shrubs can act as frames for clematis and other more fragile climbers, giving you two features in one space.

For plants with flexible backbones, secure trellis with wooden pegs securely fixed to the wall, (1) making the trellis stick out a few centimetres/ inches from the wall itself. Fix the trellis to the pegs (2)so that it can be brought away from the wall, perhaps using latches at the top (3) and hinges at the bottom supports (4), allowing for easy maintenance of the trellis and the wall.

The gap between wall and trellis is an excellent place for a house-hunting bird.

Do not limit yourself to choosing from among the more usual dark-leaved, purple-red-flowered kinds or the dark-leaved, white-flowering cultivars. These are good but can be greatly enlivened by those with brighter coloured foliage. A favourite is *Erica* 'Westwood Yellow' which is a very neat-growing, low shrub that is always a smiling bright yellow and as such makes a wonderful contrast against its neighbours. Everyone gains. It has plenty of lavender bloom at the end of the winter and the beginning of spring but it is the foliage we are investing in. There are also those kinds that have red- and orange-tinted foliage. There are a lot of these now. You would not be wrong to start with kinds such as 'Foxhollow', which has bright golden summer foliage but in winter stokes up the fires and is flushed warmly with orange-red.

New life can be injected into a group of heathers by introducing some good hellebores – species and hybrids. Spurges, too, look good. And bulbs, ranging from snowdrops and small scillas, daffodils and tulips, are effective among the low-growing heathers, as are some of the smaller and daintier lilies in summer. In this season, it is possible to add an exotic touch with *Gazania* hybrids and similar

RHEUM PALMATUM
Decorative rhubarb

Description: Strong, handsome, herbaceous perennial with a massive rootstock. The wide, sharply-lobed leaves are basically heart-shaped but the lobes are so deeply and well defined that the effect is palmate; each leaf measures 60-75cm (24-30in) long and almost as much wide. Tall strong flower stems hold substantial panicles of crowded little flowers. Fully hardy.

Uses: Fine foliage plant.

Wildlife: Shelter to birds and other animal life.

Colour: Rich green foliage, creamy flowers.

Size: Height and spread 2m (6ft).

Flowering time: Early to midsummer.

Relatives: The most desirable are those with strongly coloured leaves such as *R. palmatum rubrum* and 'Atrosanguineum' with leaves heavily suffused reddish purple.

Cultivation: Best in moist but well-drained, rich soil in sunny or lightly shaded spots.

Propagation: By division in early spring or seed sown as soon as ripe.

Thickly planted annuals have the added benefit of discouraging weed growth

SOLVING EVERYDAY PROBLEMS

GROUND COVER

Ground cover plants can be used below specimen trees and shrubs to give other seasons of colour and interest and prevent weeds having a chance to establish. This could be the place to isolate a bed of the variegated form of ground elder, *Aegopodium podagraria* 'Variegatum' or the woodruff, *Galium odoratum*, with its neat whorls of foliage and heads of tiny white stars.

---

daisy-flowered plants, such as the sun flowering South African *Delosperma (Mesembryanthemum),* with brilliant colours, or the ground-hugging alpine *Anacyclus* var. *depressus,* with very cut foliage and red buds that open to pure white daisies with yellow centres. *Anthemis punctata* ssp. *cupaniana* with its spreading mass of silvery, cut foliage looks good and is very free with flowers pretending to be ox-eye daisies. All this without spoiling the overall effect of the heather bed or garden.

Think scent

Some of the easy plants that do not need to be fussed about with are scented, so we might as well enjoy this bonus. Lavender is a favourite with everyone.

Choose shrubs and plants well endowed with perfume for use around the house. The wintersweet (*Chimonanthus praecox*) is an obvious shrub to plant close to a window; it will appreciate the support of the wall, will have its wood ripened to give larger numbers of flowerbuds and the flowers will be more generous with their perfume in the winter with the warmth of the wall to stimulate them. Seed of night-scented stock (*Matthiola bicornis*) scattered on soil below a window or by a door will produce small plants with their modest flowers but top-class scent.

Some annuals will self seed and save you the job in following years. The common wallflower has glorious perfume and should not be ignored for its late spring and early summer show.

TROPAEOLUM SPECIOSUM
Flame creeper,
Flame nasturtium

Description: Herbaceous perennial climber with a formidable creeping, stout rhizomatous rootstock. New stems arise each spring and will clamber up any support by means of fast-growing, twining stems, furnished with leaves cut into five or six oval lobes, like leaflets joined to a single point. The showy blossom, each spurred nasturtium flower with three square-shaped clearly defined lower petals and twin narrower ones above, is followed by unusual fruits. Frost hardy.

Uses: To enliven hedges, other shrubs or climbers.

Colour: Brilliant scarlet flowers, bright blue fruits splitting out of vivid red encasing calyces.

Size: Height and spread to 3m (10ft).

Flowering time: Summer.

Cultivation: Tuck its rhizomatous rootstock safely away in the shade. It can cope with a plentiful supply of moisture in the growing period but likes good drainage. Choose a warm spot where it will have scope for its clambering habit.

Propagation: By seed.

PICK YOUR OWN WEEDS

Nature abhors a vacuum: patches of soil are an invitation for some filling in with weeds. Why not select your own 'weeds'. There are a range of annuals and perennials that will seed themselves and naturalize ground that is going spare. Love-in-the-mist once sown in a border will be there every year unless you take firm action against it; other annuals such as the pot marigold, *Calendula officinalis*, or *Eschscholzia californica* are almost as easy. Perennials such as *Alchemilla mollis* are believers in large families and can soon fill their homes if allowed. Many bulbs can increase rapidly below ground by division and vegetative means and can also hugely increase their numbers by seeding remarkably quickly. Top performers are the bluebells (*Hyacinthoides non-scripta* (see page 154) and *H. hispanica*), but there are a lot of others such as star of Bethlehem (*Ornithogalum umbellatum*) and many *Allium* species. Only introduce these where you are happy to let them takeover – they can be termed invasive.

Plant associations

To build up a self-perpetuating group of plants in damp places go for a native mix. This could include willows such as *Salix daphnoides*, with violet-purple stems, and below this *Iris pseudacorus*, the yellow flag, with meadowsweet (*Filipendula ulmeria*), marsh marigold (*Caltha palustris*), lady's smock (*Cardamine pratensis*) and purple loosestrife (*Lythrum salicaria*) perhaps with some little special extras such as snake's-head fritillaries (*Fritillaria meleagris*). For a more cosmopolitan effect start with the various coloured-stemmed dogwoods (*Cornus alba* 'Sibirica', *C. stolonifera*), which grow so easily that they are naturalized in several parts of the British countryside. And use the spectacularly sheathed and early flowering, skunk cabbages, *Lysichiton americanus* and *L. camtschatcensis* in golden-yellow and white. For later colour it would not be difficult to add to the association some of the moisture-loving primulas such as *Primula japonica*, *P. pulverulenta*, *P. beesiana* and *P. florindae*.

In drier spots, dyer's greenweed (*Genista tinctoria*) can be grown in among grasses and other low herbage. It is very decorative in bloom with lots of

PAEONIA '*Bowl of Beauty*'

Description: Tough, thick-rooted perennial which will carry on in the same position for decades forming large clumps. It will reach up to 1m (3ft) high and wider. The foliage looks attractive as it grows from the ground through the spring. In late spring and early summer it unfurls large flowers from tight round buds. The wide, rounded, cup or bowl shape is formed of a ring of overlapping petals around a wide boss of narrow petaloids in creamy ivory. The flower colour is a rich satin pink. The flowers are well held and less damage-prone than the heavy double forms.

Uses: For permanent planting in borders or in light grass. Best in open, sunny spot or light shade.

Colour: Rich pink and ivory.

Size: 1m (3ft) high, but wider.

Flowering time: Late spring and early summer.

Relatives: There are many named peony hybrids. The most famous of the pink kinds is the fully double 'Sarah Bernhardt'. 'Kelway's Glorious' is a fine, single, deep pink, bordering on a salmon-red. 'Festiva Maxima' is an old one with rather informal flowers of white cut petals, some with dark crimson bases.

Cultivation: Plant firmly and then leave undisturbed. It will improve year by year. You may be well advised to arrange pea sticks or wire flower supports so that the heavy buds are not lowered in inclement weather.

Propagation: By division of the crown in late winter – but this should only be tackled when the clump is large.

PLANTS FOR SCENT

Acacia spp.

Anthemis nobilis, chamomile

Cytisus forms

Choisya ternata

Daphne spp.

Erica arborea

Eucalyptus spp.

Gardenia jasminoides

Genista spp.

Hamamelis forms

Jasminum officinalis

Lonicera forms

Mahonia forms

Matthiola bicornis

Myrtus, myrtle

Philadelphus forms

Rosa forms

Syringa forms

Thymus spp.

Viburnum forms

Viola forms

small golden pea flowers. Several of the native *Hypericum* species do well in similar positions; *H. perforatum* is a pretty little weed with upright stems and short lateral branches carrying aloft a spray of small yellow flowers usually dotted black around the edges. To change the colour introduce chicory, *Cichorium intybus*, with tall stems and a long succession of flat, doubled, daisy flowers in delightful pale blue. Bugloss, *Anchusa arvensis*, with rough hairy stems and leaves, has flowers of rich deep blue. Other plants that could be added to this native community are the field scabious (*Knautia arvensis*) the showiest of this group, though overpowered by a relative, the teasel, *Dipsacus fullonum*, standing perhaps 1.5m (5ft) high in bloom and remaining in

impressive skeleton form for months through the winter. For taller company add hazels and the field maple (*Acer campestre*), one of the most delightful natives, as a hedgerow plant or given full rein to become a mature tree of wide cloud-like form.

A basic approach to planting an association of plants that is going to maintain itself with little difficulty and maintenance means adopting nature's way. Simplified this is creating three layers: the trees, the understorey, mainly of shrubs, and the ground plants. The trees could be a mix of evergreen and deciduous. If you have space, and time, the evergreen oaks are tremendously impressive. On a smaller scale some conifers or a mix of hollies, Portuguese laurel and yew are ideal. Deciduous

The plants in this seaside garden have been chosen for their resilience to the difficult conditions

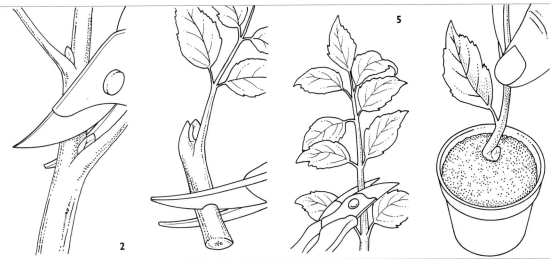

LEAF BUD CUTTINGS OF MAHONIAS

1 Select good cutting material. This is fresh young growth which has a good capacity to produce roots, unlike the old wood. If there is a lack of it you can encourage new growth by cutting back a stem and forcing new stems to grow.

2 Choose an undamaged leaf with a lively-looking bud in the leaf axil and make a neat cut directly above the bud. Use the sharpest tool you have to make clean cuts. Make your second cut 2-3cm (1-1½in) below the bud.

3 A good mahonia leaf may have six pairs of leaflets and a terminal one. Your cutting will need the support of only some three pairs of leaflets; the rest can be cut off.

4 Dip the base of the cutting in hormone rooting powder/liquid. Tap off excess.

5 Insert cutting/s into a pot of rooting medium – half peat and half grit/coarse sand. Leave bud level with the top of the compost. Firm and water.

6 Enclose each pot in a blown-open plastic bag after spraying all with fungicide and place in a cold frame or similar arrangement.

7 Keep an eye on the cuttings until you see signs of new growth from the bud. Then allow more air in and ensure the young plants do not dry out.

8 Pot off individual young plants when they have got well rooted and grow on for a year in pots before planting out.

---

trees could include quick-growing silver birches, the Italian alder (*Alnus cordata*), maples, thorns, such as the distinctive larger-fruited *Crataegus × lavallei* 'Carrierei', but even the wild hawthorn can grow into a real character tree. Flowering cherries and apple forms are useful, not-too-huge trees. *Prunus × subhirtella* 'Autumnalis' is great for flurries of blossom from autumn till spring. For really long-term thinking, you will find that apples (*Malus* species and hybrids) will outlast cherries; they will continue for decades after the cherries have given up.

Shrubs can be a glorious mix of easy kinds that need no real pruning. In moister spots the dogwoods can be left to get on doing their thing. In drier spots try hazels, including the dark-leaved *Corylus avellana* 'Fuscorubra' or the larger-leaved *C. maxima* 'Purpurea'. *Philadelphus* species and hybrids grow quickly and are always welcome with their 'orange-blossom' scent. Evergreens such as the *Euonymus* forms and *Elaeagnus pungens* 'Maculata' with vividly golden-variegated leaves will contrast with deciduous neighbours. I always enjoy the ever

healthy-looking spotted laurel, *Aucuba japonica*, in its many variegated cultivar forms.

The shrubby layer can be enlivened by introducing climbers such as wild honeysuckles; *Lonicera periclymenum* forms 'Belgica' and 'Serotina' will ensure a very long display of scented blossom.

The ground layer may be kept under control with ivies but they should not be given total control. Sweeps of naturalized bulbs should be used to lighten the whole. Introducing a few bluebells will soon produce lakes of blue flowers. *Anemone nemorosa* in white, pink-flushed and pale blue forms will steadily establish itself and small daffodils such as the wild *Narcissus pseudonarcissus* and the Tenby daffodil (*N. obvallaris*) are ideal. So are the *N. cyclamineus* hybrids – all of them; 'February Gold' is still one of the most useful and an easy naturalizer. Plant some of the large-bulbed *Camassia leichtlinii* to give spikes of blue flowers like a scilla gone mad and grown to 60cm (24in) or more. Next to this add bulbs of *Lilium martagon* and *L. pardalinum*. Once there they can manage for a century or so.

BUILDER'S SOIL

Even in the most difficult sites, raised beds and hardworking landscape materials quickly create an attractive garden

To A DEDICATED gardener, soil is a delicate and precious living thing to be treated with deference, respect and tender loving care. To a builder, soil is the rotten sticky stuff he slips around on all day, which works up his trousers from his boots, is heavy to move and is always in the way. He drives over it continually with heavy machinery to compact it further and squeeze out all traces of healthy structure with skidding tyres. He mixes concrete on it, stacks heavy weights on it, smothers it under tarpaulins, spills chemicals over it and, as a final gesture, buries all manner of detritus under it. Rubble and bricks are standard, oil drums and derelict vehicle pieces tend to reveal themselves belatedly, perhaps as the lawn sinks over rusting cavities.

LOTUS CORNICULATUS
Common bird's-foot trefoil

Description: One of the prettiest of wayside weeds and certainly worth a place in the garden with its miniature divided pea-type foliage and pea-flowers in heads of two to five blooms. Its cheerful colours and free-flowering habit make the spreading mats of stems and leaves a joyful focal point. Well-known in all countries of northern Europe including Britain.

Uses: In rock gardens, alpine meadows, wild gardens, sunny banksides and hedge bottoms.

Colour: Fresh green foliage, golden and orange flowers (the 'eggs and bacon' of children).

Size: Only 2-5cm (1-2in) high, spread 40cm (16in).

Flowering time: Late spring until early autumn.

Cultivation: Sow seed where plants are needed or sow in trays and prick out into pots before planting out. Thereafter it should look after itself, provided the position is sunny, not waterlogged and is not overgrown by much larger more dominant plants.

Coping with builder's soil

You may need to start afresh.

TOPSOIL

In very bad situations it is often the case that matters are made worse rather than better by the importation of lorry loads of material described as 'topsoil'. Sometimes it can be reasonably healthy soil, structured and fertile. More often it will have been stacked too long and much of its life will have

SOIL SIEVING

You may decide to sieve the soil to remove the smaller pieces of rubble and assorted rubbish, together with the worst of the weed roots. Be sure you really need to do this; you may be giving yourself a lot of labour for relatively little advantage.

Once you have decided to sieve, save yourself time and effort by building an A-frame sieve. This can be quite large and stand almost as high as a person.

It can be stood on clear ground or over a barrow and the material to be sieved shovelled or thrown against the top of the mesh. As it slides down, the useful sifted proportion falls through and the rejected material slides to a heap at the base. If it is predominantly weed and humus material it can be composted together with some lumps of soil. If there is a lot of rubble, this will have to be manually sorted and can then be used as hard core foundation material for paths or similar features. The angle at which you set your A-frame sieve will vary according to the material to be sieved – the easier the material the closer to the vertical.

died. Even good soil may have hidden hazards. It may not be local, it may be of very different chemical and physical nature to that naturally in your area, so making the understanding of your soil more confusing. Plants may find themselves moving from one type of soil on the surface to something totally different below. Also the imported soil may be acting Trojan horse to a whole army of weed seeds and persistent roots. Perhaps I overstate the case but it is best to be warned.

THE BACK WORK

There is no dodging some heaving and grunting when you are faced with a building site garden. The solid rubbish has to be removed together with anything unacceptable below ground and this can include chewed up tree roots and stumps. It may be necessary to fork over the entire area and make various heaps of rubbish and then ferry it sack by sack in the boot of the car to the local waste centre or hire a mini-skip to take the lot in one go – probably the better of the two options where there is a major problem. In more severe cases areas of the garden may need sieving (see box).

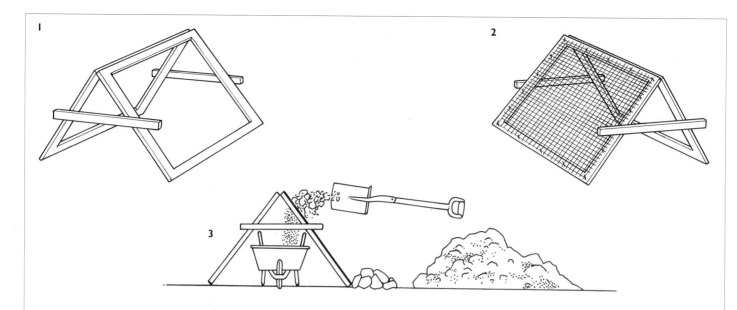

MAKING AN A-FRAME

1 Hinge together two old window frames or something similar.

2 Fix a strong grid over one side. Holes should be approximately 1cm (½in) wide by 5cm (2in) long. This should cope with normal garden soil. A coarser mesh will be needed for rougher work.

3 Allow room for a barrow under the inverted V shape.

4 Throw material to be sieved against the top stretch of the A-frame.

5 Remove rejected material; remove sieved material.

Alternatively:

1 Fit mesh over one ex-window frame.

2 Arrange the frame over two firm supports high enough to allow a barrow just below.

3 Throw material on to the grid frame and work back and forwards.

4 Tip rejected material to one side.

5 Remove rejected material; remove sieved material.

NEPETA × *FAASSENII*
Catmint

Description: Semi-evergreen herbaceous perennial that forms bushy plants of much-branched stems with the grey-green, soft leaves whose smell seems to exert a hypnotic effect on felines.

Uses: Border plant especially useful for softening edges of paths. Can be good in areas of gravel. Will grow on rough ground and is not fussy about soil.

Wildlife: Attracts cats.

Colour: Lavender-blue.

Scent: Crushed leaves have distinctive catmint aroma.

Size: Foliage to 25cm (10in) high, flowers to 40-45cm (16-18in), spread as much or a little more.

Flowering time: Early summer for several weeks. If cut back can be encouraged to give bloom later as well.

Relatives: N. 'Souvenir d'André Chaudron' (syn. N. 'Blue Beauty') can be taller and has more spacious spires of flowers; quite a refined plant.

Cultivation: Easy in most soils, best with sun and moisture.

Propagation: By division or by seed.

SOIL PANS

Building work, or your own digging, can create soil pans. These are undesirable impervious levels in the soil that can be formed in a variety of ways. One of the quickest ways in heavy soils is to repeatedly run a lightweight rotovator over the ground. While the top may become a fine tilth, below there is a flat 'pan' which can become almost impenetrable to rain or even roots. If you suspect areas of soil panning, it is better at the outset to hire a heavyweight machine to rotovate deeply or, alternatively, to bring in a contractor with really powerful machinery. If you are using a rotovator, it may help to vary the controls governing the depth to which the blades reach. Farmers plough deeply and try to break up the lower soil to avoid making or reinforcing pans, gardeners should be every bit as careful.

Digging can be a slow but thorough alternative, with less chance of creating a pan relatively close to the surface. The pan problem is more pronounced the heavier the soil so, while you may have only limited time to work on the ground, do not be tempted to try to undertake major cultivations when soil and weather conditions are bad. Trying to work heavy wet soils is difficult and unpleasant, you may do far more harm than good to the soil structure. Patience as well as elbow grease is needed.

CONTOURING AND DRAINING

Starting with a 'clean canvas', having cleared the surface rubble and rubbish, take a look at the site and do any contouring of it that may improve matters. Bear in mind surface drainage (see pages 71-75, 83-84). It might be possible to plan a pool and arrange drainage towards it. The surplus soil from the pool site can be used to build up areas, perhaps especially at the boundary of the plot as this may give a chance to elevate some of the planting and give extra height and depth to the design. The same applies to any soil removed for the foundations of paths, patio and other hard surface areas. Field drains can be laid to lower ground or to larger existing drains.

Other chapters in this book suggest designs and layouts for your garden, depending on its various uses and the prevailing condtions. Now is the time to consider where you want beds and borders, where to put in paths and patios, as well as where to site sheds, washing lines and other utilitarian objects.

Improving conditions

COMPOSTING

Now we start the garden proper by nurturing the soil and working with whatever topsoil there is. To make a really good start, try green manuring (see page 121). As much humus as possible should be incorporated into the top 20cm (8in). Continual mulches of any possible organic matter should remain a top priority for one or two seasons at least. This is undertaken to build up a reasonable soil structure, to let air into a formerly compacted soil and to aid moisture retention.

Making the most of it

The first crop of plants to be grown on a poor site could be a mix of meadowland plant of cornfield flowers. Seed could be scattered of plants such as the ox-eye daisy (*Leucanthemum vulgare*), field poppy

PAPAVER RHOEAS
Field poppy

Description: Hardy annual with hairy, narrow, serrated leaves and slender hairy stems each carrying an oval grey-green bud that bursts open to creased silk petals, quickly forming into wide open, shining flowers. Native to all countries of northern Europe, including Britain.
Uses: For covering bare spots, rough sunny areas and gaps in borders.
Colour: Orange-red.
Size: To 60cm (2ft) high, spread 30cm (12in).
Relatives: Shirley Series are the poppies of a thousand different colour shades: white, pinks, creams, yellows, oranges, and red, and many bicolour combinations.
Cultivation: Will colonize bare soil.
Propagation: By seed.

(*Papaver rhoeas*), cornflower (*Centaurea cyanus*), corn cockle (*Agrostemma githago*), black and spotted medick (*Medicago lupulina, M. arabica*), clovers and various grasses. There are also all the jolly annuals such as nasturtiums, love-in-the-mist, pot marigold, clarkia, eschscholtzia, sunflowers, asters, lavatera and poppies to add to the mix. It could be a dazzling display.

MORE TOUGH

THE PLANTS included in this section are on a kind of 'honours list' of very varied, very tough species that must be considered for a wide variety of different sites and conditions. Here you will find more ideas for difficult areas. For example, *Viburnum tinus* is included as an outstandingly useful and attractive shrub, with a long period of interest; among the other stalwarts are thyme, mint and primulas.

Eschscholzia californica

ESCHSCHOLZIA CALIFORNICA
Californian poppy

Description: Petals of pearlescent silk in all the hottest shades of summer, and grey green feathery foliage, earn this Californian annual a place.

Uses: Wonderful filler for every small gap, though you need to think carefully of colour schemes – most of these pigments are not subtle. Use their vividness to catch the heat of high summer, or pick hazy pinks to complement the blues of lavender and *Convolvulus sabatius*. It is ideal for using in a dry garden (pages 10-54) and will provide a good filler in difficult areas (see Calamitous Conditions pages 118-123).

Colour: Originally a dominant orange, breeders have created a wide palette from yellows and bronzes through many shades to red, mauve, pink and cream.

Size: 30cm (1ft) high and across.

Flowering time: All summer through and well into autumn.

Varieties: Choose seed strains to suit your colour schemes – or save your own seed.

Cultivation: Thin out seedlings and leave alone.

Propagation: Takes serious umbrage to root disturbance. Easy from seed sown in situ where it will continue to self seed for as long as there is open ground.

PLANTS

Mentzelia lindleyi

MENTZELIA LINDLEYI
(SYN. BARTONIA AUREA)

Description: Bushy annual that grows fast and has fleshy, fresh green, serrated, pointed foliage and a long succession of bloom. Half hardy.

Uses: Useful filler in beds or larger containers. Especially good in dry, sunny conditions (pages 18-31) or calamitous sites (pages 118-123).

Colour: Deep golden flowers with protruding stamens.

Scent: Well-endowed with perfume.

Size: 50cm (20in) high, spread 25cm (10in).

Flowering time: Summer.

Cultivation: Plant out in fertile soil in a warm spot.

Propagation: By seed early spring.

THYMUS SPECIES AND VARIETIES
Thyme

Description: Culinary thyme, *T. vulgaris*, occurs in several forms, all spreading subshrubby perennials. Those grown for decoration are the creepers, such as *T. serpyllum*, and the hybrid series like the somewhat more upright but spreading lemon-scented *T. x citriodorus* kinds. Fully hardy.

Uses: They are excellent in rock or trough gardens, and ideal in small gardens (pages 142-151). *T. serpyllum* is marvellous for very low carpeting of open areas such as between paving stones or in gravel (see also pages 162-169). *T. x citriodorus* forms are small scale spreading shrubs for rock gardens, troughs or herb gardens and for edging the fronts of beds/borders. *T. vulgaris* is popular and excellent in cooking.

Colour: Shades of green and many flower colours, see 'Relatives' below.

Scent: Aromatic when crushed.

Size: Up to 45cm (18in) high, spread is more.

Flowering time: Early to late summer.

Relatives: Good *T. serpyllum* forms are the bright green leaved and white flowered 'Snowdrift' and 'Minor' an even smaller-leaved kind that could be first choice for trough or other miniature gardens. *T. serpyllum albus* is white-flowered and green leaved; *T. s. coccineus* is crimson-flowered and dark-leaved; *T. x citriodorus* 'Aureus' has tiny bright golden leaves.

Cultivation: Easy in a light open spot in well-drained soil.

Propagation: Division of rooted pieces or cuttings.

Thymus

EPIMEDIUM GRANDIFLORUM
Barrenwort, Bishop's mitre

Description: A member of a hardy genus grown for its pleasing ground covering foliage. The flowers, in bunches up to a dozen or more, are spurred rather like tiny aquilegia blooms and are a very acceptable early spring bonus. The leaves are clean-cut heart shapes held horizontally by slender thread-like stems.

Uses: Distinctive ground cover and provides interest in difficult dryish corners (see pages 32-43 and 152-161).

Colour: From white and yellow to rose-pink and violet, leaves green becoming reddish brown, especially with age.

Size: Up to 30cm (12in) high and across, depending on the site.

Flowering time: Flowers appear in spring, along with the young foliage.

Relatives: *E. grandiflorum* 'Rose Queen' has deep pink flowers and bronzed leaves. f. *violaceum* has rich lilac flowers and leaves touched with brown and rich chestnut-red when young. 'Nanum' is more compact. *E. pinnatum* subsp. *colchicum* (below) is a dark green-leaved species with bunches of bright yellow short-spurred flowers.

Cultivation: Very easy if not too overshadowed and elbowed by very vigorous larger plants. To make the most of the new young foliage and the accompanying blossom, shear off the old foliage just before flowering and new growth begins.

Propagation: By division in early spring or early autumn.

Epimedium pinnatum subsp. *colchicum*

Viola riviniana 'Purpurea' (syn. *V. labradorica* 'Purpurea')

VIOLA RIVINIANA 'PURPUREA' (SYN. *V. LABRADORICA* 'PURPUREA')
Purple wood violet

Description: Clump-forming perennial with very invasive habits, but with pretty proper violet-shaped dark leaves and plentiful flat-faced typical violet flowers. Fully hardy.

Uses: Excellent for naturalizing in dry shady places where it can be given its head (see pages 32-43). Too healthily prolific for more cultivated spots. Try in woodland, wild garden, along hedge bottoms, by ditches and on banks. Also good in low-maintenance gardens (see pages 228-239).

Wildlife: Flying insects visit flowers.

Colour: Purple-blue flowers with small pale centres and the central, lower, lipped petal marked with dark lines.

Scent: Only faint.

Size: 5-8cm (2-3in) high, one clump spreads 30cm (12in) wide but a colony is indefinite.

Flowering time: Spring into summer.

Relatives: *V. odorata* is the familiar sweet violet with heart-shaped leaves and lots of flat little violet flowers in late winter or early spring, traditional violet or shining white. It is a splendid perennial for the wild garden.

Cultivation: See Uses. A plant introduced will soon set about becoming a colony.

Cultivation: Nil, given an appropriate site. You may wish to cull the outriders of the population explosion: hoes or chemicals will cope.

Propagation: By seed, usually self sown.

Ruscus aculeatus

RUSCUS ACULEATUS
Butcher's broom

Description: An evergreen shrub that can make a formidable thicket with many upright stems bearing spine-tipped 'leaves' that are really flattened adaptions of parts of the stem. All is dark green and polished. The flowers are inconspicuous but are followed by round red fruits if plants of both sexes are grown. Very tough and hardy.

Uses: One of the most reliable of plants for dark dry places (see pages 32-43 and 228-239).

Colour: Red fruits, dark green leaves.

Size: 75cm (30in) high, over 1m (3ft) across.

Flowering time: Spring.

Relatives: *R. hypoglossum* is a clump-forming evergreen of similar habit but with longer 'leaves'.

Cultivation: No bother on any soils that do not get waterlogged.

Propagation: Remove rooted portions – divisions – in early spring.

HOSTA FORTUNEI

Description: Hardy herbaceous perennial with large pointed broadly oval somewhat heart-shaped leaves. This is one of the most reliable and worthwhile species in the genus. It has glaucous grey-green leaves and standard hosta flowers – pleasing but very much a secondary matter after the splendid foliage. There are a series of different coloured forms. Fully hardy.

Uses: First class foliage plant, grouped can be a ground coverer. Especially good in moist soils and with some light shade (see also pages 54-61).

Wildlife: Popular grazing habitat for slugs and snails. (See cultivation)

Colour: Leaves grey-green, flowers lilac-mauve.

Size: Dependent on site and moisture available, height to 75cn (30in).

Flowering time: Early to midsummer.

Relatives: *H. fortunei* 'Albopicta' has pale green leaves and broad creamy primrose centres that green up in summer, 'Albopicta Aurea' has golden leaved, greening in summer, 'Aureomarginata' has green leaves boldly but unevenly marked with creamy yellow, var. *hyacinthina* has darker narrower leaves. *H.* 'Frances Williams' (below) has blue-green leaves with yellow edges.

Cultivation: Best in moist good soils but can be surprisingly good in normal soils which are not very wet. Perhaps most effective when grouped. Slugs can be a major problem, the 'small field' and 'small garden' ones being the prime offenders. By clean cultivation and tackling the potential problem in early spring when these pests are most active much can be done to eliminate or greatly curb them. In my experience shredded bark checks slugs.

Propagation: By division very early spring. Old clumps may need a spade used as a chopper.

Hosta 'Frances Williams'

Primula japonica

PRIMULA JAPONICA

Description: One of the moisture-loving, hardy candelabra primulas with flowers arranged in a series of outward-facing rings up tall stems. Growing from a tight, juicy looking crown, the leaves become larger through the spring and are widespread and as fresh as a cos lettuce. Each bloom is over 2cm (³/₄in) across so that a mass of them make an impact.

Uses: Excellent stream- or waterside plant, but can be grown anywhere there is plenty of moisture and will naturalize by seeding itself. Not worth trying in dry soils. (See also pages 82-93.)

Colour: Basic colour is a rich purplish red, but there are now a number of shades including white.

Size: 30-60cm (12-24in) high depending on site, spread of an individual 30-45cm (12-18in).

Flowering time: Early summer.

Relatives: Various strains have been bred. 'Miller's Crimson' a rich crimson shade; 'Postford White'; 'Fuji' somewhat orange. Other candelabra primulas include: *P. bulleyana*, 60cm (24in) high, bright orange; *P. florindae*, sometimes called the giant cowslip, can reach 70-90cm (28-36in) high with large heads of nodding bells in primrose-yellow for weeks through the summer and probably into autumn; *P. helodoxa* 60-90cm (24-36in) high, yellow; *P.* 'Inverewe', 60-75cm (24-30in), orange red; *P. pulverulenta* 60-90cm (24-36in), red or pink.

Cultivation: Easy in moist conditions. Plant early spring or early autumn. Allow space for growth.

Propagation: Fresh seed germinates like mustard and cress. Plants will usually sow their own to expand their numbers and territory.

TRILLIUM GRANDIFLORUM
Trinity flower, Wake robin, Wood lily

Description: A hardy, clump-forming perennial bearing large distinctive three-petalled flowers. Each is borne singly with green bracts and three-part dark green leaves below.

Uses: One of the delights of the woodland garden or grown between shrubs in leafy soils (see pages 82-93). Also good for small gardens (pages 142-151). Do not allow to dry out. Choice and very effective when a group is well established.

Colour: Snow-white but with age may blush pink.

Size: 38cm (15in) high, spread 30cm (12in).

Flowering time: Spring.

Relatives: Double *T. grandiflorum* 'Flore Pleno' (below) is more heavyweight in bloom. The other species are all distinct characters. *T. sessile* 30-40cm (12-16in) has narrow upright dark maroon flowers above collars of leaves divided into three parts.

Cultivation: Best grown in full or partial shade in conditions that are woodland or mimic it. Leafy soil either neutral or somewhat acid suits best.

Propagation: Division in early summer after the foliage has died down. If seedheads develop, harvest the seed and sow in the autumn. Seedlings will take three good growing years to reach flowering maturity.

Trillium grandiflorum 'Flore Pleno'

Ceanothus thyrsiflorus var. *repens*

CEANOTHUS THYRSIFLORUS VAR. REPENS
Creeping Californian lilac, Creeping blue blossom

Description: A rapidly spreading, fully hardy, evergreen shrub making impressive mounds of dark green that are lost under a mass of bloom formed of crowded tiny flowers in rounded heads. Special for weeks.

Uses: Grandscale ground cover that defeats any opposition (pages 152-161). Good in sunny spots or with light shade in well-drained soils and normally capable of holding out well in times of drought. Try it by steps (see pages 162-169).

Colour: Rich blue.

Size: 60-90cm(2-3ft) high, spread 1.8-3m (6-10ft).

Flowering time: Late spring and early summer.

Relatives: The genus is full of evergreen shrubs but usually more upright ones or those that are pressed against walls or other support. There are many good hybrids. Consider 'Blue Mound' a particularly free flowering one, 'Italian Skies', 'Puget Blue', and 'Trewithen Blue'.

Cultivation: In well-drained soil the featured species will romp. Taller kinds may be best with a little shelter from gales.

Propagation: Easy from summer cuttings. Seed will give varying seedlings, usually worthwhile ones.

MENTHA REQUIENII
Corsican mint

Description: A diminutive but very hardy mint; ground-hugging, much branching stems have tiny round leaves of shining bright mid-green and tiny stemless flowers. Releases strong peppermint aroma when walked on or otherwise crushed.

Uses: For a carpeting job in moist spots, perhaps in the rock garden or in paved paths (pages 162-169). Ideal for a small garden (pages 142-151).

Colour: Apple-green leaves, lavender flowers.

Scent: Strong peppermint.

Size: Only 1cm (½in) high, but spread extraordinary – indefinite.

Flowering time: Summer.

Relatives: There are plenty of mint species and forms but none so small as this character.

Cultivation: Easy in moist soils where it does not get overgrown.

Propagation: Remove rooted pieces.

Mentha requienii

Saponaria officinalis 'Plena'

SAPONARIA OCYMOIDES
Tumbling Ted, Rock soapwort

Description: Ground hugging, hardy perennial making an informal carpet of stems covered with hairy leaves that are quite lost for weeks under drifts of five-petalled flowers, each about 1-2cm (½-¾in) across, arranged in crowded umbels just above the foliage. Stems becoming woody, much branched and emanating from one central rootstock.

Uses: Obviously a good rock garden plant but extra good falling over rocks, walls or down banks, and able to manage in dryish spots once established. (See also pages 162-169 and 142-151.)

Colour: Rosy pink standard.

Size: 2.5-8cm (1-3in) high, spread 40-50cm (16-20in).

Flowering time: Summer.

Relatives: Presently available forms are 'Alba', white, and 'Rubra Compacta' which is a deeper shade. Other good carpeting species include *S. caespitosa* which is not quite so wide ranging but has lots of small flat flowers, pink to rich pink, almost purple. *S. officinalis* 'Plena' (above) is upright, to 60cm (2ft) with double pink flowers.

Cultivation: Plant firmly in well-drained soil in a sunny spot.

Propagation: Seed, sown in spring or autumn, may give different colour shades. Softwood cuttings in early summer are straightforward.

VIBURNUM TINUS
Laurustinus

Description: A common but virtually indispensable hardy evergreen shrub. Very dense growth of intricate branching and prolific foliage. Oval, pointed, dark green, persistent leaves seem to stand any amount of wind or weather. Many small individual flowers are borne in shallowly rounded clusters seemingly at the ends of every twig.

Uses: Splendid as a specimen. Excellent in a mixed planting of deciduous and evergreen shrubs (see pages 152-161). Exceptionally good as screening and can make a distinguished hedge (see pages 170-175).

Colour: Foliage darkest green, flowers pink in bud, white opened.

Scent: Rather subdued for a viburnum.

Size: Height and spread 3m (10ft).

Flowering time: Starts to profer huge quantities of posies in winter and keeps the performance up until spring.

Relatives: *V. tinus* 'Eve Price' (below) is very free flowering and dense. 'Gwenllian' has pinker flowers. It tends to produce the small blue fruits more freely.

Cultivation: Easy in almost all soils, except permanently boggy ones. Can be pruned back as required.

Propagation: Lower twigs are likely to root themselves as layers so it is hardly worth the bother of taking cuttings.

Viburnum tinus 'Eve Price'

GALANTHUS NIVALIS
Snowdrop

Description: Hardy bulb. There are over a hundred different snowdrop forms. They all have the family face, but there are variations of size, flowering period, flower form and amount of green colouring. The standard *G. nivalis* and the fractionally earlier blooming double variant 'Flore Pleno' will satisfy most gardeners' needs.

Uses: They are so welcome it is difficult to resist popping them in a variety of sites; these could include the fronts of beds/borders, the lower reaches of the rock garden, between shrubs, at the base of hedges, naturalized in grass or woodland and even in raised beds. (See pages 132-141 and 152-161.)

Colour: White with green markings on shorter inner three petals.

Scent: A sweet scent but not too obvious in very cold conditions.

Size: 10-15cm (4-6in) high, spread of individual 5-8cm (2-3in).

Flowering time: Flowers first appear midwinter, the exact timing depending on the season but they will brave really bad weather.

Relatives: Among many good variants *G. nivalis* 'Lady Elphinstone' is a prized large one, 'Scharlockii' has a long green spathe divided into two and sticking upwards, often likened to rabbit's ears and *G.* 'Magnet' is large and tall, with lantern blooms widely slung from the stems on long thin stalks. There are forms of *G. reginae-olgae* that start blooming in mid-autumn! Some clones produce flowers before the leaves. It will cope with more shade than other snowdrops. *G. plicatus* is a chubby flower with dark green, polished leaves quite unlike the traditional green-grey.

Cultivation: Try to plant in spring. If you have your own bulbs or can beg some from friends, the best time to lift and replant is when the leaves are dying down. Next best time is shortly after flowering when nursery firms will sell plants 'in the green'. Failing these opportunities try to purchase dry bulbs as early as possible at the end of the summer and plant immediately. Cover bulbs with 8-10cm (3-4in) of soil, preferably leafy, humus-rich and open in texture. They enjoy moisture together with good drainage.

Propagation: Clumps lifted can be split and replanted immediately at the times suggested above; do not leave out to dry. In good open soil the bulbs will divide fast and also send out narrow stolons at the end of which new bulbs form. Plants will also set seed which can be saved and sown in pots or scattered around the ground where bulbs are naturalized and where the young seedlings will not be disturbed.

Galanthus nivalis

INDEX

Main entries are in **bold** type

PICTURE ACKNOWLEDGEMENTS

All photographs supplied by the Garden Picture Library except pages 241, 245 (top), 249 (bottom), which were supplied by Harry Smith Collection, and page 171 Sue Berger's Garden, 69 Kingsdown Parade, Bristol, which was supplied by Clive Nichols.

List of Photographers Alan Bedding 20-1; Ann Kelley 208-9; Bob Challinor 61, 108-9; Brian Carter 18, 28, 68, 74, 79 (*Lythrum salicaria* 'Firecandle'), 122, 145, 187, 205, 214, 219, 249; Brigitte Thomas 40-1, 54, 129, 154-5, 158-9, 202-3, 230; Chris Burrows 19, 30, 104; Christopher Fairweather 20, 21, 38, 108, 113, 117, 158; Christopher Gallagher 117; Clay Perry 152, 186, 203; Clive Boursnell 133, 140-1; Buster Ancient Farm, Hampshire, 165, 225; Clive Nichols 165, 172; David Askham 148 , 179, 201, 244; David England 36, 178; David Russell 42-3, 64, 65, 100, 114, 233; Densey Clyne 204-5; Didier Willery 36, 39, 69, 77, 83, 123, 138, 139, 140, 177, 188, 193, 237, 250; Erika Craddock 12; Friedrich Strauss 217; Geoff Dann 42, 234; Henk Dijkman 70 Designed by Henk Weijers, 174-5 Tilburg, South Holland – owned and designed by Jan Van Summeren; Howard Rice 43 Monksilver Nursery, Cambridgeshire, 46, 56, 63, 91 Monksilver Nursery, Cambridgeshire, 93, 96, 103 Cambridge Botanic Garden, 107, 135 National Collection – John Drake, 184-5, 188-9, 246; Gil Hanley 235; Jacqui Hurst 247; Janet Sorrell 240; Jerry Pavia 6-7, 13, 32, 40, 58, 59, 170-1, 238, 245; Joan Dear 56; Joanne Pavia 17, 124-5; John Baker 167; John Ferro Sims 78-9, 94; John Glover 22, 24, 45, 49, 50, 51 Valley Gardens, Windsor, 55, 60-1, 71, 74-5, 88, 95, 105, 106-7, 116 Derek Jarman –

Prospect Cottage, at Dungeness, Kent, 125, 126, 131, 144-5 Designed by John Duane, 150, 151, 155, 157, 163, 182, 185, 189, 194, 214-5, 215, 218-9, 223, 228-9, 246; JS Sira *Colchicum autumnale* 'Waterlily' 26-7, 44 Designed by Julie Toll, 53, 66, 66-7 Gertrude Jekyll Garden, Van Hambeldon, Surrey, 73, 80, 85, 101, 132-3, 161, 178-9, 183, 197, 207, 208, 220, 231, 232, 235, 248; Juliette Wade 25, 100-101, 102, 129, 229, 248 Savill Gardens; Lamontagne 2, 16-17, 60, 110, 121, 130, 162, 167, 168-9, 181, 190, 198, 242; Linda Burgess 109, 149; Lynne Brotchie 111 Blakeney, Norfolk; Marianne Majerus 176-7 Sleightholme Dale Lodge; Marie O'Hara 247; Marijke Heuff 35, 141, 251; Mel Watson 99, 226; Michael Howes 4, 31; Morley Read 15 Headland, Polruan, Cornwall – the garden is open to the public on Thursdays during summer, 114-5; Neil Holmes 27, 45, 75, 92, 98, 137, 146, 154, 164-5, 168, 173, 174, 180, 204, 206, 213, 216, 218, 224, 250; Nick Meers 48, 78 Bog Garden, Chyverton House; Nigel Francis 76, 210; Philippe Bonduel 192, 202, 227, 236; Roger Hyam 90-1; Ron Evans 184, 194-5, 231; Ron Sutherland 10-11, 67, 80-1, 86-7, 128 Designed by Michael Pithie, 138-9, 148-9, 151, 221 Designed by Michele Osborne, 226-7; Steven Wooster 23 (Mediterranean courtyard), 62-3 Designed by Weerman, Holland, 82 Brooke Cottage, 92-3, 199, 222-3 Raworth, London; Sunniva Harte 34, 81 Charleston Farm, 87, 88, 90 Folkington Place, 97, 118, 144 , 147 Old Rectory Cottage, 160 Folkington Place, East Sussex, 175; Tim Griffith 15 Castlemaine, Victoria, 33; Tommy Candler 16 (*Bracteantha bracteata*), 212; Vaughan Fleming 26, 190, 196-7, 200, 243; Zara McCalmont 134;